DAY CARE FOR YOUNG CHILDREN IN INDIA

Issues and Prospects

About the Editors

Dr. Vrinda Datta is Professor, at Tata Institute of Social Sciences, Mumbai. She has extensive experience in the areas of early childhood care and development, child rights, street children and child labour.

She was a Visiting Faculty Member at University of Maine at Farrmington, USA. She received the Rockefeller Foundation's Joint Residency Fellowship at Study Center Bellagio, Italy and was selected as Global Leader for Young Children by the World Forum for ECCE. At present, she is convener of Maharashtra FORCES, and the national task force to develop quality indicators. She is also the recipient a senior fulbright Research Fellowship, USA in 2007.

Dr. Rajani M. Konantambigi is currently Associate Professor, Tata Institute of Social Sciences, Mumbai. Her current focus of research is on education of children in early years, learning disabilities, child care, non-formal education and qualitative research methodology. She is a member of the National Task Force on developing a tool to measure quality. She is also Co-convener of Maharashtra FORCES. Also, she has been a faculty member at the Department of Human Development and Family Studies, Maharaja Sayajirao University of Baroda. She is the recipient of the Rockefeller Foundation's Joint Residency Fellowship, Study Centre, Bellagio, Italy and the Fulbright Award for Post-doctoral Research at Department of Educational Psychology and Special Education, Georgia State University, USA.

DAY CARE FOR YOUNG CHILDREN IN INDIA
Issues and Prospects

Edited by
Vrinda Datta
Rajani M. Konantambigi

CONCEPT PUBLISHING COMPANY, NEW DELHI-110059

Cataloging in Publication Data—DK
Courtesy: D.K. Agencies (P) Ltd. <docinfo@dkagencies.com>

Day care for young children in India : issues and prospects / edited by Vrinda Datta, Rajani M. Konantambigi.
p. cm.
Contributed articles.
Includes bibliographical references (p.)
Includes index.
ISBN 13: 9788180694813
ISBN 10: 818069481X

1. Day care centers—India. 2. Child care services—India. I. Datta Vrinda, 1957- II. Konantambigi, Rajani M.

DDC 362.712 095 4 22

ISBN -13: 978-81-8069-481-3
ISBN -10: 81-8069-481-X

First Published 2007

Published and Printed by
Ashok Kumar Mittal
Concept Publishing Company
A/15-16, Commercial Block, Mohan Garden
NEW DELHI-110059 (India)

Phones : 25351460, 25351794
Fax : 091-11-25357103
E-mail : publishing@conceptpub.com

FOREWORD

The whole subject of day care for young children in India is a gray area, shrouded in mystery. There is hardly any documentation about it, leave alone research. This book comes like a ray of light in a dark room, bringing together, for the first time, information and insights about this neglected topic, and the autors are to be congratulated for their brave effort.

But first, why is day care such a gray area, lacking in information? At first sight, this is surprising, given the large size of the female workforce, and the large number of children below six, which make it obvious that a very large number of young children are cared for by others while their mothers are at work. How much of such child care is within the domain of the family, and how much of it is in the institutional realm of "day care"? How has this pattern changed over the years? What impact has it had? Why has there been so little interest in documenting the various ways in which children are cared for, or studying the impact on children, on women and indeed on families, of the different approaches? Why is there hardly any literature on day care in India, descriptive or analytical?

Pondering over this question at length, I have come to the conclusion that it can only be because of what I can sum up in two words as "gender blindness" on the part of policy-makers, planners, programme managers, academics, research scholars — in short, the entire educated middle class, which is collectively responsible for deciding what enters the realm of public discourse. There are two dimensions to this blindness, one related to gender, and the other to class bias. Let me dwell on each for a moment.

The gender bias underlies the widespread "invisibility" of women's work in India. In spite of the large number of women in the workforce, about 11.5 crores at a modest estimate, (even more if extended-SNA work in counted) amounting to one woman for every three men at work, women's work continues to be invisible, and hence undervalued. Recent studies indicate that both the numbers and the proportion of women in the workforce is increasing, a phenomenon often referred to as "feminisation of labour" reflected mostly in the increased number of women in the casual labour category. And this itself is part of the explanation for the blindness. The term "working women" conjures up images of women in jobs, employed women, middle-class women, women at desks, – that is, women working in the organized sector. But the reality is that this group of women form only 10 per cent of the female workforce, the rest being in the unorganized sector, which is hard to recognize, though the Indian economy is based on it. Here is the traditional iceberg, only one-eighth of which is seen above water!

Thus the first issue is this failure or unwillingness of a male-dominated perspective (shared by both men and women) to recognise that women are at work, and are productive members of society, contributing to GNP. This is compounded by class bias, since most of the women in the unorganised sector are poor and hence only marginally enter the awareness of the middle class.

Linked to this is the second issue, the failure or unwillingness to recognize that women perform multiple roles, are simultaneously mothers, workers and home-makers, and hence require day care for their young children. This attitude is also the outcome of a patriarchal perspective, (again shared by both men and women) which insists on singling out women's domestic role as their only or primary one and proceeding to glorify it.

Often there are strong moral overtones to this approach, sometimes going so far as to insist that it is woman's sacred duty to refrain from work, stay at home and care for children, and condemning those women who fail to do so as irresponsible and selfish. (Indeed a generation of working women suffered the burden of intense guilt after psychiatrists like John Bowlby purported to establish that maternal neglect in infancy could lead to severe psychological damage to the child – a finding which was later discredited because of its misapplication of conclusions drawn from one set of circumstances to entirely different circumstances. However, such reports were influential enough to lead later on to many studies in Western countries of the possible deleterious and damaging effects of day care on young children, and it is only in recent years that the emphasis has moved to the quality of care rather than the person giving it.) Be that as it may, this attitude of moral disapproval of the working woman, who is careless about her own child's welfare, lies behind the lack of interest in day care.

Here too the class bias complicates the picture, in both positive and negative directions. On the one hand, it transforms a merely patriarchal perspective into a feudal one, keeping the classes in their proper place. In spite of the moral disapproval, the needs of the newly emerged class of middle class women who work outside the home receives some sympathy, and is seen as ideally being met by the joint family, or by devoted servants, an attitude often justified by pointing out its employment-creating potential for poorer women. But the needs of working class women, who have been working in the fields and forests and doing artisan work from time immemorial, are conveniently ignored. Feudal values have little time for those at thc bottom of the ladder.

Combine class with gender, add a dash of caste, and we have a really smoky brew, turning the sky from gray to black. No wonder that in this thick fog, day care has not found its place in the tomes of academe. There is need for much more class, caste and gender analysis to isolate the reasons for the present state of affairs and to begin locating day care in its socio-cultural context.

A beginning can be made by trying to study the historical origins and development of day care, which began with the early post-Independence legislation (1948-51) mandating crèches for the care of children of women working in factories, mines and plantations, who were even then recognized as "working class" females in need of such services. This was a legacy of British colonial policy, based on thinking forged in an industrialising Britain which was not only providing reluctant services for its working class, but at the same time, at the ideological level, carrying out the domestication of the middle class "non-working" woman and creating the concept of the "housewife" which has come to trouble so many later generations of women. By the later part of the nineteenth century, this distinction had been made clear, as the literature of that period in Britain clearly points to the existence of both the elegant middle-class housewife who was a model mother to her numerous children (aided by working-class household help, of course), and the working class woman who slaved in factories and sweatshops, with little leisure to pursue either the maternal or housewife role.

However in India, the application of this simple dichotomy failed to come to terms with the reality of the unorganized sector, in which the vast majority of its people, both men and women, laboured. The Maternity Benefit Act (1961) a few years later, fell into the same trap, defining eligibility in such a manner that fewer than 10 per cent of working women stood to benefit from it. In fact, of course, even fewer than that number actually availed of the benefits, for various reasons. Once again, the vast majority were left out. Both maternity relief and child care, basic components of support services for working women, received short shift under the benign gaze of a patriarchal, feudal and deeply gender-blind State.

Numerous examples could be given of how these attitudes not only manifest themselves in day to day life but unwittingly determine programme and policy towards the care of children. Some examples are — "naturalizing" the role of the crèche or day care worker, as something which every woman with a maternal instinct should just "naturally" be able to without the need for any training; denying the need for any training in day care, or to acquire any special skills — in fact, pooh-poohing the whole idea of skills for child care; in consequence, neither the day care worker nor the *anganwadi* worker has up to now been recognized as a skilled worker and hence cannot lay claim to the wages due to skilled labour; child care being seen as a personal problem of the woman alone, and not as a social issue or a concern for the family as a whole; the common prejudice among both employers and lay people against the employment of married women, because they are perceived as neglecting their primary duty; and the very recent and grudging acceptance of the fact that the education of girls who have to care for younger siblings is adversely affected by the lack of day care facilities.

All of the above explain the late arrival of day care on the Indian research scene, and its slow growth and lack of meaningful models for emulation. It is perhaps true to say that even today, the bulk of children are cared for in their homes, by different family members; while the small numbers in day care are distributed in a variety of programmes. The tone of early research also is apologetic, some of it reflecting the early Western concern for the possible ill effects on children of care by caregivers other than the mother. The lack of interest in exploring the care offered by different types of Indian families, spanning the full range from single parent through nuclear to the various kinds of extended and joint families, and their impact on children is also evident. So is the lack of interest in a variety of institutional alternatives, again ranging from informal arrangements by siblings or mothers themselves on a rotating basis, to more formal structures.

The field, therefore, is wide open and there is much to be done. One cannot but congratulate the two young authors for their courage and determination in beginning to tell the untold story, to look at micro-level programmes as well as macro-level perspectives and to document the efforts to run crèches in a variety of settings, ranging from the mandated statutory crèches to private and NGO crèches and above all, to set down what is known through accounts of research, much of it their own.

Starting with broad overviews, first, of the socio-economic context by Vandana Prasad, and then of the development needs of young children by one of the authors, they make it clear from the start from what perspective they are approaching the issue, and their own concern as Child Development specialists to assess day care in terms of its impact, if any, on children's development. This is followed by a section containing descriptive studies of day care in different settings — agricultural communities, women in the unorganized sector, women in mines and urban middle class settings. Having set the scene, the next section goes on to examine, with the help of rigorous research tools, the outcomes for mothers and children of different day care provisions. It would have been valuable if the findings of the two sets of studies could have been linked by a discussion of the implications of such researches for day care in the Indian context, but this could not be expected since the papers have been written by different people at different times for different purposes, and the aim of this book is mainly to bring together the available literature on the subject. The penultimate section contains essays on some of the important issues in day care — the workforce, the question of training, the ensuring of quality and strategies for advocacy and networking. The concluding chapter by the editors pulls together the threads and tries to look into the future.

This book makes a splendid start with its rich material which throws up many issues both for research, documentation and dissemination and for advocacy, and provides valuable insights for policy makers and programme planners. It would be especially useful to students because of its extensive and carefully compiled bibliography. I can only say that I am delighted to be associated with this publication and hope that it will be as widely read and used as it deserves.

Chennai
January, 2006

Mina Swaminathan

PREFACE

Over the past decade the issue of child day care in India has been in focus among the academicians, researchers and advocates of early childhood investment. Our interests in the issue of day care emerged when we pursued our Ph.D. in the area of child day care and from then on our efforts have been to contribute to the understanding of the field of child care.

For some time now we have been strongly feeling the need to have a book which will focus largely on empirical researches done in India on child day care. Though there is not an overflow of researches in this field but there are a few who have studied this issue across the country. We indeed are privileged to have authors giving perspective papers, research papers and also papers based on field experiences. But we still had to depend on some reprints as they are important studies in our field.

The book has taken quite some time to put it forward for publication. During this period papers from authors were received at various points of time but we have not asked authors to update their papers as it would further delay the publication.

The format of the varied papers have been retained by and large. As editors we have given authors the liberty to write in the format they wanted to. Therefore, we have papers that read as research papers while many of them are narratives of the experiences of authors.

The aim of the book is to serve as an important reference book to researchers, practitioners, policy makers, teachers and students of home science, early childhood education, social work and psychology. It is hoped that the book will also have relevance to international organizations, who are planning for early childhood intervention programmes in South Asia. Today, with globalization, there is a need to reach out to the international community by giving them this academic literature.

We hope this book is the beginning of many more efforts by us and others who are working in the field of early childhood care and development.

Vrinda Datta
Rajani M. Konantambigi

ACKNOWLEDGEMENTS

The stalwarts in child and human development, namely, Mrs. Mina Swaminathan, Prof. Veena Mistry and Prof. T. S. Saraswathi had been urging us on to publish our Ph.D. work. It never got off the ground. Finally, when we put our heart to it, it was kind of late to publish the work as articles in current journals. We also found that there were a number of researches coming up. We decided to put them together in a volume. The credit for making this book happen goes to Mrs. Swaminathan, Prof. Mistry and Prof. Saraswathi for believing in us. Thank you!

The Tata Institute of Social Sciences provides an atmosphere and a scope for open thinking and creativity and the time to pursue them. We are grateful to the Institute for supporting such freedom. This support has also been experienced in terms of bearing with our absence from the Institute while we were away on the Team Residency Fellowship of the Rockefeller Foundation, at the Bellagio Study Centre, Italy in 2000. The fellowship was to edit this volume. We would also like to thank Mrs. Gianna Celli and her staff at the Bellagio Center for excellence in playing host — we enjoyed the comfort and facilities provided to facilitate academic and creative work.

We thank all the authors for their contributions, and also for bearing with the long delay in bringing out this volume. We are thankful to the editors of the journals, Economic and Political Weekly, Trends in Social Science Research, to M.S. Swaminathan Research Foundation, to CLAP, Orissa, FORCES and OMVS for permitting us to reprint articles by Sriram and Ganpathy, Gupta and Konantambigi, and Arulraj and Samuel Raja for Chapters III, IV, V, IX respectively.

At various points of time, our friends and colleagues have provided feedback a big "thank you" to them. A special thanks to

Ms. Joyeeta Sengupta for a careful screening of the volume and assistance in adapting and editing the Chapter by CLAP, Orissa, FORCES and OMVS. Professional editing was undertaken by Mrs. Sudha Raghvendra. She helped us unite the difficult knots in the book. We are very grateful to her.

Ms. Bhargavi Mohan and Mr. Rakesh have typed copiously and re-typed articles due to the computers crashing! Their pains taking endeavour needs a special note!

Our families bore with our absences and continued involvement in the work, and they emotionally provided the moral support — a big thank you to them !

Finally, we thank the publishers for recognizing the importance of the issues in child care and publishing the volume.

June, 2006 **Editors**

CONTENTS

SECTION-V

FUTURE PERSPECTIVES

LIST OF TABLES

LIST OF BOXES

LIST OF FIGURES

INTRODUCTION

The current issues in child care stem from the history of the family as it affects women's multiple roles and children's needs for growth and development. In India, till the recent past, irrespective of the social class, and the working status of the mother, the mother was by and large the primary caregiver. In the middle and affluent classes the mothers were assisted by the older women in the family or the community. In the lower classes, then, as of now, child care was either neglected or delegated to siblings, or the child was carried to the work spot, the safety and care conditions not withstanding. Children in the lower classes have suffered double neglect, both physical neglect and psychological deprivation.

With women's employment, especially employment outside the home, child care in middle and upper class homes has changed. Though joint families lent some support, the conflicts within joint families have not been seen as conducive for children's development. However, child care in the form of grandparent care has been seen as the next best alternative to mother care, and acts as a great physical and psychological support for a number of mothers. Today there are large sections of mothers in nuclear families who seek alternate forms of child care outside the home, and are plagued by issues ranging from non-availability of any kind of care to issues in quality of alternate care. The scenario is compounded by the pressure for early stimulation and education in middle and upper class homes. Nurseries, pre-schools, play groups/play schools help, but are not adequate to fulfil the needs of harried, ambitious parents. There is pressure on child care centres to provide "home-like" care, "home-like" food, "home-like" affection, and an efficient, effective stimulation or "pre-school like" activities. While parental expectations are high and their guilt and anxiety soar, various forms of child stimulation centres and child care centres make the most of the situations. It is a seller's market. Child care is looked at as a low investment, high-returns, business, and women with some school or pre-university education feel that they are competent to run the centres.

In the lower socio-economic strata, the situation has not changed much in terms of care for young children. Women in the unorganised sector suffer the most, and are forced to rely on low quality government run centres or carry their children to work. The State attempts to provide for some basic health and nutrition needs, but child care by and large continues to be ignored.

As researchers pursuing an interest of change in child care contexts in India, quality of child care and impact on child outcomes, the issue of availability and care for working mothers, we found that a number of studies were coming up, and training for child care personnel was being initiated. The decision to bring the research together under a single volume was undertaken about four years ago. As we further explored the field various other issues came forth and a need was felt to look at the issues in child care in a holistic manner. The need to look at the macro situation of child care in India, that is the State's role in promoting child care, at the micro level looking at what do children need for development, the various issues in quality, what kind of child care is available to women from various strata and whether they are satisfied with care, what are the implications for parenting, how could child care services and providers be organized so that they cater to the needs of children and parents, issues in the child care work force and their training were some of the dimensions of child care we thought needed to be included. The issues in care by members of society other than close relatives has come full circle, and like a parent-teacher association in the schools, in some localities/cities we have or have had Day Care Associations or Parent-Caregiver Associations addressing the needs of working parents and their children, and at the national level there are efforts for advocacy for child care. These are not common features of out of home substitute care settings.

The various concerns raised about child care are represented in five sections:

- Macro and micro issues in child care.
- Women, work and child care
- Effects of substitute care on children
- Current issues: Child care quality, personnel training and advocacy.
- Future perspectives

Section I: Macro and Micro Issues in Child Care

Section I is represented by two chapters. The macro one dealing with the state of child care in India and the role of the State, "Socio-Economic Context of Child Care in India" is by Vandana Prasad. The other, the micro perspective one, discusses the developmental needs of children and how the various agents, the parents, child caregivers and the State try to fulfil them, titled "Development Needs of Young Children: Home, Day Care and State Linkages" is by Rajani Konantambigi. The rationale of Prasad's Chapter is that various facets of the society impinge on the family which meets the needs of growing children. In the context of industrialisation, modernisation and now globalisation, the state needs to play an increasingly important role. So there is a need to look at the state's role critically in the past and the present, and what could be/should be the role for the future. The future role of the state will have to take cognisance of not only the child's needs, but also those of the family and the emerging job market and its demands. The first chapter will address these issues. It draws from secondary data, and existing policies and programmes in child care.

The second chapter discusses the developmental needs of the children and their fulfilment by the agents of socialisation, the family, the child care set up, and the state. Parents work in organised and unorganised sectors, and children in marginalised groups are deprived more. Developmental needs addressed here have also paid attention to the basic nutrition and health care needs of children; needs of children at the different developmental stages, like infancy, toddlerhood, pre-school age and school-age. Different types of day care do not ensure that the requisite quality is present in day care centres. The quality parameters are addressed in another chapter. This chapter draws from theoretical premises, review of literature and the authors' research and her experience with day/ child care settings.

Section II: Women, Work and Child Care

This section on child care needs of women has three papers, one in the rural context, one in the urban, semi-urban, unorganised content and the third in an urban middle class locale.

In Chapter 3, Sriram and Ganapathy have examined the changing circumstances of women's lives and work, the consequent burden of multiple roles and the child care support system utilised by them in the face of practical constraints. Focusing on child care, it presents evidence from four unique research studies which have studied not only the child care supports used by employed mothers but also women's perceptions about these, their preferences and the options viewed by communities as viable. Drawing from this, conceptual issues pertaining to child care have been raised and a strong argument made in favour of adequate child care services.

In the next chapter Arulraj and Raja Samuel take a close look at the child care needs of women in varied unorganised labour settings in Tamil Nadu. They have brought out the stark realities in terms of deprivation and difficulties faced by women as they manage triple roles and that of child care, as they struggle to make provisions for breast feeding and basic care, the time consumed in travelling and distance factors, problems in carrying children to work, lack of services for children below two years of age, and the needs for and in quality care expressed by women, and the relief such measures would bring to girl children. The chapter highlights the gap between needs and services, the participation required by employer and the policy issues that can be initiated.

Maternal satisfaction about the quality of day care is crucial. Since there are other protagonists in the scenario making up the child care service, the day care personnel, the parents and the children themselves, a holistic perspective is taken by Konantambigi and Sriram (Chapter 5). A series of studies were conducted in Baroda city, and the children in the sample were 3-6 year olds from various day care centres. Findings revealed a few gaps in the expectations of parents; day care personnel tended to project a very positive image of their centre. This chapter delineates the role of subjectivity and its interfaces and implications for determining quality care in the functioning of centres.

Section III : Effects of Substitute Care on Children

An empirical study based on the child care quality and its impact on child outcomes. Konantambigi's study (Chapter 7) has drawn from Gamble and Zigler's (1986) premise that poor quality of one setting of child care is compensated for another of higher quality. The study has considered various aspects of the day care and home environment, and their relationship to the social and cognitive development in pre-school. The sample of 71 pre-schoolers with a control group comprising 32 children and their parents was drawn from different crèches in Bangalore city. The study using a combination of interview and observation methods, along with putting together a kit for assessing cognitive development found that child-centred, caring and concerned interaction by the adults in both the settings was highly positively related to social and cognitive developments. Socio-economic status notwithstanding, physical parameters, like, hygiene practices, adequate availability of space, lighting and ventilation in day care were related to development in the child. Home and day care environments both contributed significantly to development, and Gamble and Zigler's contention holds good to a significant extent. Implications for practice are drawn.

In Chapter 8, Datta's study draws on an urban metropolis, Mumbai. Here a large number of educated women continue to work even when they are married and have young children. The dual earner families have to find alternate child care arrangements when they are at work. Grandmother care, maid care and family day care are some of the child care arrangements made by them. For the child they offer a different environment for growing up. The author in this chapter reports about her research which studied the intellectual development and social maturity of children of working parents under these various types of child care. Using psychological tests and interviews with parents and caregivers this study has revealed the differences in the children's development because of exposure to various forms of child care. The author through this study has pointed out the advantages and disadvantages of the forms of day care under study.

The authors Gupta and Konantambigi, in Chapter 9 have situated their study in Baroda city. The sample in the study are children in preschool, their mothers and teachers. As expected, positive maternal perceptions about the setting and different dimensions of child care (child care support obtained through in-laws, parents, friends and neighbours) was related to better socio-emotional behavioural adjustment in children. Adequate financial security, time-management for various tasks through the day and strategies at handling guilt induced because of their working and need for alternate child care were again related to socio-emotional behavioural adjustment. The study revealed that a working mother tended to feel anxious and guilty especially if alternate child care was provided outside the home to her children. The anxiety was generally passed over to the child, and so also she tried to overcompensate because of the guilt. The main problem though was anxiety due to alternate care, and this was accentuated if this care was of poor quality. Psychologically the issue was not actually how good or poor the care was. It was one of perception and it was positive!

The researchers in the field of child care show that group settings for young children have the capacity to enhance the development depending upon their distinctive ecological character. The extent to which caregivers interact with children, engage in behaviour that stimulate, sustain and encourage task oriented activities, will influence the development of children. Thus understanding the day care environment becomes essential to know what kind of impact they can have on children. The author in this Chapter 10, details out her in depth work on family day care (29) and Day Care Centres (13) and 120 children in these child care centres. The researcher developed scales for measuring quality, developed indicators of quality and studied what factors have an impact on children's interaction pattern and play patterns. In depth observation of children and interviews with caregivers gave detailed understanding of the quality in day care programmes and children's development.

Section IV : Towards Quality in Child Care

Child care quality, personnel training and advocacy and quality parameters, form the important links to quality. Making sure that child care has adequate parameters of quality and that the parents and caregivers interact fruitfully to meet the needs of children are the various, current issues. These are addressed in Section IV.

Considering that personnel is the most important component of a programme in determining its quality, it is very essential that enough inputs are given into their training. In chapter 11, Mridula Bajaj basically discusses issues like, why train child care workers, who should become child care workers, can we have a common training programme across all types of programmes, and methodology and programme content? These issues have been discussed against the backdrop of experience in training by Mobile Crèches. The chapter also highlights the issues of concern in training and ways to augment this aspect.

Earlier research on day care tried to establish the impact of day care by comparing day care children to non-day care children. The diffused results in the various studies led to the next decade of day care research which tried to see what parameters of day care programmes have an impact on children. This Chapter 13 by Datta analyses what parameters need to be emphasised in the Indian context, and how does one develop minimum standards for day care programmes. It also chalks out the roles that the State, parents and personnel can play in ensuring quality day care programmes. The author draws from her research on child care quality and experience in training personnel at various levels.

The single most important factor determining the quality of a day care programme is the personnel in the programme. The misconception that any woman/mother can be a caregiver in a programme has led to inadequate understanding about recruitment of staff and their training. With no job descriptions in hand, programmes are mismanaged due to duplication or neglect of certain duties. These factors have had a direct impact on the work conditions of the day care staff as they are not getting recognition as professionals and also their remuneration and other work-related facilities are poor. Datta in this Chapter (12) through her own research and field experience has highlighted the situation of the personnel in day care programmes by reviewing the existing training programmes and has chalked out appropriate model of staff development. Datta's paper has addressed the overarching issues concerning the work force.

In India, day care for young children has taken various forms and is being managed by governments, employees, voluntary organisations and individuals. The services today are inadequate in meeting the needs of large number of working women and children. Linked with day care services for the marginals are larger problems of malnutrition, poor retention in primary schools and child labour. It is important that the young children do not get neglected because of non-availability of the mother or day care services and that appropriate and adequate sources be developed and advocacy is, therefore, essential for ensuring this. Though day care services are now picking up, they work in isolation having no platform to interact and enhance their professional skills and services. Therefore, network becomes very essential and could have multiple functions like standards in quality care, programme parameters, etc. The author has initiated networking in her own city and has highlighted the process in this Chapter 14. In addition her experience with the national advocacy group has brought out issues in advocacy for field of child care.

Shanmugavelayudham's Chapter 15 is another example of building a networking and advocacy group. The premise of his writing is that considering the types of child care programmes, it becomes important to establish whether networking is needed, whom do we network with and for what objectives? Is advocacy a part of networking issue? How does one network and do advocacy work in the field of child care? These issues are tackled and the strategies for networking and advocacy explained with the help of Tamil Nadu experience.

Section V : Future Perspectives

In the last Chapter (16), an attempt has been made to gather all the strings, and the authors have attempted to put various concerns of child care in perspective. In a country where 91 million women are working, it is imperative that we be concerned with what happens to children when women are at work. The issue of what kinds of day care will be pursued from two dimensions: the urban and the rural. The need for child care exists, but of different kinds. The urban set up and lifestyle, the school system and its functioning exert certain pressures on child care. The rural set up, though allows the child to be in the work set-up of the mothers, invariably does not guarantee high quality child care. This chapter has drawn from experiential information of the editors (field experience), a review of literature, and other chapters in this book. The nature of problems in child care, and the developmental needs of the child point to a community based child care. Another challenge for the future is mobilising the people for community based care and training the child care personnel for high quality, child oriented care, and personnel who would be able to meet the challenges of supportive care, that is, meeting the familial needs.

To meet this challenge, the state, the employees, parents, members of the community and child care personnel have to come together and take responsibility. The magnanimity of the problem of children's care warrants a deeper involvement of the State.

SECTION-I

Macro and Micro Issues in Child Care

1

SOCIO-ECONOMIC CONTEXT OF CHILD CARE IN INDIA

— *Vandana Prasad*

How well any given society cares for its young is an important benchmark of its 'humanity' and its concern for human rights over and above the utilitarian considerations. The years of early childhood have been understood to be vital in determining the future physical, mental, cognitive and social development of a person. They are also directly related to school preparedness and retention. Significantly, these also happen to be the years of maximum vulnerability. The growing body of research and publications on early childhood care and education reflects its significance.

All major indicators of human development use indices that reveal the status of survival of the very young child. Infant Mortality and Under Five Mortality Rates are time-honoured indices of the general human development of any country. More recently, the Human Poverty Index uses the percentage of malnourished children under five as an index of 'decent living standard' (Human Development Report, 1997).

This Chapter looks at the existing situation of children in India in terms of basic health and nutrition indicators, economic policies and practices, migration and industrialisation, women's work, the role that older children play in child care and the resulting scenario for child care in India. Statistics that throw light upon the existing situation of very young children in India must, therefore, be interpreted in full understanding of their relationship with and implications for children and society as a whole.

Existing situation

In the report on, "State of the World's Children" by United Nations Children's Fund (UNICEF, 2000) India ranks 140th, on the basis of under-five mortality rate (UFMR), which is 105. Wasting, stunting, infants and children with low birth weights, breast feed availability and vitamin A deficiency are also still high compared to the USA or China (Table 1.2).

On comparing India with a developed country and a developing one, it ranks high on IMR (Table 1.1) and the percentage of infants with low birth weight is 33 per cent. Basic amenities, such as, safe drinking water is not accessible to 19 per cent of the population, adequate sanitation is available to only 29 per cent of the population, immunization for measles 66 per cent and availability of Oral Dehydration Therapy is for 67 per cent, immunization for DPT, TB, polio, and tetanus for pregnant women is in the range of 73 per cent to 80 per cent (Table 1.3). There are still 25 per cent of the children out of the ambit of basic health amenities. A point of enthusiasm is that the routine immunization programme funding is being undertaken by the Government of India from 1998. While the health indicators need improvement, the population continues to rise and the fertility rate in India is higher than that of China or the USA Expenditure on health and education continue to be poor in comparison to expenditure on defence (Table 1.5).

Relevant comparative statistics are as follows:

Table 1.1 : Basic Indicators (UNICEF, 2003)

	USA	*China*	*India*
Infant Mortality Rate 2003 (IMR) (under one)	7	37 (25) 39 (21)	63
Total population (thousands)	294043	1304196	1065462
Annual number of Births (thousands)	4262	18706	25052
Annual number of under 5 deaths (thousands)	34	692	2180

Table 1.2: Nutritional status of children: Comparison with China and the USA

	USA	*China*	*India*
% of infants with low birth weight (1998-2003)	8	6	30
% of children who are exclusively breast-fed (0-6 months) 2003	–	67	37
% of children who are breast-fed with complementary food (6-9 months)	–	–	44
% of children who are breast-feeding (20-23 months)	–	–	66
% of under five suffering from moderate and severe under weight (1995-2003)	1	10	47
Suffering from severe under weight (1995-2003)	0	1	15
Wasting (moderate and severe)	1	2	16
Stunting (moderate and severe) (1995-2000)	2	14	46
Vitamin A supplementation coverage rate (6-59 months) (2002)	–	–	27

Source: UNICEF, 2003.

Table 1.3 : Health Status

% of Child Population with access to:	*USA*	*China*	*India*
% of population with access to improved water sources (2002) Total	100	77	86
" " Urban	100	92	96
" " Rural	100	68	82
" " adequate sanitation (2002) Total	100	44	30
" " Urban	100	69	58
" " Rural	100	29	18
% of routine Expanded Programme for Immunisation (EPI) vaccine financed by government (2003)	56	100	100

Contd . . .

Table 1.3 Contd . . .

% of Child Population with access to:	*USA*	*China*	*India*
% of fully immunized 1 year old children for TB (2003)	–	93	81
” ” ” DPT (2003)	96	90	70
” ” ” Polio (2003)	93	84	67
” ” ” Measles (2003)	93	84	67
” ” Pregnant women for Tetanus	–	–	78
% of Oral rehydration therapy (ORT) use rate (1990-98)	–	–	67

Source: UNICEF, 2003.

Table 1.4 : Demographic indicators

	USA	*China*	*India*
Population under 18 (2003) (thousands)	75893	369191	395791
Population under 5 (2003) (thousands)	20794	92555	115615
Population annual growth rate (%)(1970-90)	1.0	1.6	2.1
” ” ” ” (1990-2003) %	1.1	.9	1.8
Crude death rate –1970	9	8	17
” ” ” – 2003	8	7	9
Crude birth rate – 1970	17	33	39
” ” ” – 2003	15	14	25
Total fertility rate –1998	2.1	1.8	3.1

Source: UNICEF, 2003.

Table 1.5 : Economic indicators

	USA	*China*	*India*
Gross National Product (GNI) per capita (US $) – 2003	37610	1100	530
GNP per capita average annual growth rate (%) – 1960-1990 (%)	2.2	5.5	1.7
" " " – 1990-2003	2.0	8.5	4.0
Annual rate of inflation (%) – 1990-2003	2	5	7
% of population below $1 a day–1990-96	–	17	35
% of central government expenditure allocated to (1998-2003) – Health (1992-2007)	2.2	0	2
" " " – Education	2	2	2
" " " – Defence	16	12	15

Source: UNICEF, 2003.

Table 1.6 : Women and maternity

	USA	*China*	*India*
Contraceptive prevalence (%) 2003	76	87	47
Ante-natal care coverage (%) (1995-2003)	99	90	60
% of births attended by trained health personnel – 1995-2003	99	97	43
Maternal mortality ratio reported – (1985-2003)	8	50	540

Source: UNICEF, 2003

Birth registration (Government of India, 1998, 2000) may be seen as an important strategy to provide identity to the child and also protect her rights. This may have special significance during periods of displacement and rehabilitation (or lack thereof). Coverage varies considerably from state to state (Table 1.7).

Table 1.7 : Classification of States of level of Birth Regstration Coverage (Government of India, 1998, 2000)

Registration %	*Name of States*
30 and less	Assam, Bihar, Rajasthan, Manipur
31 – 50	Andhra Pradesh, Meghalaya, Madhya Pradesh, Manipur, Uttar Pradesh
51 – 70	West Bengal, Orissa
71 – 90	Arunachal Pradesh, Haryana, Himachal Pradesh, Kerala, Maharashtra, Karnataka
91 and above	Goa, Gujarat, Mizoram, Punjab, Tamil Nadu, Tripura, All Union Territories

The broad picture thus illuminates a massive denial of the basic rights to survival, development and protection. Participation in the processes of decision-making and development remains a distant dream since even those with the welfare of children closest to their agenda, the Government continues to ignore the basic rights of children. The phenomena of displacement, migration and other aspects of urbanisation add to the already grim scenario.

Displacement, Migration, Urbanisation and the Young Child

Both 'push and pull' factors have been operating to create a situation in which 30 per cent of the population now lives in urban areas (Census of India, 1991 and 2001). Of the 30 per cent living in cities, 50 per cent live in urban slums in conditions hardly fit for animals. India's total slum population in 1991 was 46.3 million and this is likely to be 62 million by the end if the century. This would imply that nearly 7 million children under six live in urban slums. Basic amenities like housing, water, sanitation, transport and electricity have hardly been tackled. The State has responded by further cutting back on the budgetary allocations for urban poverty alleviation and employment schemes. In actual terms, the budget for 1998-99 is 13 per cent less than even that in 1990-91.

Families are forced to migrate as a result of poverty and deprivation in rural areas caused by a failure of development. Even those who were small landholders are dispossessed of it by processes of insurmountable debt or processes of 'development' itself which acquires land for the 'larger public good' without any or adequate compensation with land. Processes of rehabilitation being manifestly unjust, long drawn and inadequate, many lakhs of families are likely to face displacement. In essence, these processes ensure that previously self-reliant families migrate and enter the market as daily wagers.

Environmental lobbies and the Supreme Court have wittingly or unwittingly contributed to a heavily inequitable situation in cities like Delhi by engineering the closure of industries said to be polluting the environment, thus denying thousands of workers their right to livelihood. The fact is, of course, that vehicular pollutants contribute more than four times to air pollution as compared to industries.

Women, Work and Childcare

Within the family, the onus of child care has traditionally with women, specifically the mother. This perspective has been thoroughly exploited, or remained unchallenged at best by most agencies dealing with the issue. It is convenient to all but the targeted mother, that she remain not only the root cause of all the ills that befall the young child, but also the key to all solutions. It is not surprising, therefore, that feminist groups have often reacted against this maternal image of the woman. Even today, women carry the triple burden (Swaminathan, 1995) of child bearing and rearing, housework and economic activity.

One of the main problems in enumerating women as workers is the all pervasive patriarchal attitude that assumes that women do not work at all or that women do not work outside the home. This bias also influences the Census. If one goes by the premise that all underprivileged women are perforce *working women*, ninety three per cent of these (over 12 crores) would be working in the unorganized sector (Government of India, 1989), which is also the main source of livelihood for Indians. One of the main problems in 'quantifying' women's participation in the economy, and therefore planning for and supporting it, has been the inadequacy of the Census process itself. In 1991, the Work Participation Rate (WPR) of women was 22.3 per cent as compared to 51.6 per cent for men. However, studies done with greater sensitivity to the types of work women do reveal a vastly different picture as indicated in Table 1.8. Obviously, this has significant repercussions on policy formulations to do with labour and social security, as well as

Table 1.8 : Gender and employment patterns

Year	*Round*	*Self-employment (In percentage)*	*Regular employment (In Percentage)*	*Casual Employment (In Percentage)*
Persons				
1972-73	27	41.2	46.3	12.5
1977-78	32	42.4	41.8	15.8
1983	38	41.8	40.0	18.2
1987-88	43	42.8	40.3	16.9
1993-94	50	42.3	39.4	18.3
Males				
1972-73	27	39.2	50.7	10.1
1977-78	32	40.4	46.4	13.2
1983	38	40.9	43.7	15.4
1987-88	43	41.7	43.7	14.6
1989-90	45	42.3	41.3	16.4
1990-91	46	40.7	44.2	15.1
1993-94	50	41.7	42.1	16.2
Females				
1972-73	27	48.4	27.9	23.7
1977-78	32	49.5	24.9	25.6
1983	38	45.8	25.8	28.4
1987-88	43	47.1	27.5	25.4
1989-90	45	48.6	29.2	22.2
1990-91	46	49.0	25.9	25.1
1993-94	50	45.4	28.6	26.0

Source: S.S. Suryanaryanan, Level and Pattern of Female Employment in Gender and Employment in India, 1999, Delhi and Urban Statistics of India, 1996. NSSO DATA.

allocations of resources to support services such as child care services. Though trends in (un) employment take many years to show clearly, some trends have gathered enough evidence from a variety of sources. Organized employment is growing at a 'snail's pace (Kabra, 1999) compared to demographic growth. There is an increasing casualisation of work with a rise in contractual work. Urban trends in Delhi were revealed by a survey by the Women's Commission (Box 1.1).

Box 1.1 : Some facts about women and employment

- 94 per cent of the working women in Delhi are in the unorganized Sector. A report by the Delhi Commission for Women states that 90 per cent of the rural and 70 per cent of the urban women are unskilled labour and also perform their domestic duties. (Delhi Commission for Women)
- At an average most women spent 7 hours outside the house and 4 hours working inside the house thus making their workload of 11-12 hours per day. This leaves them little time to attend to their young children who require attention during the early years.
- There is no social security for these women who start working one month after their child is born.

Source : Indu Pathak and Pushpa Patnaik, Women in the Informal Sector, NIUA, 1991.

The State has been the largest employer of women in the public sector but, where women working in the organised sector are concerned, privatisation has led to a decline in women employees from 8 per cent in the eighties to below 2 per cent in the nineties (1999a). More and more women being pushed to self-employment or the unorganised sector are unable to prove their status as workers. This means that less and less women are able to avail of maternity and child care benefits or any kind of social security at all. They also find no protection from the law. Simultaneously, wage security is seriously endangered and already meagre earnings are further compromised. Thus the trend is one of an increase in the relative and absolute poverty of women. Where one-third of all households are already women headed (National Council of Applied Economic Research, 1994), the repercussions upon the very young child of these trends in employment are grave. Women who must work for the survival of themselves and their families have to do so regardless of how and by whom their young children would be cared for. Images of a tiny six month old left alone covered in faeces and flies, crying in a jhuggi or being carried around by a pot bellied three year old with a grubby bottle in the other hand are not at all unusual. Those that choose the devil's alternative of staying at home eat less and their children probably eat even lesser. Either way, there seems little hope for a situation in which one of three babies is born of low birth weight and one of two children are malnourished. For the poor, it is a catch-22 situation.

On the other hand, the State's present role here needs to be highlighted for the wrong reason. The Central Government had a scheme of crèches for children (0–6 years) of working and ailing mothers. This scheme provided funds to the NGOs to start crèches. Along with the supplementary nutrition component it was difficult to run a meaningful programme. The scheme was under review, the financial details had to be reworked since it had not been reviewed for 20 years or more. The review was under progress, and in the meanwhile the IX Plan funds meant for the purpose was diverted to a counselling programme (personal communication with FORCES Delhi, 2002). Such is the priority that is accorded to child care by our Government.

From the point of view of the very young child, it must be said again that in most circumstances, the child is best looked after within the family and not in institutions. However, the family does not exist in a socio-economic vacuum. If the function of caring for children is to be given the recognition due to it, society would have to provide the circumstances and systems by which a family is enabled to stay out of the 'market' for that period of time. In reality, the concept of paternity leave hardly exists though some State statutes have now provided 15 days paternity leave. Maternity leave and benefits can only be accessed by women working in the organised sector which is only about 7 per cent of all working women. The leave itself does not even provide for the 4–6 months of recommended exclusive breast feeding. Crèches on worksites thus become one important way in which parents may continue to contribute to the care of their young children while earning their livelihood. Recently there have been some encouraging moves to extend maternity entitlements to the unorganised sector; a recent Supreme Court Judgement pronounces that muster roll workers of the Municipal Corporation of Delhi are entitled to maternity entitlements and the Construction Workers Act of 1996 also potentially provides for similar rights for construction workers.

However, generally speaking, far from gaining universal recognition and support, the 'triple burden' of women's work is further compounded by the sharp rise in prices of food and health care.

Child Care and the Older Child

The number of young children not receiving adequate care can also be estimated through a number of micro studies on the issue of sibling care. It is estimated that 98.2 million children were 'invisible' in 1991, that is, they were neither counted in the workforce nor in the educational system. Of these, 58 million were girls (Chaudhary, 1996). A study of children of agricultural workers in Gujarat, Mizoram, Kerala and Meghalaya shows that 60 per cent of the siblings under the age of six were left in each others' care. In 37 per cent of the cases when the mother was not available, the caregiver at home was the older sibling and in 19 per cent of the cases the caregiver on the field was the older sibling. (Sriram and Ganapathy, 1998; also see this volume).

Another study of over 600 households from an urban slum showed that 40 per cent of children in the age group 6–14 years were out of school. Of these, 20.5 per cent were involved in sibling care and of these 70 per cent were girls (Prasad, 1997). Another study looking at the household chores performed by young girls notes that of 8.6 per cent girls who had to fetch water for the household, 80 per cent were able to attend school, whereas of the girls looking after younger siblings, only 61.4 per cent were in school (Anandlakshmy, 1994).

Obviously, a large number of children, young and old are growing up without adult inputs or supervision at the cost of their childhood, care, development and education. Equally obvious is the fact that the lack of child care services is a serious hindrance to universalising elementary education, especially for the girl child. Simultaneously, the young child is left handicapped in her development due to inadequate early stimulation and care.

Child Care and Breastfeeding

The inability of the mother to be present through the day also has an impact on breastfeeding (Prasad, 1999). The *National Family Health Survey* for the post-reform period revealed that at least half the infants of the country were not being exclusively breast-fed during 1992-93 (Table 1.9).

Table 1.9 : Infant Breast Feeding Practices (Percentages of 0-12 month Children Breast Feeding Status)

Age in Months	*Not Breast feeding*	*Breast Feed Only*	*Breast Feeding And*				*% Breast-Fed*
			Water	*Other Liquids*	*Solids*	*Others*	
URBAN							
0–3m	8.7	33.6	29.8	30.5	1.8	0.5	16.2
4–6m	7.0	14.4	23.0	42.5	12.9	0.2	29.3
7–9m	9.4	6.3	14.2	30.1	39.6	0	28.7
10–12m	14.9	1.7	8.1	21.4	53.9	0	25.6
RURAL							
0–3m	1.5	55.4	19.9	21.5	1.3	0.4	7.7
4–6m	2.5	29.7	27.1	30.7	9.8	0.2	13.6
7–9m	3.4	10.4	18.9	31.1	35.9	0.3	12.2
10–12m	5.6	4.8	10.0	20.8	58.7	0	11.9
TOTAL							
0–3m	1.9	50.9	22.0	23.4	1.4	0.4	9.5
4–6m	3.5	26.4	26.2	33.3	10.5	0.2	17.0
7–9m	5.0	9.4	17.7	30.9	36.8	0.3	16.4
10–12m	8.0	4.0	9.5	21.0	57.5	0	15.4

Source : NFHS Introductory Report, 1992-93, p.81.

The NFHS survey identifies that the problem of breast-feeding is more severe in urban areas than in rural ones. This is further buttressed by a study in Delhi and Haryana that shows that 60 per cent of the children in these areas receive no breast-feeding (Khosla, 1998). The NFHS survey further shows that the trend in the Northern, Western and Eastern states, except for Rajasthan and U.P., is one where the exclusive breast-feeding rate was less than the average breast feeding rate in India. It is only in the Southern states that the breast-feeding rate is considerably higher than the national average. In at least 10 states out of the 25 surveyed by the NFHS less than one-third of the children below 3 months were exclusively breast fed. This data is significant in the context of an increase in the unorganized female labour force in some of the northern and eastern states.

As far as the duration of breast-feeding is concerned, the NFHS data shows that exclusive breast-feeding is very common for children during the first month even in the post-reform period, but more than one-third of the children are given water at this stage also. Though breast-feeding continues up to the age of three years supplementary nutrition is given by the age of 6-7 months (National Family and Health Survey, 1992-93). However, the quality of the feed often depends on the health of the mother and the type of nutrition that she is getting. The need for crèches and day care facilities is highlighted when one looks at the statistics on breast-feeding and views breast-feeding as the basic right of the child.

Child Care and Malnutrition

There is sufficient data to show that the age between 6 months and two years makes children most vulnerable to malnutrition. This period is one of perpetual hunger where the child is dependent on someone else to feed it. Demographic distribution of criteria of malnutrition is shown in Table 1.10.

The state-wise estimates of under-nutrition, show that the prevalence of severe malnourishment is much higher in the northern and the eastern states as well as Gujarat and Maharashtra. The

Table 1.10 : Nutrition by Demographic Characteristics (in Percentages)

Characteristic	*Weight for Age*		*Number*	*Height for Age*		*Weight for Height*		*Number*
	Below –3SD	*Below –2SD*		*Below –3SD*	*Below –2SD*	*Below –3SD*	*Below –2SD*	
Child's Age								
> 6 months	2.8	15.6	4406	5.7	15.7	2.0	9.5	3225
6–11 months	14.1	43.3	4792	14.3	34.3	2.9	15.7	3176
12–23 months	26.3	63.4	9560	30.7	56.6	5.6	28.0	6945
24–35 months	25.9	62.2	8406	34.6	60.2	2.5	16.6	6033
36–47 months	21.8	58.5	8643	40.7	66.7	1.8	11.6	6204
Sex								
Male	20.2	53.3	18208	28.4	52.3	3.7	18.8	13040
Female	21.0	53.4	17599	29.4	51.7	2.6	16.1	12543
Urban	14.8	45.2	8464	22.0	44.8	2.9	15.8	5584
Rural	22.4	55.9	27543	30.9	54.1	3.2	18.0	19750
Total	20.6	53.4	35807	28.9	52.0	3.2	17.5	25584

Source : NFHS India Report, 1992-93, pp.282-83.

National Nutrition Monitoring Bureau (NNMB) data on nutrition of pre-school children in urban areas reveals that only 10 per cent of such children had a normal nutrition status. The rest were faced with mild, moderate or severe malnutrition. A study by Voluntary Health Association of India (VHAI) also states that severe to moderate malnutrition pervades in nearly half the population of children in the country and accounts for nearly 60 per cent of the deaths of all children. Thus breast-feeding, malnutrition and infant mortality can be linked to each other in a significant way.

India has one of the highest mortality rates amongst young children. Even though statistics show that mortality rates have been declining steadily, regional and demographic trends are quite disturbing. The average mortality rates of young children for 15 years preceding the NFHS survey of 1992-93 are given in Table 1.11. The survey holds that the effect of ante-natal and delivery care mortality rates in the first month of life and the mortality rates of children and mothers who do not receive such care is almost twice as high as others who do receive such care. Births delivered at home have a higher rate of infant and child mortality than those delivered in clinics. As far as the demographic composition of the mortality rates is concerned, female death rates are 5 per cent higher than male ones for the age group 0-4 years. During the neo-natal period males have a higher risk of dying, whereas in the post natal period, females have higher rate of mortality by 43 per cent. This reflects the discrimination practiced in nutrition and medical care of the girls.

Table 1.11 : Average mortality rates from 1978-1992

Years	*NN*	*PNN*	*IMR*	*CM*	*UFMR*
URBAN					
1988-92	34.1	22.0	56.1	19.6	74.6
1982-87	38.8	25.7	62.4	20.6	81.8
1978-81	42.5	26.5	68.7	29.0	93.7
RURAL					
1988-92	52.9	32.2	85.0	33.4	119.4
1982-87	62.2	40.7	102.9	43.3	141.8
1978-81	65.1	46.2	111.3	55.0	160.2
TOTAL					
1988-92	48.6	29.9	78.5	33.4	109.3
1982-87	56.4	37.2	93.6	37.7	127.8
1978-81	59.5	41.2	100.7	48.2	144.0

Source: NFHS Introductory Report, 1992-93, p.87.
NN: Neo-natal Mortality PNN: Post-neonatal Mortality
CM: Child Mortality

The trends that may be observed from Table 1.12 are the following: The state mortality rates are considerably lower than the average where more than 20 per cent of the female workforce works outside the house for cash. Kerala, Andhra Pradesh, Karnataka, Tamil Nadu and Maharashtra are some prominent examples of this. This development has been attributed to the social

Table 1.12 Mothers employment and infant and child mortality

STATE	*Per 1000 IMR*		*Per 1000 UFMR*		*Employment Status Percentage*			
	Total	*M/F Ratio*	*Total*	*M/F Ratio*	*Not Employed*	*Employed at Home*	*Not for Cash*	*For Cash*
INDIA	78.5	1.06	109.3	0.95	67.2	5.1	10.3	17.3
NORTH								
Delhi	65.4	1.06	83.1	0.94	88.4	2.9	3.6	5.0
Haryana	73.3	0.79	98.7	0.67	61.6	3.9	25.5	9.0
HP	55.8	1.41	69.1	1.39	30.0	3.4	58.7	7.9
Jammu	45.4	0.95	59.1	0.86	58.5	3.6	32.1	5.8
Punjab	53.7	1.16	68.0	0.90	88.4	2.9	3.6	5.0
Rajasthan	72.6	0.83	102.8	0.94	67.7	4.8	19.6	7.7
CENTRAL								
MP	85.2	1.15	130.3	1.05	66.7	5.2	12.5	15.5
UP	99.9	0.99	141.3	0.84	85.6	3.8	5.3	5.1
EAST								
Bihar	89.2	1.07	127.5	0.93	74.8	2.2	11.1	11.6
Orissa	112.1	1.24	131.0	1.09	73.1	3.9	1.2	21.7
W. Bengal	75.3	0.87	99.3	0.80	77.0	7.2	3.6	12.1
N. EAST								
Arunachal	—	—	—	—	53.1	1.5	25.3	20.2
Assam	88.7	1.71	142.2	1.08	80.3	3.5	0.6	15.6
Manipur	—	—	—	—	56.9	3.8	30.0	36.3
Meghalaya								
Mizoram	—	—	—	—	64.9	3.8	8.9	22.4
Nagaland	—	—	—	—	56.4	6.6	21.2	16.4
Tripura	—	—	—	—	74.2	6.7	5.3	13.8

Contd...

Table 1.12 Contd . . .

STATE	*Per 1000 IMR*		*Per 1000 UFMR*		*Employment Status Percentage*			
	Total	*M/F Ratio*	*Total*	*M/F Ratio*	*Not Employed*	*Employed at Home*	*Not for Cash*	*For Cash*
INDIA	78.5	1.06	109.3	0.95	67.2	5.1	10.3	17.3
WEST								
Goa	31.9	1.53	38.9	1.36	69.6	3.7	5.2	21.6
Gujarat	68.7	0.82	104	0.79	56.4	6.1	16.2	21.3
Maharashtra	50.5	1.35	70.3	1.16	49.7	5.0	17.5	27.7
SOUTH								
Andhra Pradesh	70.4	1.21	91.2	1.09	45.7	7.6	11.6	35.0
Karnataka	65.4	1.33	87.3	1.08	52.2	6.7	14.1	26.9
Kerala	23.8	1.16	32.0	1.22	74.2	4.4	0.6	20.5
Tamil Nadu	67.7	1.39	86.5	1.49	52.7	8.0	8.2	31.0

Source : Kishor and Parasuram, 1998. *Mothers employment and infant and child* mortality, NFHS, April 1998, p.12.

and cultural change that is brought about by the fact that these women improve their social and economic position because they earn money and they are also exposed to liberal values much more than women who stay inside the house. Advanced by a NFHS study, these factors are said to be important reasons for non-discrimination between female and male children. As we have already observed, the female mortality rates are higher than the male ones. The second major conclusion that emerges from these two tables is that the UFMR is higher than the IMR and the NN figures show that more than 40 per cent of the deaths occur in the first month of birth. Significantly this figure is high for states like Bihar, UP, Orissa, West Bengal and MP where the unorganized sector has grown over the years. The UFMR is also significantly higher in these states than others.

These conclusions are more or less supported by the Report of the Independent Commission on Health sponsored by VHAI. The Independent Commission on Health in India stated that even though there was a marked decline in the infant mortality rate from 146 in 1951 to 74 per 1000 in 1995, the regional variations showed that states like Madhya Pradesh, Bihar, Assam, Orissa, Rajasthan and Uttar Pradesh still had an IMR that varied from 83-110 per 1000. If we take the regional trends for under five into account then the same trend is found with Assam, Madhya Pradesh, Orissa and Rajasthan having a considerably high average than the Indian average of 109. It is significant that about 60 per cent of these deaths occur in the first month of birth. Almost 60 per cent of these deaths occurred due to malnutrition, respiratory diseases, measles and causes associated with improper antenatal, natal and post-natal care (VHAI, 1997).

Day Care and the Special Needs Child

The lack or inadequacy of adult presence is also a key factor in the late recognition and intervention for the special needs of children. Sensitive and trained child care workers can become the critical bridge between the community and presently specialised services for children with disability, and facilitate the vital function of coordination, integration and further training of the community. On the one hand, the Disability Act (1996) has facilitated the creation of systems for persons with disability like, funds, statutory schemes, resource centres and rules for mainstreaming of children with disability. Simultaneously, the inadequacy of norms recently amended by the Rehabilitation Council of India, are proving detrimental for those trying to set up good quality services.

Food Security, Women and Child Care

Fifty three per cent of our children are malnourished. Eighty eight per cent of all pregnant women in India are anaemic largely due to inadequate nourishment. One-third babies born are of low birth largely due to the chronic and acute malnourishment and anemia of the mother. Though these statistics have been quoted so frequently as to lose their shock value, nobody who has dealt with hungry children and frail mothers can fail to see the degree of mortality, morbidity and sheer human suffering behind these statistics. The prices of food have increased sharply in the years of economic 'reforms'. The change in copping patterns favouring cash crops as a result of the policies and inducements of liberalisations of agriculture, lack of implementation of land reforms, the removal of the Essential Commodities Act, the State's growing reluctance to ensure a basic minimum security net has led to a situation of growing food insecurity.

If we look at the food doled out through the various 'welfare' schemes for women and children the problem of access crops up again since the vehicle remains the inadequately construed Integrated Child Development Services (ICDS) Scheme.

The Mid Day Meal Programme which occupies a major part of the elementary education budget may have done much to attract children to school but certainly fails as a measure to tackle malnourishment which sets in soon after weaning and has maximum impact by three years of age. Further the quality of the nutrition provided, leaves much to be answered.

Questions must also be raised about the ethics of supplying such programmes with pre-processed food such as corn-soya blend imported from the USA as part of the World Bank assistance to ICDS projects. Apart from defying norms of quality that recommend the use of freshly cooked, locally available food that is culturally acceptable and that may provide the community with income generation, the concern is that we have no way of telling whether the soya is genetically engineered or not. While there are doubts about the ill effects of such food on the immune system (*The Sunday Times,* 1999), surely we have a duty not to foist them upon our children in the name of welfare.

Recently, the Government at the Centre has directed all States that Rs. 375 crores from the Pradhan Mantri Gramodaya Yojana is to be earmarked for supplementary nutrition of the under threes through the ICDS and that Rs. 50 could be added to the Anganwadi worker's honorarium for this extra work. However, by not tackling the systemic problems of the ICDS, it is doubtful whether this money will find the required response. In any case, the chronic hunger of women and children cannot be tackled by these piece meal measures.

While the family must have basic food security through a functional and strengthened PDS, the child needs an aware and well-supported adult caregiver to ensure access to food. Once again, there is no evading the need for comprehensive child care services to support both the working mother and the young child. It also needs to be highlighted that morbidity (specially in the young child) due to rising food insecurity is further compounded by the situation of environmental degradation and the inadequacy of government health services.

Women, Health and Child Care

Figures 1.1 and 1.2 inform us about the existing gaps in the medical and related personnel. On an average there is an immediate need of 25 per cent more staff (as per the graph figures). Health expenditure remains low and the country is not able to provide for basic health services. More than 75 per cent of our health care lies in private hands with no regulation upon costs to the 'consumer'. The cost of drugs have spiralled in some cases to almost threefold in the last few years. At the same time foreign funds (on credit, of course), (For example, US$ 248 million is being provided by International Development Association — the IDA, for the Reproductive and Child Health Programme (World Bank, 1997), are flooding into the health sector ostensibly in the name of Mother and Child Health or RCH, but in effect skewing priorities towards population control rather than general health measures.

Significantly, many micro studies confirm that casual workers, both rural and urban, spend a high proportion of their income on health care. Apart from contributing in general to the poverty of the family, the impact on the child, and specially the girl child (Prasad, 1998) is one of greater morbidity. Once again, all the relevant National programmes such as the RCH are compromised in terms of outreach and impact due to a lack of basic care services, which would provide the vehicle for such programmes. It is apparent that the seemingly simple issue of child care services is inextricably tangled with the

Figure 1.1 : Health personnel (all India).

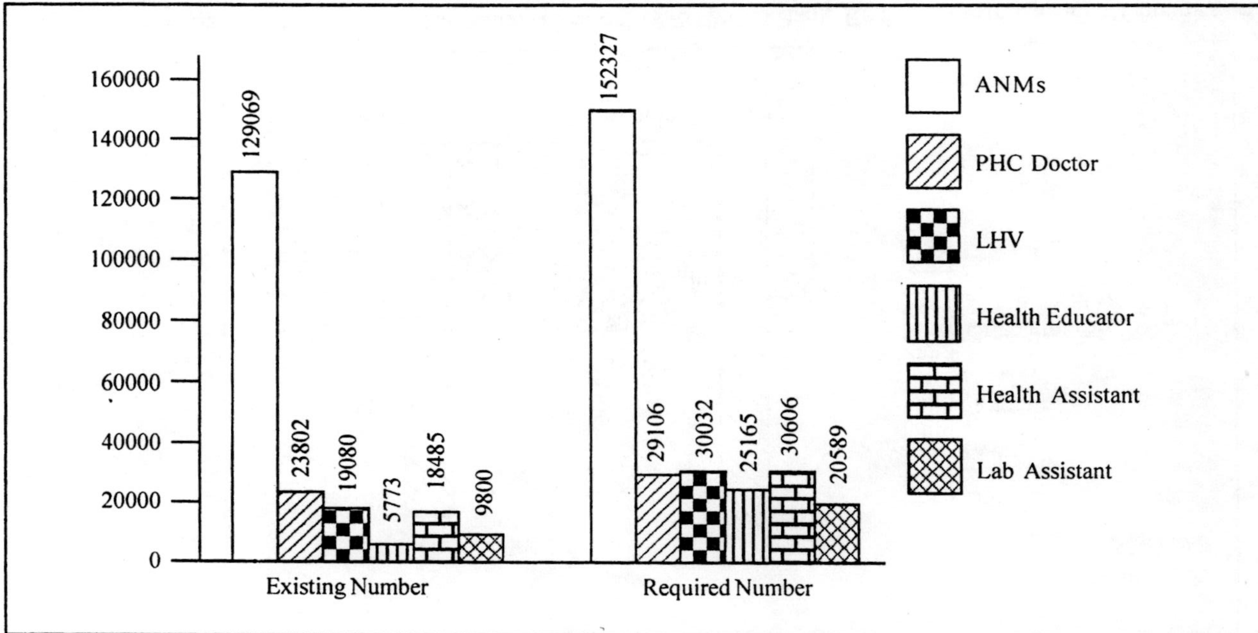

Source: A New Agenda for Women's Health and Nutrition, 1996, World Bank Report of the Independent Commission on Health in India, Published by : Voluntary Health Association of India, 1997.

Figure 1.2 : Health personnel (all India).

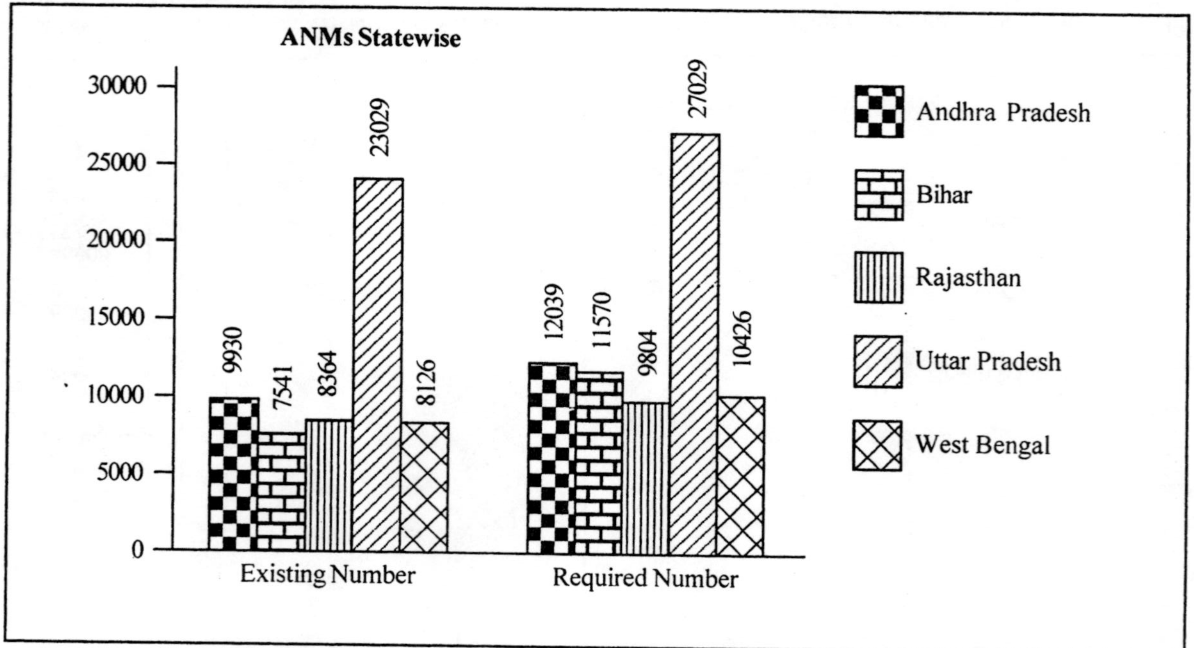

Source: A New Agenda for Women's Health and Nutrition, 1996, World Bank. Report of the Independent Commission on Health in India. Published by: Voluntary Health Association of India, 1997.

overwhelming and complex socio-economic and political processes that are consuming the country today. Net effects on labour, health, environment, food, status of women, education and poverty on the whole impact the young child in viciously cyclic ways to hamper their survival, growth and development. At the same time, systems for addressing all the needs of the very young child are like an enormous inverted pyramid coming to rest upon an inadequate system of care at best exemplified by the ICDS or Crèche Scheme. Clearly, unless the basic foundation of care is strengthened and widened, even the inadequate measures that do exist cannot operate.

The State's Response

Government Schemes

The State has paraded the ICDS as sufficient proof of its commitment to children under six for the last 25 years. This assertion itself is debatable going by the various evaluations the scheme has undergone. At the moment, a nationwide ICDS evaluation study is on under the aegis of the National Council of Applied Economic Research (NCAER). The pilot for this study was carried out in ten ICDS blocks and shows some significant trends. Three-fourths of the Anganwadi Centres (AWCs) were functioning in temporary spaces like open spaces or cattle sheds. 54 per cent of them had no separate cooking space and 13 per cent had no toilet facilities. 40 per cent of the Anganwadi workers had received no training at all. Its main impact seems to have been on the prevalence of severe malnutrition (NCAER 1997-98).

However, as far as the very young child is concerned, the main criticism against the ICDS scheme is that it has remained fundamentally unchanged since its inception 25 years ago. This is one of the main reasons for its limited outreach and impact, specially *vis-a-vis* the child under three. Granted that the scheme does not lay claim to be a day care service aimed at supporting a working mother. However, the socio-economic reality of poor women is that they are all working and contributing in minor or major ways to the economy of the family and the country. Their young, non-ambulatory children cannot be accessed without taking this fact and the logistics of the arrangements for their care into consideration. To put it simply, a centre that has little relationship to the working hours and working places of women cannot be of use to the children who are either carried to work or left behind with other children. The programme cannot be taken to the doorstep of these children because it depends upon a single child care worker who is paid a pittance has a host of responsibilities including managing the centre and the children within the programme, filling in records, fund raising, community work and other sundry tasks like economic surveys, TB and malaria programmes, Census work, etc. This partially explains why a programme that has been 'universalised' for the 16 crore children under six reaches out to only 2.3 crore in any way at all (be it only to give drops of polio vaccine twice a year) and only 1.1 crore participate in centre based pre-school activities. (Department of Women and Child Development, 1997-98).

It seems obvious, therefore, that the needs and rights of the very young child cannot be addressed without simultaneously addressing the requirements for *care*. In the case of the children of the over 90 million women working in the unorganised sector, and the 60 million children under six under the poverty line whose parents necessarily work or need to work, this is a requirement for day care services.

The only specific arrangements for day care services derive from the scheme Providing Crèches For Working And Ailing Women (Central Social Welfare Board) since 1974 and National Crèche Fund (NCF) Scheme (Department of Women and Child Development) since 1995. The setting up of the NCF, can fairly be attributed to pressure exerted by various women and children groups. However, even the tiny corpus of 19.9 crores set apart for it (only the interest derived from this can be spent on the scheme itself) has been acquired on credit from the World Bank in the name of 'development'.

These schemes have a limited outreach and cater to only about 3 lakh children through 14,313 crèches. By the government's own estimation 8 lakh crèches (Department of Women and Child Development, 1997-98) are required while the estimation of activists in this area of work is that the requirement is for about 2.4 million. The rate of increase of the number of crèches over the last five years has also been minimal, from 12,470 crèches in 1990 to 14,313 in 1998 (Prasad, 1998) since the scheme is fundamentally a non-expanding one. Similar to the ICDS Scheme in structure, the scheme suffers from many deficiencies.

Apart from this, a detailed study on Crèche Services in India, done by the National Institute of Public Cooperation and Child Development, (Gopal & Khan, 1998) highlights a number of other issues that need urgent attention. Only 7 per cent of the children enrolled were under one year of age, the average space provided per child was an appalling 3-6 square feet and almost all centres had a dearth of play material. Seventy-three per cent of the centres did not have toilet facilities for the children who had to defecate in open drains, fields or roads. Of even greater concern is the fact that the child care worker (still called a volunteer despite much agitation for worker status) is paid a measly Rs. 400 to Rs. 500.

The two changes of note to the scheme itself have both been negative. The budget for health checks has been removed (consequently, 58 per cent of crèches do not arrange for health checks) and the budget for supervision has likewise been slashed (79 per cent of crèches do not have an earmarked supervisor).

A detailed report of child care services in seven states and case studies from the "government, statutory and voluntary sectors" had raised identical issues of limited outreach, poor and generally custodial quality of services, lack of community participation and lack of training and inadequate remuneration of child care workers many years earlier. Significantly, all the studies showed that there were very few instances of children under two attending these centres (Khullar, 1991).

The Suraksha Series looks at nine case studies of day care centres in diverse settings and provides further insights into these issues at a micro level (Swaminathan, 1995b).

Significantly, many of these points have been repeatedly raised by activist groups since 1977 with concrete recommendations for changes at the schematic level. Thus, it has been clearly understood, articulated and accepted that the crux of a successful crèche programme rests upon:

(a) a sensitive, trained and well supported child care worker who receives adequate recognition, both social and monetary, and
(b) a flexible, decentralised scheme that closely corresponds to the needs of the community, and in particular, the working mother.

Clearly, neither condition is being met by any of the government programmes created for the young child. In view of the fact that day care services have hardly expanded in the last many years, we must look at the wider scenario to be able to analyse the situation of day care services and project their future.

ECCE and the Voluntary Sector

Trade Unions and Women's Groups have long realised the value of child care services, not just as a support to the working women, but as an encouragement and empowerment for women to participate in economic and political activity. Child care has become part of their demand charters and has also found its place in the political manifesto of a progressive political party or two. Child care lobbies have gained even greater momentum and strength through the use of advocacy exercises such as public hearings on the issue and through their widespread support for the rights of the Anganwadi and Crèche worker. The recent move to ignore Early Childhood Development, a vital and essential component of education with potential to impact schooling, enrollment and retention, in the proposed Compulsory Education Bill has further intensified mobilisation around the rights of the very young child and placed ECD at the centre of the 'Education' debate. Simultaneously, question marks are being posed on the quality of 'pre-school' education and efforts are on to 'regulate' the burgeoning private pre-schools and crèches being run primarily for business purposes.

It has been widely recognised that effective child care contributes significantly to population stabilisation and that fertility rates drop hand in hand with child mortality rates. A nationwide health campaign for 'Health for All : Now!' identifies female foeticide and population policies as the burning health issues of the day. Effective child care also prevents child labour and child abuse and permits the earliest identification of disability.

Thus, groups of people working on health, education, labour, economics, gender, and at ground level with women and children have come together to think of maternity and child care within the larger context of development as a whole. They have validated again and again the significance of the issue, not just in terms of the scope of the problem, but also in terms of the human and financial costs of ignoring it. The government spends a major portion of its budget for the 'social sector' on poverty alleviation. It can be logically argued that prevention of poverty by focusing on children is ultimately less expensive than poverty alleviation. The Ninth Plan has acknowledged the need to focus on the very young child and has accepted recommendations (at least in theory) made by groups concerned with child care in the Ninth Plan Approach Paper.

The Convention on the Rights of the Child demands a commitment to the survival, protection, development and participation of all children but specifically mentions the role of the State in rendering 'appropriate assistance to parents and legal guardians in the performance of their child rearing responsibilities' and in ensuring 'the development of institutions, facilities and services for the care of children'. The State is also to take all appropriate measures 'to ensure that children of working parents have the right to benefit from child care services and facilities for which they are eligible.'

The rights of the young child to health and nutrition have been defined in Article 24 of the CRC. However, the rights of the child to breast-feed have not been clearly linked to the provision of maternity entitlements and child care services to all working women.

India has also committed to child care at other international conventions and platforms such as Convention for Elimination of All Forms of Discrimination Against Women (CEDAW) and the Beijing Platform for Action. In fact, Article 11 of CEDAW clearly enunciates the working woman's rights to maternity entitlements and child care services, and in a significant statement, places the rights of the child first and foremost. However, ratification to both these important Conventions has not produced much visible or radical change in laws, programmes or schemes relating to the issue.

Addressing the Issues

Within this framework, how is labour viewed, how health and education are viewed, how women and children are viewed, and, indeed, with what perspective human life itself is viewed may provide answers to why child care has not become an agenda in the last many years. If we analyse trends within policies, laws and budgets it becomes evident that the State is seeing its major role in, on the one hand, creating circumstances conducive to an open market, on the other, as 'protector' of its physical boundaries. Providing social security is simply not a priority except when it comes to wooing voters. Many views exist on what strategies a country like India should adopt. Each side is usually impassioned and armed with its own 'argumentarium' of data. The plea for balance between liberalisation and social safety as two sides of the development coin has found many an impressive champion (Sen and Wolfensohn, 1999). Many of us live and work in the belief (though it gets increasingly difficult as each new generation grows up entrenched in the assumptions behind this paradigm of development), that it is for us to continue to provide exposure to an alternative view of the goals and processes of human life; one in which all children will be valued greatly for themselves regardless of their future utility.

2

DEVELOPMENTAL NEEDS OF YOUNG CHILDREN
Home, Day Care and State Linkages

— *Rajani M. Konantambigi*

The Indian society faces changes and challenges in the child care scenario. The primary, the secondary and the tertiary systems of care, that is, the family, the neighbourhood and the state make efforts to meet the developmental needs of children. This Chapter presents the context of care and discusses how the various developmental needs of children can be met. Developmental needs are viewed from practical as well as conceptual/theoretical perspectives.

The Context of Care

Care and development of young children has been the primary responsibility of the family, supplemented by society through strong community bonds, and cultural mores and values. The context of care and socialisation is defined in a very significant way by the goals of care and the adult roles that one is preparing the child for. LeVine (as cited in, Sigelman and Shaffer, 1995) talks of a hierarchy of goals that are set by parents with preparation for economic goals at the top, followed by social and moral ones. There are also long term and short term goals that parents have for their children.

However, there are a number of factors that impact how these developmental needs are met — the work situation, the attitude of the family towards the mother's/women's working, the kind of day care facilities, the economic background of the family, whether it is low, middle or high income group, whether it is an urban/rural locale, whether it is a nuclear/joint family.

The micro, meso and exosystems also influence how the needs are met. The parent-child dyad, triad and complex interaction systems in the family and what individuals bring to the situation determine the means and extent of need fulfilment. While the long term goals are of great importance, the short term goals have to be fulfilled too. In most societies around the world, women and mothers combined multiple roles of work and care of the family members. Their roles were not controversial, and by and large they did not have difficult choices to make between work/career and children. They could concentrate single-mindedly on meeting the developmental needs of children. In the present context of an industrial society, the career/work roles of women demands a number of adjustments and arrangements so that the developmental needs of their children are met. The effect of multiple care on children (Konantambigi 1990; see also Konantambigi, this Volume) is a subject of grave concern. Research studies on the subject reveal findings that should quell certain fears of the parents. Babies not only adjust to multiple primary caregivers but are also capable of forming multiple attachments. Besides, children's temperaments vary; some children are fussy and take time to adjust to routine, or are sensitive to different handling by caregivers. In such instances, the primary caregivers (parents/grandparents of the baby spend more time and have to take full responsibility for the care and development of children). Childcare literature is replete with mothers saying that they opted to quit their jobs to care for their children. Most of the time women take such decisions because they believe that they are the best caregivers for their children. Beliefs in this regard exist in India, i.e. that mothers and immediate family of the child should take care of their child and it should not be entrusted to others/strangers (Thakkar, 1991). While beliefs about child care pertain to preferred care by parents and family of the child, research also reveals that mothers are on the lookout for caregivers who show care, love and affection for children, and provide cognitive stimulation At times they prefer alternate care by people other than their relatives (including in-laws of the women) because they do not want to be obliged to them. It depends on the attitude of the family towards the mother's employment. A supportive one which recognizes the earning needs for the family or the career needs of the woman. The attitude sets the tone for the guilt that the working mother is made to experience. There is also the role that the fathers play in society, and new supportive child care role they are willing to take up in the light of the changing scenario.

The mothering/caring variable is not the only one influencing child development needs and outcomes. It is dependent also on the child-parent match; that is, on the match of their personalities as the parent goes about the task of caring and rearing and the manner in which the child's developmental needs are fulfilled. The way nurturing/caring takes place is also strongly influenced by cultural beliefs and prevailing practices. The larger context of urban India looks at women's employment as an economic necessity and not as a job or career that the woman wants to pursue. She is up against the societal ideal and perhaps even the familial expectations. Add to this the fact that a mother has to work; work where it takes her away from the baby and the home for about 8 to 10 hours on a continuous basis everyday for 5 to 6 days a week, and also consider the fact that a mother might have to return to work when the baby is just about 3 months of age. In most organised work settings the maternal leave is for 3 months. Women especially from the lower strata are in the unorganised sector where maternity leave is not uniform, and/or the young mothers because of poverty, cannot stay from working for long periods of time.

Child care depends not only on the nature of work, especially of women, but the socio-economic strata the family belongs to. This determines the kind of substitute care available and what kind of care parents are able to buy and arrange for their child.

The rural/urban locale impacts day care too. While alternate child care may not be available in rural areas, generally the choices are limited in urban areas and care is more of a custodial type

(Datta,1995; Konantambigi, 1990). The Government funded centres, run by the NGOs are of low quality, and function like custodial care centres. Moreover, the attitudes and motivations of caregivers towards the care of another's baby are of significance in influencing the child care outcomes.

The story of the dynamics of care is a continuous one. The dissatisfaction with alternate child care generally has two dimensions, one is the physical care dimension or the custodial type of care that includes the satiation of basic needs of shelter, protection from physical harm and abuse, and food/nutrition needs. The other is in the realm of satiation of social and psychological needs. Some of them are the dynamics of parent-child, and child-caregiver attachment (and the way the parent/mother handles it), match of parental goals for child development and care, and those of the alternate caregiver. While parental goals and objectives in caring and discipline of the child have a long-term thrust, those of a substitute caregiver are temporary and may change with each caregiver in the same place/centre, or may change as parents may be forced to change the caregiver for various reasons. Professional and personal attitudes of the caregiver, her/his child care beliefs and practices determine how care of children in a group takes place.

This chapter aims to discuss how various developmental needs of children are met. The discussion on developmental needs is based on Erikson's (1950) psychosocial theory of development, Kagan's work (1984, 1979), Piaget's theory of cognitive development and my own observations (parent-child interactions) and interactions with parents and children. Children here mean infants or babies (from birth to 2 years of age), toddlers and pre-schoolers (2 to 6 years of age) and school-going children (aged 6 to 13 years). Depending upon the stage of life, their needs could vary. In the discussion to follow specific reference to these groups is made wherever necessary, and the discussion will pertain more to infants, babies and younger children. However, the discussion of various developmental needs would be proceeding needs wise. Physical, cognitive, re-creative, social, psychosocial and emotional needs will be the sections under which the elaboration would follow.

The Physical Needs of Children

The physical vulnerability of a child at birth requires that a hygienic environment be provided, immunization of the baby be ensured, constant physical care be available and regular routines of feeding, sleeping and physical warmth be ensured. Young infants also require this nature of care at very short, constant intervals. This is especially so in the first five to six months of the baby's age. There is no gainsaying the fact that all babies would require the routine care mentioned above. This routine care is of primary importance to the baby's adjustment to her environment. The provision of routine care poses no problems when primary caregivers are devoting their time exclusively to their babies. The mother of the child may be required to be gainfully employed (due to forced choices, like the economics of the situation, or self-imposed condition like the pursuance of a career). As per the terms and conditions of employment or her own situation that might require that she report to work while the baby is very young. This also has implications because young babies are fed exclusively on breast milk. Child care settings are away from the work place. This segregation and the facilities available to facilitate breast-feeding are of prime importance in the first year of the child's life. Women may also have to give up their careers if their child does not adjust at all to alternate care. Such instances were brought to the attention of the author during data collection, and other research reveals so too (Datta, 1993). Adjustment to new child care set up takes time. Parents and caregivers may be willing to spend time and make the efforts. But when children experience intense anxiety and refuse to accept food from others, parents are forced to heed to these distress signals and give-up their employment.

Mothers on their part experience anxiety because they are worried whether their child will be fed adequately, whether they will catch infection, etc. (Konantambigi, 1990; Konantambigi and Sriram, in the present volume). The provision of food for the child in the early years is of great concern for the parent. She has to plan out a whole days menu and provide it; pack it safely so that it can be used through the day. If the food is being provided by the day care centre, issues of whether it is prepared under safe and hygienic conditions, whether her child will find it palatable, and whether child will eat adequate quantities, would probably be some worries of the parent. Parents find it difficult to trust the caregivers, because our set-ups do not offer professional services, and it is assumed that being a woman is a good enough qualification to be a substitute caregiver. The food policy of the centre is of significance, as it could mean a proper one with the requisite variety of food or a limited one which has monotonous menus which may not be appetising enough. Programmes that do provide food are lacking in meeting the required needs (Datta, 2001).

The scenario is more alarmimg in lower socio-economic strata. Feeding and clothing, protection from the vagaries of nature, hygiene and attention are all sacrificed at the altar of basic survival. The baby sleeps in a makeshift bag; a cloth swing improvised by tying some strings to a nearby tree, to a pair of poles or whatever supports that can be garnered. If it is lacking, the baby's bed is on the hard ground or even on a stone! An older baby, generally half naked, plays in the mud, and consumes some dirt! (also see Prasad, this Volume). The mother is aware and is probably striving to keep an eye on the child. The mother also has to take care of the food needs of her children as she toils in difficult circumstances. In such situations basic provisions for children are absolutely essential to ensure minimum safety and care. Safety and care assume great significance because the child could pick up various infections, which could turn fatal.

Economic constraints, job requirements, work conditions and government policies regarding paid maternity and paternity leave influence what kind of care children get. Breast-feeding frequency and schedules are interrupted due to the nature of job — day jobs as well as the night shifts. Lack of privacy in crèches/day care centres influences feeding patterns. One of the existing beliefs is that strangers should not see the child being breast-fed or fed. The underlying belief is that an evil eye will be cast on children who are healthy and have healthy appetites, and subsequently, the child's intake and health is expected to suffer. (This is a child care belief prevalent in many communities in India. However empirical evidence for the same is lacking). Similarly, there is a belief, especially in South India that menstruating women from outside the home should not touch and feed babies. It is called "*muttu dosha*" in Kannada. Ramesh, B.M., personal communication, May 2001. Lack of provision for childcare near the work place and lack of adequate privacy for breast-feeding have their consequences. Early weaning has its consequences, not only on the health of the child but also on that of the mother. She experiences anxiety and guilt for not being able to breast feed the child. Provisions for expressing breast milk, its storage and feeding mechanisms need to thought about and implemented. A further consequence is that her anxiety and guilt affect interactions and bonding. The caregivers on their part can utilise the feeding situation to provide security and stimulation. Involving the child through eye contact and verbal interactions not only can ensure caregiver-child bonding which is crucial in the care giving process, but also act as a base for further stimulation and socialization. For the physical wellbeing of the child, the alternate care set-ups could make efforts to introduce variety of weaning foods and ensure that children do eat adequate quantities. The same dimension of feeding in public will change if the child belongs to a very low socio-economic status.

In the rural set-up too, the care scenario is bleak because mothers have a very demanding role to play as housekeepers and mothers. Families cannot ensure total hygiene because of the preoccupation with fulfilling survival needs and getting some food everyday. However, in work set-ups that are home-based, or are informal, there is frequent demand for breast-feeding. Lower SES parents do not have the luxury of attributing the "evil eye" to their child's feeding/eating. So they might be willing to participate in nutrition programmes of the centres and when they breastfeed their baby they are not necessarily looking for privacy and space. How much nutrition will the child get if the mother herself is not healthy is another issue altogether. But the case for childcare provisions at various contexts and work places especially where women work, cannot be reiterated enough.

As babies grow to be toddlers and pre-schoolers they can actively make choices in what they want to eat and can become fussy about eating. They can give a tough time to the caregivers, and the parents on their part could interpret this as indifferent care on the part of the caregivers. Dialogue and understanding of the needs of children at different stages, and how well they can be met need to be agreed upon by both the parties concerned. Communication regarding the nature and quality of food children consume should take place almost on a daily basis between caregivers and parents. This could quell the parental anxiety about the child's eating and ensure nutrition of the child. Furthermore, adequacy of nutrition has an effect on mental/cognitive functioning. Immediate effect of inadequate nutrition is lack of concentration on the tasks on hand. Over a period of time it has a cumulative effect leading to lowered academic performance. Khalakdina (1974) has well conceptualised as to what factors need to be considered if nutrition programmes have to be successful. Hygiene maintenance in groups could be an issue of contention if caregivers do not realise that inadequate care in this regard results in the spread of infections.

Children's feeding schedules have to take into account the fact that some children come to the centre from school, or go to school from the centre. The schedules should cater to children's eating needs. Moreover paying attention to children's individual sensitivity in asking the caregiver for food, asking the child whether he/she needs another helping need to be built into the feeding programme at the centre. Children express their needs differently and the caregivers need to be sensitive to it. Generally the attitude of the centres is that a schedule or practice is fine if it does not inconvenience the caregiver. Routines should not get regimented; in fact no aspect of care should attain the proportion of regimentation.

Feeding practices, in addition to physical dimensions have a psychosocial dimension. Physical feeding by the adults fulfils the dependency need in children. As they grow into pre-schoolers, efforts are generally done to encourage feeding by self. This enhances independence training. At times during early childhood a balance between catering to dependence needs and independence training for self-reliance need to be maintained. Intense early pressures for independence training may be harmful, burdening children with responsibility of their care.

At times some diseases/infections that children and caregivers carry could be dangerous with life long implications. There needs to be a separate room or the sick room or isolation practices should be enforced strictly. It is difficult to keep children from mingling, so a policy statement by the centres helps every one concerned. Sick children could also mean extra demands on the caregivers and additional responsibility. Babies and toddlers who are ill could take up a lot of the caregiver's time. Isolation practices are difficult to follow if sick children are allowed to attend the centre. It is next to impossible to keep children from interacting. Physical routines may take away time that needs to be spent on other activities and interactions. Sufficient number of caregivers, and support from parents needs to be elicited.

While at the issue of child's physical well-being, one needs also to focus on health care and medical attention; the medicines that children need to be given. This is another area where the parents and the caregivers need proper exchange of information as to when, what and how medicines need to be given to children. Allergies and reactions to medicines need to be clearly spelt out. In contrast to situations (middle and upper socio-economic strata) like the above, in caring for children in lower SES group, medical attention needs to be monitored by the caregivers. They should be empowered to handle such a situation.

Child health in terms of the immunisation programmes in the country has made great strides. But the mortality rate for India is around 63 for every 10,000 births (UNICEF, 2005). Differential mortality rates exist for urban and rural areas in India, the rates being higher in the rural areas. Our health system has a long way to go; and our government has yet to ensure basic health and hygiene system to its citizens. The government has the responsibility of ensuring systems that address survival of its citizens which has implications for the population growth of the country. The NGO and Government partnership has addressed some issues in child health and care (see Prasad, this Volume). This needs to translate into policies of care and training of caregivers.

Health and hygiene, physical amenities and quality of the physical environment together constitute the nature of the physical ecology that the child is in. In certain respects even some urban middle class homes may be lacking in appropriate physical environment, perhaps because of space constraint in metropolitan cities, like Mumbai (Balu, 1996). Awareness generation could come from the centres and formulation and implementation of policies for the functioning of centres. They are however in the purview of the quality of life that society sets to provide for its younger generation. The issue arises when day care centers or crèches and childcare places, which are set up by various agents of society and the government, do not heed to basic necessities. Studies show that centres, especially those that cater to lower economic groups are lacking in basic physical amenities (Konantambigi, 1990; Datta, 2001). A similar situation was observed in certain Municipal Schools in a Mumbai suburb (Konantambigi, 2000). The government, the custodians of care need to build these issues into policies, and related monitoring and regulation of the early childhood care is required. The significance of the policies, need to be reiterated because it means survival, health, lower mortality rates, and reduced anxiety for a great number of parents.

Routines of care are intense and frequent when children are babies. In the group care set up this calls for adequate child to staff ratio, and adequate hygienic amenities and practices for cooking, washing, etc. The parents of course take care of linen and clothes in private day care centres. Physical care of babies and young children needs careful, sensitive and tactful handling. The manner in which routine care is regulated has implications for feelings of psychological security and acceptance that are vital to the self concept of children. In the physical care too, exchange of information and practices between parents and caregivers is required, which resolves the differences, or each of them gets to know the developmental niche of the child better. The state on its part needs to ensure that trained caregivers are given these inputs, because the so called simple aspects of physical care have significant implications for development of children.

Safety needs of children of all ages need safety in the environment. They need space free of physical and chemical hazards; they need safe equipment and toys, safe drinking water and the like. Providing adequately for the safety of the child relieves the mother/family of the guilt and tension she would experience on leaving her child at a centre/entrusting the care of her child to others/ strangers.

The alternate care set-ups are very likely to lack in the extent of space available (especially in the urban areas) and the partitioning of space for various child and adult activities. Kitchen, adult work areas, and movement or activities for children might be taking place in the same room or in cramped spaces. Infants might be lying down and toddlers and pre-schoolers might be blissfully moving about and playing in the same area. There may not be safety grills and doors, perpetuating scope for accidents and children's unprecedented movements. There may also not be adequate locks and latches. Outdoor play areas may not be fenced and may not be free of hazardous materials. There may not be adequate supervision. Conditions like these have been noted in surveys and studies where the editors of present volume have participated (Datta, 1989). To add to the parental woes, safety issues could take on nerve racking monstrous experiences if there is a hint of physical and sexual abuse of the child (Datta, 1989; Konantambigi, 1990).

Adequate space for sleeping, crawling, walking, running around, playing and other indoor activities, a pleasant and bright environment and devoid of leakage and dampness are not only desirable features, but essential from the physical and mental health view of children and adults working in the set-up. In spite of research (Misra, Jain, and Bhargava, 1990) and experimental knowledge in this regard, crowded, dull and drab settings are found characterizing some of our centres. Research reveals that majority of such structures belong to our government (Datta, 1989; Gopal and Khan, 1998; Konantambigi, 1990; 2000).

A part of physical well-being requires adequate space for movement and play of children; older the age group, more is the space required. Most day care centres in Bangalore, had less than 12 square feet space per child (Konantambigi, 1990). Our urban locales on the whole lack adequate space for the free movement and play of children. This is reflected in the buildings and homes where our schools and child care centers are housed. When the society/the government do not plan to provide basic requirements, the private sector takes over. Once such resources are in the hands of the private sector, it means that one has to pay for the basic needs, which are to be the basic rights of children and citizens. It also means that only the rich, who can pay for those services will avail of them, further increasing inequitable division of resources in society. Economic reforms in the country are headed the Structural Adjustment Policy way and it implies a seller's market for the fulfilment of basic needs of children. The children's right to basic needs of care and play are left to the vagaries of market economy. The State needs to intervene.

Cognitive and Recreation Needs of Children

In the previous section, the issue related to play space and facilities has been discussed. Provision of play space and recreational facilities gives scope for a healthy body, mental relaxation and stimulation. Physical activities are known to stimulate certain cortical areas in the brain too. Manipulation of various kinds of objects, giving expression to curiosity and exploring the world are the hallmarks of childhood. Learning and cognition based on the exploration and handling objects in the physical world is essential. Play and explorative activities are grist for the cognitive mill. In the light of such facts, we need to pay serious attention to the provision of play spaces and facilities for both indoor and outdoor play. The educated middle and upper SES families do provide for play during the child's early years. But as the child enters school, more emphasis is placed on academic learning, and play and learning are segregated. This practice stems from the belief that academic performance is more important to learning and that play is separate from and less important to the realm of learning. After all the day-to-day school related learning is done, only then is a child expected to indulge in play.

Developmentally, sensory and cognitive stimulation to children needs to proceed from low to more variety in stimulation. The existing environment should be having an optimal level of variation (Kagan, 1984). More stimulation does not work in an additive or a multiplicative fashion (Gamble and Zigler, 1986; Konantambigi, Chapter 7). Middle class homes generally have variability; the environment is not lacking in things around the house and should suffice. Of course, interactions to facilitate babies' and children's interactions with the physical world have to take place. Adults do this, some more efficiently that others. In Vygotskian (Vygotsky, 1978) terms we should know the child's zone of proximal development for the learning that is taking place, and we should know when to scaffold. Conceptual learning too is taking place as the child encounters the environment à la Piaget. One needs to provide enough variability and experiences for both accommodation and assimilation to take place. Adult interventions which are facilitative and do not rob children of the joy of discovery and learning will go a long way in instilling the love and need for learning in general. Strictly enforced stimulation, recreations and even play will disrupt the natural process of continued learning. The need is for having an open facilitative attitude towards learning, and this comes from knowing how children learn. Caregivers need this information.

In child care settings the personnel could be preoccupied with the maintenance of the place; with the management of routines. The administrative concerns could over rule the needs of the child, and therefore, there could be limitations placed on exploration by children and on the kinds of play that is permitted. It needs reiterating that the concern has to be providing for the development of children.

Cognitive growth, however, does not take place in a technical set-up devoid of social and emotional support, especially in early years (Vygotsky,1978). The approving support and acceptance of adults is required. When caregivers and teachers have such an insight into children's behaviours, or as individuals are sensitive to the overall needs of children, are they able to provide for the overall growth as well as learning in children (Konantambigi, 1990; 2000).

In a society at a given period of time in its development, certain skills and knowledge are valued. Society directly or indirectly encourages the learning of those skills. In India, for the past four decades at least, academic learning and professionally oriented skills which fetch lucrative jobs and career opportunities have been encouraged. The encouragement has started early. In the urban middle and upper classes it begins with the pre-school child at times it starts during the late toddler-hood itself. Toddlers are sent to play groups. The overemphasis on academic learning and learning through the rote method continues. Parental awareness in this respect is the need and parents could be made conscious of their duty of facilitating development and not imposing certain kinds of learning on the child. However, the more cognitively savvy middle and upper SES families want their child to learn at the conceptual level, through the experiential and other less didactic means. They are willing to provide the play materials and opportunities and expect the centres to do likewise (Konantambigi and Sriram, this volume).

Generally physical care routines take up most of the time in centres. If the programme is not balanced, cognitive stimulation may take a back seat. Providing experience and stimulation and valuing a child's learning means a willingness to put up with the mess they create as they play and accept a grubby dirty child for most of the day. They need to be allowed to participate in the chores and activities that go around in the setting, be it at home or the centre/alternate care arrangement. The child may indulge in fantasy, make believe play, but he/she knows that the real thing is out there, where the adults are! Young, curious children want to know and learn the activities that adults indulge in around the house. This means that caregivers/parents should spare time and have patience, and it means one has to tolerate delays; a difficult proposition if one is following a scripted schedule. Babies and children are not expected to understand this. The parents and caregivers, while they cannot possibly give-in every time, need to provide the scope for child-paced activities. One also needs to accept the tasks as completed by children. They are learning and cannot be expected to be perfect. Saying "its fine" and then going on to do a number of corrections in front of the child definitely gives the wrong messages to children. One would drive them to perfection and discourage initiative and experimentation. Some children are more sensitive than others. More the corrections more are the damage to the child's initiative. In the management of activities and schedules for children, practical aspects of care and staffing pattern are to be considered, so as to provide the requisite care and stimulation.

Stimulation provided to children should also follow the growth patterns/neuromuscular maturity (milestones in development). Keeping pace with their growth and their needs ensures the required stimulation. Forced stimulation could create a burden on the child, and kill his/her natural instinct for dealing/manipulating the environment. Burn-out is something we keep hearing about. The child cannot be made the conduit for one's own unfulfilled aspirations.

Considering that the family is the basic unit of society, and a primary locale for initial learning and socialisation, cognitive development is facilitated by the family. This does happen in the middle and upper class homes. The family especially provides for it knowing that caregivers/teachers in alternate care settings and pre-schools/schools do not have the required time, or the strength of children is too large to warrant enough adult attention and interaction. In this regard, children from lower SES lose out, because these families are not adequately equipped to deal with this situation. In addition to this, problem occurs when settings/pre-schools/schools for the lower SES children are deficient in programmes providing cognitive and re-creative facilities. Research has already demonstrated time and again that providing the required early cognitive stimulation can make a difference to the learning required in early school years. The benefits of early stimulation last for at least three years in school (Head Start, ICDS). There are additional costs involved in terms of trained personnel and other resources. The focus needs to be the overall development of every child, and providing for the requisite developmental needs. Simple low cost materials, adult supervision and guidance when children cannot proceed ahead, are the basic guidelines to enhance cognitive stimulation. Cognitive needs and recreational needs are viewed in isolation. They could be merged, and a single activity could be catering to multiple needs of children. A point of caution for middle and upper-middle class families is over protection of children. It can be extremely limiting, and thwarting of children's natural flair and interest (aptitude) for certain skills and activities. Inclination for work with children and willingness to experiment with simple materials may be the key to stimulation of children in centres catering to lower income groups.

Certain programmes in early childhood care and education in the country, for example, the government run Integrated Child Development Services Scheme (ICDS) has incorporated some of these features. How it is translated into action and how effective it is, is not in the purview of this chapter. (See Prasad for this volume for some discussion on ICDS).

Research has revealed that parents expect day care centres to provide for academic and some cognitive stimulation, and where such stimulation is given the parents are satisfied with it (Konantambigi and Sriram, Chapter 5, this volume). In earlier studies too observations had revealed that some cognitive stimulation is provided for (Datta, 1993; Konantambigi, this volume) some specific goals may more easily be met by the centres. However, most centres tend to have highly structured, fixed activities. They may view activities as means of keeping children engaged, and out of their way rather than recognising play and activities as means of learning, and therefore, a serious business of childhood. This recognition is something which needs to be instilled in both parents and caregivers. Policy and programme guidelines need to take cognisance of this.

Social Needs

Childhood in the human species is a fairly long period of dependency in the lifespan compared to other primates and mammals. This period is the stage for learning. The learning of social skills through observation, imitation, vicarious learning and socialisation is more intense during the early period. The growing baby needs adult voices (of reassurance, security and warmth), adult interactions for social as well as other kinds of learning. The child needs them to learn language, and to imitate adult behaviours and nuances of social interactions. Social development would encompass being able to communicate, get along with others and get what one wants out of the social world, learn to be self-reliant too and give support when others require it. These behaviours take place so naturally in social interactions that we take them for granted. But a growing child imbibes all these as she/he interacts with the social world.

Early period is not only the training ground for social interactions but also a stage where the young elicit social support from others. The dependent, helpless nature of babies makes other adults and older children to have a protective, more giving stance towards young children. As these babies and toddlers grow-up and begin to interact with their peers, the relationship is one of equals and by the time children are in school they are expected by and large, to hold their own. For this need fulfilment, they need the company of children of their own age. As children grow, they also need to learn emotional control. Emotional control and the proper controlled expression of emotions aids fruitful interactions in the peer world and protect the child's ego. Exposed emotional weakness leaves the child vulnerable to further hurt in social interactions. This is more so with children who are temperamentally more sensitive. Relating to adults is also a needed opportunity for social interaction.

The Indian joint family provided/provides a number of adult role models. Cousins of similar age acted/act as a peer group to train in the social skills and their nuances. They act as models who if available for the whole day can provide guidance too. If such is the situation, children can constantly watch the adults in action. Large joint families provided for social interactions, sharing, providing support to others. (The large joint family though has not been the norm in Indian society, and even today one finds that various family forms exist. However, there is a tendency to believe that the joint family was the norm in the past and that there is a movement towards nuclear family as the norm). But constantly being in groups does not provide scope for the fulfilment of individual needs; and may not also provide adequate scope for the growth of individual abilities and skills. Similarly, if the child of today spends most of the time in such group care, and if there is also no scope for individuality and the growth of skills at home, she will be the loser.

But families with the small family norm and maternal employment may be balancing the various developmental needs and the socialisation goals of their child. The nuclear family with small family norm, without the mother being employed outside the home has the advantage. This makes the mother available to the child all through the day. In the context of the nuclear family, where both the parents hurry to work, and if the child does not have other significant adults he or she can emulate then he or she is deprived of role models. However, this does not mean that child parent-bonding gets affected. Under such circumstances, one of the prevailing anxieties in mothers (expressed informally during data collection, Konantambigi; 1990) is that children will get attached to the caregiver and not to them, the parents! The social construction of family reality is such that, children very early in life know who the significant others are, what is the hierarchy of these significant others, and that she is expected to emulate these people. The child on entry into the childcare centre or alternate care may and does develop attachment to other caregivers if they are caring and affectionate enough (Kagan, Kearsley and Zelazo, 1979; personal communication to the author by parents and caregivers in research studies, and supervision of day care programmes). But the child knows that the significant others are his family members and it is them that he is going to look up to.

When the child is put into day care or alternate care, the caregiver is up against this barrier, that is, that the child is not attached to her and does not accept care and is not amenable to socialisation. She has to care for, provide affection, discipline, and run the show smoothly in the group care situation. She has to manage the child through the day. At the end of the day, the child nor the parent may consider her to be the "significant person". She may be seen as providing a valuable service, and may be well regarded if the child has formed an attachment. The "significant others" for the child are most likely to be the parents. Whether the caregivers are accorded the exalted status of "significant other by the child depends on how the parent/family views the caregiver, and what behavioural message, rather than the verbal message the child is given. This issue is of importance because it determines the kind of habits, disciplining and inculcation of moral values that the child will imbibe, and whether the caregiver will be in a position to impart them. The caregiver may consciously keep the child at arms length for fear of attachment. Attachment could bring in more demands from the child as well as the parents, the caregiver views her role on a short term basis — manage child care for the day or for some days to come, and does not dwell on the impact of her behaviour on the child. It will also influence the nature of relationship that the parents and the caregivers will have. However, there will be other dynamics involved in this situation. It is problematic if the child is attached to the caregiver and the parent views it as a threat to her bond with the child. Insecurities generally bring a difficult stance to the interaction situation, and the parent could be constantly finding fault with the caregiver. In her/his relationship with the child, instead of parenting by setting limits and reasonable control, the parent might end up giving in to the child's unreasonable demands most of the time which in turn is not in favour of the child's development. Bribing the child when s/he is young may seem the easy wayout to keep the child happy. In the long-run, the child may start blackmailing the parent emotionally and may get on to the socially undesirable trajectory of development.

Another issue is of a match between the child rearing/ socialisation goals of the parents/family and the caregiver. A fairly good match is expected. Otherwise they may be at loggerheads, and depending on the severity of need for caregiver, the parents may decide to let things be, and do the needful socialisation, disciplining, moral teaching, on their own. Parents and caregivers may deal with these issues on a practical level. But it could instill feelings of confusion regarding how to behave and result in insecurity in children. Open disputes could also mean that caregivers might pick on the child. The children may also learn to behave in more opportunistic ways.

In contrast to the situation mentioned above, a lack of adequate socialisation from the home front, the child may benefit from being in alternate care. This would obviously be more so if the caregiver is from a higher social stratum than the child. Benefits do accrue to children hailing from home backgrounds lacking in language, and limited social skills due to the milieu of their life and the parent's work situation. The elaborate language code, the disciplining, inculcation of good habits and routines, and opportunity to observe children/adults from a higher SES above them help. 'Sanskritisation' of kind will definitely take place; and add to the child's social skills.

One of the needs of young children as they are disciplined and limits set, requires that there be regularity, and there be security in regularly reinforced discipline and habits. Here too, a match of the parental and caregiver discipline is required. The issue may be more serious if morality is involved. These issues would definitely arise with educated parents who have a definite disciplinary and moral agenda for their children's development. At such times, an openness of mind and a will to dialogue to solve the problems needs to be present in both the parties concerned.

In this regard a prevailing belief about childcare needs is in order, which has been mentioned in an earlier part of the chapter. By and large one is not expected to entrust the care of one's child to others, to strangers. The mother and the women folk of the family are expected to perform the role, the duty. In situations where the parents are availing of childcare services the parents on their part are experiencing the guilt. The caregivers on their part may not have the openness and maturity to give of their best to others' children. If they view it like a job and mechanically go about their duty, it is not going to be in the developmental interest of children. The parents' experience of guilt has another dimension. It makes them behave in ways to overcompensate for leaving the child away for the day. Disciplining becomes weak; certain habits, which they know are unwanted, may be inculcated. These issues may be ignored when children are small, but certain habits, messages and life styles that are given to children could become a part of them and their life. This has further implications for the development of inner limits for life, the concept of "parents" that is developed and the dynamics of parent-child relationship.

The joint families of yore or those of today have multiple caregivers (significant others) involved in the care of children (Gore, 1978). Differences existed and they had to be sorted out. Individual differences in the inculcation of morality existed. There are also instances of jealous display of love and affection for favoured children. But they taught the value of caring for others in a group, learning to live in groups, to share, to give and take. The issue is not of just giving and taking. These values are the ones which balance individualistic and collectivist feelings and practices and build social support networks of a society. Societies need to ponder deep, and foster values for cohesive community values. The state could facilitate this by incorporating such values in child caregiver training (Sinha, 1984).

Under the prevailing circumstance of maternal employment and alternate childcare, group childcare provides a regular platform for peer interaction in early life. With family size norm being small, and joint families not being the order of the day, day care centres play a crucial role in providing for peer interaction of the intimate kind. Children spend time together on a variety of day-to-day activities. It also provides opportunities for the development of self-reliance. Peer play cuts across various aspects of developmental needs, not just for social skills learning. Provisions for them to be made, one cannot reiterate the point enough. However, I am of the view, taking from Erikson (1950) that in the process of peer interactions and social skills learning, children should not prematurely assume responsibility for themselves and others. They need to experience the dependent stage of childhood. Only then would they become equipped, after having received adequately, to become independent and to become good nurturers. Deep rooted social and emotional needs have to be fulfilled during childhood. Otherwise, a phenomenon akin to burnout in early education can take place. This does not mean that children do not participate in the daily chores going on in the house or at the centre, but that children are not put into Hamlet-like situations.

Psychosocial and Emotional Needs

During the course of social development the child goes through various phases. Some of the phases have implications because parents decide to put children in alternate care whenever circumstances seem favourable. One of the circumstances that they should consider is the age of the child. By the time the baby is six months old he/she has developed an attachment, cognitively misses the mother/other people in the environment who have played a significant role in the child's care. The child is capable of being and of experiencing the loss of the person; distress is expressed. So if one has to resort to child care this early in the child's life, it is before the child recognises familiar others and forms an attachment. Beginning at four or five months of age the child could get used to ecology where alternate caregivers do care for the child. The concern at this stage should be providing stable care; not changing the centre, and hopefully a few caregivers taking care of the child for the following couple of years at least. Before the child is admitted to the centre, the centre practices could encourage parents and babies to spend some time at the centre and with the caregivers. One can strive to provide continuity in the environment.

Another crucial age at which the child could be disturbed is around one year of age when stranger anxiety is at its peak. The child could be distressed at being left with strangers. One needs to also take into account individual differences in the exact age at which they experience stranger anxiety. Generally, if children do not experience alternate child care early in life, then it is perhaps better to wait till the child is around three years of age. However, there is no adequate research to support the above contention. In one study, pre-school aged entrants to day care were better adjusted than children whose mothers returned to work before children were one year of age (Moskowitz, Schwarz and Corsini, 1977). A long-term longitudinal study of 25 years by Easterbrooks and Goldberg (1985) supports the ecological viewpoint, where early entrants to alternate care were well-adjusted because that was the nature of the environment in which they grew up. At times, mothers may have to quit jobs if their child is extremely sensitive to be being left with others. If care is taken to ensure early bonding with the father/ or other adults as well then it may be possible for both the parents to work part-time and care for the baby. The State could instill employment policies which would provide for paternity leave and let couples have flexible work schedules.

The provision of stability in childcare, how childcare is provided (how babies are handled and played with), the way norms are enforced and disciplining goes on have deeper significance as they are related to the fulfilment of psychosocial growth and emotional needs of children. While discharging these needs I am going to elaborate on Erikson's (1950; 1967) theory of psychosocial development as it applies to the early stages of childhood. From birth to about six months of age, through the way babies are cared for and played with, the basic trust is instilled. Handling the baby with care, timely fulfilment of the basic needs for food, warmth and comfort, conveys the message that the baby is a valued person and she/he can trust the world to care. Erikson says that this instills not only trust in others, but a trustworthiness about ourselves; it instills hope which is required throughout life.

Children develop attachments to persons who care for them regularly and people who play and are sensitive to them. It is not necessary that only biological parents care for children. Any sensitive, caring adult can play the role and the child will develop attachment and develop trust. If for some reason trust has not been instilled, it can be instilled through sensitive care. Parents and caregivers can rectify the situation if something has gone awry in the process of early care.

In the next stage where the neuro-muscular system of the child is maturing, as she/he is mastering bowel and bladder control, again sensitive handling of a baby/child is required. Through the maturation of various neuro-muscular systems the individuation/separation processes are also on. Treating toilet accidents harshly, severely curbing the autonomy of the child, and making fun of the child and insulting the child as the child grows older are going to instill feelings of shame and doubt about one's autonomy. Early autonomy plays an important role in the development of self-esteem and self-concept. Inner doubts about the muscular control in bowel and bladder movements instill doubt, harsh parental toilet training enforce doubt. A lack of respect for the child and the treatment accordingly are anathema to the concept of fair dealing. Early equations between children and the adults determine the base for democracy according to Erikson. A part of this equation is already not in favour of the child as there are gross physical differences between a child and a parent. So from infancy through to toddler-hood and childhood parents need to ensure that they are fair in their dealings with their children.

During late toddler-hood and early childhood, the child has mastered locomotion and language and is eager to explore the environment. The accidents of spilling, breaking and dirtying things, of hurting oneself accidentally, and the way the odd and difficult questions that he/she asks especially related to sex are answered, all induce guilt in the child. The guilt is for the initiative he takes in things, and for being punished when things go wrong according to adult standards, or when in actuality things break/spill and the child does feel bad about it. Accidents have to be accepted, the initiative of the child has to be accepted to give scope/impetus for her growth.

This, however, does not mean that children should not be disciplined. Setting limits and providing guidance, giving a shoulder to cry when they make mistakes help instill the superego. Parents who do not set limits and do not discipline the child will be viewed as a weak parent; a parent to be ashamed of, says Harry Stack Sullivan (see Chapman and Chapman, 1980). The child requires guidance and limits to reduce the anxiety that is created in taking initiatives/decisions in the development of the individuation process and in the experiencing of freedom. A weak parent/caregiver will not be looked up to, will not be identified with, and this will hinder the individuation-separation process anchor. For reasons like this, parents and caregivers need to have a dialogue regarding limits and limit setting. Consistent limits of certain kinds, which might appear not to be in favour of the child, must still be set-up. No limits means the society loses a person who could have become a good citizen.

In this context of discipline too, cultural beliefs play a role (Kakar, 1978). Indian scriptures and folk beliefs advocate intense care, relaxed toilet training (there is almost a lack of it) and no strict disciplining till the child is five years old. It is believed that children only need unconditional love and care, and no disciplining. But discipline is definitely to be enforced in an older child. Practices which do not break the basic spirit and self-esteem of the child are to be inculcated. Cultural beliefs that play crucial roles in child rearing have to be discussed between the parents and the caregivers.

Beliefs about disciplining have also to be kept in mind because according to Erikson during the childhood stage, the child realises the physical inequality in the anatomy of the self and the adult/parent. He/she also realises that what is given to him or what he/she is engaged in doing could be taken away from him by the adults. In such instances initiative and industry on the part of the child suffer. Again, for a democratic society, industry, and the belief in 'I can become what I want to' through efforts, needs to be supported. However gender differences have prevailed in childcare beliefs, and industry in girls and boys are differentially supported.

One can discuss SES differences in setting goals for their children. Lower SES groups will invariably tend to set-up only survival goals, and activities to support such a living. Middle and higher SES families set economic and self-actualization goals (Sigelman and Shaffer, 1995). They do this through disciplining children, through providing for the education and exposure, and through moral training. Together with the families, the alternate caregivers need to work towards supporting higher order goals of socialisation. The government support to centres that are set up or public funding to centres is justified if higher order socialisation rather than the mere custodial care of the children takes places. The state has a very significant role if it gets down to enforcing quality care for children.

Generally, without our knowledge, we are role models for children as well as models for emotional learning in children. Parents, caregivers and significant others are especially models for such learning. Children (individual differences in this regard exist) vicariously take in our emotional reactions and the way we handle emotion-laden situations. Emotional socialisation that takes place at the centre is, of course, significant for the child, but it portrays the whole personality of the caregiver. He/she is watched by the parent or the community and the person is expected to be a good model for everyone concerned. The caregiver sensitivity in terms of attention s/he gives; his/her listening ability especially when the child is upset; and providing scope to experience and label the emotion, and then to present the consequences of possible action; and guiding the child to take constructive action would be some of the behaviours that would enhance the emotional capabilities in children. Characteristics of caregivers assumes importance, and there is a need for the state to take cognizance of such aspects in the recruitment and training of child care personnel.

Acceptance of the child, providing an emotionally secure base, respecting the child as an individual on the path of development, who needs an empathetic friend and guide, rather than a self-centred adult are some of the basic ingredients for healthy emotional development. Empathy and understanding create an acceptance and provide security to pursue higher self-actualization goals. A significant indicator is the eye-contact that the caregiver/teacher has with the child and the rest of body language of the caregiver/teacher that tell us about the acceptance of the other. My hypothesis is that this is further related to the SES and appeal value of the other. We gaze and maintain eye-contact more with children from our own SES, or with children/persons belonging higher SES. In the contexts of alternate caregivers/teachers of children hailing from lower SES, the caregiver/teacher belongs to a relatively higher SES. It affects the caregiver-child interaction, and does not provide the basic requisite input for child care, wellbeing and learning in children. The State, therefore, needs to give importance to micro issues in caregiver/teacher-child interactions and inculcate such aspects in the training of child care personnel.

In conclusion, forms of the family may change, but adults have to cater to the various developmental needs of children. For this purpose we, the parents and the caregivers, that is, all of the adult population need to dwell on long term and short term goals for the child as well as for the society. The child care profession needs to help articulate the goals and provide a platform for a dialogue between the parents and caregivers and even at the level of policy makers. A holistically healthier ecology for human development needs to be created.

The State has to focus on some of the following to make the environment more child friendly, and also to instill continuity of the fulfilment of basic needs so that holistic development of human beings can continue.

- Balancing individualistic and collectivistic ideologies.
- Sensitivity in handling children, basic acceptance of children and recognising the importance of understanding how emotional socialisation can go on in the child care sets-up is of significance. The state can play a role by setting/ emphasizing standards in the functioning of centres, and in the recruitment and training of caregivers.
- The issues raised in the chapter need to reach the parents too. The child care centres, play groups, early childhood education set-up could play the role of outreach. Again state norms for training in this regard could help.
- Regulation, monitoring, professionalism, advocacy, networking and coordination requirements need to be addressed.

SECTION-II

Women, Work and Child Care

3

CHILD CARE OPTIONS IN AGRICULTURAL CONTEXTS*

— *Rajalakshmi Sriram* and *Hemalatha Ganapathy*

Women work

I've got the children to tend
The clothes to mend
The floor to mop
The food to shop
Then the chicken to fry
The baby to dry
I got company to feed
The garden to weed
I've got shirts to press
The tots to dress
The cane to be cut
I got clean up this hut
Then see about the sick

Shine on me, sunshine

Rain on me, rain
Fall softly, dewdrops
And cool my brow again.

— *Maya Angelou*

---

* Reprinted with permission of authors and publisher, EPW, 1998, XXXII (43), WS-64.

This article examines the changing circumstances of women's lives and work, the consequent burden of multiple roles and the child care support systems utilised by them in the face of practical constraints. Focusing on child care, it presents evidence from four unique research studies that probe into not only the child care supports used by employed mothers but also women's perceptions about these, their preferences and the options viewed by communities as viable. Drawing from this, conceptual issues pertaining to child care have been raised and a strong argument has been made in favour of adequate child care services.

The issue of women, work and child care, the role conflicts that employed women are confronted with, the limited options they have, their attempts to make the most of whatever supports exist and the effects of these on children have been the subject of debate over the last two decades by nutritionists, psychologists, child development professionals and feminists. This topic was focused upon because of:

— a series of researches and debate worldwide which concentrated on extricating and explaining the variables implicated in the issue of women's work and child care.

— workshops, seminars, discussions and individual attempts at piecing together the factors into a more coherent and multi-perspective whole.

Genesis and Evolution of Debate

The origins of the debate can be traced to the early 1980s when international definitions of work were examined and found wanting (Dixon-Mueller and Anker, 1988; Mukhopadhyay, 1981). These definitions considered the productive and reproductive roles of women as mutually exclusive and implied that women could choose between the two. Actually, in poverty contexts, women can ill-afford the luxury of choosing between productive and reproductive roles (Doan and Popkin, 1989; Leslie, 1989). There are over 91 million women in the labour force, of whom 24-26 million have children below the age of two (*Shramshakti*, 1988). Economic constraints demand that they earn an income, especially as they happen to be sole providers in more than 30 per cent of the households (Prasad, 1997) and that they perform nurturing roles simultaneously. Women are viewed as the main providers of child care and feel guilty and anxious if unable to do so. This scenario is unfortunate in the light of historical facts which have been scrutinised by Lamb, Sternberg, Hwang and Broberg (1992) in a book titled *Child Care in Context*. Studies of hunter gatherers and agricultural societies show that exclusive mothering was never an option for women in Homo Sapiens history. Depending on the task, the season, children's ages, availability of alternatives and women's working conditions, children accompanied one parent or the other or were left under the supervision of others. Child care was shared by family members and neighbours. By some quirk, exclusive maternal care, which was a luxury for a few, came to be viewed as the typical practice. The difference today is that with average household sizes shrinking (as a result of male migration and decreasing fertility), consequent reduction in support, environmental degradation (entailing travel over long distances for fuel, water and fodder), women's lives become more demanding (Lamb *et al.* 1992). While industrialisation has created opportunities on the one hand, it has, on the other, disrupted familiar cultural practices and patterns that women had developed over the years to cope with their multiple roles. Modern day work is much more regimented and less easily adapted to child care needs. This leads to an incompatibility between mother's productive and reproductive roles. Such incompatibility affects many women as female labour force participation peaks at 25-44 years — the very years when child care responsibilities also at peak (Jain & Chand, 1981; *Shramshakti,* 1988). A host of other factors complicate the issue further. Women work long hours because of unstable or absent male incomes or reduced access to the same. Battling for time, energy and financial resources, child care is done concurrently with other tasks,

Nutritional Status

A number of research studies in the 1970s and 1980s concluded that maternal employment jeopardises the child's nutritional status. While some studies reported Vitamin A deficiency (Engle, 1981), others reported a decline in the nutritional status of children of employed mothers because of deprivation from breastfeeding time (Kumar, 1978; Ramalingaswami *et al.*, 1996). However, few nutrition studies found significant relationships between maternal work status and infant feeding practices thus rendering them questionable.

Employed mothers sometimes resort to the use of formal child care support in order to cope with their burden. When crèches and day care centres were examined, they were found to be lacking in certain aspects:

- Poor quality of services rendered as surmised from poor adult child ratio, low emphasis on training in developmental and educational aspects and inadequate attention to effective materials and approaches (Khullar, 1991; Swaminathan, 1993).
- Inflexibility of service models (Government of India, 1986).
- Absence of women's participation in designing the service models (Sriram, 1998; Swaminathan, 1985).

The implications of these for the development of the child were discussed and the verdict was adverse. It was concluded that poorly designed and delivered services have a negative effect upon child development.

Women in Development Studies

Studies of women in development came to starkly different conclusions. Many found that mothers who are employed spend a greater proportion of their incomes on the welfare of their children as compared to the fathers. They focused on women's and children improved decision-making powers and self-confidence (Chaudhari, 1990; Huffman, 1985). Hence, they took the diametrically opposite stand of summarising that maternal employment is, in fact, beneficial to children.

While the first two perspectives viewed the issue from the standpoint of children, the last viewed matters from the woman's angle. None of these studies examined both sides of the issue. What was common to all three was the study of the effect of maternal employment on child welfare, of factors guiding choices and consequences. For instance, in nutrition studies, maternal employment was assumed to be the cause and the child's nutritional status, the outcome. An alternative interpretation that anxiety over the child's well-being may have motivated the mother to seek employment was not taken cognisance of. According to Ramalingaswami *et al.*, (1996) rather than the presence or absence of the mother, it is the timing and quality of feeding, i.e. feeding practices that eventually decide whether or not a child is going to be well nourished. Similarly, in Early Childhood Care and Education studies, the conditions that force a woman to opt for an ill-equipped, poorly-functioning crèche or day care centre or an unreliable neighbour or relative were not given due consideration.

Overall, evidence has been inconsistent indicating sometimes conceptual and at times methodological flaws (Himes, Landers & Leslie, 1991). The complexity of the woman's work-child care situation was viewed for a long time in a fragmented manner and seldom in its entirety.

Towards a Holistic Conceptualisation of Child Care

A significant milestone in understanding women's work patterns was '*Shramshakti*', the Report of the National Commission of Self-employed Women and Women in the Informal Sector, 1988. It drew attention to the magnitude of the problems related to women's work and their lives in the informal/self-employed sector that had been completely neglected so far. The plight of these women and their child care situation were highlighted. The National Perspective Plan for Women (Government of India, 1988) took cognisance of this and made recommendations for expansion and inputs into support services, one of which was childcare.

After 1991, a national study covering six states (Gujarat, Delhi, West Bengal, Maharashtra, Madhya Pradesh and Rajasthan) was co-ordinated by the Centre for Women's Development Studies (CWDA). Results indicated high levels of inadequacy in coverage and quality of child care services. For the first time, child care was conceptualised as a support to women's development. Action was initiated through the formulation of the Forum for Crèche and Child Care Services, FORCES, a national network to bring the issue of child care to the forefront. The main purpose was the welfare, development, education and empowerment of women, girls and children. This initiative was followed up by individuals and institutions is some parts of the country.

The first was a collaborative research which was part of a larger project under the aegis of the International Development Research Centre (IDRC), Canada through the Department of Human Development and Family Studies (HDFS), M.S. University, Baroda from 1983 to 1993. Co-ordinated by Saraswathi, a study on women's work and child care was conducted by five researchers in four different regions of which Ganapathy (1992) was one. A key concept in these studies was that of 'Availability'. Child care has traditionally been viewed as the actual activity of caring for a child such as feeding or bathing. What has to be understood is that child care needs change with the age of the child. Direct care is necessary only during the first 2-3 years. It gradually changes into more indirect forms such as verbal instructions or reprimands. At any time, though not engaged in active childcare, people may be present in the vicinity of the child. They are 'potential caregivers' and their presence is called 'availability'. The concept of availability supplemented and expanded the concept of childcare.

Besides this effort, the Department of HDFS undertook a series of small-scale research studies co-ordinated by Sriram (1987-93) to understand the childcare needs of urban middle class working women of Baroda and women in rural agricultural sectors in Gujarat and two north-eastern states. Simultaneously, a collaboration project was initiated with Mahila Samkhya, Baroda (a programme for women's empowerment) to assess needs and evolve flexible models and training packages that are friendly and empowering to rural women (documented in Suraksha Series "Another Kind of Child Care", 1995). Results proved that provision for women-friendly action for child care can empower women by fostering leadership, creating a 'space' for women including greater voice and better image in the community.

The comprehensive research and documentation work undertaken by the M.S. Swaminathan Research Foundation, Chennai, in examining how women balance multiple roles (Arulraj and Samuel 1995; Narayanan, 1997) among others reinforce the crying need for child care supports and programme and policy alternations. Of these and aside from them, very few studies have scrutinised the problems and needs of women *vis-à-vis* child care together with their perceptions about existing child care arrangements and the options perceived by them as viable.

Child Care among Women Agricultural Workers: Primary Research Findings

The present section integrates findings from four studies. Of these, three studies viewed all the above mentioned components in conjunction — Sriram (1992), Garrey (1993), and Fanai (1993). A fourth study by Ganapathy (1992) investigated the child care management strategies adopted by women tea pluckers. All four researchers studied women in different agricultural settings. They covered disparate geographical regions and used a variety of tools and techniques (Table 3.1). While three of these represented the unorganised sector, the fourth represented the organised sector.

The Settings

Gujarat

The nine rural and tribal villages comprised landholders and a few landless labourers. Men and women worked on their own farm or as farm labourers or combined both when produce from the land was insufficient. Jowar, cotton, rice and tuver were the main crops. Most

Table 3.1 : Sources of data

Place, Researcher, Year, Study Details	Gujarat - Sriram, R. (1992)	Meghalaya - Garrey, W.M. (1993) Mizoram - Fanai, H. E. (1993)	Kerala - Ganapathy (1992)
I Primary Sources - Four Research Studies			
	• Understanding rural women's and children's lives and examining CC* with respect to available supports, services, perceptions, satisfaction needs.		• Identifying alternate CC arrangements made by tea plucker mother. • Examining differences in availability of people for CC. • Examining plantation crèche.
Objectives	• Evolving participatory, processual training modes for village workers, women to facilitate field level action and implementation. • Documentation for replicability.	Including strengths + weakness (Fanai) and suitable alternatives.	
Subjects and Sample	9 rural tribal villages. ★ 148 mothers ★ 24 fathers ★ 40 other caregivers ★ 115 girls	4 + 4 village 43+50 mothers 12+34 fathers 52 other caregivers 7 other functionaries	1 tea plantation 43 0-6 years old from 30 families.
Tools and Techniques	Indepth Interviews and Observations (in all 4)		
	• Meetings • Trainings • Workshops • Visits	Focus group discussion	• Spot observations • Yesterday Recall Interviews.
II. Secondary Sources : Review of literature, research studies, government reports, seminar proceedings.			

* CC - Child care

of the families (60 per cent rural and 50 per cent tribal) were nuclear. Most of the women were illiterate or were not prepared to reveal their educational level or did not know it.

Meghalaya

The four villages represented the traditional villages of Garo Hills. Families were mostly low-income and nuclear, 63 per cent of the mothers were illiterate. The main occupation of the sample was agriculture with rice, millet, cotton, ginger, chillies and a host of vegetables dominating the produce. Some of these were retained for home consumption while the rest was sold in markets. Income depended on landholdings and for some, on subsidiary occupations such as government job or private business.

The Garos of Meghalaya follow the matrilineal family system and matrilocal residence pattern. In addition to this special feature, another characteristic that merits mention is their style of Jhuming cultivation or slash-and-burn cultivation. In recent times, due to the increase in population, availability of land close to home has declined thereby increasing the distance from home to workplace. Men and women work side by side but despite this and the matriarchal social order, women have to bear the burden of domestic work in addition to work on the fields.

Mizoram

The four selected villages were representative of North, South, East and West Mizoram and were densely populated. Of the sample, 62 per cent of the families were nuclear and though comparatively better-off when compared with the Meghalaya sample, they lived under monetary constraint. Here, 91 per cent of the mothers were literate. The chief occupation was agriculture with jhum cultivation as the norm.

Kerala

The tea estate which formed the study site was located in Peerumade, Idukki district. What set this locale apart was that this was representative of the organised sector. Estate residents were

Tamilians or Malayalees all of whom worked on the tea factory or as coolies on the estate. Living quarters were provided to them. Almost all the women were literate and all tea pluckers. Tea plucking is a full time job with long hours involving rapid, delicate work done standing on hilly terrain with tea baskets slung on the back. Hence unlike in the other three settings, tea pluckers were forbidden from taking their children with them to the worksite.

Activity Profile of the Women

In keeping with regional variations, in terms of customary practices, lifestyle and geographical terrain women in each locale exhibited activity profiles that were different in certain ways. In Meghalaya, for example, women had kitchen gardens which required daily care. Cattle care was the task in Gujarat and Mizoram. In Kerala, women read magazines and newspapers in their free time.

What bound the women together by a common thread was the unremitting hard work that characterised their days (Figure 3.1). All the mothers spent about one-third of their day in work on

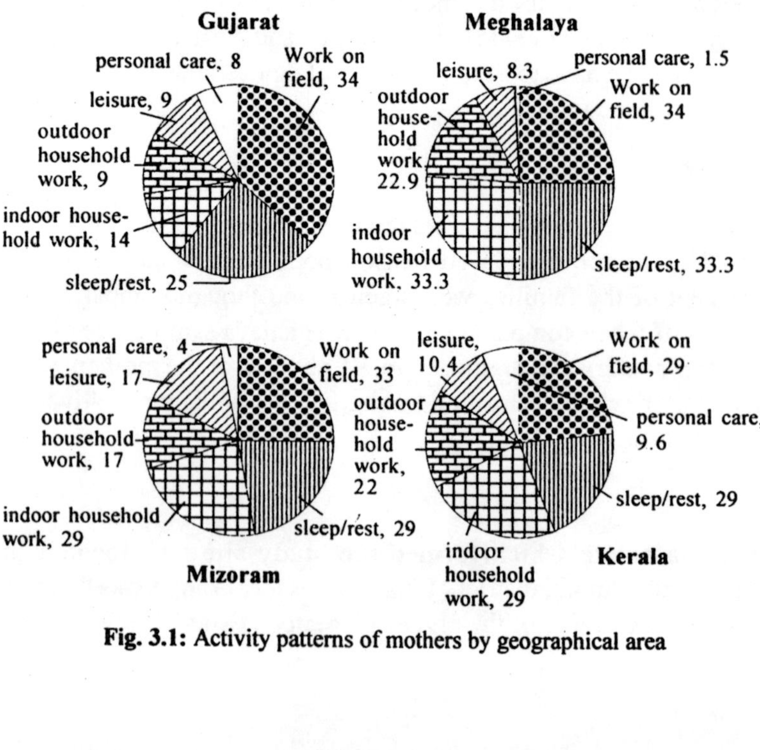

Fig. 3.1: Activity patterns of mothers by geographical area

the fields or the estate, as the case may be. A fourth of their day was spent in attending to a variety of household chores some of which were done indoors while others took them outdoors. All tasks were energy-consuming leaving little or no time for leisure. This raises questions about the unequal division of labour. It is normative and so society fails to recognise that women are overburdened. This also raises queries regarding the nature and quality of care and attention children receive because of multiple demands on women's time.

In developing countries, just as women have always worked, they have also supplemented maternal care with non-maternal care. This fact has been acknowledged and described in literature. As put forth by Myers and Indriso (1987), child care arrangements can be classified into four types:

- Doing it yourself, where the woman extends her day or combines child care with other tasks.
- 'Delegating tasks' were she takes the help of relatives or neighbours.
- 'Delegating responsibilities' were, she takes the help of a crèche or day care centre for child care.
- 'Leaving child unattended' where child care is non-existent when the mother is otherwise occupied.

Table 3.2 indicates that a wide range of individuals, namely fathers, older siblings, relatives such as grandparents, uncles, aunts and cousins as well as neighbours contributed in varying degrees to child care.

Relatives: The percentage of children left at home with relatives other than parents and sibling such as grandparents, uncles, aunts and cousins ranged from 27 per cent (Meghalaya) and 29.73 per cent (Mizoram) to 43 per cent in Gujarat and 54.18 per cent in Kerala. Some relatives resided in the child's family; others lived separately but still helped in child care. Of the relatives, grandparents showed a high degree of involvement despite the fact that they were either ill or desired to earn an income or were not motivated for undertaking the responsibility for care.

Table 3.2 : Prevalent Child Care Arrangement of Working Mothers by Age of the Child.

Locale	*Caregiver at Home when Mother is Not Available*						*Caregiver on Field when Mother is Available*						
	Age of the Child	*Father*	*Siblings*	*Rela-tives*	*Neigh-bours*	*Paid Ser-vants*	*Mother*	*Father*	*Siblings*	*Rela-tives*	*Neigh-bours*	*Left alone*	*Sum-mary*
Gujarat N = 295	0.1	0	1 (5.55)	10 (55.5)	0	1 (5.55)	5 (27.77)	0	1 (5.55)	0	0	0	18 (6.10)
	1-3	0	17 (14.65)	53 (45.68)	1 (0.86)	1 (0.86)	20 (17.24)	0	13 (11.20)	0	0	1 (0.86)	116 (39.32)
	3-6	0	24 (14.90)	64 (39.75)	2 (1.24)	2 (1.24)	25 (15.52)	0	10 (6.21)	0	0	34 (21.11)	161 (54.67)
	Sub-total	0	42 (14.23)	127 (43.1)	3 (1.01)	4 (1.35)	50 (16.9)	0	24 (8.13)	0	0	35 (11.86)	295 (100)
Megha-laya N=73	0.1	2 (15.38)	2 (15.38)	3 (23.07)	0	0	3 (23.07)	0	1 (7.69)	2 (15.38)	0	0	13 (11.01)
	1-3	2 (3.50)	23 (45.83)	18 (31.57)	4 (7.01)	0	7 (12.28)	0 (1.75)	1 (3.50)	2	0	0	57 (48.3)
	3-6	0 (45.83)	22 (22.91)	11 (22.91)	2 (4.16)	0	8 (16.66)	0	3 (6.25)	1 (2.08)	0	1 (2.08)	48 (40.74)
	Sub-total	4 (3.4)	47 (39.83)	32 (27.11)	6 (5.1)	0	18 (15.3)	0	5 (4.23)	5 (4.23)	0	1 (0.84)	118 (100)

Contd . . .

Table 3.2 Contd . . .

Locale	*Caregiver at Home when Mother is Not Available*						*Caregiver on Field when Mother is Available*						
	Age of the Child	*Father*	*Siblings*	*Relatives*	*Neighbours*	*Paid Servants*	*Mother*	*Father*	*Siblings*	*Relatives*	*Neighbours*	*Left alone*	*Summary*
Mizoram N=198	0-1	26 (35.61)	6 (8.21)	31 (42.46)	10 (13.69)	0	0	0	0	0	0	0	73 (13.82)
	1-3	55 (33.74)	21 (12.88)	59 (36.19)	13 (7.97)	0	2 (1.22)	1 (0.61)	1 (0.61)	0	0	11 (6.74)	163 (30.9)
	3-6	64 (21.91)	40 (13.69)	67 (22.94)	22 (7.53)	0	28 (9.58)	16 (5.47)	18 (6.16)	3 (1.02)	0	34 (11.64)	292 (55.30)
	Sub-total	145 (27.5)	67 (12.7)	157 (29.73)	45 (8.52)	0	30 (5.7)	17 (3.21)	19 (3.6)	3 (0.6)	0	45 (8.52)	528 (100)
Kerala N=417+ 477 Observation	Sub-total	32.37	82.01	54.18	13.42	0	71.27	37.94	60.79	88.42	2.72	0	322 (100)
(per cent)	(Summary)	15.81	37.2	38.53	7.01	0.3	27.29	10.28	19.18	23.31	0.7	5.30	316 (100)

Older Siblings: Older siblings particularly girls who were in their childhoods themselves and of school-going age shouldered a considerable share of child care responsibilities, particularly in nuclear families. In Mizoram and Gujarat, sibling involvement was about 13 per cent but was nearly 40 per cent in Meghalaya and upto 82 per cent in Kerala. In Kerala, data showed that siblings in the age range of 6-14 years showed an involvement of 24.7 per cent. That nearly 60 per cent of the siblings below the age of six were left in each other's care was a matter for worry. In general, parents exhibited little worry over older siblings missing school on account of child care responsibilities or being burdened with adult work at a young age. But in Meghalaya, 17 per cent of the older siblings voiced distress over their inability to concentrate in class due to fatigue and worry and frustration over the lack of playtime.

Father: The participation of fathers in child care showed interesting variation according to geographical area. From being non-existent in Gujarat to a mere 3.4 per cent in Meghalaya it was substantial 27.5 per cent in Mizoram and 32.37 per cent in Kerala. This variation could be because high father involvement might be a function of three factors: family type, degree of patriarchy and educational level of the community.

In Meghalaya and Gujarat, the nuclear family was the model pattern; individuals other than the parents were not available for child care. Matriarchy was the norm in Meghalaya implying greater power to women. Yet father involvement was low indicating that family type and degree of patriarchy are not predictors of paternal involvement. What set Mizoram and Kerala apart was the high literacy levels of the community. Father involvement was also high. It seems, therefore, the community literacy level has direct link with paternal involvement, a fact that needs further examination.

Mother: The scenario changed when mothers took their children with them to the fields or when they stayed back at home with their children. In up to 17 per cent of the cases, the mother was responsible for child care when she took the child to the farm.

This was especially true when children were below the age of one and were, therefore, being breast-fed. The contribution of other individuals including siblings proportionately declined indicating that everything said and done, when the mother is around, social sanction dictates that others seldom engage in child care. In rare case or for short periods, children were left alone on the field in 8.5 per cent of the cases in Mizoram and at home outside locked houses in 12 pėr cent of the cases in Gujarat. This occurred only when children were above three years of age.

During the foregoing discussion, the conceptualisation of child care as availability *versus* actual care was dwelt upon. The Kerala study examined child care from this perspective. In terms of availability, when mothers were at home, they remained the most available people (71.27 per cent). The availability of father showed a slight increase (from 32.37 per cent to 37.94 per cent) while most other declined in availability. The trend on the tea estate was to remain within earshot of children irrespective of the absence or presence of mother. Analysis of actually observed child care activities revealed a kaleidoscope of activities (feeding, washing, pacifying/petting, guiding and so on). Of these, pacifying dominated the activities, followed by consversing and asking questions to check on the child. In a telling finding, it was discovered that most of these activities were done by parents (mainly mothers when they were at home). Clearly, availability does not signal actual child care unless under extenuating circumstances. Overall, it was common for mothers to take the help of resident and non-resident relatives and neighbours, the strategy referred to as "desperation tasks" by Myers and Indriso (1987). "Doing it themselves" by extending their day or taking the child to the field was also resorted to while some mothers, in sheer desperation, left their children alone. It has to be reiterated at this juncture that prior to drawing any evaluative conclusions, the variables implicated in the issue have to be recognised.

Family and Community-based Care: The Maladies

Given contexts and circumstances, employed mothers create their own childcare support systems which are informal, often not guaranteed and based upon arrangements, several problems pertaining to work and child care were enumerated by mothers, other caretakers and fathers (Table 3.3).

Table 3.3 : Perceived problems with respect to Child Care in three* Communities.

Problem Perceived	*Gujarat* *N = 198*	*Meghalaya* *N = 73*	*Mizoram* *N = 118*
Child health and food habits	28 (14.14)	13 (18)	82 (69)
Child's Safety	30	—	—
Carrying child on back affects caretaker's health heavy workload of caretaker	— (19.33)	12 (16) (22)	49 (42) (79)
Caretakers unfit for child care	20	3	—
Decreased work eficiency due to concurrent child care	—	9 (12)	69 (58)
Lack of Child care time	(19) (8.96)	—	—
Lack of leisure time	—	3 (4)	73 (62)
Inability to work because of Child care responsibility	60 (28.30)	—	—
Inability of concentrate	—	2 (3)	16 (14)
Constant worry and anxiety about child	21 (9.90)	—	—
Difficulty in commuting with child to workplace because of long distances	—	3 (4)	—
No caregiver	—	—	71 (60)
No problem	6 (2.83)	16 (22)	—

Note : Precentages exceed 100 because of multiple responses in individual interview. Findings were echoed in Focus Group Discussions (FGDs).

* The Kerala study did not examine this dimension.
Bracketed figures are percentages.

The problems can be roughly clustered as pertaining to child caretaker health and welfare; related to efficiency and time use of caretaker and connected to caretaker psychology.

The first query that employed mother's raise is 'who will look after our children while we work?' As low incomes mean that everyone has to work, unavailability of caregivers becomes a problem (Mizoram 60 per cent). Only those who are compelled by age or ill-health to remain at home are available for caregiving. As reported by 9.43 per cent of the Gujarat and 4 per cent of the Meghalaya sample, child care by itself is hard work and caregivers handicapped by physical constraints find it difficult if not impossible. On the other hand, able-bodied adults staying back for child care means blocking of employment prospects for the individual and loss of an income for the family. This was voiced as a problem by over 28 per cent of the Gujarat sample. In Meghalaya and Mizoram, the heavy workload of the caretaker was pinpointed as the single biggest problem. This was also reported by caregivers in Kerala during informal conversations. Caregivers' inability for child care can rcsult in casual child care or translate into neglect. Not surprisingly, in the Mizoram study, high incidence of accidents due to falls, burns, knife cuts and fights was recorded. Many children did not receive timely medical help because of neglect or practical constraints such as lack of facilities or unaffordability.

For employed mothers who can only make compromises with their difficult circumstances, leaving their children behind causes great anxiety over their safety and well-being. (Gujarat 14.15 per cent, Meghalaya, 18 per cent; Mizoram 69 per cent). For instance, tribal mothers of Gujarat reported worry because of the proximity of the village river to their homes. The option for them was to take their children along to the workplace. This too is beset with pitfalls.

Long distances between home and workplace can pose a health hazard to children. In any case, commuting with a child is difficult from a practical viewpoint. This has been discussed by Leonard and Landers (1995), who elaborate that when women travel with young children, sacks of merchandise, baskets and tools, accidents are common and they are powerless to defend themselves against thieves and sexual harassment. Even if this barrier is crossed, for

58 per cent of the Mizoram sample, the presence of children on the worksite impairs work efficiency. Women from tribal Gujarat reported that mothers of young children are not preferred as employees and if at all they are hired, they are paid less or have to work intermittently. Often in north-east India, women carry their young children on their backs as they work. This has an adverse effect on women's physical health and slows down their work. Also, caregivers at home find that child care has to be jointly done with other activities leaving time for little else.

The anxiety of mothers who leave their children behind is justified in view of the fact that while neighbours and other family members may "look out" for the child, they shy away from "taking the responsibility", because that entails accountability. If they take on the responsibility, they remain unsure about the "correctness" of the child care they give. Frustration is also experienced because they feel tied down. This is especially true of grandmothers who feel that they are past the age of child care. The dropping out from school of older siblings, particularly girls, in order to care for younger children, their inability to concentrate due to fatigue and preoccupation if they continue to be school going, their longing for play time, and the unawareness of parents to this wordless torment are poignant facts that cannot be underscored enough.

An interesting observation pertained to 22 per cent of the Meghalaya sample who said that they had no problems with respect to child care. Closer examination revealed that these were mostly men who concerned themselves little with child care. The question then is, what role do fathers play in parenting especially when their better halves struggle with a surfeit of work and worry incessantly about child care?

Women's Work and Child Care

Arrangements: Factors that Mediate

Choice of substitute child care arrangement is guided by a number of variables. Observation, discussions and interviews led to preliminary conclusions about the following:

- Typically, large, extended families offer more choice in terms of caregivers. But even in joint families, substitute care is not guaranteed. This was evident from the fact that 25 per cent of mothers (Gujarat) from such families had to take their children with them to the fields. The situation being thus in joint families, it was worse for mothers in nuclear families, 75 per cent of who had to take their children with them to the worksite.
- Where caregivers are only guests, relatives are not a dependable choice for the mother. When work is on a daily wage basis, potential caregivers go for work whenever possible. This makes worry over child care arrangements a daily feature in the lives of employed mothers.
- The younger the child, the more sustained, intensive and dependable the care required. When the child is being breast-fed, mothers prefer to take the child to the workplace. As the child becomes older, other options are considered. For example, toddlers are accident-prone and need constant supervision. Child care arrangements have to be made accordingly. Lack of other caregivers force women to use older children as caregivers. If they are available, that is, non-school going or non-employed, they become an easy choice. However, if siblings themselves are under six, mothers remain anxious and insecure.
- Stability of family income is a major determinant of the kind of child care arrangements made. The lower the income, the more limited the choice.

In poor families where incomes are low and unstable, all family members work whenever they can. In agricultural contexts, earnings made during the peak season have to last through the year. Hence, everyone works, leaving few caretakers available. Besides, there is usually little income to spare for substitute arrangement.

All communities in some form or the other idealise motherhood as all-powerful, thus making it a woman's sole responsibility. Many mothers continue to believe that they somehow have to "manage"; "Care at home is the ideal form"; "All women can care for children well"; "Child care is a natural skill for the mothers". "The woman has to care because she breastfeeds", are other beliefs that haunt women and hinder their choices for non-maternal care.

Women who view the informal childcare arrangements as unreliable and who prefer not to or cannot take their children to the work place turn to the strategy of 'delegating the responsibility' of child care to crèches or day care centres run by the government or voluntary bodies.

Status and Community Opinions

All four areas studied had some formal child care facilities (Table 3.4). While Gujarat, Meghalaya and Mizoram were covered by the ICDS, the crèche in the Kerala plantation came under the statutory sector. Everywhere, supplementary nutrition and partial support with respect to child was offered. The provision for nutritious food, the support they provided for child care, educational input, health check-ups and the improvement it caused in terms of the child's socialisation were identified as strengths of the support systems.

However, a number of problems surfaced during individual interviews with mothers, other caretakers and crèche functionaries (Table 3.5). They can be conceptually viewed as belonging to

- Infrastructure and physical environment
- Timings
- Funds and remuneration
- Teacher variables.

The most common problem expressed was poor infrastructure (buildings, furniture, cooking utensils) and insufficient and irregular supplementary nutrition. Mention was also made of unsuitable meal timings and the tendency to devalue local food. Workers engage in

Table 3.4 : Formal Child Care Services Available in Gujarat, Meghalaya, Mizoram and Kerala

Components of Quality	*Care and Issues*	*Gujarat*	*Meghalaya*	*Mizoram*	*Kerala*
Agencies Implementing Services	Integrated Child Development Services (ICDS)	✓	✓	✓	
	Others				
		• Balwadi run by private Group		* * MHIP	Statutory Plantation Crèche
Components of Care provided	Supplementary nutrition	✓	✓	✓ (ICDA MHIP)	✓
	crèche/			✓ (MHIP)	✓
	Anganwadi pre-school education			✓ (MHIP)	✓
Coverage	Poor	✓ 59 children attend out of 361	✓ 255 villages of out of 1943	✓ (ICDS)	✓ (12 attended 52 registered)
Teacher-Child Ratio	Good	✓ 1:10 for 0-3 year old 1:25 for 3-6 year olds	✓	✓ (MHIP)	
	Poor			✓ (ICDS and MHIP)	
Training Level of Teacher	Optimum Anganwadi trained pre-schools	✓	✓	✓	

Contd . . .

Table 3.4 Contd. . . .

Components of Quality	*Care and Issues*	*Gujarat*	*Meghalaya*	*Mizoram*	*Kerala*
	Trained			✓	✓
	Balsevika				
	Trained				
Funds	Government	✓	✓	✓ (ICDS)	
	State Other			✓ (MHIP)	✓ (Plantation)
Duration	2-3 Hours	✓	✓	✓ (ICDS)	
	3-6 Hours			✓ (MHIP)	
	> 6 Hours				✓ (all daylight Hours)
Accessibility	Accessible		✓	✓	✓
	Inaccessible	✓			

Note : Tick (✓) indicates presence while empty blocks indicate absence of any in that category.

* Details pertaining to the private balwadis were not available.

** Mizo Hmechhia Insuihkhawm Pawi (Mizo Women's Integrated Association)

Table 3.5 : Formal supports — Hurdles and hindrances*

(*Per cent*)

Weakness	*Meghalaya*	*Mizoram*
Infrastructive problem	—	100
Sub-optimal environment	37	37
Inadequate, irregular food	35	100
Irregular timings	44	95
Inconvenient timings	—	100
Low remuneration	—	75
Lack of or inadequate funds	—	52
High teacher-child ratio	—	62
Low teacher motivation	—	24
No resource person in village	—	33

* *Sources:* Individual Interviews
Garrey, W. (1993)
Fanai, E. (1993)
Total percentage exceeds 100 because of multiple response.

round-the-clock duty and are entrusted with large numbers of children. Yet they are paid abysmal wages and are, therefore, demotivated. Delayed and inadequate funds compound the problem, e.g., one of the crèches in Mizoram was sanctioned the paltry annual sum of Rs.1,500.

In additional to those overarching concerns, a plethora of others came to light:

Services mostly catered to 3-6 year olds, leaving the needs of mothers with children less than three years of age unaddressed. Also, the emphasis was on custodial rather than developmental care. For example, though the plantation crèche catered to infants, care was purely custodial. Khullar (1991) in "Whither child care services" highlights the superficial nature of statutory services. If evading child care responsibility is easy in the organised sector, it is not difficult to imagine the situation in the unorganised sector.

Often, services are free of cost or a token fee is charged. This leads to their being devalued by the community. Open for only two-three hours during the day, crèche timings are inadequate as mothers work 10-12 hours.

Crèche workers are trained in information heavy, rigid programmes that pay scant attention to regional and individual variations. Support material is scarce and follow up, non-existent. What loses out in the bargain is worker motivation. In the absence of enthusiasm and participation from parents, workers feel that they are doing what is essentially a thankless job. With this exception, all others reported low satisfaction levels. The problem can largely be attributed to the neglect given to the child care needs and preferences of women and other caregivers. These key individuals possess insights about viable options which programme planners fail to consider.

What do Communities Want?

It emerged from the Gujarat study that more than 50 per cent of the women needed some form of part-time or full time substitute care for their children under six years. A closer look at disaggregated data about women's daily routine indicated that one in three women had no help for any of their activities. The others were being supported by in-laws or daughters. Women expressed a strong desire for organised substitute care arrangements so that they could engage in productive activities related to their household or farm, free of anxiety over their children's well-being; and be relieved from child care for three-four hours per day and have the freedom to seek employment.

The demand for full time child care supports was high among nuclear families (Meghalaya, 72 per cent and Mizoram, 96 per cent) where children were left in unsafe surroundings. In 70 per cent of the extended families where caretaker availability was unpredictable or where they were unfit, there was a need for part-time substitute care. This it was felt, would take the physical and psychological pressure off women.

In Meghalaya and Mizoram, parents clearly articulated several needs of their children and expressed discontentment over their inability to meet the same due to lack of facilities or time constraints. Therefore, it was felt that a child care centre could effectively meet the children's need for nutrition, health care, play, stimulation and education. However, group opinion was divided over the issue of responsibility for implementation. Nearly half of them felt that child care arrangements should evolve by collective actions at the village level. Even within this, 22 per cent of mothers and 34 per cent of fathers viewed it as the mothers' responsibility which is a reflection of their socialisation that upholds the sanctity of motherhood and tries to absolve fathers of their responsibility. About one-third felt that the government should extend its ICDS to include day care as it has vast resources at its disposal.. Religious leaders and the health department were other options cited by about 20 per cent. A noteworthy feature was the emphasis on contextualised services and upgradation of the existing services.

Innovations with a Vision

The community needs, opinions and perceptions formed the source for alternate child care models which the north-east Indian studies evolved in theory. The first opinion was to append day care to existing ICDS by recruiting new staff or paying additional remuneration to Anganwadi workers. Villages without ICDS could have the following three alternatives — mothers could care for children on a rotational basis; a village mother or grandparent could regularly care for the children; and a village volunteer could be trained for care giving with help from an aged caretaker.

Going much beyond suggestions, unlike the Meghalaya, Mizoram studies, Sriram's Gujarat study which was an action research actually evolved a model for child care. A collaborative project directed by Sriram (1991-93), it was the effort of Mahila Samakhya (a women's programme), the Department of Human Development and Family Studies and the Women Household Development Research and Information Centre, M.S. University.

The stage was set by identifying potential clientele for child care services. A situational analysis of women, girls and children was done to infer needs. Then, through discussions, consultations and simulated activities at different levels, models suited to village needs were constructed with the in-built features of fulltime or part-time care as needed; pre-school education; provision for the service in more than one location per village if needed; and flexible timings suited to needs and work patterns.

As needs were being inferred, facilitators who were specially trained worked at creating awareness about women's situation in society and mobilising the women's collective (Mahila Sangha) for action. Building on this, later, collective decisions would be taken on details such as type of child care supports, formation of committees, place, time, choice of payment for caregivers, and follow-up and resource mobilisation at different levels. The final step comprised initiating the child care centre and the gradual process of its stabilization to achieve financial sustainability.

In 1995, 28 centres, were being run in Baroda with or without financial support from Mahila Samakhya. This was a small venture supported strongly by grassroots level women. By no means was it the first. The precedent was set by pioneering endeavours such as Mobile Crèches and Self-Employed Womens Association (SEWA) catering to the children of migrant construction site workers mainly in Bombay, Delhi and Pune with support from contractors through approximately 362 centres. In SEWA, on the other hand, in 1972, tobacco workers in Kheda district of Gujarat started with bargaining for better working conditions and were helped to organise their own child care anganwadis in slums through local women and SEWA members. It has been the first Trade Union to provide child care support and the first to focus exclusively on children under three years of age. These programmes have powerfully demonstrated that creating need-based child care supports is possible and necessary, provided the communities, more specifically women, are involved in the process as partners.

It is now beyond doubt that "child care" needs to be viewed in its totality as is summarised in Figure 3.2. This leads us to critical concerns, which form the concluding part of the paper.

Fig. 3.2 : Child care in agricultural contexts

SALIENT FEATURES

Family and Women's Contexts

- Need to earn an Income
- Work Overload
- Limited options
- Anxiety,
- Guilt
- Insecurity
- Poor Health status

Problems Associated with Available Options

Implications for Caregiver

- Constraint to work
- ➔ Inability to seek employment
- ➔ Marginalisation
- Health Hazards
- Lack of personal options/denial of right
- Devaluing of child care work

Implications for the Child

- Neglect
- Tragedy and Health Hazards
- Lack of Stimulation

Forms of Substitute Care

- Doing it herself (Overcompensating)
- Non-Guaranteed care from
  - Fathers
  - Siblings
  - Grandparents
  - Other relatives
  - Neighbours
- Inadequate institutional care

Possible Solutions

- Political will that views child care as women's and childrens rights, a priority area for resources.
- Inclusion of 'Day Care' into the minimum needs programme and materinity benefit to women in agriculture.
- Promotion of flexible models and decentralized approaches to service delivery.
- Advocacy incentives for community participation
- Recognition of 'Child Care' as a mainstream issues.

Critical Concerns

Social Change: Implications for Child Care

The changing social scenario and economic forces have propelled large-scale changes in the family making it grossly incapable of meeting the needs for child care from within. Nurturance of the idea of 'maternal care' coupled with the notion of availability of substitute care within the family has led to disastrous impacts on women and children which can no longer be ignored.

A greedy market sucks in needy women in return for piecemeal employment, long hours, distant travel, low wages and hazardous environment. Most work (including some forms of home-based employment) is incompatible with child care; hence the option is of leaving children behind or exposing them to multiple hazards. This weaves in persistent worry, strong guilt and insecurity about the wellbeing of children into the overworked woman's life.

Research has repeatedly indicated that the backlash of maternal employment is felt most by siblings especially girls, who are forced to manage child care and household work thus elbowing them out of education. Being school going with adult responsibilities means poor performance, low motivation and a high drop out rate. On the other hand, emphasis on education means unavailability of older children to share the mother's burden.

The involvement of aged, often ailing caretakers in an energy-consuming task, and the inability of otherwise healthy caretakers to contribute to household incomes owing to child care duties adds another dimension to what is already a multifaceted issue.

Families in this scenario have options "only between the devil and the deep blue sea". Hence full time substitute day care is no more an option, welfare or luxury but a long-term investment into the well-being of women and children.

Quality of Child Care

Non-parental care outside the family is still not a well accepted fact in the Indian context and hence is swept under the carpet, begetting the notion that available support networks (as opposed to none) can meet the needs for substitute care effectively. What is to be noted is that availability of potential caregivers does not in any way guarantee quality care. The major components that have consistently emerged in relation to quality care are:

- The ability of arrangements to cater not only to survival but developmental needs of children, which means that custodial care must be augmented with stimulation, education, recognising the differential needs of infants (0-2), toddlers and pre-schoolers (2-6 years).
- They should be "mother, child and family friendly", that is easily accessible, concurrent to mothers' working hours, affordable and dependable. Meeting the intersecting needs of women, children and girls is a priority.
- Good quality "daycare" if assured is, in fact, supportive to the overall development of the child especially in social, cognitive and language skills (as demonstrated by research studies in Indian and other contexts).

Hence the debate is not of replacement of existing supports (and perhaps losing whatever support is already available) with a two caretaker 25 children centre based model of day care, but of drawing the positive features from existing supports to build alternative/flexible models. Sensitivity to social contexts, situation of women and children, economic and cultural realities is an overwhelming need. Some examples of creative solutions could be training of healthy elderly caregivers for child care, part-time support to elderly caregivers for stimulation activities for children, devising a model of care by mothers on rotational basis (For example, Entry point — Nepal), downward extension of ICDS and primary schools to include daycare; and evolving models of family day care with support networks.

A Right or Welfare?

Till date, child care has been treated as a welfare issue and has, as a result been accorded back seat. Left-overs after expenditure on high-profile areas such as defence and industry are allocated to child care and other human development areas. As a market place response to neighbourhood child care needs, unlicensed, cheap child care arrangements are available for some sectors. Women who have to look outside their families for support, fall back on them in the absence of better alternatives. The use of a poor quality service does nothing for their peace of mind. The question is, why must women be forced to accept, poor quality options? In a patriarchal structure, girls and women accept their status as inferior. Low self-esteem and the stresses of survival engage them so completely that they do not demand even their rights. With no resources or support to attend to them, the self-perpetuating cycle continues. Acknowledgement of the right of a woman to education, health care, rest, time and resources implies according a high priority to guaranteed day care for children under six.

Viewed from the standpoint of personnel, a poorly trained, poorly paid and unmotivated child care worker functioning amidst personal and practical constraints cannot by any means perform effectively. Child care in crèches and day care centres is a job like any other if not more difficult and has to be viewed as such. Child care workers have a right to status, respectable salaries and adequate infrastructural facilities that will help rather than hinder them in their duties. Why should the rights of women, children and child care workers be sacrificed under the guise of lack of resources?

Who is Responsible for Child Care?

Motherhood has always been idolised. Its ever-coping ideal has been reinforced by religious institution and kinship structures. As a part and parcel of this ideal, child rearing is considered as the mother's exclusive responsibility. Accepting this, women have sacrificed a great deal and have worked single-handedly at child care when in fact, the responsibility should be shared by men. While fathers view child care as being the mothers' responsibility, the state delegates it to the family. The men, state, religious units — all do their bit to the so-called "noble cause of children" in different ways. These *ad hoc* and piecemeal interventions do little good except for catering to a collective conscience in absolving them of responsibilities.

While the government has accorded separate positions to health, welfare and education in the list of minimum needs, providing it through different departments, day care receives no mention. The ICDS touted as an example nationwide of an integrated programme does not include 'day care' among its numerous objectives.

Communities blame governments and the government in report after report points to the lack of "community participation". The blame directly shifts towards the women, who in reality have no "time or space" to think of their primary concerns, lack of awareness, low status, overload of responsibilities, obligations to family and society and lack of access to resources. Though the demand must originate from the communities, the state must take on strong ideological commitment and financial support. Such a step complemented with decentralization, flexibility, ownership by community where fathers are sensitized and participate along with mothers, and adequate training is the only answer to make services sustainable.

Cost Benefit Angle

The debates related to quality and cost centre around a host of issues—the basic requirements for providing efficient services, honorarium to caregivers, provision for meals, hidden costs of burnout, infrastructural leakage and under-utilisation among others. Critical analysis has shown that minimal cost of good quality care amounts to about Rs. 5 per child per day and has demonstrated that at no instance can we expect low cost endeavours to yield high quality services (Swaminathan, 1996). 'Low services' is only eyewash that glorifies voluntary community service but fails to support the family in the true sense in child care.

Effective child care will no doubt be expensive, but will be a minuscule portion of total government outlay. Inadequate child care means greater expenditure in the long run on intervention programmes to combat malnutrition, school drop-out and low enrolment. While these expenses cannot be done away with altogether, they can be controlled by investing in sound provision for user-friendly child care services. Is there any doubt then that good child care support will not only support women by creating time and space but will also be a long-term investment for ensuring the welfare of over 300 million children in the country?

4

CHILD CARE STRATEGIES OF WOMEN IN THE UNORGANIZED SECTOR*

— *M.R. Arulraj* and *S. Raja Samuel*

Introduction

Who is responsible for taking care of children: mother, father, parents or society? This simple question has acquired poignant meaning today, given the rise in the number of working women and the everyday conflict they face over balancing their roles as workers and mothers.

Today, despite the large number of women in the workforce, the basis of all labour welfare legislations is the traditional family unit where the man is the breadwinner and the woman is involved in housekeeping, child bearing and child rearing. There are a large number of families where both the husband and wife work. There are also many families in which the woman is the sole or main breadwinner, and families where, although both the husband and wife may be working, it is the woman's contribution alone that sustains the family, because the husband's income is either meagre or is often spent for other purposes like drinking. Frequently, under such circumstances it is difficult for the woman to reconcile her roles as a mother, worker and home maker as these roles conflict with each other.

---

* Reprinted with permission of author and publisher; first printed as *Balancing Multiple Roles*, Research Report No. 1, M.S. Swaminathan Research Fundation, 1995.

Triple Roles for Women

Labour legislation does not allow for the complexity of needs and responsibilities of a woman in performing her triple roles as worker, mother and home-maker. The issue of providing child care outside the home has not been addressed seriously. Moreover, legislation covers only those working in the organised sector, who account for about 10 per cent of the total workforce of women (Swaminathan, 1985). The problem is many times more complex when one takes into account the plight of women in the unorganised sectors (89%), who are left out of the purview of such legislation.

The average woman worker in the unorganised sector constantly balances the quality of attention she can devote to her three major roles, resulting in the inadequate performance of all three roles or a drastic negative impact on one particular role. Often, the mothering role suffers as this is the only one that can be compromised, however unwillingly. The working/earning role of these women as workers is of paramount importance to their basic survival and hence difficult to neglect, and home-making, which is again the responsibility of the mother, also demands attention.

However, the mother in the unorganised sector has been coping with the care of her young child with whatever resources she has at her disposal. The coping strategies she adopts may not be termed as ideal and frequently may have detrimental effects on both the mother and the child, but she cannot help it.

Apart from the problems faced by the mother working in the unorganised sector, the young child too faces a serious threat to development, even survival. Preoccupation with work separates the mother from the young child for a considerable period of time every day, right from birth. When the child is sick, the mother has to take time off work, which is not compensated for by the employers.

Unanswered Questions

Several questions have to be addressed with regard to the child care needs and problems of women working in the unorganised sector:

- Who takes care of the young child when the mother goes to work?
- What are the occupational constraints faced by the mother in relation to child care?
- How does her occupation influence the child care strategies adopted by her?
- How does work affect breast-feeding? What is the extent of siblings' involvement in child care and its impact on them?
- What are the child care services used by these mothers?
- What is their opinion regarding the services which they use?
- What is their opinion of other caregivers in the family?
- What assistance do they need for child care, particularly in the context of their occupation?

Apart from the National Sample Survey conducted in 1978 which detailed the child care strategies adopted by working women, there have been no micro-level studies to address the questions raised above. There is a need to go into all these issues as it concerns the welfare and development of a majority of the working women and above all the young children who are the future of the nation.

This study attempts to provide information which would portray the real situation about the child care needs and strategies of women working in the unorganised sector.

Objectives of the Study

- To study the working conditions of women in various occupations that have a bearing on child care.
- To portray the problems in child care encountered by working mothers.
- To find out how working mothers cope with child care.
- To study the outcome of the responsibility for child care placed on siblings.

- To examine the factors related to breast-feeding practices of the respondents in the context of their occupation.
- To establish the pattern of utilisation of available child care facilities by working mothers.
- To study the opinion of the working mothers regarding the quality of child care provided by the government and voluntary organisations.

Methodology

This study intended to focus on working women in the unorganised sector in Tamil Nadu. According to Census 1991, there are 57 lakh working women in Tamil Nadu, of whom 50.73 lakh (89%) are in the unorganised sector. The percentage of women in this group who are mothers of young children (below six years) is not known and the possibility of getting the exact number of such mothers was remote. There are also several differences in the type of job activity carried out by women working within a occupational category. These were some of the factors that shaped the methodology adopted for this study.

The Respondents

The unit of study in this research is the working mother in the unorganised sector involved in any one of the following occupations as her primary income-generating activity, and having at least one child below the age of six years. The occupational sectors are as follows: agriculture, plantation, quarrying, fishing, domestic work, beedi rolling, construction, urban petty trade, and weaving/artisan.

Though they do not belong to any particular occupational category, gypsies were included in the study to find out whether they have any specific child care needs, different from other women in the unorganised sector.

Criteria for Selection

Two major considerations governed the selection of respondents. One was the objective of the study, which was to get an overall picture of the child care problems faced by women in the unorganised sector and the strategies adopted by them to meet their needs. The study was not designed to obtain estimates for projection. The second consideration was the limited amount of resources available — both time and money. The resources needed to identify the sampling frame for a study of this nature covering such a large population were not available.

Keeping these considerations in mind, the researchers decided to select 1000 respondents from all over Tamil Nadu. The number of respondents to be selected representing each occupation was decided based on the need to give some representation to all the occupational categories within the sample of 1000 persons.

The selection of districts, the blocks in these districts, and the villages, was based on the strong presence of respondents belonging to the listed occupations in these places, as well as the availability of local support in the form of non-governmental organisations.

While selecting the respondents, the differences in the nature of the activities of the respondents in the same occupation were also taken into consideration. For example, respondents in agriculture sector were selected both from irrigated and rain-fed areas. Similarly, casual labourers, migrant workers and contract labourers were included as respondents from the construction sector, to ensure sufficient representation of the wide variety of workers within the sample. The districts of Madras (now Chennai), North Arcot, Tanjore, Madurai, Tinneveli and Ramnad has samples of 100 or above. South Arcot, Dindigul, Salem, Kannyakumari, Nilgiris and Trichy had samples ranging from 20 to 50 drawn from them. The sample drawn from each district varied as all the occupational categories were not present in certain districts. Occupation-wise representation of the sample is presented in Table 4.1.

Table 4.1 : Occupation-wise Sample Distribution

Agriculture	300
Construction	100
Weaving/Artisan	100
Beedi rolling	100
Quarrying	100
Urban petty trade	75
Fishery	50
Plantation	50
Domestic work	75
Gypsy	50
	1000

To cover more villages within a block, it was decided to take only 5 or 10 respondents per village depending on the size of the population belonging to one occupational category from each village. To reduce bias to some extent at this final level of selection, systematic sampling procedure was used to obtain 5 to 10 respondents each from the selected villages. In each village, a list of working mothers of young children was prepared with the help of animators from local NGOs or the health personnel attached to the PHCs. This list included only those who were involved in a particular occupation. From this list 5 to10 respondents were selected using systematic sampling method. The same procedure was followed to select respondents from wards in urban areas.

Tools for Data Collection

The major instrument, for data collection was an interview schedule containing structured questions.

An interview guide containing five open-ended questions was also used by the researchers to collect data from secondary respondents such as crèche workers, nutrition workers, teachers, local leaders and junior level government functionaries. The tool contained questions on general information pertaining to child care needs and problems as well as suggestions for improving child care among women in the unorganised sector.

The interview schedule was subjected to a pilot study with 25 respondents covering four occupational categories in both rural and urban areas. Necessary changes in the questionnaire were made.

Data Collection and Analysis

Graduates in social sciences were trained for data collection. The primary respondents for the study were mothers with children aged between 0 to 6 years. Data on the functioning of the centres was collected from crèche workers, nutrition workers, teachers, local leaders and junior level government officers.

Of the data collected from 1000 respondents, 46 schedules were rejected because of incomplete data. Four schedules containing information from tribal respondents were not included as the original intention of grouping them with gypsies was not found appropriate. The remaining 950 schedules were analysed in a computer using a statistical package (Number Crunching Statistical System). Cross tabulations and descriptive analysis have been used.

Definition of Terms Used

Child Care comprises the whole gamut of activities carried out by the biological mother or a mother substitute to address the developmental needs of a child.

Caregiver is a person who attends to the developmental needs of a child for a considerable period of time per day. The caregiver may be the mother herself or any other person entrusted with the responsibility of child care.

Working Mother of Young Children is a mother having at least one child below 6 years of age and involved in an income-generating activity for at least 6 hours per day.

Unorganised Sector comprises all the occupational categories not included under the public sector and not covered by statutory provisions in the private sector.

Child Care Centre (CCC) is an institution run by Government, voluntary or private initiative, where child care workers are employed to take care of enrolled children for a fixed period of time during the day.

Child Care Worker is a caregiver employed in a child care centre to take care of children entrusted to her for a fixed period of time during the day.

Child Care Services **(CCS)** includes Child Care Centres run by Government/private/voluntary initiative, Noon Meals Centres and the Mother and Child Health Progamme.

Working Conditions Affecting Child Care

The unorganised sector is characterised by a multiplicity of occupations in which women are involved which differ from each other in several ways. These differences contribute to the unique nature of the problems faced by the mothers of young children in each occupation in relation to child care and evolve a holistic picture of the working mother in the unorganised sector to gain a comprehensive understanding of the issues currently being discussed. The researchers attempted to do the aforesaid through an analysis of the demands placed on the working mother by a set of occupational factors. In doing so, the research concentrated only on those factors that have implications for child care.

The Time Factor

Time is a major occupational variable that has a bearing on the home-making and child care activities of working women. If the time involved in income-generating activities increases, it cuts into the time allotted for essential home-making and child care activities. Similarly time available before going to or starting work may, to a large extent, influence the quality of child care efforts, especially in the morning.

The mean time available before work was 3 hours. For 31 per cent of the respondents, only 2 hours were available before work.

Within this time they may have to manage household chores, grooming children and cooking, apart from preparing themselves for the day's work.

A majority of the respondents (80%) left for work by 8 a.m. Most of the respondents (75%) returned home by 5 p.m., while the average returning time was 5.20 p.m.

The demands of work that keeps the mother away from her child throughout the day and throughout the week may have serious consequences for the growth of the child, unless it is amply compensated for by a surrogate caregiver. Finding a surrogate caregiver for the child frequently proves to be a difficult task for the mother.

The Distance Factor

Distance to the work spot is another occupational factor that has a bearing on child care. Mothers who live farther from the work spot spend more time commuting than mothers who live closer. The greater time in commuting means more time is spent by these mothers away from their young children, if the child is not taken to work and greater inconvenience if the child accompanies the mother. While 53 per cent of the respondents travelled a distance of only 2 km. to the work spot, a considerable percentage (28%) travelled more than 6 kms. The average distance travelled was 4.8 kms.

The Income Factor

Though the respondents work for a period of 8 hours on an average, the income reportedly earned by them per month is strikingly low. Only 24 per cent of the respondents stated that they earned above Rs.400 per month. The average stated income was Rs.332 per month.

Another dimension in income is the perceived contribution of the respondent's income to the total income of the family per month. Sixty-four of the respondents stated that they earn fifty per cent of the family's total monthly income, while about 6 per cent of the respondents stated that they contribute to more than 75 per cent of the family's income. This group of respondents, being the primary or sole breadwinners of the family, may be under pressure to relegate the welfare of the child to a lower priority.

Child Care Options

Four main strategies are adopted by working mothers to cope with child care: child care at work spot, child care centres, care at home by others and care at home by mother in home-based occupations. At home the child may be cared for by elders (grandparents), other relatives, neighbours, siblings or even left alone. The respondents were also asked to mention an alternative strategy that they adopted if the first option was not available.

Of the 37 per cent of respondents who leave their youngest child at home, it is significant to note that 12 per cent left them with siblings, while five per cent left their children alone with no one to take care of them. The other common strategies were taking the child to the work spot (25%) and leaving the child at the child care (29%). An outstanding feature of the picture of child care strategies is that almost 50 per cent of the respondents did not have any alternative other than the strategy they adopt most of time.

Occupational Variations

The child care strategies adopted by the women varied considerably among the various occupations (Table 4.2). In the agricultural sector a majority of the respondents (67%) leave their children at home while at work. A sizeable per cent of respondents in the construction sector (43%) and 30 per cent in the quarrying sector take their children, especially the younger ones, to their work spot, though doing so may be more hazardous in these sectors than in any other. Domestic workers (26%) and agricultural workers (22%) also follow this strategy to a large extent. About 50 per cent of all who leave their children at home are in the agriculture sector.

It is important to note that though Tamil Nadu has an extensive network of child care centres (CCC) spread out throughout the

Table 4.2 : Child Care Strategy by Occupation (N = 950)

Occupation	*Child care strategy*				
	Taken to work spot	*Left at child care centre*	*Left at home*	*Self (home-based occu-pation)*	*Total*
Agriculture	19.9	13.2	66.9	—	100
	22.8	13.4	50.9	—	29.5
Construction	42.5	29.2	28.3	—	100
	20.1	11.2	8.6	—	11.1
Weaving/artisan	25.3	27.6	10.3	36.8	100
	10.4	8.7	2.6	39.8	9.1
Beedi rolling	—	16.3	5.8	77.9	100
	—	5.1	1.4	49.6	9.0
Quarrying	29.7	56.4	13.9	—	100
	14.9	20.6	4.0	—	10.6
Urban petty trade	12.0	34.7	46.7	6.7	100
	4.8	9.4	10.0	5.9	7.9
Fishery	1.7	79.3	12.1	6.9	100
	0.4	16.6	2.0	4.7	6.1
Plantation	19.5	26.8	53.7	—	100
	4.4	4.0	6.3	—	4.3
Domestic work	26.0	23.4	50.6	—	100
	10.5	6.5	11.1	—	8.1
Gypsies	42.9	31.0	26.2	—	100
	8.7	4.7	3.1	—	4.4
Total	26.6	29.0	36.7	9.7	100
	100	100	100	100	100

state, not all respondents send their eligible children (3-6 years) to the CCC. Only 20 per cent of the respondents in agriculture, 21 per cent in weaving/artisan, 17 per cent in beedi rolling and 13 per cent in agriculture sent their eligible children to the CCC. Child care centres run by the government and voluntary organisations generally close by 3 or 4 p.m. In this situation, the option of leaving the child at the child care centre becomes unattractive. The mother has to find alternative arrangements for the care of the child until she returns from work. Again, the fact that very few children below two years of age can be left at child care centre may also be reflected in this choice. In spite of the wide network CCCs are not catering to the working needs of mothers.

Quarry workers and fisher women make the maximum use of child care centres for children aged 3-6 (over 70%), while urban petty traders, plantation workers, construction workers and domestic workers are next in the use of centre for children of 3-6 years (32-40%).

Child Care at the Work Spot

About 25 per cent of the respondents take their children to the work spot. The average age of the child taken to the work spot was 25.1 months and the average distance these respondents travelled to their workspot was found to be 3.4 kms.

It was found that 80 per cent of these respondents take their children to the work spot because they do not have any other alternative. Another significant reason was the feeling that the child would be safe only under the care of the mother (49%), while 31 per cent stated that the child is too young to be left under the care of siblings. The link between the age of the young child and these reasons is presented. Reasons such as lack of alternatives (72%), young age of the child (89%) and 'the child is safe only with me' (75%) were mentioned more by mothers of younger children (0-2 years).

At the work spot, most of these respondents (85%) took care of their children themselves, while 7 per cent said that their children were cared for by co-workers and the remaining by siblings and other children (8%). The siblings, apart from looking after the child, ran odd errands such as fetching water, buying betel-nut, for the respondents and co-workers. Deprived of formal education, they may end up in the same occupation as their mothers. None of the respondents had the privilege of an employer-arranged facility for child care.

Inability to feed the children on time (73.2%), accidents (43%) and natural hazards (40%) were the major problems faced while caring for the child at the work spot. About 53 per cent of these respondents stated that taking the child to the work spot interferes with the quality of work. However, this did not attract the ire of either the employers or the co-workers as 80 per cent said that neither their co-workers nor their employers objected to bringing the child to the work spot. In spite of this, devoid of adequate supervision and care at the work spot, infants and young children frequently consume mud or other hazardous material which causes diarrhoea and sometimes death according to the respondents. There were also instances of children falling into irrigation wells or ditches. It is thus evident that though the mother is available near the child, she is unable to provide adequate care.

The Child Care at Centre

Twenty nine per cent of the respondents send their children to the nearby CCC. Of these respondents 74 per cent send their children to Government-run CCCs, while the remaining 26 per cent send them to CCCs run by voluntary agencies or private persons. However, it is interesting to note that the percentage of children 0-2 years old is greater in the centres run by voluntary/private agencies (70%) than in Government run centres (41%).

Fifty three per cent of the respondents send their children to CCC primarily because there is no one else at home to look after them. Sending the child to the CCC is the only option available for child care for these respondents. Again, it is noteworthy that 83 per cent of respondents send their children to the CCC with the expectation that the latter will learn to read and write or at least learn the basics that might help them to read and write later on. For 28 per cent of the respondents, the inability to take the child to the work spot was the distance from home, and therefore, the reason for sending them to the centre. The availability of a CCC nearby also prompts the mothers to send their children. This reinforces the finding that more respondents send their children to the CCC if it is within 1/2 km from home.

Respondents were asked about the satisfaction with child care service. The responses have been presented in Table 4.3.

Table 4.3: Level of Satisfaction with the functioning of Child Care Centres

Area of functioning	*Level of satisfaction*			
	S	*N*	*D*	*Total*
Timing	32.2	15.7	51.1	100
Feeding	60.1	28.8	11.1	100
Toilet care	34.7	43.6	21.7	100
Sleeping	50.4	42.7	6.9	100
Play activities	37.6	46.2	16.2	100
Skill training	48.1	44.7	7.2	100
Pacifying the child when the child cries	48.4	40.2	11.4	100
Physical protection	42.4	43.9	13.7	100
Child care worker	45.0	35.9	17.1	100

N = 227 S - Satisfied N - Neutral D - Dissatisfied

The food provided at the CCC also prompted the respondents to send their children (23.1%). The other reasons mentioned were that the CCC provides a chance for the child to spend time usefully rather than roam around in the village and some respondents stated that caregivers at home were either sick or unwilling to be involved in child care.

Studying the opinions regarding various activities of the CCC, it was found that with the exception of 'feeding' activity, less than 50 per cent of the respondents were satisfied with the other activities at the CCC (Table 4.3). The least satisfaction was expressed for CCC timings, with just 33 per cent expressing satisfaction, and 51 per cent dissatisfaction.

This lack of satisfaction is understandable as the CCCs start functioning at 8.30 or 9.00 a.m., while most of the respondents leave for work by 7.30 a.m. Similarly several CCCs close down at noon after lunch or by 3.00 p.m., while most respondents return home only by 5.00 p.m. About 48-50 per cent of the mothers were satisfied with sleeping time, play activities and skill training which refers to teaching of the three R's.

Child Care at Home by Others

It was seen that the young child left at home by the respondents was cared for by the siblings, relatives, neighbours and aged relatives. Some children were even left alone. The average age of the child left at home was 21.3 months.

More than 50 per cent of the respondents were satisfied with the quality of child care provided by caregivers at home in terms of various child care activities such as feeding, toilet care and preparing for crèche. Maximum satisfaction was expressed for 'feeding' (69%), while more respondents were dissatisfied with 'preparing for school/crèche (21%).

Reasons for dissatisfaction were lack of adequate time spent with the young child, inattentiveness of the care giver, ill-health, old age, lack of affection and young age of the siblings.

Most of these respondents completed activities such as washing, grooming and feeding the children before they go for work so as to reduce the work of the caregiver at home. Most respondents (70%) said that they have very little time for these activities before they leave for work, while quite a few (53%) complained that the caregivers do not assist them in the morning with child care activities. All these exert considerable pressure on the respondents as they hurry for work.

About 10 per cent of respondents were from home-based occupations such as *beedi*-rolling, weaving and pot-making. These respondents may have a significant advantage over other occupations with regard to child care as they are normally near their children at all times of the day which may facilitate the smooth conduct of several child care activities. The child may also grow up with a feeling of security.

However, 60 per cent felt that child care interferes with income generating activity to some extent and 89 per cent stated that the impact is mostly on the quality of the output.

One of the problems as stated by these respondents (47%) was that the demands of their occupation interfered with what they considered normal child care activities eventhough they were at home. Health hazards posed by the occupation to the young child was also a serious problem mentioned (70%).

Siblings in Child Care

It is also seen that 46 per cent of all sibling caregivers were in the age-group 4-8 years and that 70 per cent of children below two were in the care of 'tender' caregivers. The responsibility of child care at such an young age may have serious implications for the development of both the child and the sibling.

The age of the sibling caregivers ranged from 4 to 16 years. The mean age was 9 years. A majority of all sibling caregivers (67%) were girls. However, almost 68 per cent of the male sibling caregivers were below 8 years while a majority (64%) of the female sibling caregivers was above 8 years of age. At the same time, 3/4 - 4/5 of all sibling caregivers above 8 years of age were female. This suggests that male children 8 years of age or above are more likely to be in school than female children of the same age, and hence are not available for child care. It is also possible that male caregivers of such a tender age are roped in for this task only when there are no female children available. These findings draw attention to the considerable gender differences in the involvement of siblings in child care.

Fifty-four per cent of the siblings are involved in full-time child care, which means that the siblings were in charge of the young child till the mother returned from work. Among these full-time caregivers, the majority is girls (78%). This again implies that the burden of child care is borne more by girl children. It is interesting to note that the proportion of full-time to part-time caregivers is exactly reversed as between male and female caregivers.

Fifty-six per cent of all sibling caregivers did not attend school. However, the proportion of those attending school is almost exactly reversed as between girls and boys. Among those not attending school, 81 per cent were girls. This again reflects the fact that the burden faced by girl sibling caregivers is more than that of the boys.

Out of these non-attenders, 51 per cent stopped attending school before they completed the primary level. The foundation for further learning is laid at this level so discontinuation may make it difficult for the child to pick up the threads and continue education later.

Differences among sexes were observed in the level at which discontinuation of studies occurred. A majority of the female siblings (64%) has discontinued before completing primary level of education while only 25 per cent of the male sibling care givers had discontinued studies at this level. Among the non-attenders at primary level, girls constituted 84 per cent. It is evident that the girl child is most affected when one considers the overall impact of the responsibility of child care on the siblings. Seventy-one per cent of the non-attenders had dropped out of school exclusively for the purpose of child care. Among these, the percentage of girls was 86 per cent and boys 14 per cent, reinforcing the perception that girl siblings are more burdened by child care than boys. While among boys, 56 per cent had dropped out for child care, 75 per cent of the girls had done so for this reason. Among the many factors that influence children's retention in the school system, one needs to add the realities of child care (or a lack of it). Hence the pressing need to enhance care facilities in the country, especially for mothers in the unorganised sector.

Difficulties and Problems

About 59 per cent of the respondents fully or partially make use of the child care services available in the state, including MCH. Though a majority is satisfied with these services, they mentioned several shortcomings of the services.

Table 4.4 : Stated Assistance needed for Child Care by Occupation

Occupation	*Assistance needed for child care*					
	A	*B*	*C*	*D*	*E*	*F*
Agriculture	5.0	69.4	7.9	1.8	47.4	68.7
Construction	49.1	33.9	2.8	—	27.4	86.8
Weaving artisan	6.9	67.7	8.0	2.3	44.8	70.1
Beedi-rolling	5.8	75.7	7.0	2.3	51.2	58.2
Quarrying	37.7	49.5	5.0	4.0	29.7	74.3
Urban petty trade	1.3	64.0	2.7	—	56.0	76.0
Fishing	39.6	44.8	8.6	3.4	31.0	72.4
Plantation	7.3	78.1	—	—	51.2	63.4
Domestic work	9.1	67.6	5.2	3.9	53.3	61.1
Gypsy	90.5	7.2	—	—	7.2	95.3
TOTAL > 100*	19.6	59.3	5.6	1.9	41.9	71.5

N = 950   * Multiple Choice Responses

A— Child care programmes that cater to other needs

B— Child care services with quality

C— Medical assistance

D—Awareness generation programmes

E— Infrastructure/administration

F—Financial assistance

Though accurate statistics were not available, about 2/5th of the respondents said that the children have to put up with the poor quality of the CCCs. But the major hurdle seems to be inappropriate timings of the child care services as about 4/5th of these respondents cite this as a major problem.

Another problem is related to the programme personnel, who, according to the respondents, are not very cordial and friendly with the beneficiaries. Frequently they are told to wait or are shouted at by the programme personnel. A few respondents mentioned about the unfriendly attitude to some CCC workers. Nearly a quarter of these respondents felt that the programme personnel are not very helpful when approached by the beneficiaries. Only about 5 per cent did not face any of these problems.

Perceptions about Child Care Needs

The respondents were asked a direct question as to what assistance they would need to take care of their children below 6 years of age. Most of the respondents initially were unable to answer as they had never thought about it earlier. However, after some thinking, about 72 per cent said that they wanted financial assistance from the government, and that they would take care of their child's nutritional, health and educational needs themselves, better than at present. Quite a few respondents wanted financial assistance at least during maternity and after delivery. A few were more specific and asked for assistance at the rate of Rs. 400 per month for a few months before delivery, and for at least six months after delivery! According to them such assistance would facilitate their presence near the growing child throughout the day and promote breastfeeding for longer duration.

Some respondents wanted the government to provide them with Rs. 50 per month for each child below 6 years of age in the family. This, they say would be enough for them to provide the child one nutritious meal per day in a hygienic and palatable manner and which according to them, would be much better than the nutrition provided at present by the CCCs.

The second major felt-need of the respondents was in the domain of child care services. Fifty-nine per cent of the respondents wanted a reoriented and a qualitatively improved CCC. The primary need in this category was CCCs that would function full-time, and would be linked with the work duration of the mother. Some respondents in this category require CCCs that would start functioning at 6 a.m. or at least at 7 a.m. and wind up only after 6 p.m. Apart from the extension of CCC timings most of the respondents stressed the provision of a qualitatively better service. Cleanliness, good and hygienic food in sufficient quantities, play materials and a safe atmosphere were the elements grouped under quality.

The respondents wanted the CCCs to concentrate more on education of the young child including the teaching of three 'R's. According to them, a child attending the Government run CCCs is at a disadvantage in terms of knowing the three 'R's, when compared to children attending pre-KG classes or CCCs run by voluntary organisations and private persons/institutions. Hence the respondents wanted a strong educational input in the services offered by the CCC.

Forty-two per cent of the respondents' needs can be put under the infrastructural and administrative domains. With regard to the administrative aspect of the CC services, these respondents want the Muthulakshmi Reddy Childbirth (M R) Scheme to be extended to the third child too. Some respondents want additional inputs for children of families below poverty line though they are unable to specify what these inputs can be. A few respondents wanted additional benefits for the girl child. A strong appeal was put forward to simplify the procedure for obtaining assistance under M R scheme.

Another infrastructural value addition demanded by the respondents is the proximity of CCCs to the work-spot. This would help the mother to monitor her child as well as facilitate breastfeeding. Respondents in gypsy communities and those involved in plantation work wanted more CCCs in remote areas where they go for work.

A few responses can be grouped under other needs (20%). A primary need expressed here is CCCs for children aged six months onwards. The mother may not be in a position to stop working for more than six months, and hence needs support services for child care, particularly in the absence of other caregivers. The respondents strongly felt the need for such CCCs as they found it difficult to balance their work and child care, till the child reaches two years of age. The fact that existing services are unsuited to meet this need is beyond dispute. Hence the demand for better infrastructure and changes at the policy level.

Implications

The Gap between Needs and Services

A major issue concerning the child care services presently

available in Tamil Nadu, is that the availability of the elaborate infrastructure is not equally matched by a recognition of the genuine needs of working women in the unorganised sector, nor are the day care services geared to this diversity of needs. Most centres function for six hours only when the actual need is for 10 to 12 hours a day.

The findings clearly indicate that the child care needs of working women vary among the different occupational groups. Flexible timings for child care centres would address some of those varying needs.

Another important finding relates to the unmet needs of the age-group below two. Most of the child care centres admit children after they have completed two or three years of age, because they are not equipped in terms of staff, space, materials etc. to handle younger children.

There is a need for an alternative child care system, not necessarily centre-based, to meet the needs of infants aged six months onwards. The different approach to services indicated has radical implications for policy.

Quality of Services

Another issue is that of quality. Lack of quality of care has been a recurring theme of the findings related to child care centres. Satisfaction of respondents who utilise child care centres was low with regard to several activities of these child care centres such as feeding, toilet care, timings, play activities and education. Strong efforts need to be made to improve the quality of services provided in child care centres. Improvement in quality pertains to an improvement in the quality of the food provided, in the infrastructure such as furniture, play materials, safe building and play space, in the activities of the child care centres and in the allied services such as nutrition and health care, all of which have implications for the training, remuneration, timings and working conditions of child care workers.

Relief for the Girl Child

The provision of maternity assistance and adequate child care services will lead to a substantial decrease in the involvement of siblings in child care—especially the girl child—at the cost of their own education and development.

This has also been emphasised by the national plan of action for children (Government, 1992), which had "universal access to primary education with special emphasis for girls" as one of the major objectives. Creation of child care services to release girls from sibling care responsibilities in order to participate in education was one of the activities suggested to fulfil this objective.

There is an urgent need to think in terms of child care services, particularly in close proximity to school, which will play a significant role as a support system for girls' education. This would brighten the prospects of continuing their education.

Alternative systems of child care need to be explored. Family based, community based, women's group-based and school-based day-care centres (as suggested by *Shramshakti*, 1988) to name a few can become viable alternatives. Vast human resources remain to be tapped. Voluntary organisations can perhaps explore possibilities to address the issue of child care at the village level.

Employer Participation

The 'employer' in the unorganised sector denotes a difficult area for intervention, because the employers are small, numerous, scattered, changing and often 'invisible' in the multi-layered system of contracts. Yet it cannot be neglected. Employers can play a very significant role in making the work spot as mother and child-friendly as possible. For this the employers need to be sensitised about the needs of the mothers employed under them. Employers can also make a financial contribution, even if indirectly, to the maintenance of child care services.

Policy Level Changes

All the above call for a paradigm shift in the present orientation of child care policies. Both government and policy makers and also employers have continued to look at the child care as an individual problem of women and their families and not as a social responsibility. They fail to recognise that maternity and child care are not the sole responsibility of the concerned individual, but that in the long-term interest of the nation, the state, the family, and society at large have a major responsibility for taking care of working mothers and children. This also involves efforts to involve men to a greater extent in accepting responsibility for child care in the family.

The policies need to be given a pro-child and a pro-mother emphasis rather than a pro-resources and a pro-administrative one. This is necessary because, frequently, adequate resources are not allotted to child care in the name of structural adjustments, and administrative considerations gain emphasis over the needs of the mother and the child. Child care cannot be compromised. There is a need to consider it as a national priority on par with perhaps poverty alleviation. Progammes must shift from a service-delivery approach to a need-based flexible child-and-mother-sensitive one.

Conclusion

The issue of child care is a complex one involving several areas of concern and action. However, one cannot afford to be hesitant in investing in child care, as the spin-offs from such an investment are tremendous. This has been the experience of most ex-socialist countries as well as some developed countries which are reaping the fruits of investing in a supportive and mother-friendly child care system.

The fundamental change that is required is a change in attitudes among employers, policy makers and the public. The first step in this direction is the recognition that women are performing a socially relevant function when they bear children. Secondly, children are a valuable resource for a nation and hence providing good child care is a national responsibility. And thirdly, it is the fundamental right of every child to have adequate care. These implications if understood properly will be instrumental in revamping the existing child care system to take a giant step towards one that is comprehensive and child-and-mother-friendly.

5

CHILD CARE IN THE SERVICE SECTOR
Perception of Multiple Stakeholders

— *Rajani M. Konantambigi* and
Rajalakshmi Sriram

Child Care Services — An Introduction

In India, as in most societies of the world, child care in the past had been confined to the mother, and/or to the family (nuclear or an extended one). Women's, more specifically, young mothers' entry into the world of work which took them away from home has brought forth problems and issues in the 'who and how of child care'. These problems and issues are diverse depending on a variety of factors. Mothers from socio-economically deprived backgrounds have not only to care totally for their children, but also play a part in the survival of the family. To begin with, the rate of women's participation in interaction with the economic forces of a society creates a need for child care facilities/providers that need not be a part of the child's family. Not only have the needy mothers to be aware of the existing facilities, they should also be able to afford the services. By and large, in the Indian context, it is a seller's market. Those mothers who have to seek child care service outside the family have to agree with the terms and conditions laid down by the providers.

Vis-à-vis the types of care available, there seems to be some variety. The available forms of child care are a full-time domestic helper taking care of the baby/child at the child's place or the helper's place, grandparent care (at the child's own home if cared for by the paternal grandmother or at the place of maternal grandmother), neighbour care (a lady in the immediate neighbourhood may agree to care for one or two children), family day care (informal child care at the provider's place for about 6 to 8 children), crèches functioning under government schemes and day care centre – formal child care centre/crèche provided by the employer or established privately (Datta, 1991; Gupta,1994; Konantambigi, 1990; Sriram, 1991; Thakkar, 1991).

The various other factors apart from the economic and social that determine the type of child care sought are listed as below:

(i) *Developmental Stage of the Child:* Infants/babies' developmental needs would tend to be more of a routine nature. Custodial care with the satisfaction of basic needs for food, elimination and hygiene could be perceived as satisfactory. Whereas, in the Indian context, if the child is aged 3, he/she begins to attend a formal pre-school centre. The child needs to physically get ready for the purpose; he/she has to be dropped off to the center and be picked up from there. Parents would look for care that would include this facility.

(ii) *Propinquity factors:* How close is the facility to home or the work place of at least one parent. This also depends on the nature of the city. In Bombay (Mumbai) respondents who generally commute long distances wanted the facility closer to home (Datta, 1995, Thakkar, 1991) and respondents in a relatively smaller city like Baroda wanted it closer to the work place so that they could supervise child care better (Sriram, 1991). In the former case it implied that they did not want the child to travel.

(iii) *Physical and custodial care facilities:* Respondents invariably sought facilities that provided a proper hygienic environment; one where they perceived child's safety, and a place where the child would be fed properly (Sriram, 1991; Thakkar, 1991; Datta and Maheshwari, 1997).

(iv) *Cognitive and academic factors:* Parents sought places, though this was not a priority, where the basics of alphabets and numbers were taught, children were prepared for entry into pre-school, and provided some cognitive stimulation through play activities (Konantambigi, 1990; Thakkar, 1991).

(v) *Affective factors:* Like attention, love, and the ability to understand children were mentioned as important aspects of basic care (Sriram, 1991; Thakkar, 1991). Another dimension here is the overall satisfaction of the mother/parent with the centre and the caregiver (Gupta and Konantambigi, this Volume; Sriram, 1991). In the past, research has shown that the felt satisfaction of the mother/parent together with the perceived positive qualities of the centre are positively related to child outcomes (Vanaja and Venkataramaiah, 1990; Greenberger and O'Neil, 1990a; Crockenberg and Litman, 1991). However, most studies concentrated on the quality of day care centres and its relationship to child outcomes (Atkinson, 1987). Of the former kind, Gupta and Konantambigi (in this volume) found perceived global maternal satisfaction to be positively related to socio-emotional behavioural adjustment in pre-schoolers of Baroda city.

Perceived Satisfaction with Child Care

By and large, studies on quality of day care centres and its relationship to child outcomes have not considered the dimension of parental satisfaction. Parental and children's satisfaction with care and the caregiver completes the loop in understanding the effects of child care for the target group. If such perceptions are positive they could help in better-child caregiver/centre relations, which in turn feed into positive outcomes for children's development. The maternal or parental perception about childcare *per se* and satisfaction with alternate care is also related to maternal guilt. Negative perceptions about childcare centre and the caregiver could make the parent (mother) feel that they have not chosen alternate care well for their child and thus induce guilt. (From this stage of the paper the term "maternal guilt" is used as child care in the families is still perceived as the major responsibility of the mothers). Maternal guilt in turn determines coping strategies. Adaptive strategies work well for the child, but not necessarily the extreme feelings of guilt. Mothers learn to handle the overall situation to their satisfaction and by and large, their guilt too (Gupta and Konantambigi, this volume). However, what was not studied here was whether the guilt gets translated into certain behaviour and feelings that could affect their child.

Caregiver and Parental Perceptions and their Interactions

Another important dimension to child care has been brought to focus by Atkinson (1987). The caregivers, she says, also have a perception of the services that they provide; these perceptions should match with what the parents are expecting and perceiving regarding child care services. This in turn, she says, is related to the nature of caregiver-parent interaction, which in turn has a bearing on the functioning of the child care centre. The primacy of the family-child care service interrelation is being recognised as such, and it is also believed to have a bearing on child outcomes. These views of Aitkinson (1987) are put forth in Figure 5.1.

Atkinson (1987) further adds that there is scope for match of the perceptions of parents and caregivers and for satisfaction if quality care exists, and if there is variety and option in care. One tends to think that this could be the case in the West. Relatively speaking it could be true, but problems exist. Atkinson (1987) has explored the perceptions of both caregivers and the parents, and has tried to see if there is a match. There was more similarity in the ratings of mothers (N = 43) and caregivers (N = 13) in the evaluation of parental and child care needs than on mothers' reason and providers' perceptions of mothers' reasons for choice of child care. The providers exaggerated on the social opportunities (76%) for the child, preparation for school, characteristics of the staff. Mothers' reasons predominantly were programmes and planned activities at the center, social opportunities for child (35%), and convenience

Fig. 5.1 : Child care set up and its functionong as conceived by Atkinson based on Atkinson (1989)

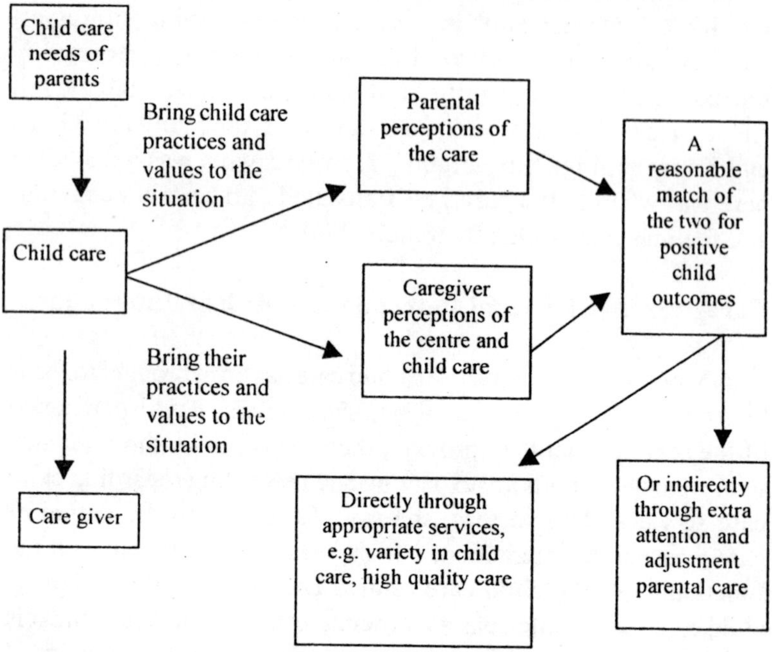

and location. Since multiple open reasons could be given, there have been wide variations in what parents perceive as important.

There is also the issue of decision making when there are choices. To look at the decision making process in the choice of child care, Bogota and Gensheimer (1986) studied 167 parents who had called day care service. They were telephonically interviewed. The following were the desired features mentioned by the parents. "Of the ten features listed, health and safety" was endorsed as important by 99.3 per cent of the callers. This was followed closely by "the way in which children got along with each other and with the adult supervising them" (93.4%) and "the provider's child rearing philosophy (93.4%)". Callers felt that coordination between their home and the child care provider (89.0%), physical space and surroundings of child care facility (86.8%), materials, equipment, and programme activities (85.3%), and "distance of the child care facility from their home" (80.2%) were also quite important. Other factors such as "cost" (72.1%), "distance of the child care facility from their place of work" (64.4%), and "recommendation of the facility by other people" (59.2%) were other important considerations to many respondents (Bogota and Gensheimer, 1986, p.164).

A host of other features which pertain to the caregivers came forth when Bogota and Gensheimer (1986) asked respondents to list any other feature that was significant in decision making. The spontaneously generated features included "personality of the provider", "credentials or experience of the provider", "convenience", "general atmosphere", "meals", "heterogeneous balance of children", "educational component", and "location" (p.164). The single most important factor that influenced the child care decision was "the way in which children get along" (11.2%) and "convenience" (10.4%). In this study the use of checklist, consulting others, prior enquiries and actual visiting of the child care facility, and behaviour of the parents were also studied in conjunction with the decision making process involved. It was found that parents using the checklist were as well satisfied as the non-users. The non-users concerns were more practical like cost and location of the facility (Bogota and Gensheimer, 1986). Practicality and cost seem to be the features. Families who had mothers who earned more per hour, higher incomes and income other then mother's earnings tended to look for centre care (Hofferth and Wissoker, 1992). They also found that lower the cost of child care, more was the probability that a particular mode of care would be chosen (N=971).

Studies exploring the desired type of child care facility and the requisite features there in have been limited to the urban context in India. Grandparent care is still considered the most appropriate form of care as seen in both the studies of Mumbai (Datta, 1994 and Datta and Maheshwari, 1997). It has also been seen that maid care continues to be used as alternate child care arrangement, as parents feel that there is no difference in the quality of care provided by maids and that provided by child care centres. This is in spite of the fact that research showing that children of the maid care group fared most poorly on Kamat-Binet Intelligence Test and the Vineland's Social Maturity Scale (Datta, Chapter 8, this Volume). In the study by Datta and Maheshwari (1997) not only were mothers satisfied with child care (whatever be the type of care) but most of them (79%) did not also have difficulty in finding child care and convincing elders in the family. Child care decisions in the Indian context seem to be a familial decision; including especially grandparents, and at times the children too. Seeking alternate care for the child is a serious decision as is a commonly held belief, and practiced too, that one should take care of one's children, and that the care should not be entrusted to members outside the family (Thakkar, 1991). The reasons for satisfaction with child care were cleanliness of the centre, a loving atmosphere, "taking good care of the child" and teaching the child new concepts. In this study most of the parents were satisfied with child care (Datta and Maheshwari, 1997).

In a series of short surveys over 1990-91 (N-393) Thakkar (1991) found that family day care (FDC) was relatively the most preferred facility, because it was available in the neighbourhood, caregiver was known to the mother, and smaller number of children were present in the center. Of the total respondents, about 35.8 per cent had their children in FDC, 29.5 of the cases availed of formal day care centre and other types of alternate care were utilized by 31.2 per cent. The latter point scored well with these parents, and they said that it ensured adequate attention to their child. In FDCs hot meals were served, sometimes supplementing home food and at times providing complete meals, and drinking water provided was safe too. Parents had to pay more for such care in comparison to a day care centre, but they were willing to. In contrast to these findings, Thakkar (1991) notes that FDCs were not perfect, they were better places of custodial care but lacked stimulating and planned activities. Parents opted for full-day care, a clean and a safe environment. The study also revealed a need for awareness regarding the existing facilities.

In a study on the child care needs and satisfaction with the child care services in a comparatively smaller city like Baroda, Sriram (1991) found that about 50 per cent of the respondents

(Primary School Teachers, N=100; Nurses, N=100; and Office Workers, N=100) resided in nuclear families and that there was a need for alternate services. They (about 50%, especially the school teachers and nurses) expected the employer to provide affordable child care services, and a majority expected the facility to be nearer the work place like the other studies (Datta and Maheshwari, 1997; Bogota and Gensheimer, 1986; Thakkar, 1991). The available facilities were few, and the affordable ones were not of good quality. The good quality services were expensive and also not close to their homes. The majority of the respondents desired good quality care, and centres where they could exercise some control over its functioning — a novel feature as compared to the findings in the Indian context, as well as a well articulated factor considering that the Indian child care scenario is a sellers' market. However, such a need to exercise control in the functioning of the pre-school set up was voiced in a Japanese study. Kaneda, Suwa and Hijikata (1994) got different groups of day nursery teachers (caregivers from public and private centres, and also caregivers of an Association — the Aichi Prefecture Caregivers Association) from Japan to elaborate on what constitutes "good care" and "what currently are the best things about care in their schools". This part of the study has been like the one carried out by Atkinson (1987). However, Kaneda, Suwa and Hijikata went a step further and queried on "what in their schools bothers them", and "how they proposed to work on the things that bothered them".

The following five central categories emerged:

- The relationship of teachers to each other
- Teacher's attitude towards child care
- What child care should be
- The relationship between parents and teachers
- Child-care environments and conditions of care (Kaneda, Suwa and Hijikata, 1994.

The exploration of "teachers" attitude towards "child care" in the same study revealed the following three sub-categories.

- Child-centred care (including care that considers the child's point of view; care that starts from the child; and care that values the child's individuality).
- Care that accepts children as they are (including close care on a one-to-one basis; care that allows children to be themselves and care that they can depend on; and care that is sympathetic to children's feelings).
- Care that fosters children's initiative (including care that promotes children to be lively; and care that allows children's active concentration).

The authors summarise "good care" as coming from the "basic relationship between teachers and children" (Kaneda, Suwa and Hijikata, 1994). The responses of the three groups of respondents however were not uniform, the teachers in the public school on the whole tended not to see problems in care as stemming from their attitudes or the way they were' the other teachers tuned inward to seek solutions and better the care. This research study which has not only focused on helping the caregivers to reflect on "good care", but also on "what of their practices/facilities are good or not good for children", is a very good example of a hiatus between research and practice to enhance the quality of child care.

It seems possible to cull out certain common denominators (from the various studies conducted on the Indian sample) that articulate expectations regarding child care: Generally, child care should take place at the child's home by close relatives, though at times it is under debate when the paternal grandmother looks after the child. Alternate care is needed by close to 50 per cent of the respondents, due to reasons like nuclear family, not wanting to burden the grandparents or to expose the child to academic/cognitive stimulation. Though at the cognitive and belief level, parents would want to consider a number of characteristics while choosing/desiring day care for their child, but they end up making the choice by considering one or two factors. Mostly the factors were location and cost (Bogota and Gensheimer, 1986; Datta and Maheshwari, 1997, Sriram, 1991; and Thakkar, 1991). Some of them consider the personality of the caregiver (Bogota and Gensheimer, 1986), a loving and caring atmosphere, safe and hygienic environment (Datta and Maheshwari, 1997; Thakkar, 1991); and cognitive stimulation (Datta and Maheshwari, 1997). Only in one study did respondents speak of control over functioning of the day care centre (hence the quality of care) (Sriram, 1991). The respondents at times spoke of "good quality care", without elaborating on what "good care" is (Sriram, 1991).

The preceding review of relevant studies reveal that research has been carried out on:

- Child care needs of parents.
- Parental expectations from child care; and to some extent the decision-making process that parents engage in.
- Maternal perception/satisfaction regarding the quality of care.
- Observers'/experts' evaluation of child care "quality" and its relation to child development outcomes, and parental perceptions/satisfaction (the review here has not covered this aspect, see other Chapters in this Volume).
- Caregivers' perception of the services that they offer.

Objectives

Keeping in view the stakeholders of child care services and the role that multiple perspectives play in enhancing the quality of care and satisfaction to the parents, following were the objectives in the studies conducted between 1994 and 1998:

- To understand the commonalities in motivations of providers in initiating centres and those of parents in availing of the services and the perceived roles and qualities of the caregiver.
- To develop an overview of expectations of parents with reference to childcare and parental satisfactions/dissatisfactions.

- To know caregivers perceptions and problems related to childcare services.
- To present an overview of existing features related to quality of services based on observations.

The present chapter makes an attempt to put together available data, from interviews with parents, care providers and observations carried out at centres, to evolve a meaningful picture of the existing situation from multiple perspectives. It highlights the gaps that exist in meeting the needs of parents and children in India to identify appropriate approaches and strategies for intervention.

Method

An attempt has been made to integrate data from a series of small studies conducted between 1994 and 1998 in Baroda city. The universe comprised of 28 child care centres who were members of a day care association named "Shishu Palak Vrund". The sample comprised of parents and care providers who were representative of the group and were purposively chosen in view of the goals of the study. Table 5.2 describes the sources and methods for procuring the data.

Procedure

The study used multiple method to obtain the needed data. During the first phase in 1994, data was collected by a group of 4 students, who were conducting this research as a part of their course under the guidance of the author. In the second phase of data collection in 1996, data was collected by an M.Sc. student as part of her dissertation and the third phase of 1997-98 data was collected as a part of a project under the guidance of the second author. Discussions took place in the homes of parents and in the centres during parents' visits. Providers' interviews were conducted during their free time, all with prior appointments, thus offering scope for freedom of expression.

Table 5.1 Tools and methods used for the study

UNIVERSE : 28 Urban Day Care Centres Located in various parts of Baroda city.		
Total centres	*Parents*	*Providers*
15/20 urban centres	1994 – 58 (mothers)	In charge of the centre – 14
	1996*– 20 (10 fathers 10 mothers)	In-charge – 5 Other Staff – 9
	1997 – 100 (75 mothers 25 fathers)	C.C. Worker – 22 and helpers – 13 In-charge – 15

Table 5.2 : An Overview of Sample and Tools used for the Study

	Purpose and Timeframe	*Tools and Methods*
1.	Parental beliefs, expectations, satisfactions 1994, 1996, 1998.	• Questionnaire and in-depth interview of parents at their homes.
2.	Care providers' perceptions of centre and parental needs 1994 and 1998.	• Checklist to develop a profile of the centre covering all aspects. • Detailed interview with providers at the centre.
3.	Details about the centre 1994, 1996 and 1997.	• Bradley and Caldwell (1989) Home Observation checklist adapted to suit Day Care Centre. • Recording spot observations at the centre on all aspects.

Data analysis

Interviews were transcribed into recording sheets. These helped in preparation of response clusters and summary charts in line with the study objectives. The data from various sources have been integrated under subheads and presented evolving appropriate formats that are both pictorial and the results are presented in an integrated manner in view of the four objectives. An attempt is made to integrate data from providers, parents and observations as need be.

Results

A Closer Look at Existing Child Care Centres

Different types of childcare centres are operational in the city of Baroda such as day care centre, play care centre, family day care, etc. All the day care centres, family day care centres, or day care centres-cum-nurseries were catering to mostly a middle-class clientele; the range being lower-middle class at times to upper middle class.

These centres were privately managed by their own resources and those generated through charges collected by the clientele. There were only three family day care centres (FDCs), others were large, and four of them had nursery sections also attached to their DCs. At least 5 centres in the sample had babies younger than one year of age; the providers did not prefer babies in the centre.

The trend of 5 out of the 14 centres catering to babies is different to those reported by Thakkar (1994), where caregivers did not entertain admitting babies. Most of the centres have been in operation for 4 to 5 years on an average, a couple of them have been around for the last 10 years; only a couple of them were a year older.

Play centres are spread all around the city catering their services to children between the age 1½-2 years to 3-3½ years are, where as in family day care, children from 6 months to 10 years are admitted ; specially children of working parents use this facility. Many centres are housed in the residence of the care provider and some centres have a special place where children come. Most of the centres are well equipped with open outdoor and spacious indoors for play, activities like story telling, creative work is also done. Where as some of the centres are less equipped or do not have outdoor space for play, activities, storytelling, etc., their caregivers provide the same activities inside

Table 5.3 : Overview of the centres in Vadodara

No. of Children in a centre	*N-21*	*N-12*
	*Play Care Centre**	*Day Care Centre***
15 – 25	5	4
25 – 40	—	4
40 – 50	4	1
50 – 100	3	2
Above 100	—	1
Age Range of Children		
Infant (Less than 2 yrs)	9	9
Toddlers (1½ - 3 yrs)	6	9
Pre-schoolers (3 – 6 yrs)	2	7
Older children	0	9
Child – Staff Ratio		
5 : 1	—	1
12 : 1	8	1
16 : 1	1	—
20 : 1	1	1

* Play Care Centre: Centres for toddlers 1½ to 3 year olds to play, generally function for about 2 hours a day.

** Day Care Centre: Centre for the care of mostly pre-schoolers (3 months to 6 years of age) for the entire day to facilitate working mothers.

Note: Total is not 100 per cent due to multiple responses. Day care centres also have a play centre as a part and therefore, the number in day care may sometimes be not very accurate.

the centre. The staff child ratio varied from 1:7 to 1:15 to 1:25/30 according to the quality and space of the centre. (See Table 5.3) Play centres are open for 2½ to 3 hrs where as day care are open for 9-10 hrs and family day care is open 12 hrs in a day.

Day care and family day care provides the child with the food and less than fifty per cent of the play centres provide snacks/food, the others ask the children to get snacks from their homes.

How do Parents and Providers look at Child Care Services: The Motivations

Parents, in addition to the factors that would influence their choice of a centre, were asked as to what they thought were the benefits of sending a child to a day care centre. The responses varied from practical such as, "they do not have to be absent from work" to the overall development of the child. "It helps working parents", "provides opportunity for socialisation, helps in the care, and safety of the child", were some of the popular responses. Gain in terms of becoming independent and becoming confident for the children were also mentioned. It is evident that parents have awareness about children's needs and are concerned about their child's development. The fact that a majority of the parents perceive safety (custodial care) to be important speaks of what actually is expected of alternate care. In subtle ways these kinds of messages are conveyed to the caregivers. These determine the nature of services that are provided by the daycare centres.

While examining data from two sources (Tables 5.4, 5.5 and 5.6), it is quite evident that there is convergence in the primary motive of the service to support working mothers and offer inputs into overall

Table 5.4 : Reasons for Initiation of Child Care Centres

Reported Reasons	*No. of Caregivers 28*
To support working mothers	52%
Interest in supporting children's development	42%
Provide homely environment in absence of parents	35%
Hobby and make use of one's knowledge	21%
Earning income and independence	17%
For being busy (Time pass)	25%
To prepare children for school	7%
To provide good food	3.5%

Table 5.5 : Parental Expectations from Child Care Centres

Reasons for Sending Children to Child Care Centre	*N=100 (1998) %*	*N=56 (1994) %*
Centre helps child		
To be social and adjust to other children	38	33
For overall development	35	14
Giving security in absence of parents	21	89
To form and develop good habits	13	28
To get habituated to school, teachers and keep child away from parents vicinity	12	16
By giving freedom to play and enjoy	08	—
To develop imagination and creativity	05	—
Expectation from the Centre		
Parents expect centre to		
Support pro-social behaviour	77	
Support learning through play	33	
Provide safe, healthy and clean environment	47	
Prepare child for age appropriate activity	23	
Provide soothing, loving and caring environment	17	
Support proper molding of child	16	
Employ trained staff	10	

development of the child. It is obvious that parents explicitly state the nature of support expected in terms of environmental features and the programme. Providers though concerned about children's development did not state its features.

Investment in Initiating Child Care

Only a couple of caregivers invested heavily in setting up the centres. Most of the FDCs reported that they did not need to make initial heavy investments; they started the centres because some space was available. Some of them spoke of their qualification as an added advantage. The caregivers also voiced certain dissatisfactions, for instance, parents' misuse of the creche timings, their wanting to send children on holidays too, and misunderstandings that took place between them and the parents. It also seemed that most caregivers did not ask for adequate participation; however, they said that they do consult the parents in the functioning though no formal meetings were held. The FDCs mostly and some other centres too, did not keep any records of children's development, etc. Some of the larger day care centres did so (4), and some (3) had medical check-ups. One of the safety measures followed was having identity cards for children (which were to be pinned on to their dresses while coming/or being dropped to the centre) (6 centres).

Parent's Satisfaction with the Services

As in other aspects of respondents' replies, satisfaction with child care has also been expressed on a variety of aspects. These are listed in Table 5.6.

Table 5.6 : Perceived (N = 56) Satisfaction with Various Aspects of Child Care

	Satisfied with	*N=100 (1998)*	*N= 56 (1994)*
1.	"Good care" at the Centre	54%	58%
2.	Variety in the programme	23%	33%
3.	Habit formation	14%	33%
4.	Facilities – food, play	–	30%
5.	Social development of children	34%	23%
6.	Good teaching, Formal learning	14%	52%
7.	Toilet training/discipline	14%	10%
8.	Clarity in speech/Vocabulary increase	–	17%
9.	Independence training	29%	14%
10.	Manners taught/learnt	14%	12%
11.	Happiness and Adjustment of child	54%	8%

From the data, it is clearly reflected that a majority of the parents are satisfied with centre and child's development. The administration, policy and staff of the centre are sensitive to children's and parents' needs. The qualities of the centre enhance the child's development. Parents have also observed positive changes in their child. For example, they said that they became social, sang songs and developed healthy habits.

Perceived Influence on the Child

Parents have also reported on some behavioural changes in their child as a result of being in the Centre (for about a year) or immediate changes that were noticed by them. Many of the children looked forward to going to the Centre. Some however did not (12%); they cried at times (21%) especially in the initial days of attending the Centre and were stubborn too (21%). 71 per cent of the mothers said that their child eats adequately at the Centre; only 12 per cent felt that they did so sometimes.

Perceived Influence on the Family

Mothers were asked if they had noticed any change in their relationship with the child — 16 per cent experienced some change; 9 per cent a positive one and the remaining and 7 per cent a negative one.

Some parents (4) spoke of anxiety that continued even after initial adjustment of the child; anxiety was about aggression from other children in the centre and accidents; 'child being hit/pushed by other children'. Other apprehensions, though mentioned by one or two parents were 'child contracting an infectious disease', 'over-eating or under-eating by the child', 'whether the child would be comfortable without mother', and 'whether the child will cry'. All parents spoke of the initial adjustment problems; specifically of children crying. The majority of the parents (75%) stated that they did not experience any anxiety in sending their child to the day care centre.

In view of the prevailing cultural belief that children should not be cared for by non-family members, the grandparents in this sample, according to the parents (46%), felt that day care effects were positive for children, while 17 per cent said that there were negative effects, 26 per cent said that there are no effects, and that there are mixed influences (8% of the sample said so).

Thus it can be said that the positives of a centre must have helped in developing positive characteristics in children. Some of the negative features are highlighted in dissatisfactions and observational data that is presented further in the paper. There is a need for providing different incentives to the staff, which leads to child positive development.

Choice of Childcare Centre: What do Parents Look For?

It is interesting to note that proximity is the first factor, followed by features of good care especially provider's nature and a homely atmosphere, rather than the type of programme, thus reflecting a parental belief about safe and secure environment as the primary feature of care. However, what is note worthy is the variation between expectation and satisfaction which reflects clearly "acceptance of existing services by parents as they are." Such an attitude indirectly influences childcare quality, as supply is always related to the demands of the market.

Table 5.7 : Salient Factors in the Choice of the Centre (Parents Reports)

Reasons for choice	*Percentage of parents*	*Parental Satisfaction %*
Proximity to home	50%	—
Facilities: space timings, food, food/toys	45%	30%
Good individualized care, nature of care provider, habits, activities provided	76%	Ranged from 30 – 58%
Stimulation and teaching	21%	52%
Reputation and molding child's behaviour	21%	7-10% on different features

Care Providers and their Role

Most of the women running these centres were middle-aged; two of them had a master's degree and a bachelor's degree in education, one had only a bachelor's degree in education, only two had a diploma or a certificate in child development, others were high school or pre-university graduates. That is, majority of the caregivers had no special training or orientation to child development. The directors of the centres in urban areas are women above 25 yrs. More than 70 per cent are 35 yrs and above. However, teachers and helpers (*bais*) in urban centres are in the age range of 15–35 yrs. This shows that teachers and helpers are in such an age group that it would help them to be actively involved more with the children, and children can also relate to them in turn.

Twenty-three per cent helpers are illiterate. A majority of helpers in the urban centres (65%) have education up to 10th class or less. Half of the teachers in urban centres have completed either matriculation or higher secondary, and another forty per cent are graduates. The persons in-charge (10 of them) are graduate/post-graduate. This shows that the persons in-charge have better qualifications as compared to teachers and helpers. But very few are trained/educated in field of childcare/development. A majority of the care providers run the childcare centre without any training qualification of child development; the teachers are educated up to Standard XII (52%).

It is evident from the Table (5.8) that care givers perceive their major role as a substitute to parents. Though loving and caring was mentioned as a quality and general knowledge and ability to give input with children's development, it is quite clear that providers do not emphasise specific professional skills either in staff or for conducting the programme. Therefore, we see a clear difference between intention and action that is only 1/3 to ½ the parents express satisfaction about care provided and only about a fifth expressed satisfaction with reference to sensitivity of care providers and their relationship with the child.

Table 5.8 : Care Providers : What do they Perceive and how do they Function?

Roles	*N= 14*	*Quali-ties*	*N=14*	*What parents appreciate*	*N= 14*	*What is observed*	*N= 21*
Discipli-narian	71%	Loving & kind	78%	Loving care	47%	Warm loving attitude	70%
Substitute to mother	42%	Under-stan-ding nature	35%	Clean cooperative punctual	12%	Little or no formal training	All
Promoting Indepen-dence in child	42%	Patient gain trust of child	78%	Cheerful, patient	7%	Both positive and negative mode of interaction	All
Habit formation	42%	General know-ledge	28%	Sensitive to child's needs	16%	Casual unprofes-sional attitude	All
Individual attention	28%	Coura-geous and bold	7%	Child trusts and relates well	6%	Multiple responsi-bilities	All
Toilet train children	7%					Limited staff	All
						Sometimes rigid ineffective use of materials space.	All

Interactions between Caregivers and Children: Some Observations

Despite the fact that the caregivers do not have professional training, they clearly responded to children's basic needs, but they were not always conscious and hence it was done intuitively. Also the observers' presence might have had an impact. Keeping the child happy, quiet/not too mischievous was the main aim. It was noted

Table 5.9 : Caregiver-Child Interactions : An Overview of Observations

Nature of Interactions	*Total centres (N=19)*
• *Responds to children's needs*	
– Encourages children's expression of thoughts and feelings	94%
– Help child in routine personal tasks	68% (when the caregiver is relaxed)
– Play and affectionate responses	100% (most of the time)
• *Discipline*	
– Control, restricts, commands	Most of the times 100%
– Negative strategies such as threatening, shaming, ridiculing, comparison, blaming	instances observed (22)
– Positive strategies	100%
– Assurance, reason, answer questions, appreciate, cuddle, direct attention etc.	instances observed (15)
• *Others*	
– Partial	2
– Pleasant	12

that most caregivers used both positive and negative strategies of interaction. On questioning, there was greater acknowledgement of the positive practices. Some negative strategies such as "the child tied to the slide", 'the child is threatened' were also seen. However, quarrels between children were resolved fairly, in 80 per cent of the centres and children were observed to be reprimanded for their misbehaviours in more than 40 per cent of the centres.

Observations and discussions further reflected that despite sensitivity to children's needs, the caregivers' attitude to interactions and programme is very casual. The coordinators reflect this as "they take leave without informing" or "delay in changing or washing of children". As most of them learn on the job, wherein there is a frequent turnover at the level of the helper, inputs into skill development seem to be an ever emerging unsatisfied need. Since getting trained staff for low salaries is not possible, many had to fulfil multiple responsibilities and in the process some became rigid in their attitude and behaviour. The chief providers put up with the limitation as the salaries are meagre and services are indispensable. Parents as they have limited option develop an attitude of tolerance which is culturally ingrained.

Programme

Since the picture is a combined one for day care and play centres, apart from routine custodial care for babies and infants, the slightly older children (12+ months) are provided with various activities. Despite the verbal denial, it was noted that preparatory activities for schooling and school admission are included not only as a

Table 5.10 : An Overview of Activities Carried out in Centre : Caregiver Reports and Observations

	Routine activities (care-giver reports)	*N=24 (%)*	*Occasional activities*	*Observation*
1.	Free play (indoor/ outdoor)	95	• Clay modelling	• Idea of music limited to songs.
2.	Play with toys	62.5	• Video show/puppet/ magic show	• Story telling a mechanical activity.
3.	Songs / rhymes alphabets / numbers	75	• Sand and water play.	• Absence of a plan or schedule.
4.	Common art activities	100	• Music and dance	• Activities do not cater to different age or level of children.
5.	Stories	95		• Children play alone.
6.	Books, picture reading	50		• Equipment is sometimes only best for show and not used for fear of loss, depletion.
7.	Formal Education	29		

means to attract parents, but also on demand of families for such training to children to be able to perform for admission tests. However, the availability of appropriate activities to all children is questionable. Also, there is lack of stimulation by involvement of the care provider due to her multiple responsibilities.

Availability of facilities/conditions of the centre, and some behavioural observations were made by adapting Bradley *et al.* (1985), Home Observation Inventory (Konantambigi, 1990) and also on the spot observations.

Table 5.11 : Features of the environment and facilities : A Summary

Environment	*N= 21*	*Facilities*	*N= 14*	*Hygiene*	*N= 14*
– Adequate indoor space	14	– Drinking water	14	– Washing hands before meals	10
– Outdoor space	12	– Food	10	– Wash after play	5
– Sufficient Lighting/ ventilation	18	– Toilet	14	– Immediate actions to maintain cleanliness	3
– Aesthetically pleasant	9	– Sleeping arrangement	8	– Cleanliness not always attend to immediately	3
		– Milk	6	– Attending to children when soiled	7
		– Outdoor equipment	11	– Separate utensils for each child	10
		– Dolls corner	5	– Separate napkin	4
		– Games	11		
		– Puppets, blocks, house materials	10		
		– TV, VCR Music system	5		

Observations point to abundance in material facilities at the centres, while only nine centres actually gave all the materials to the children to play with, three of them gave the materials sometimes and two did not give at all. It was heartening that a majority of the centres had various indoor games and materials, and that they also allowed/facilitated the play of and the stimulation for children.

The centres followed various hygienic practices except one centre. However, the issue of separate napkins continued to plague most centres. Group care involves such intricacies and our centres do not seem to be paying heed to certain issues (dealing with sickness behaviour). Other features included appropriate furniture and parental cooperation.

Expectations from Parents, Policies, Procedures

Observation and discussions conducted at nineteen centres revealed that all the providers (directors) and the caregivers did have some expectations from user parents, though they were not explicitly stated and given to parents in a written form. Some key features are summarised in Table 5.12.

All the centres had simple procedures to be completed in terms of filling in an admission form that is distributed for a nominal sum

Table 5.12 : Cost of Child Care

Type of service	*Average fees/month in rupees*	*Range of fees in rupees*
Play care with snack provision (3 hrs.)	300 – 350	250 – 400
Play care without Snack (3 hrs.)	200 – 250	150 – 300 (if care is for 2 hrs. then Rs. 100)
Day care (Toddler/pre-schooler) (5-7 hrs.)	Around Rs. 600	400 – 700 Maximum about Rs. 800 if care is for around 8 or more hours
Day care (infant)	Additional cost of about Rs. 50-100	

(Rs. 10/-), payment of some deposit, advance or term fees. The charges for the services are varied depending on the facilities of food. The average costs for different types of care are provided in the Table 5.12. The parents in the sample did not have any quarrel with the amount charged for the purpose. The fees ranged from Rs.100 to Rs.400 per month, in play centre and was slightly more for day care. Each of the parents (98%) earned Rs.3000 and above per month. Roughly, family incomes ranged from Rs. 6000-12000 per month.

Most providers ran their centres in their homes or a place which they own/or is available to them and therefore, do not incur expenditure for rent. Different patterns of charging for food was observed in day care, which corresponded with the amount charged. A few of them served meals and children brought snacks from home, as a way of cutting cost and workload. In addition, some parents believed that "home food" was better.

Formal communication with parents was limited. It was observed that the trend of organising parents' meeting had set in. Two large centres have parent teacher associations and about 50 per cent conducted at least one parent meeting and about 20-25 per cent up to two or more meetings, the purpose of which was, to either make parents aware of children's needs, centres programme or clarification of some issues, such as future school admission or behaviour problems of children and the like.

Dissatisfactions: The Flip Side of the Coin

For the smooth functioning of child care centres providers expect parents to cooperate with them. Since many of them are small enterprises, running on user fees, they are sometimes unable to exert an authoritarian or disciplinary approach for the fear of loss of children to other nearby centres. Providers concerns are summarised in Table 5.13.

Providers maintained this as "parents expect the best from us, but are not willing to pay". They bargained for condoning of fees for uninformed absence (which occurs due to many

Table 5.13 : Providers' expectations: To what extent care they fulfilled

Types of expectations	*Responses* %	*Problems Faced* %
• Regularity and punctuality in attendance	90	38
— in pick up or dropping of children	86	57
• Fees to be paid on time and regularly	100	76
• Children to come after finishing routines, clean and neatly dressed	100	20 of parents do not comply
• Parents not cling to children or disturb during nap time	48	80 Especially prevalent in initial stages
• Children should be instructed not to leave premises	52	80 parents do not follow up
• Not send children even when parents have holiday	100	52

family reasons, such as travel, family functions, birth of second child and so on). One provider said, "it is not a vegetable or fruit market". Fear of unpopularity stopped them from taking firm action. The larger centres, take either a "deposit" or "term fees" to compensate for the loss. Certain practices that arise out of parental insecurities, like dropping in unannounced or peeping from windows made caregivers feel felt that there was a lack of trust. One caregiver expressed it as, "I am not God to do miracles in a day. Children take time and parents should cooperate".

Concerns of Providers and Parents: Two Sides of the Same Coin

Interviews with directors of day care centres, the staff and parents, taken separately, yielded interesting results and highlighted similarities and differences (Refer Table 5.14).

A noteworthy feature is that the lack of adequate staff and

Table 5.14 : Overview of Key Concerns of Parents and Providers

Provider's concerns	*Response % N=50*	*Parents concerns*	*Response % N=100*
Staff related		*General issues of concern*	
– Lack of knowledge of Child Development and Activities	100	– Absence of activities (Activities for children to enjoy)	40
– Unprofessional attitude	200	– Lack of individual attention	52
Parents related			
– Demand academic programme	61	– Over crowding in centres and low no. of staff	52
– Demand for food, milk, snack	52	– Rude behaviour or carelessness of care provider	20
– Lack of involvement in child's progress	80		
– Expectation of dramatic changes	38	– Refusal to allow parents in centre	18
Others		– Aggression & foul words	6
– Neighbours demands/ Finance interference	28	– Addiction to TV	2
Children's problems		– Frequent illness – Lack of health facilities, clean drinking water – Provision of healthy food	1
– Behavioural problems	60		
– Hyperactive children	53		
– Slow learners	60		

lack of training was recognised and accepted both by providers and parents. Only a small percentage of parents were unhappy about staff's behaviour. Providers were very dissatisfied that parents demand that children be taught recognition, reading, numbers, colours, rhymes "as they consider it smart" and necessary for success. They find it difficult to find ways to provide enough stimulation due to their own unawareness and limitations. Care givers are unable to handle either hyperactive or aggressive children, though they manage. It is also related to staff-child ratios that are not adequate in about 50 per cent of the centres.

The caregivers (chief supervisors/proprietors) said that there were no drawbacks in their centres. However, observations (by student trainees) revealed that 5 centres had inadequate outdoor space, 4 centres had inadequate indoor space and in 2 centres the staff-child ratio was as high as 1:16, and 1:20.

Another drawback pertains to the type of children admitted to the centres. All caregivers would not want to cater to children with special needs. In this study, 9 out of the 21 did not admit such children, and moreover, they did not have any special programme for such children. Non-involvement of parents in their programme by caregivers could also be viewed as a limitation of the service.

Parents expected centres to provide with food so that children learn to eat in a group and by self rather than being fed, and also to learn to accept all types of food. Food they felt is a must, as children are for long hours in day care/family day care. Few parents (21%) preferred home made food, so that diet and quality of foods can be monitored. These were mostly from a play centre with limited hours.

Most parents prefer activities for children so that they can develop optimally. Activities provide fun enjoyment (39%), independence and creativity (29%), satisfaction (2%) and it also helps in clearing admission test to school (1%). Parents expect an overall improvement in health facilities like hygienic environment (13%), medical checkup (10%), clean water and food facilities (5%) etc., for ensuring healthy development of the child. Parents expressed their strong views regarding overall changes in centre, which are minor but very important for the centre and child. The infrastructure, policy, trained staff; loving environment of the centre helps in good rearing which helps in overall development and proper molding of the child.

The observations conducted at various points in time revealed that there were differences between parental and caregiver perceptions and that they were certain limitations in the way caregivers carried out their tasks. There have been highlighted in Table 5.15.

Discussion

The findings of the present study continue to support what was found in earlier researches in the Indian scenario. It is a seller's market —

Table 5.15: Perceptions of researchers, parents and caregivers where change/input is required

Researcher's Observations	***Caregivers perception***	***Parents perceptions***
Physical Environment	*Problem areas*	*Dissatisfactions*
• Need better use of physical facilities	• Worry about safety and misuse	• Facilities provided over-crowding.
• Improvement in hygiene	• Difficult to maintain hygiene, too much load.	• Inadequate hygiene
• Caregiver child interactions adjustment problems	• Children's adjustment.	• Difficulty in adjustment because of caregiver's interactions.
• Inadequate training of caregiver	—	• Untrained staff/poor ratio.
• Inadequate knowledge of child development.	• No knowledge of child development difficult.	• More in all attention / stimulation needed.
• Lack of effective communication parents / providers.	• Communicating with parents excessive parental demands.	• Children's reports, not given daily.
• Lack of monitoring of activities	• Difficult to give activities in mixed age groups.	• More fun and enjoyment needed for children.
• Inappropriate furniture equipment.	—	• Centre overcrowded.

the cost and the nature of the service is given; the customer takes it or leaves it. The stakeholders, that is, the parents have no say (Sriram, 1991). In the present study the respondents have reported that affordable services are of low quality (tend to be those run through NGOs/Government aided schemes), and better quality care costs are on the higher sides. In the researches done on the city of Mumbai it was found that parents did not complain about cost.

The parents in Mumbai preferred family day care for their children. The parents in the Baroda sample (of the present study) preferred good quality centre care to that provided in family day care. Either way the parents favoured a home-like environment for their children (Datta and Maheshwari, 1997). The difference though in the case of the current sample has been that they were not too concerned about the distance between the home and day care. In most studies in the West, too, the concern has been proximity as a desired index. The Baroda sample also did not ask for grooming and dropping and picking up children from the centres. This goes to show that parents either have the time or other persons in the family or neighbourhood provide these services.

Centres of care were not crowded. The adult to child ratio was 1:5 at the upper end. This scenario is heartening and is not expected to be found in the metros. This also comes closer to the ideal ratio expected by ECCE professionals, and associations that research has found between children's age and developmental outcomes. In an urban city like Baroda, the scene has probably not changed, though space is slowly becoming a highly priced and sought after commodity. This aspect also does not feature in parents' reporting on child care centres. A number of expectations featured in the current sample and were similar to the Mumbai sample. The features expected are a good quality, developmentally appropriate programme, good physical and custodial care, a home-like environment that provides cognitive and academic inputs and attention, love and affection (Datta, 1991; Datta and Maheshwari, 1997; Sriram, 1991; Thakkar, 1994).

Certain matches in expectations were there. However, certain phases like initial adjustment of the child to the centre, cooperation in terms of how long the child is left at the centre, child's absence, etc., were not coordinated. The phase of adjustment took time, and parents were expected to trust the caregivers. This is an important dimension for good quality care to continue. There were certain bones of contention and issues that need attention in parent-teacher or caregiver association meetings. Parents on their part were concerned about the rude behaviour of the caregivers, and lack of an adequate academic programme.Better physical infrastructure, better health, hygiene facilities, provision of food and snacks were the other demands. Caregivers felt that the expectations of the parents were very high. There were differences in the concerns of the caregivers and parents (see Tables 5.13 and 5.14); the former were caught up in the administrative aspects, slow learners and the high demands of the parents, and the parents were concerned about the lack of activities, lack of individual attention and overcrowding in the centres.

Though the findings do not very explicitly state so, the parents wanted to exercise more control over what happens to their child at the centre. For example, they wanted privileges like visiting the child often (which is not generally encouraged by centre personnel). A similar felt need was found by Kaneda, Suwa and Hijikata (1994). The second author of this Chapter, has initiated a child care association, Shishu Palak Vrund, to enhance interaction and understand each other's expectations and perspectives. In Kaneda *et al* (1994) too, the teachers in public school did not see the problems in child care as coming from their attitudes. Observations of teacher/caregiver behaviours, parents, satisfactions and dissatisfactions point to such a view. This seems to be happening across certain contexts. This has been observed in our school settings, too (Konantambigi, 2001). Atkinson's model should be used to depict the various factors in child development outcomes as it helps the caregivers to see their own short comings, and the parents to reduce their expectations or have realistic expectations of child care and cooperate in the functioning of the centre.

6

STATUTORY CHILD CARE PROVISIONS FOR WOMEN IN THE MINES*

Committee for Legal Aid to Poor (CLAP)
Orissa Forum for Child Care
and Crèche Services (FORCES)
and
Orissa Mahila Vikash Samiti (OMVS)

Introduction

Child care services are important as a supportive service for women and also as an essential service to provide for care and development of young children. From the time of independence of the country, when the constitution was drafted, there has been emphasis on the right to work, right to education and protection for child within the family. For this, various provisions were made in terms of welfare services. Industrial registration too was being formulated and within this the concept of child care as an essential element in liberation of women was emphasized (Swaminathan, 1985). Thus the Factories Act (1948), the Plantation Act (1951) and the Mines Act (1952) were specifically identified where women were in large

* With the author's permission, the report, Crèche Services in Mines — A Fact Finding Report from Orissa, was reorganized for this book by Joyeeta Sengupta.

numbers and so child care would be needed as a support service. Swaminathan (1985) observes that by its nature, statutory crèches are for women in organised sector only. The employer is obliged to provide crèche facilities if the number of women exceeds fifty. A study by Rane (1979) shows that there is reduction in factory crèches as many employers employ less number of women or older women and thus escape from the law. It is therefore said that such laws may only serve to limit women's entry into the formal sector. The numbers of children attending these crèches are often very few. Within the law, the crèche is a facility for working women and very often when male employees do want to use these facilities they are unable to do so. Further, in cities like Mumbai due to distances between workplace and homes many mothers find it difficult to carry the child to the work place (Datta, 1995). Women are employed in large numbers in the plantation as it requires fine work and stamina. It is expected that plantations would have two types of centres; one with educational facilities and the other, called satellite crèches, spread across plantations where young children are cared for and the mothers can visit. However, evaluation studies (Gopal, 1982) showed that crèches just existed in name; there were no provision of services. Parents were reluctant to use the services as the quality was poor. Lack of training, poor monitoring and the reluctant employee, all make the statutory crèches almost non-existent.

The crèches under the Mines Act also face a similar problem. An evaluation in 1977 showed that of the 87 units studied, 70 units -were obliged to provide statutory crèches and only 35 were actually providing them. Nearly half these crèches were in places which had poor lighting, ventilation, equipment and cleanliness. The staff too was inadequate and untrained. Since statutory crèches is one of the first attempts to address needs of working women and their children, it is important to see their functioning and relevance in today's context. This chapter gives details of a fact finding study done on crèches in Mines in Orissa.

The Committee for Legal Aid to Poor (CLAP) is a non-profit, specialized, professional and legal support NGO operating in the state of Orissa in India. It originated to facilitate the process of accomplishment of human rights through legal support services and activism. CLAP places high priority on the rights of the children. 'In Defence of the Child' is a special programme for children, launched by CLAP to develop a set of legal intervention strategies which address the needs of children living in difficult circumstances and/or who are more vulnerable due to their disadvantaged position.

CLAP is concerned about children of women workers in mines. Women who belong to the lower strata of society and who need to work to meet their day-to-day economic needs are bound to be outside their house. Children of such working mothers become vulnerable and highly neglected. Child populations below the age group of 6, therefore, need special care in the form of crèche services.

These children have been endowed with facilities and opportunities by different laws such as Mines crèches which was framed under the Authority of the Mines Act, 1952.

G.S.R. 516 — In exercise of the powers conferred by clauses (d) and (w) of section 58 of the Mines Act, 1952 (35 of 1952), the Central Government hereby makes the following rules, the same having been previously published and referred to every Mining Board concerned as required by sub-sections (1) and (4) respectively of section 59 of the said Act, namely :-

MINES CRÉCHE RULES, 1966

1. Short title and application:
   (a) These rules may be called the Mines Crèche Rules, 1966.
   (b) They shall apply to all coal mines and metalliferous mines to which the Mines Act, 1952, applies.

2. Definitions : In these rules, unless the context otherwise requires, —
   (a) "Competent authority" means, in respect of coal mines, the Coal Mines Welfare Commissioner and, in respect of metalliferous mines, the Chief Inspector of Mines, and includes any person authorised in writing in this behalf by

the said Welfare Commissioner in the case of coal mines or by the Chief Inspector in the case of metalliferous mines to perform all or any of the functions of a competent authority under these rules;

(b) "Crèche" means a room or rooms with ancillary accommodation reserved for the use of children, under six years of age, of women employed in a mine;

(c) "Medical Officer-in-charge" means a qualified medical practitioner employed, whether on a whole time or part-time basis, by the owner of a mine to perform the duties assigned to such officer by these rules.

3. Provisions of Crèches.

(1) Save as otherwise provided in this rule, the owner, agent or manager of every mine (hereafter in this rule referred to as the 'said person') wherein any women are employed or were employed on any day of the preceding twelve months, shall within such period as may be specified by the competent authority, construct thereat a crèche in accordance with the standards prescribed under rule 4:

Provided that where the competent authority is of opinion that the situation, nature and extent of the workings or other places where women are employed are such as to tender compliance with the provisions of these rules not reasonably practicable, the competent authority may be order in writing exempt the said person from the provisions of these rules for such period as may be specified in the order subject to the condition that the competent authority may require the provision and maintenance of suitable room or rooms with an attendant and necessary equipment at or near any working place or part of the mine :

Provided further that the competent authority is satisfied that by reason of shortage of building material or of labour, the said person is unable to provide within the stipulated period a crèche in accordance with the specifications in these rules, that authority may approve of the erection of a temporary structure to be replaced by a permanent structure within such time as he may prescribe.

(2) If the competent authority is of opinion that the conditions in any mine or part thereof are such as to render compliance with the said rule unnecessary, he may by order in writing and subject to such conditions as he may specify therein exempt the mine from the provision of a crèche.

(3) If in any case the competent authority is satisfied that no inconvenience will be caused to the employees concerned, if a single crèche is provided to serve neighbouring mines, he may authorise by order in writing the owners, agents or managers of such mines to provide jointly a single crèche and on such conditions as he may specify in the order.

[Vide the Gazette of India, Part II, Sec. 3 (i), dated the 9th April, 1966 at p. 591.]

(4) On the production of a certificate from the Chief Inspector of Mines the productive capacity of a mine will be exhausted within three years from the date of the certificate, the competent authority may on condition that the said person shall provide a temporary structure to serve the purpose of a crèche and on such other conditions as the competent authority deems fit, grant by order in writing exemption from construction of a crèche in accordance with these rules.

(5) Subject to such relaxation as may be considered necessary by the competent authority the provisions of rules 5 to 13 shall also apply to every room or rooms provided under the first proviso to sub-rule (1) and to every temporary structure provided under the second proviso of sub-rule (1) and under sub-rule (4).

4. Standards for crèches –

(1) There shall be four types of crèche according to the number of women employed, namely, Type 'A', Type 'B', Type 'C' and Type 'D'.

(2) The plinth areas of different types of crèches and the type of crèches which shall be provided shall be specified on Schedule I.

(3) Every crèche shall conform to the following standards:

(i) It shall be contained in one building, built of brick and mortar, adequately lighted and properly ventilated and affording, effective protection from all kinds of weather : provided that, with the previous permission in writing of the competent authority, it may be built of any other material which the said authority may approve.

(ii) It shall be constructed on a suitable site selected by the mine management with the previous approval of the competent authority.

(iii) The flooring shall be of cement or stone and the ceiling shall not be less than 4 metres high from the floor.

(iv) The interior walls shall be lime-washed once in six months and the woodwork shall be painted or varnished once in every three years.

(v) It shall be maintained in a clean sanitary condition to the satisfaction of the inspection staff :

Provided that the competent authority may permit variations in the standards specified in clauses (iii) and (iv) having regard to local conditions.

5. Provision of latrines –

(1) Three shall be provided one latrine in each 'A', 'B' and 'C' types of crèches and two latrines in each 'D' type of crèche :

Provided that a separate latrine or commode shall also be provided in all types of crèches, wherever considered necessary by the competent authority, for the use of children affected by any infectious disease.

(2) The latrine shall be kept in a sanitary condition to the satisfaction of the inspecting staff.

(3) The competent authority may permit variations in the standards specified in sub-rule (1) having regard to local conditions.

6. Provision of bathrooms –
   (1) In every crèche there shall be provided a closed bathroom with separate space for washing and drying soiled clothes or bed lines. The bath room shall be equipped either with a sink or masonry tubs and the quantity of water to be provided shall be on a scale of at least 15 litres per child attending the crèche.
   (2) The competent authority may permit variations in the standards specified in sub-rule (1) having regard to local conditions.

7. Amenities to be provided at crèches –
   (1) Medicines for, first aid, cradles, cots, beds, linen, bedding, feeding bottles, cooking utensils, toys, furniture and other equipment for the use of children shall be maintained at each crèche on the scale specified in Schedule II.
   (2) A supply of cool and wholesome drinking water shall be provided for each crèche on a scale of at least two litres per child attending the crèche.
   (3) Milk and diet for children attending crèches and clean clothes for the crèche staff shall be supplied on the scale specified in Schedule III.
   (4) The competent authority may permit variations in the standard envisaged in sub-rules (1), (2) and (3) if considered necessary.

8. Times when crèches shall be kept open – The crèche shall remain open at all times both by day and by night when women employees are working at the mine and it shall be properly lighted at night.

9. Use of the crèche – The use of the crèche shall be restricted to children, their attendants; the supervisory staff and such other persons as may be related to or concerned with children in the crèche.

10. Medical arrangements –

    (1) A medical examination of the children attending the crèche shall be made every month by a qualified medical practitioner and a record of such examinations shall be maintained in Form A.

    (2) A medical examination of the nursing mother attending the crèche shall be made once in every month by a qualified medical practitioner preferably a woman, when the examination is conducted by a male doctor, it shall be made in the presence of the crèche nurse. Records of such examination shall be maintained in Form B.

    (3) The Medical officer-in-charge of the mine, or the welfare officer of the mine, shall be responsible of the general supervision of the crèche.

11. Provision of staff –

    (1) The owner, agent or manager of a mine shall employ, at every crèche, staff on the scale prescribed in Schedule IV :

        Provided that only such women as have successfully undergone training as a crèche nurse at an institution approved by the Central Government shall be eligible for appointment as a crèche-in-charge :

        Provided further that in the case of a woman in employment on the 1st June, 1965 as a creche-in-charge in a mine, this provision may be relaxed with the approval of the competent authority subject to such conditions as may be specified.

    (2) Where by reason of temporary absence, illness, or any other similar cause, the full time crèche-in-charge is unable to perform her duties, the owner, agent or manager of the

mine shall authorise in writing any one whom he considers competent to act in her place:

Provided that no such authorisation shall have effect for a period of more than thirty days except with the previous consent of the competent authority.

(3) The crèche-in-charge shall ensure that the crèche is kept in a clean and sanitary condition, that all children attending it are properly looked after, washed and fed in accordance with the provisions of these rules and that they and the nursing mothers are taught clean and healthy habits.

12. Maintenance of records –

(1) A register giving particulars of children attending a crèche shall be maintained in Form C.

(2) A register of complaint shall be maintained for inspection by the Medical Officer-in-charge and by the management of the mine.

13. Inspection of crèche – A crèche may be inspected at any time by the competent authority or by an officer authorised by the said authority for the purpose.

14. Repeal – The Mines Crèche Rules, 1959, are hereby repealed except as respect things done or omitted to be done before such repeal.

It is pertinent to mention here that in 1984, the Honourable Supreme Court in writ petition No.2135 of 1982 in the matter of Bandhua Mukti Morcha *vs.* Union of India, in paragraph 16, observed that Mines Act, 1952 and other Rules and Regulations made under the Act are bound to be enforced for the benefit of the workmen. In view of this order, the provision contained in Mines Crèches Rules, 1966, to the appropriate governments are under an obligation to take necessary steps for the purpose of securing compliance with this provision by the mine leasers and owners.

The law that governs operation of crèche in mines needs to be analysed. Like other social registration, the laws concurring crèche services do not get translated into real implementation. Even though the laws are rich in spirit, the legislative intention gets diluted when it comes to implementation.

The non-enforcement of the legal provisions can be attributed to the ignorance of the workers about the entitlement, lack of united demand and ineffective role played by labour officials. The mine owner has the sole responsibility and is under legal obligation to provide crèche in their mines. Improper monitoring mechanisms, lack of bureaucratic will and soft penal provisions compound the problem.

Whatever may be the reason, the undeniable fact is that non-enforcement leads to deprivation of rights conferred on the children by law. The soft state approach towards issues of children in the mines has generated a concern amongst civil society groups working towards advocacy of child rights in Early Childhood Care and Education.

Forum for Crèche and Child Care Service (FORCES), an advocacy network lobbying for promotion of crèches and child care services for children of working mothers in the informal sector, has expressed its concern regarding the ineffective implementation of crèche provisions in different identified sectors, including mines. Therefore, CLAP, as a member of FORCES took up the matter for further investigation in the field so as to influence policy. A fact finding mission was sent to make an on-the-spot review and collect first hand information concerning the present status of crèches in mines in Orissa.

The rationale for constituting the fact finding mission was the latent need to collect first hand information from the grassroots and to give shape to an advocacy strategy to protect the best interests of children who belong to working mothers in mines.

Efforts were made to forge an alliance with the Orissa Mining Area Peoples Action Network and Orissa Mahila Vikash Samiti (a local NGO) which has a stake in the mining area of Sukinda, Jajpur.

The objectives of the fact finding team was:

- to ascertain the status and coverage of crèches in Sukinda mining area;
- to understand level of awareness of women mine workers regarding their legal rights and entitlements; and
- to observe fulfilment of legal obligations.

Fieldwork included on-the-spot enquiry in crèches, observation of beneficiaries (children) and interviews with mothers, caretakers, Mines Welfare Officer and Supervisor of the crèche. The fieldwork was conducted in April, 2002.

Profile of Area

Sukinda valley of Jajpur district is the leading producer of chromite ore in the country. The total proof reserve of chromite of the state is of the order of 140 million tonnes. Thus, 95 per cent of the reserve is located in the Sukinda Valley. In the field of Chromite, M/s TISCO Ltd. were the pioneers in the Sukinda Valley and they obtained lease as far back as 1953 from the erstwhile *Zamindars* of Sukinda Estate. The Sukinda Valley possesses the only known commercial deposits of nickel ore in the country. There are also some iron ore mines in Sukinda Valley.

Sukinda is one of the 10 blocks of Jajpur District. Sukinda Block consists of 24 Gram Panchayats and Kaliapani is one of them. The Fact Finding Mission visited Purunakalapani which comes under Kaliapani Grampanchayat, a newly constituted Gram Panchayat. Sukinda is surrounded by Dhenkanal to its west, Keonjhar on its north, Danabir to its east and Dnagadi and river Brahmani on its south. In order to understand the demographic situation of Sukinda Block, the following information may be of interest. A profile is given here below about the area visited by the Fact Finding Mission.

(a) Area : 597.04 Sq.Km.

(b) Villages : 129 (105 Revenue Villages)

(c) Households : 23,800

(d) Population : 1,01,888

(e) ST Population : 52,268 (Women —27,351)

(f) BPL : 14,118

(g) APL : 9,662

(h) Literacy : 19%

(i) Primary School : 74

(j) UGME School : 14

(k) M.E. School : 27

(l) High School : 22

(m) Asram School : 04

(n) Colleges : 03

(o) Total student enrolled in Primary School : 13,507

(p) IMR : 122/1000

(q) Forest produce : Kendu leaf, Jhuna, honey, cashew, Sal seed, Mahul etc.

(r) Mines : Chromite and Iron

(s) Economy: People largely depend upon the forest produce for their living. Almost all the people belong to the labour class. Some work in the mines, some work in the agricultural sector while rest of the population either sells country liquor along the roadside or engage in animal rearing.

Status and Coverage

The fact finding team met and discussed the need and present status of crèches in the area with around 300 men and women representing different communities. Though authorities were invited they were conspicuous by their absence. The inhabitants informed the team that there were no ICDS functioning in this Panchayat. Since the tribals have their own dialect, interpreters from the community were sought for communicating with the people. In some habitations, children under the age of 7 were seen roaming around. They looked demonstrably malnourished wearing no clothes or dirty clothes. The environment looked dirty. Older children, particularly girls aged 6-10 years were engaged in sibling care, washing utensils, cooking, bringing water or selling country liquor along the roadside. There were 800 women labour (contract labour = 507, casual labour = 201, regular labour = 92) working in 7 mines and 1 washing plant in Kaliapani Gram Panchayat. Of these 319 women, they had 491, 0-6 year old children (0-3 year olds = 335, 3-6 year olds = 156). Only 3 mines had crèches.

It was found during the visit that in this particular pocket, an elder sibling, invariably a girl child escorts the younger child of the family to the crèche and continues to be present all through the day. The crèches take children between 3-12 months of age. This phenomenon might be happening in other mining areas too. A working mother said, "There is no extra benefit in sending the children to the centre. The staff do not take care of our child. Those who have a grown up child in their family are sending the older child to keep an eye on the younger one. So it is better for us to leave the child at home. Moreover, we are instructed to send an older child to take care of the other child in the centre."

Another finding was that the crèche is far from the habitations. In many cases, the mother has to travel over hills without any available transport service. The work conditions of the women worker is exploitative as they earn Rs.10-20 less than men for the same amount of work; crèche facility is only for the regular workers eventhough 90 per cent of the workers are either contract or casual labourers. Though there is a provision for availing 15-30 minutes nursing break, most mothers cannot breastfeed as that time is not enough (they need at least 1-1½ hours to come out of the mines to feed their children).

Level of Awareness of Rights and Entitlements

The women workers do not know their right to have a crèche in their working place. Where there is a crèche, they consider it as a charitable support given by the owner. Therefore, they have never demanded nor complained about the poor condition of the crèches. The poor service at the centre has not generated interest among the working women to send their children to the centre.

Facilities at the Crèche

In most cases the crèches in the area conform to the required space and construction (see Mines Crèches Rules, 1966). Other facilities like separate latrine, closed bathroom, medicines, drinking water etc. were not seen by the team. The crèches only provide *chuda* and *gur* with milk powder (Amul) and that too occasionally. There were no play materials or minimum sleeping facilities in the centres. Centres were often not maintained in clean and hygienic condition.

Centre Staff

A crèche worker gets Rs.1500 salary per month. The staff is not trained in Early Childhood Care and Education. Amongst her duties is sweeping the centre and giving food to the children. Ironically, one of the crèche workers does not bring her own 3 children (under 5 years of age) to the centre as the facility and accommodation does not satisfy her!

Implications

A review of the legal framework *vis-à-vis* the Mines Crèches Rules, 1966, reveals the rich spirit of legislation beneficial (a) to the care and development of children; and (b) as a support service for mothers working in the mining area. The Rules give ample scope for the owners of the mines to take advantage of the loopholes so as to avoid their legal obligation. The wider benefit given to owners in sub-rules 2, 3, 4 and 5 of rule 3 of the Mines Crèches Rules, 1966 creates enough scope for manipulation to escape from their responsibility. A more stringent implementation *via* a Monitoring Agency can be developed for regular supervision and verification.

In case the owner is given benefit under rule 3 of the Rules, reasonableness of such benefit should be well in place.

Lack of awareness of women workers about the right to childcare services for their young children has led to poor utilization of the services. On the other hand, the inaccessible location and the poor quality of services provided in the crèches have discouraged the working mothers to use the service.

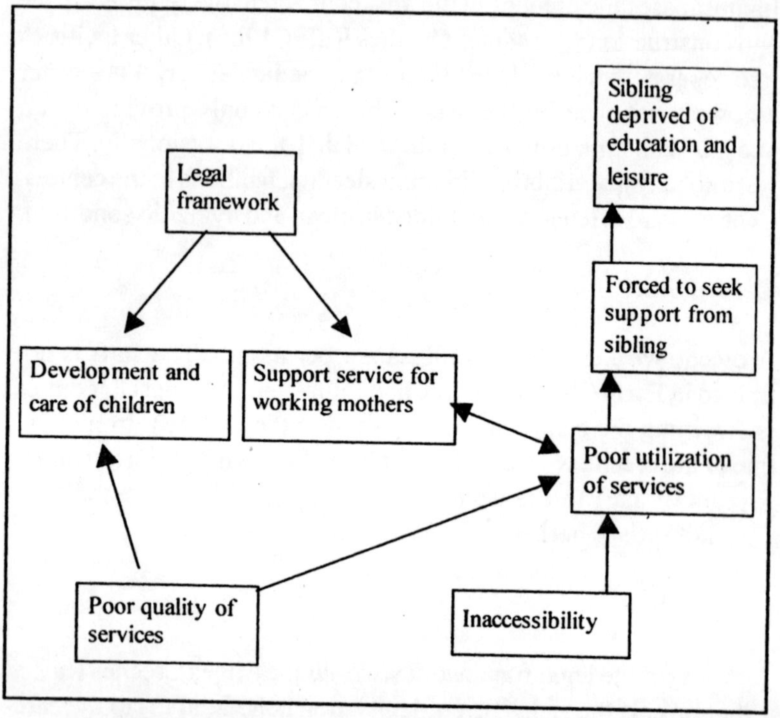

Fig. 6.1 : Implications of Ineffective Child Care Services.

Quality is universally recognised as the essence of childcare services. The investigation proved that amenities and basic facilities like hygienic surroundings, sanitation, drinking water, first aid and food have either not been taken care of or are provided inadequately. This speaks of gross neglect and violation of basic rights of the children.

There is an urgent need to help in capacity building of the child care worker. Empowering her would lead to a direct improvement of her interaction with children. She can also become the focus for bringing in awareness amongst the mine workers regarding their right to have a crèche. She can ensure better facilities at the centre too.

As has been noted earlier, the poor quality of services has led many working mothers to send an older sibling, mostly the sister, with the younger child. This may be because the family is not convinced about the protection and appropriate care of their child in the centre. For the child care worker, having a sibling in the centre reduces her workload. This leads to depriving the girl child from education and leisure. This is a serious implication and needs attention. The State needs to show due diligence and play a more proactive role in executing legislation, funding, monitoring, capacity building and advocacy.

SECTION-III

Effects of Substitute Care on Children

7

HOME AND DAY CARE CONTEXTS
Social and Cognitive Development of Children

— *Rajani M. Konantambigi*

Care and development of children have been studied in the context of emerging maternal employment, substitute care of children, especially from a centre based care and their effect on development of children. This empirical study begins with the review of literature, establishes the need and theoretical premise for the study, followed by methodology, findings and a discussion of the findings.

Introduction and Review

Review of literature for the past five decades has been screened, and the review mainly focuses on maternal employment outside the home context, children's attendance of day care and its impact, if any, on the development of children. Issues and reviews pertaining to maternal perceptions and satisfaction with substitute care have been touched upon because the aim of the study was to look at the effect on children's social and cognitive development. Further on in the review, effects/relationship of maternal employment and day care attendance to socio-emotional and cognitive aspects of development have been discussed in two separate sections.

The impact of growing industrialization on the occupational world whose effects later spread to the spheres of family functioning and child socialization is a historically well watched and well studied topic of research. The anxieties and fears of the society ran deep as the nature, speed and extent of industrialisation changed societal functioning to dramatic lengths after the world wars with women entering the world of work outside the home context. These anxieties and fears in the sphere of child socialisation ran strong in the industrialised countries, especially in USA. This is evidenced in the vast amount of research on the effects of maternal employment and substitute care on the development of children from the 1950s to the early 1990s. The state of transition, the further impetus to industrialisation during the two world wars and the developments in the field of psychoanalysis evoked the concern of social scientists in general and the psychologists in particular regarding the effects of maternal employment and substitute care on the development of children. Various explanations have been provided to understand the influence of maternal employment and substitute care on children's development. Some premises of psychoanalytic thought, ethology (role of the critical period on development), role-theory, and the widespread almost sanctimonious belief that maternal care is the best for the child have been utilised as explanations.

The psychoanalytic school of thought emphasised the importance of the mother-child bond. The intense mother-child bond was expected to provide continuity of security and to promote emotional development in the child. Mother-child separations would instill a sense of loss of the basic person in life, which could later produce anxiety and insecurity. Maternal employment according to the psychoanalysts would result in maternal neglect which in turn could also produce delinquent children. Parental figures, the psychoanalysts emphasised, are of paramount importance in the development of the superego. Findings of ethological studies also support the Freudian premise. According to the former, there are critical periods in development which require certain environment and nurturing from the parent for optimum development. Failure to provide such an environment could distort growth and compensations at a later date cannot reverse the damage done. These thoughts, in the period of intense upheaval during the world wars and industrial growth, had influenced researchers too. This view was popular enough to evoke anxiety among parents and provide an impetus for research in the field (Etaugh, 1980).

The premise of role-theory is that when an individual has two or more roles, each making incompatible demands, not only is there role-strain for the person involved, but role-effectiveness is reduced as well. This could be termed the classical role theory. Role conflict, the critics of maternal employment feel, is what happens with working mothers who have to play the roles of an employee at work and those of wife and mother at home. If there are other individuals in the family, many other roles have to be played as well. The classical role theorists maintain that the mothering role needs a lot of time and investment, which an employed mother cannot provide. There have been empirical studies to prove role-strain in employed mothers, especially in a transitional society (Kapur, 1970; Rani, 1976; Mane, 1983; Ranade and Ramachandran, 1970).

Changes in family functioning have brought about stress which a working mother faces; she has to cope with, work and home demands without much assistance and support from the men of the house. The prevailing conditions help perpetuate the belief that maternal employment is *per se* bad for children's development. The economic changes, the accompanying social changes, the social upheavals, the perception that maternal employment adversely influences children's development, the advances in the psychoanalytic field and the tenets of classical role theory created a *fait accompli* of an antagonistic atmosphere *vis-à-vis* maternal employment (Fein and Clarke-Stewart, 1974; Kagan, 1984). Research studies of the 1940s and the 1950s supported the hypothesis that maternal employment and substitute care produced more delinquent and psychoneurotic behaviour in children (Perry, Jr., 1963; Hoffman, 1963). However, when the background variables of the home of the child were taken into consideration, delinquent and problematic behaviour were related to the broken home condition and not to maternal employment *per se* (Perry Jr., 1963; Hoffman, 1963; 1979; Etaugh, 1980; Nye, 1963). Subsequent studies have also revealed the adverse effect of stress that a family may be undergoing (Howes and Stewart, 1987; Main and Cassidy, 1988).

These results led to a search for factors that could lead to adverse child outcomes, including home environment and substitute care dimensions.

Researches in the 1960s concentrated on studying adolescent children of employed and non-employed mothers on various aspects of academic skills and social development. The findings may be summarised thus:

- Daughters of part-time or full-time employed mothers fared the best in contrast to the daughters of non-employed mothers.
- Sons of non-employed mother fared the best in comparison to the sons of part-time and full-time employed mothers.

The findings have been interpreted in the light of prevailing social norms and role perceptions of children, that is, their academic performance and social adjustment depended on how the children perceived their mothers' working (Hoffman, 1963; Poresky and Whitsitt, 1985; Gold and Andres, 1978).

Research emanating from the role theory perspective provided a diagonally different dimension to role theory itself. Yarrow, Scott, Leeuw and Heing (1962), Caldwell, Wright, Honig and Tannenbaum (1970), and Lerner and Galambos (1980) in their studies have shown that maternal satisfaction in the non-mothering roles influences child rearing and not the working/non-working status of the mother. Mothers who wanted to work and were working scored higher on mothering roles (and their children in turn were more cheerful and happy) than mothers who did not want to work and were employed and *vice versa* in case of non-working mothers. A few studies that have been conducted in India regarding satisfaction with substitute care show that parents are not satisfied (Rani, 1976; NIPCDD, 1978; Mane, 1983). However, this does not mean that substitute care quality is absolutely low. Parents do want the best for their children, and therefore, the satisfaction levels tend to be low.

Maternal Employment, Day Care and Effects on Socio-emotional Development of Children

Concern over the adverse effects of maternal employment on child development spurred by psychoanalytic influence directed research into another channel. A spate of studies were initiated on the effects of mother-child bonding and on the child's behaviour and development (Ainsworth, 1980; Ainsworth, *et al.*, 1978; Cummings, 1980; Vaughan, Gove and Egeland, 1980). Most of these studies were with infants and toddlers and they utilized the strange situation technique in studying the impact of mother-child separation, evoked a lot of controversy. At the initial phase of research, child temperament, which can alter the effects of mother-child separation and the consequent adjustment on the part of the child was not considered. According to McCartney and Galanpoulos (1988) who conducted a meta analysis of the studies, whether the effects on children's behaviour and development are positive or negative depends on the researchers' bias! As reflected in Vaughan, Gove and Egeland's (1980) study, life stresses in the form of single parenting that is, mothers having to return to work early, was the factor associated with insecure attachments and anxious/avoidant behaviour in toddlers. Schwarz, Krolick and Strickland's (1973) findings revealed contradictions—infants whose mothers returned to work early continued to have secure attachments at three and four years of age, and were in day care, did not have any adverse effects. Children entering day care at three and four years were more disturbed in this study. In yet another sample of children, initial disturbances at day care attendance tended to disappear (Roopnarine and Lamb, 1977). Easterbooks and Golderg's (1985) long term longitudinal study is a pointer towards the adjustments that parents and children make towards changes in their environment; adverse effects are countermanded as coping strategies are developed. Longitudinal studies of this type are few and far between and a number of studies at a single point of time have been conducted. No definite trend in the findings was revealed (considering that some of them could have methodological limitations). The following are some of the examples of the varied and mixed findings: No significant differences on the socio-emotional aspects of development have been found between children of employed and non-employed mothers and day care and non-day care children (Caldwell, *et al.,* 1970; Datta, 1993; Moore, 1963; Moore, Snow and Poteat, 1988; Nye, 1963; Stith and Davis, 1984). Findings of studies by Schachter (1981) and Venkataramana (1987) found that employed mothers' children fared better on social development.

Schachter's (1981) observational study revealed that employed mothers' toddlers were likely to initiate approaches to peers. Non-employed mothers girls were more likely to initiate speech to teachers than to peers. Employed mothers' group was significantly more self-reliant and the non-employed mothers group was more jealous.

In Venkatramanna's (1987) study, the relationship between employment status and interaction with children has been examined (N1=99; N2=98). Employed mothers had significantly more positive interactions with their children. This finding is part of a larger study where personality trait differences between employment status and within employment groups were studied. Employed women's children were most often significantly on the side of the positive traits of Catell's 16 PF Questionnaire.

Studies by Rubenstein and Howes (1979), Schachter (1981) and Schwarz, Krolick and Strickland (1973) again found that the results were in the positive for working mothers' children and those by Douvan (1963), Marantz and Mansfield (1977), Pasquali and Callegeri (1978), Poresky and Whitshitt (1985) and Gold and Andres (1978), were in the positive only for the daughters of working mothers.

In a sample of day care and home care children, aged 17 to 29 months, Rubenstein and Howes (1979) found positive affective exchanges being exhibited more often in day care situations with more reciprocal smiling, holding/hugging, mutual play, both with and without objects. More negative affects were expressed at home by both infants and mothers with more crying. Reprimanding helped more positive affective interaction in both situations, that is, day care and home situations. Toddlers enjoyed the company of their peers. Children at the centres also sought more visual attention and were more ready for social interaction.

Children attending day care from infancy were compared with those entering day care at 3 and 4 years of age by Schwarz, Krolick and Strickland (1973). Affection and social interaction of children were rated as they entered a new centre. The ratings obtained on the day one and the fifth week dispelled the view that day care leads to emotional insecurity. However, children entering day care at 3 and 4 years were more disturbed than those attending day care from infancy. The authors interpret this difference as arising from the fact that the children in day care from infancy moved over to the centre almost *en masse*. They had familiar peers around them. These children through a prior study were similar on mother-child and child-mother attachment. So attachment was not the cause of early group care being more relaxed and happy on the first day.

There are many studies which have not found any difference between children in day care and those not in day care. Caldwell, Wright, Honig and Tennenbaum (1970) found no adverse effects on socio-emotional development. Stith and Davis (1984) did not find any difference between employed mothers children in day care (N1=10), non-working mothers children not in day care (N2=10) and children of employed mothers in family day care (N3=10) on socially mediated stimulation, contingent responsiveness, positive affect, and overall level and activity of social stimulation.

In Datta's study (1993) on pre-school children, aged 4 to 6 years of family day care (N1=12), grandmother care (N2=23), home care non-working mothers children (N3=23) and servant care (N4=22), there were no statistically significant differences on social maturity quotients as measured by Vineland's Social Maturity Scale.

Rural (North Carolina) Caucasian, middle to upper-middle class, intact families children aged 5 and 6 years, who had attended day care (N1=33) or family day care (N2=26) for 18 months (six or more hours per day for five days a week) were studied by Moore, Snow and Poteat (1988). A sample of 33 children not attending day care was also included. No hyperactive or disabled children were in the sample. Though all centres (24) were not evaluated, the two centres evaluated ranged from scores of 130 to 150 on a possible range of 35 to 217. Vineland's Adaptive Behaviour Scale, measuring skills for communication, daily living, socialisation and motor skills were used. ANOVA revealed that the three groups did not differ significantly on any of the adaptive skills.

Bojrkman, Poteat and Snow (1986) in a study on day care environment and social behaviour ratings in four-year-old found no association. The authors explain this by the possibility of the scale not being sensitive to changes in day care quality related to social behaviour in children. Possibility of day care not varying in quality was also there as the facilities and provisions were similar in the centres studied. In contrast, Vandell and Powers (1983) found a distinct association between quality of day care and the amount of time children spent in solitary play and unoccupied behaviour.

In a study of pre-school children (N=166), Philips, McCartney and Scarr (1987) controlled family background, child-care experience (of day care giver) and age of the child. Verbal interaction, overall day care quality and director's experience (of day care) emerged as predictors of children's social development. Social development comprised one scale containing the factors, considerateness, sociability, task orientation, dependence and intelligence, and another comprising aggression, anxiety, and hyperactivity (social adjustment).

Vandell, Henderson and Wilson (1988) in a four year longitudinal study related day care quality experiences to interactions with peers, adults, solitary play and unoccupied behaviour. Observations of these types of behaviour were videotaped in a laboratory play room when they were eight years old. Triads were formed for the purpose, in such a way that a child was chosen from each strata of day care quality group or from among other eight year olds from the community. No two children from the same strata of day care or same centre were chosen. Children did not know one another before this play session. The tasks in this play session consisted of cooperative, competitive and conflict resolution tasks and a free play session with specified time limits. Quality of day care was positively related to friendly interaction and children from high quality day care were rated as more socially competent, happier and received fewer "shy" nominations from peers. The behaviour of the four year old and their later functioning at eight years of age were significantly related. The interaction of four year old with adults was positively related to ratings of empathy, social competence and peer acceptance when the children were eight years of age. Unoccupied behaviour at four years was negatively related to these types of behaviour.

Studies reveal that security of attachment, maternal satisfaction with working or not working, age of entry coupled with the adaptation of the child, quality of care and a lack of socio-emotional tensions at home influence the sociability, social adaptability and secure behaviour on the part of toddlers and pre-schoolers.

Maternal Employment, Day Care and Cognitive Development in Children

The unanimity in the research findings continues here too. Two major studies (one a longitudinal type by Cherry and Eaton, 1977 and the other by Farel, 1980) on the impact of maternal employment on cognitive development of children show that there were no significant differences between children of employed and non-employed mothers. Studies by Cheung and Chau (1984), Datta (1993) and Robinson and Robinson (1971) also revealed no differences. In Caldwell, *et al.'s*, (1970) study the day care children had an edge, while in studies by Kagan, Kearsley and Zelago (1978); Sinha (1979; c.f., Naidu and Nakhate, 1985) definite effects on cognitive development were seen in day care children.

Twenty-three home reared children and 18 enrolled in day care centres and from low SES formed the sample of Caldwell, Wright, Honig and Tennanbaum's (1970) study. The mean age of children was 2 to 5 years and they had been attending day care for 1 to 5 years. Day care did not have negative effects on socio-emotional development, on the contrary had a positive effect on their cognitive development. Robinson and Robinson's (1971) study was a longitudinal one, and extended over a period of 2.5 years. Nineteen infants (admitted in day care between 2 and 5.5 months of age) and 12 pre-schoolers formed the sample. But it was found that culturally deprived children benefited from day care.

Kagan, Kearsley and Zelago's (1979) longitudinal study covered (N=116) two ethnic groups, two classes of SES and day care, home care and mixed care and children aged 3.5 to 30 months of age. Low SES day care children performed better on concept formation index with no difference between Caucasian and middle class Chinese children. The home environment was more facilitating with home reared children scoring higher than day care children. This study highlights the importance of a facilitating environment for the group of children concerned, be it home or day care.

Cherry and Eaton (1977) conducted a longitudinal study on 200 low income families (the sample slightly decreased at the end of 8 years). They assessed the impact of maternal employment in the first three years of the child's life; an eight year follow up was maintained and the comparisons for children of working and non-working mothers were made on weights, heights and measures like I.Q., reading, arithmetic and spelling achievements. There were no significant differences between children of employed and non-employed mothers when controlled for maternal variables (age, education, work status, etc.). Thirty differences in outcomes were found, out of which 27 favoured children of working mothers. Crowding had a deleterious effect on the heights, weights as well the performance of children.

Sinha's (1979 : C. F.: Naidu and Nakhate, 1985) sample (N=100) covered children of educated part-time and full-time employed women in the age group 6 to 12 years. Measures of concept development in the children who where in school were markedly better. The mother's employment condition whether part-time or full-time did not make a difference to the children's cognitive development. The importance of environmental stimulation is highlighted since the sample covered a low SES. However, reactions and responses to deprivation are to an extent unpredictable. There is some evidence that intellectual and cognitive sub-systems growth in an individual are less influenced by variations in environment and more by internal factors (Jensen, 1983; Kagan and Klein, 1956).

Piotrokowski and Katz (1982) studied the effect of mothers' employment status on the academic behaviours of children in low

SES, black families. The sample comprised children in the age range of 10 to 17 years (mean age = 12.8 years). The nature of mother's employment, job autonomy and skill utilisation were positively associated with academic behaviour. The findings of this study indicate that a specific relationship may exist between the employment condition of parents and aspects of children's behaviour at school. Satisfaction in one sphere of life affects another sphere. Satisfied women make better mothers.

Cheng and Chau's (1984) pilot study (which was part of a project on cross-cultural study) examined the influence of different types of care-taking styles and their relationship to development. The care taking forms considered were extended family care, individual paid care, group and mother care (group care is day centre care). These children (N=46), aged three years belonged to four geographical locations also indicating their SES. Naturalistic observations in simulated conditions formed the main mode of assessing children. Mother-child interaction, caregivers-child interaction, productions on dough-play and skill in problem-solving tasks did not vary in the four care-taking forms. SES and educational levels contributed to differences in these aspects. Irrespective of the caregiver, the mother played the key role in making decisions about the child's development. This study shows that maternal employment does not imply low investment by the mother on the child's development and welfare. In the high SES group, the mothers were educated, the stimulation and facilities provided and fathers' involvement in the child's upbringing was higher as compared to that in groups where the mothers' education levels were lower. The latter emphasised traditional academic abilities in reading, writing and memory, but no facilitation was provided. Differences in the three groups of children to read and write English, Chinese and number existed. More children from the two lower SES groups were unable to read, write and count.

Two matched groups of 60 children, one group attending day care for 8 to 10 hours a day in Sweden and the other-home reared, were compared in a naturalistic setting (Cocharan, 1977). The children were matched on a number of variables such as geographic location, income level of parents, sex of the child, and number of siblings from four SES levels. Attitude of the parents towards the value of experience of day care was held constant. The observations showed that experiences for the two groups of children were similar, but own and day care-home children were exploring their surroundings more than centre-care children and were interacting with adults more in cognitive verbal situations which led the adults to limit their activities. However, no developmental differences were found on an infant scale nor in a separation situation. According to Cochran (1977), the findings stress the varying roles played by adults in the several settings as they are reflected in environmental design differences.

Caldwell *et al.'s* (1970) study showed that day care did not have negative effects on socio-emotional development but had a positive effect on their cognitive development. So was the case in Robinson and Robinson's (1971) study, Kagan Kearsley and Zelago's (1979), Cheng and Chau (1984) and Datta's (1993) studies.

Robinson and Robinson's (1971) longitudinal study, referred to earlier in the Chapter, of 2.5 years covered 19 infants (who were admitted in day care between 2 and 5.5 months of age) and 12 pre-schoolers. The study revealed that culturally deprived children benefited more from day care programmes. Cherry and Eaton's (1977) also found similar results. In Kagan, Kearsley and Zelago's (1979) study, low SES day care children performed better on concept formation index. There was no difference between Caucasian and middle class Chinese children. Among the Caucasians, both working and middle class children, the home environment was more facilitating, and the home-reared children scored higher than day care children. This study highlights the importance of a facilitating environment for the groups of children concerned, be it the home or day care.

In Datta's study (1993) on pre-schoolers in Greater Bombay, there were no differences among the four groups (servant care, grandmother care, family day care and home reared children), on the Indian adaptation of Binet's Intelligence Test — the Binet-Kamat Test.

As revealed in studies on socio-emotional development, home environment in terms of maternal employment and the day care set-up, age of entry of the child into day care and adaptation, have been related to positive child outcomes; no definite relationship by maternal employment status and day care attendance to cognitive development was found. Positive effects of quality day care programmes were seen on children hailing from lower SES background.

Home Environment, Day Care Quality and Development in Children

In some of the studies quoted above (for instance, Farel, 1980), when the sample is not controlled for family stress or demographic variables, analysis is performed by statistically keeping these variables constant and on such analysis, results revealed that there are factors other than maternal employment or day care attendance that influence the development of children. More recent studies have taken care to control such variables, and study the day care environment. Howes and Stewart (1987) have shown that stressful life experiences are related to low competitive play in children. In Main and Cassidy's (1988) study, parent-child attachment was related to the absence of life stress experience and quality of relationship, and not to the change either in job situation for the parent or the child-care situation for the child. Philips, McCartney and Scarr (1987) found verbal interaction between the caregiver and the child, caregiver's experience on the job and overall day care quality to be the predictors of a child's development. Day care quality was related to different aspects of social development in a longitudinal study by Vandell, Henderson and Wilson (1988).

Employed mothers in McBride and Belsky's (1988) study were more sensitive to their children's experiences and related to them in sensitive ways by providing security. Maternal anxiety was related to them in security mother-child attachment. Personality characteristics of the mother/parents could also be a significant variable. Oppenheim, Sagi and Lamb's (1988) longitudinal study on Kibbutz children which revealed that infants with secure attachment to their metaplot, were at five years, more empathic, dominant, purposive, achievement oriented, independent and self-controlled than non-securely attached infants. Their measures of socio-emotional development were closely associated with their behaviours at their Kibbutz than at their parents home. Majority of the infants had secure attachment to their parents. This study shows that the residential environment of the child and secure attachment to significant care-taking adults are significant determinants of socio-emotional development.

The dimension of parenting *vis-à-vis* not just the employment status but the maternal satisfaction with overall care and management of her family the extent of job-involvement and commitment has begun to be explored (Demeis, Hock and McBride, 1986; Gupta and Konantambigi, 1998; also Chapter IX, this volume; Levitt, Weber and Clark, 1986). Though a large amount of research on various aspects of maternal employment and substitute care effects on child development exists, no adequate research exists to quell the anxiety of working couples to the issue of whether it is absolutely safe to adopt substitute care for their child and what concrete evidence one can provide regarding the various factors that influence child development in the present context. While some answers are forthcoming (Howes, 1990; Galambos and Maggs, 1991) the issue *per se* is fraught with problems as attitudes towards maternal employment and substitute care are undergoing change and they in turn influence parents' anxiety, parental values and child upbringing. A very significant answer could be culled out from the way Belsky (1994), Lamb and Sternberg (1990) and McGurk, Caplan, Henessey and Moss (1993) categorise research on day care. The work of the earlier few decades could be viewed in terms of "waves". These waves provide clues to the advances in the study paradigms and shifts in focus in research on substitute care, impact on children.

Wave 1, the 'Experimental Day Care' in the 1970s was concerned with whether substitute care had adverse influences on children's development. High quality, university based day care centers formed the sample, and therefore, the conclusion was since quality of care was high, one need not be concerned about adverse effects (Belsky, 1990).

Wave 2, "Beyond Between —Group Comparisons", the focus was on the various socio-structural features of substitute care arrangements and the prevailing environment there. Again, the conclusion pointed to features of substitute care like well-trained and experienced staff, small groups of children in reasonably specious, safe and well-equipped settings predicting favourable outcomes for children (McGurk, Caplan, Henessey and Moss, 1993).

Wave 3, "The Issue of Age of Entry", pertains to the issue of every young babies entering day care, the ensuring separation and effects on mother-child bonding. Various methodological criticisms were levied on these particular sets of studies, and a review of them (McGurk, Caplan, Henessey and Moss, 1993) concluded that the quality and consistency of care in substitute care arrangements, in equipped settings predicting favourable outcomes for children (McGurk, Caplan, Henessey and Moss, 1993).

Wave 4, "Family, Work and Child Contexts", goes beyond the substitute care contexts and age of entry into substitute care; and gets into an understanding of the family ecology as encompassing family, attitudes, processes and parents' occupational experiences (Belsky, 1990).

Wave 5, talks of "Distinct Ecologies", for the children of working and non-working mothers who are in substitute care and who are not availing of such care. The ecologies in each setting are specific, and the processes are not comparable. Howes (1990) has added on the dimension of developmental stage, as she found that when children are in full-time substitute care in the first year of life, quality of substitute care predicts later development, whereas when children entered out of home care in their second year of life, subsequent development was predicted by family factors and processes rather than quality.

A child's temperament further confounds the picture. Given the current status of research in the field and the prevailing paradigms for interpretation of results, Bronfenbenner (1979; 1986) and Gamble and Zigler's (1986) views on the ecological context for children's development need to be heeded to. The findings then need to be put into the larger framework of cultural history of child rearing (Kagan, 1984; McGurk, Caplan, Henessey and Moss, 1993; Super and Harkness, 1987). The role demands that working mothers have to deal with, calls for plans to empower the women as well as the family in tackling the stress. Culturally, women are expected to play it adequately, but guilt operates and hinders in the various roles that she has to play. Applying the ecological perspective one needs to look at not only the factors and contexts of development, but to see the process of adjustment that the family is going through and whether the child's development needs are being fulfilled. The studies reveal that ecology of development is of concern. One cannot use maternal employment or day care attendance *per se* as factors determining child outcomes. Lack of familial stress emerges as a crucial variable. Day care quality has definitely emerged as a factor, though not in all studies. The findings of research like the present one would inform us about whether parents are doing fine by their children, and whether there are enormous differences between children who go to the centre from those who do not may also help quell the anxiety of the working parents. It also helps reduce the anxiety of parents who are wont to believe that child upbringing should take place exclusively in the home under the exclusive care of the biological mother.

Objectives

There is a need to address the lack of unanimity in existing research findings. In this regard, the contributions from the child care contexts of the home and day care need to be studied. In addition to lack of familial stress, there is a need to unpack the home environment. Bronfenbrenner (1986) taking stock of day care research and applying his ecological perspective to day care research has suggested home environment, one of the significant micro-systems, as a variable to be included in examining the impact of day care on children. Gamble and Zigler (1986) proposed a model that combined the effects of the quality of home and day care, where, if home environment is of poor quality it is compensated for in a day care centre of high quality and *vice versa*. Studies in the preceding review have also established that day care quality of high/adequate standard is not harmful for the child's development if not totally beneficial, and certain studies have delineated the aspects of day care that contribute to development. Studies examining the contribution of home and day care to development and aspects of home care that determine development are scarce.

This study aims

- to control family stress in its sample, compare some developmental indices between children of employed/non-employed mothers; these were also children in day care/ and not in day care (only home care group) respectively.
- to test Gamble and Zigler's hypothesis, to determine the extent of contribution of home and day care to development.
- to test the hypothesis that development depends not on maternal employment and substitute care received per se but on the stimulation and psychological environment of the home.

Method

The Setting

The study was conducted in Bangalore, the capital city of the state of Karnataka in South India. Day care centres which functioned regularly, except for holidays and vacations, at least for the past year, and which admitted children aged three to six years were included in the study. The 18 day care centres in the sample were managed by different organisations in Bangalore city and their distribution was as follows: three centres were managed by the employees' unions of service oriented organisations (hereafter referred to as EU type of crèches), six by the public sector industrial establishments (or factory day care centre, F-public) two by the private sector industries (F-private), two by the Karnataka State Council for Child Welfare (KSCCW) and five by Christian Missionary Organisations (CMO). The latter two categories were exclusively for low income families' children.

The non-day care children and their families were selected on the basis of physical proximity (neighbour of the day care child) as it would match the two groups of sample, to some extent, for the socio-economic status variable (hereafter referred to as SES).

Sample

The sample consisted of the 18 day care centres that could meet the research criteria and two groups of pre-schoolers and their mothers. The target groups of pre-schoolers for the study were in day care with employed mothers. In the comparison group the children were not in day care and had non-employed mothers; that is, mothers not gainfully employed outside the home and for whom there was no necessity of using any form of substitute care. Child care for the comparison groups was confined to the home by their natural parents. The age of the pre-school children varied from three to six years. The criterion for all children to be in the sample was absence of family stress. In addition to this, the day care children had to meet other criteria: they should have attended the day care centre continuously for the past year and should have spent at least five hours a day for days a week. Seventy-two day care children and 36 non-day care children and their mothers formed the sample.

Measures

A preliminary interview schedule prepared by the researcher was utilised to screen the sample for family stress and to obtain information on SES and other family related issues. It was pre-tested, as were all the other tools used for the study. Bradley and Caldwell's (1979) Home observation for the Measurement of the Environment Scale was adopted to assess the physical and psychological environment of the home and day care. It consisted of subscales, namely, physical environment (PE), stimulation through academic behaviours (SAB), stimulation through toys, games and books (CE), language stimulation (LS), disciplining methods (DP), autonomy given to the child (AG), stimulation through out-door activities (OA) and parental pride warmth and affection (PWA).

Each sub-scale was made of eight items. A total scale score as well as sub-scale scores could be obtained. In the original scale, all the items were observation items. The researcher converted some of the items to interview items. Thus a combination of interview and observation techniques was utilised. After the adaptation of the scale, the maximum possible score was 68 for home environment and 64 for day quality. The maximum possible scores of the subscales varied from 14 to 8. They have been calculated for a maximum score of 10 so as to make them comparable. The minimum possible score in the scale is "zero". To facilitate comparison the day care quality score was adjusted for 68. Internal consistency coefficient of scale as reported by Bradley and Caldwell (1979), derived by the Kuder-Richardson formula —was .93 for the total score and ranged from .53 to .83 for the subscales. Stability coefficient after a period of one and one-half years ranged from .05 to .70. Validity measures with SES and mental tests were from low to negative but were highest and positive with Q scores (Bradley and Caldwell, 1979). For the present study sample, the split-half reliabilities of the scale using the Kuder-Richardson formula (KR-20) are .87 and .84 for the measurement of home environment and day care quality respectively. Factor analysis of the scales did not reveal factors delineated in the original scale; nevertheless it has shown the scale to be homogeneous. Factor loadings for the measurement of home environment scale varied from .71 to .31. In the case of the measurement of the day care quality all items pertaining to stimulation obtained out-doors and one item pertaining to the physical environment had extremely low factor loading, low commonality scores and low correlations with the total scale score. The rest of the items were homogeneous with factor loadings varying from .89 to .39.

To assess social development, Mallin's Indian Adaptation of the Vineland's Social Maturity Scale (Doll, 1963) was used. The scale is made up a variety of self-help skills and the extent of self-direction/self-reliance an individual develops. Scale values are convertible into social development quotients. Split-half reliability for the present study sample was .72. This scale is widely in use in the child guidance clinics especially in Bangalore and Bombay cities.

Muralidharan and Kaur's (1986; 1983) Cognitive Development Test was used with slight variations to measure cognitive development. The kit had to be reassembled by the researcher as no ready kit was available. The kit was developed with some assistance from the first author of the test. The test was subject to the scrutiny of three psychologists and later pre-tested. The Cognitive Development Test includes functions such as identifying familiar objects and actions by the child, sequential thinking, listening comprehension, language proficiency, knowledge of the environment, identifying body parts and their functions and Phatak's Draw-a-Man Test (Phatak, 1967; 1987). No norms are available for the Cognitive Development Test. Hence standardized T-scores for each age level with a gap of half-year were utilised. They were calculated separately for the day care and non-day care children. However, the IQs on Phatak's Test have been utilized separately for analyses with the independent variables.

Procedure

After permission was granted to visit the day care centres and interview the caregivers, preliminary enquiries (as to the age-group catered to and if the centre had been functioning regularly for the past year) were conducted. If they fulfilled the criteria, the caregiver was interviewed regarding the functioning of the day care centres. Interviews normally lasted for about an hour. In addition to this, the researcher spent another half-hour or more visiting the centre and making observations. Observations for a behavioural item were conducted three times, that is, observations were time sampled thrice. One observation period was during the visit for the interview and another two when the researcher visited the day care centres to be introduced to and to collect the addresses of the sample —the children and their parents.

During the first visit to the child's home with the help of the preliminary interview schedule, the mother of the child was interviewed regarding the home background and child related aspects. If the family was not undergoing any stress, it was to be the study sample. Home environment had to be assessed by interviewing and observing mother-child interactions. Observations were to be done thrice. The need to visit the home a number of times was explained to the respondents by saying that a good rapport had to be established with the child as an intelligence — like test was to be administered. They were not informed that their interactions with the child were being observed. During a visit, an interview, and/or testing was conducted in addition to spending time for observation. The schedule of interviews, observation and testing the child as planned and executed is presented in a tabular form (for details see Table 7.1).

Table 7. 1 : Schedule of observations, interviews and testing at the child's home

Visits	*Sessions*		
	Nature of researcher's activity	*Respondents*	*Observations*
First	Preliminary interview	Mothers	Mother's interaction with the child
Second	Interview to assess home environment and obtain responses for Vineland's Social Maturity Scale	Mother	
Third	Testing the Child's Cognitive Development	Children	

Result

Background Variables

The result reported in tabular form in this section are only for variables that have emerged as significant variables or for differences between groups that are significant either for dependent or dependent variables. Before comparing the children in day care and those not in day care (hereafter referred dc or dcg and ndc or ndcg respectively) on the developmental indices one would like to be certain that the two groups are comparable. During sample selection it was not possible to control the background variables. In lieu of such care, it was seen to that no characteristic of the sample was over-represented. T-tests or Z-tests were conducted to be sure that they were comparable. There were no statistically significant differences on the background variables like age of children, parents' education and their occupation, number of siblings of target child, family's monthly income, gadgets and vehicles in the family, and the family's SES between children of dc and ndc. Significant differences existed between the two groups on paternal occupation, on which the samples vary (it is a part of the variables "SES") and was considered in the analyses of the factors contributing to development in children. "SES" is a composite of parental education, paternal occupation, family's monthly income and gadgets and vehicles in the child's family. A comparison of the background variable, proportion of female children (girls), has shown that their proportion is the same in the dc and ndc groups. In addition, it is necessary to check if boys and girls as groups differ on developmental indices before a comparison of dc and ndc groups is undertaken. No significant development difference between the genders exist. T-values for difference in cognitive development was .91 ($p<.10$) and social development it was 1.3 ($p<.10$). The two groups of dc and ndc did not differ significantly on the home environment (HE) and the subscales of HE (mean scores of HE for the two groups are 46.4 and 47.1 with a t-value of 0.13, $p<.10$).

Developmental Differences between the Study Groups

Statistical results of comparison between dc and ndc groups on social and cognitive development (c.d.) and sub-scales of c.d. is presented in Table 7.2. The day care children fared better on the social development index mean social maturity score being 113.2 in comparison to 106.8 for the ndcg. There were no developmental differences on cognitive development test and its subscales and on the subscales of social development between dc and ndc groups.

Table7.2 : Development in Day Care and Non-Day Care Children

Development-al aspects	*Day care children*	*Non-day care children*	*t-value*	*Significantly different at .05 level of significance.*
Social maturity quotient	113.2	106.8	2.11 (p .05)	Yes
Cognitive development	49.7	50	.15 (p .10)	No
Sub-tests of the cognitive development test				
Language test	49.7	49.1	.10 (p .10)	No
Cognitive test	49.8	50.0	.04 (p .10)	No
Awareness of environment	49.8	50.0	.07 (p .10)	No
Phatak's Draw-a-man test IQ	111.1	117.0	.88 (p .10)	No

To test Gamble and Zigler's (1986) model, home and day care environment were both classified as low and high. Home and day care quality (dcg) scores between 20 and 35 were classified as low and those between 52 and 68 as high. Scores between 35 and 52 were moderate scores.

Controlling either quality of day care or home care, corresponding home or day care and developmental mean scores were computed. -Two-way analysis of variance was also carried out for the dependent variables; namely, cognitive development and its subscales and social development. A comparison of means shows that development is the highest in high care environment. Table 7.3 presents these means and Figure 7.1 depicts them graphically.

Home Environment, Day care Quality and Development

Analysis of variance revealed that only the means of social development in the four combination of home care and day care

Table 7.3 : Mean Scores and Standard Deviation on Development of Children in Home and Day care Situations

Aspects of development	*Low home care quality with moderate quality day Care = A* (N1 = 11)	*High home care quality with quality low day Care = B* (N2 = 12)	*Low day care quality with high quality home Care = C* (N3 = 23)	*High day care quality with moderate quality home Care = D* (N4 = 26)
Cognitive development	44.0 (8.34)*	53.06 (10.4)	48.1 (9.6)	49.2 (8.6)
Social development	102.2 (14.8)	121.2 (14)	115.3 (15.1)	112.6 (13.5)
Subscales of cognitive development				
Language test	46.2	51.7	47.1	50.3
Awareness of environment	45.4 (10.1)	51.9 (9.9)	48.9 (10)	48.9 (12.6)
Cognitive test	44 (6.2)	54.5 (11.1)	49 (10.7)	48.7 (8.9)
I.Q.**	104.6 (27.2)	120.9 (18.9)	113.5 (19.5)	106.8 (25.8)

* Figures in parenthesis are standard deviation.
** I.Q. as measured by Phatak's Draw-a-Man Test.

were significant (F-ratio = 9.84; p > .001). ANOVA also revealed that the interaction of home care and day care quality and its contribution was significant only for social development (F-ratio n = 4.25; p > .049). Home environment scores (mean 46.4) of the dc children was significantly higher than the day care quality scores (38.1) (See Table 7.4). Subscale value of language stimulation (LS), stimulation of academic behaviour (SAB), democratic disciplining (DD), autonomy given to the child (AG), outdoor activities (OA) and parental pride warmth and affection (PWA) were significantly higher at home than in day care. Day care had significantly higher

Fig. 7.1 : Mean Scores on Cognitive and Social Development of Children with Varying Quality of Home and Day care Environment

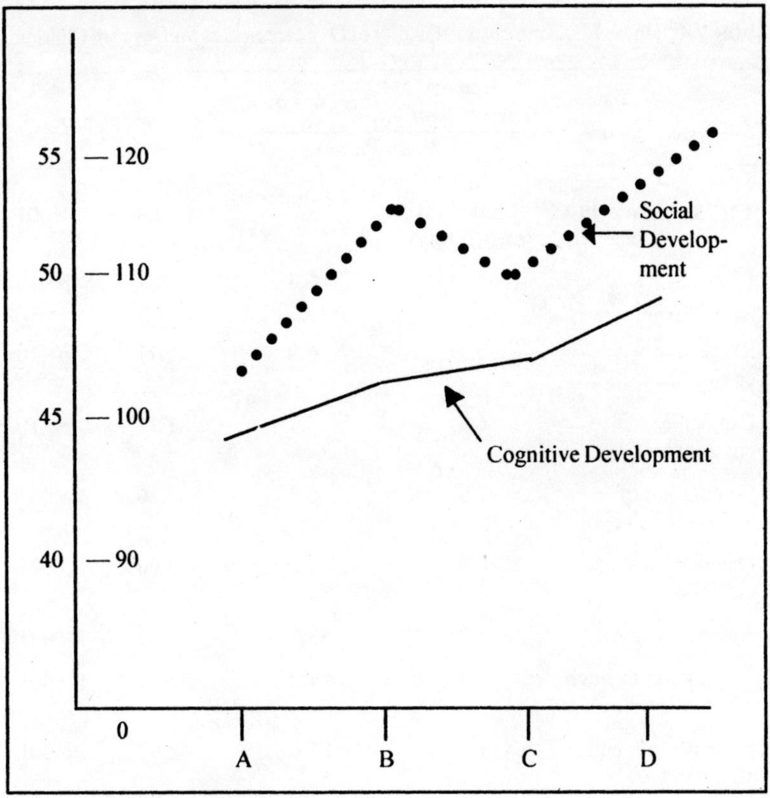

Index: On the Y-axis:

A = Children group with low home care score and corresponding day care score which happens to be moderate.

B = Children's group with low day care and corresponding home care score which happens to be high.

C = Children's group with high day care and corresponding home care score which happen to be moderate.

D = Children's group with high home care and corresponding day care score which happens to be low.

On the X-axis: 3 cms = 5 scores of cognitive development, and 3 cms = 10 scores of social development.

scores on physical environment and recreative environment or stimulation through toys, games and books (CE) (Table 7.4).

Table 7.4 : Home Environment and Quality of Day care Scores for Day care Children

Aspects of care	*Home environment*	*Day care quality*	*t-value*	*p*
	Mean Values			
Total environment	46.4 (Mode=58) (Median=49)	38.1 (Mode=30) (Median=39)	15.4	p>.001
Physical environment	5.5	6.3	1.71	.05>p>.10
Recreative environment	5.9	6.8	1.71	.05>p>.10
Language environment	6.3	5.7	1.71	.05>p>.10
Stimulation of academic behaviour	7.0	6.5	3.66	P>.001
Democratic disciplining	6.0	4.5	3.90	P>.001
Autonomy given	7.0	3.3	10.76	P>.001
Stimulation through outdoor activities	6.4	1.2	15.71	P>.001
Pride warmth and affection by caregivers	7.9	5.0	8.97	P>.001

Note: Maximum Values of the Subscales' Totals varied; they have been calculated for a value of 10.

To test the nature of relationship of day care quality and home environment to development in children, in addition to DCQ and HE, other day care related variables, the intervening variables, namely SES and years of pre-schooling of the child and other background variables were also included. Multiple step-wise regression was utilized. Results are tabulated in Table 7.5; the variables which have not contributed significantly to development have not been represented in the Table.

Table 7.5 : Home Environment, Day care Quality and Development

Aspects of development	*Partial correlation of coefficient with*	
	Home environment	*Day care quality*
Cognitive development	.69 (p>.01)	.66 (p>.01)
Social development	.76 (p>.01)	.69 (p>.01)
Sub-tests of cognitive development		
Language development	.30 (p<.05)	.60 (p>.01)
Awareness of environment	.68 (p>.01)	.66 (p>.01)
Cognitive test	.66 (p>.01)	.69 (p>.01)
Phatak's Draw-a-Man Test	.75 (p>.01)	.69 (p>.01)

Day care quality contributes to the development in children as much as home environment does. DCQ has a higher correlation coefficient for cognitive development ($r = .69$, $p > .01$) than HE ($r = .66$, $p > .01$) and in the case of social maturity, HE has higher partial correlation coefficient ($r = 0.76$, $p > .01$) than DCQ ($r = .62$ $p > .01$). The independent variable, number of hours spent in crèche has contributed to some subscales of cognitive and social development. In case of cognitive development its contribution is not significant ($r = .26$, $p < .25$), but is, in the case of social development ($r = .34$, $p > .05$). For the subscales of social maturity and cognitive development, the contributions of HE and DCQ were approximately equal.

SES conventionally considered a significant factor, has not featured in majority of the partial 'r's. It featured in three cases and was significant in self-help eating and self-help dressing skills ($r = -.38$, $p > .05$ and $r = -.34$, $p > .05$ respectively). It implies that in these instances it is a significant variable. The negative sign implies an indirect relationship. In partial 'r's, if two independent variables are related, then the sign of the less significant variables changes (Blalock, 1979). It implies that for these two cases, self-help eating and self-help dressing, HE and DCQ are the more significant variables, but that SES has an influence or is related to HE and/or DCQ. Similar finding has been reported by Howes and Stewart (1987).

The independent variables, years the child spends in crèche featured in three subscales and was significant only in the case of self-help general, partial (r = -.44, p > .01). The negative sign implies its relationship in DCQ, since it is an aspect concerning DCQ. Spending more hours in a good quality day care is beneficial for leaning self-reliance. Its contribution, however, for this sample is minimal as it was significant in only one subscale of development. The independent variable, years the child spent in pre-school, featured in "communication", "language" and "cognitive tests". In case of communication, years in pre-school (r = .53, p > .01) contributed more significantly than HE (r = 51, p > .01) and DCQ (r = 21, p < .05, not significant). "Communication" items in the scale are "narrating events", "writing alphabets, "words", etc., i.e. pre-school contribution to the extent of .43 (r) (p > .01). HE was not significant (r = .30, p < .05) for language development and years in pre-school was not significant (r = .27, p < .05) for cognitive tests.

Aspects of Day Care and Development in Children

To answer the question, "which are the salient features in day care that contribute to development", partial 'r's between aspects of DCQ and day are variables to development in children were obtained through the step-wise regression analyses. As regards cognitive development, the variables that emerged significant were physical environment (PE) of day care (r = .76, p > .01) caregiver's pride warmth and affection towards the child (CPWA) (r = .45, p > .01) and hours the child spends in creche (4 = -.39, p > .05) (Table 7.6). Stimulation through academic (SABA) had a partial 'r' of .30 (p < .05 not significant). Number of hours the child spends in a day care had a negative sign to its 'r', implying an indirect relationship to development. From the partial 'r' it is not possible to detect the aspects of DCQ to what it is related. For social development, number of hours the child spends in crèche does not feature as a significant variable. PE (r = .88, p > .01); SAB (r =.42, p > .01) and PWA (r = .39, p > .05) were the aspects of DCQ that had a significant bearing on social maturity on social maturity in children.

Table 7.6 : Aspects of Day Care and Development in Children

Aspects of development	*Partial Correlation*	*Coefficients with*	
	PE	*SAB*	*CPWA*
Cognitive development	.76 (p > .01)	.30 (p < .05)	.45 (p > .01)
Social development	.88 (p > .01)	.42 (p > .01)	.39 (p > .01)
Language test	.70 (p > .01)	.39 (p > .05)	
Awareness of environment	.88 (p > .01)		.53 (p > .01)
Cognitive test	.78 (p > .01)		.53 (p > .01)
Phatak's Draw-a-Man test	.81 (p > .01)	.41 (p > .01)	.43 (p > .01)

As regards the relationship of independent variables to sub-tests of cognitive development, the pattern observed in case of cognitive development holds true (Table 7.6). PE and CPWA feature significantly in all the sub-tests languages test, awareness of environment test, cognitive test and Phatak's Draw-a-Man test. Recreative environment and stimulation through toys, games and books (CE) (r = -36, p < .05) and hours in crèche (r = -35, p < .05) are related indirectly to language test; but not significantly, i.e. CE and hours in crèche influence some other independent variables in the equation and that independent variable contribution to performance on the cognitive test.

Independent variables related to day care like SES of the child, caregiver's education, caregiver experience, years in pre-school, staff-child ratio and years in day care have not contributed significantly to development. Aspects of day care quality, such as autonomy given to the child (AG), DD and stimulation through outdoor activities (OA) were not related to development. These were entered in the equations but did not feature in them. CE has contributed to only three aspects of social maturity, and was significant once (in case of self-help dressing, r = -40, p > .05).

Home Environment and Development in Children

To determine the saliency among the independent variables, namely HE, SES and the number of years the child has attended pre-school, partial 'r's to different aspects of development were computed. When controlled for SES and years in pre-school, in case of non-day care children group (ndcg), HE emerged as the single salient factor contributing to development and its subscales (Table 7.7).

Table 7.7 : Home environment and development in children

Aspect of Development	*Non-day care children*		*Day-care children*	
	Partial correlation coefficient with			
	Home Environment	*SES*	*Home Environment*	*SES*
Cognitive development	.97 (p > .01)		.88 (p > .01)	
Social development	.91 (p > .01)	-.45 (p > .05)	.93 (p > .01)	-.20 (p < .05)
Sub-tests of cognitive development				
Language test	.98 (p > .01)		.87 (p > .01)	.43 (p > .01)
Awareness of environment	.97 (p > .01)		.86 (p > .01)	.38 (p > .05)
Cognitive test	.97 (p > .01)		.88(p > .01)	-.42 (p > .01)
Phatak's Draw-a-Man test	.96 (p > .01)		.91 (p > .01)	-.54 (p > .01)

The partial 'r' was above .90 ($p > .01$) in all the instances. Social maturity, self-help eating and locomotion were influenced indirectly by SES, but the partial 'r's are not significant. The 'r's being -.45, -.44 and -.35 respectively (all with $p > .05$).

In the case of day care children's group (dcg), in addition to the HE, SES was also a significant factor (Table 7.8). Since it has negative sign, it means that it has an indirect effect on the development of children. SES determines home environment of children and HE in turn influences development.

In both the target groups of the study autonomy given (AG) and parental pride, warmth and affection (PWA) emerged as the salient features of home influencing cognitive development (Tables 7.8 and 7.9). Social maturity was in addition significantly related to stimulation through out-door activities in both the sample groups.

Table 7.8 : Aspects of Home Environment and Development in Day Care Children

Aspects of development	*Aspects of the home environment*	
	AG	*PWA*
Cognitive development	.37 (p > .05)	.62 (p > .01)
Social development	.47 (p > .01)	.41 (p > .01)
Language test	.30 (p < .05)	.61 (p > .01)
Awareness of environment	.40 (p > .01)	.51 (p > .01)
Cognitive test	.33 (p > .05)	.64 (p > .01)
Phatak's Draw-a-Man test	.48 (p > .01)	.55 (p > .01)

Table 7.9 : Aspects of Home Environment and Development in Non-day Care Children

Aspects of Development	*Aspect of the Home Environment*	
	AG	*PWA*
Cognitive development	.52 (p > .01)	.55 (p > .01)
Social development	.52 (p > .01)	.45 (p < .01)
Subtests of cognitive development		
Language test	.42 (p < .05)	.45 (p < .05)
Awareness of environment	.58 (p > .01)	
Cognitive test	.40 (p < .05)	.31 (p < .05)
Phatak's Draw-a-Man test	.48 (p > .05)	.53 (p > .01)

With respect to sub-tests of cognitive development, the two groups of respondents, dcg and ndcg varied to some extent

(Tables 7.8 and 7.9). In case of dcg, AG and PWA were the two factors determining development. Only in the case of language development is AG not significant ($r = .30$, $p < .05$). The case of ndcg, in addition to AG and PWA, CE and democratic disciplining were also the factors salient in determining aspects of cognitive development.

As far as the subscales of the social maturity scale, the factors influencing them varied between the dcg and ndcg. In the dcg, autonomy given to the child and PWA were cannot fathom the reason for these differences in the two groups of dcg and ndcg.

Discussion

The present study was undertaken as a response to the varied, mixed and lack of unanimous outcomes of research on the effect of maternal employment and day care attendance on the development of children. A group of day care children with employed mothers and another of home care children with non-employed mothers were chosen. Before they could be compared on the developmental indices, family stress was controlled through sampling, and statistical testing on family characteristics and socio-economic background was carried out. The sample has differed only on paternal occupation. Paternal occupation is a part of the SES variable, which in turn has been used an independent variable in examining the relationship between home environment variables and child development. It was an interesting phenomenon that the two samples did not differ significantly on the home environment variable. While the samples did not differ significantly on the cognitive development indices, the day care children fared significantly better on Vineland's Social Maturity Quotient. This could be due to the day care environment making it imperative for the children to indulge in various self-help skills which the Vineland's is made up of. Similar findings have been reported by Phillips, McCartney and Scarr (1987). No differences on the cognitive development indice may be attributed to similar stimulation in the home. However, the artifact of the t-scores computed on a relatively small sample could have also contributed to the no differences in the cognitive development between the dc and ndc groups. On a significant variable like behavioural problems, Howes (1990) did not find any significant difference between day care children and those in the general population.

The arithmetic means on development for different home and day care situations have supported Gamble and Zigler's (1986) hypothesis that developmental deprivation in one environment can be compensated for in a more enriching one. The hypothesis however cannot be considered to be totally supported as the variance among the means for the groups was not very high as shown by ANOVA. F-ratio was significant for social development scores for interaction of home and day care environments. ANOVA not being significant for the cognitive development could be that they are computed for a small sample. Gamble and Ziglers' (1986) hypothesis needs to be tested in more varied deprivation conditions; longitudinal studies need to be undertaken as individual development reactions to deprivation are varied and could be more genetic in origin (Kagan and Klein, 1956). However, as various early childhood stimulation programmes in USA and elsewhere have shown, early intervention could induce more optimum overall development.

Home environment scores of children were significantly higher than their day care quality scores. Home is a very significant setting providing love and affection, and as yet, in the Indian context, also provides stimulation for the child's development. The salience of home environment has emerged in a number of American studies also, notably in Bradley, Caldwell and Rock's (1988) study. Howes and Stewart (1987), Lamb *et al.* (1988), have also shown that supportive role of the family is of significance in determining various aspects of child development and performance on various tasks. Galambos and Maggs (1991) have found that parental acceptance and firm control was instrumental in preventing girls in self-care from engaging in problem behaviour. Vandell, Henderson and Wilson's (1988) study support these findings. Rodman, Pratto and Smith (1985) have found no difference on social and psychological functioning between self-care and adult-care children.

In the present study, day care has contributed as much to development in children as did home environment. In the day care settings as a group, physical environment and stimulation through toys, games and books were significantly higher. Substitute care contexts where children spend at least three to four hours of their waking time should be expected to influence certain aspects of their development. Studies by Howes and Stewart's (1987), Howes' (1988) and Vandell, Henderson and Wilson's (1988) have also delineated quality of day care as a variable significantly influencing child care and development outcomes. Day care quality as revealed in the present study is of low quality in a number of settings and therefore calls for enhancing their quality. The need for taking measures to enhance the quality was viewed as imminent, because the Government of India planned to provide more funds for expansion of early child care services (Government of India, 1986; Ministry of Human Resource Development, 1986). The Government as well as the Voluntary Sector needs to respond to the situation.

Socio-economic status variables, conventionally considered a very significant variable influencing development does not group to a large extent under the variable "home environment" and "day care quality". However, SES has some contribution in the day care children's groups and not in the home care only group (in non-day care groups). The author has not been able to fathom any reason for this difference. One possible explanation is that working parents may need to invest more in child care, definitely in terms of finances if not anything else, to provide substitute care for their children. But then, most centres in this study were financed by either the public or the private sector and most parents did not have to pay for substitute care. Bradley *et al.*, (1988) did not find SES to be predictive of the child's developmental status; aspects of home environment like parental responsibility and availability of stimulating play material were related to developmental status. SES as a variable distinct from other psychological variables, also was not found to contribute as significantly as is conventionally believed. In a study on factors that contribute contraceptive behaviour use, it was found that SES does not contribute to this behaviour as significantly as expected (Ramesh, 1987). This implies that SES *per se* cannot be used to represent psychological and other social activities and processes.

The intermediate variable, hours spent in a crèche was significant to an extent especially to social development in the day care. The number of years the child has spent in school was significant for the dependent variable of "communication" (an aspect of Vineland's Social Maturity Scale) and was not significant for the cognitive tests (subscale of the Cognitive Development Test used in the study). Interestingly, home environment was not significantly contributing to language development (another subscale of Cognitive Development Test). The role of the dependent variables influencing the two different aspects of cognitive development differentially cannot be completely explained. Perhaps, day care, by providing for a number of interactions enhances language development and home environment being more focused on the child, was perhaps not fulfilling its role.

Physical environment and caregiver's pride, warmth and affection towards the child emerged as the two most significant variables of day care influencing development. Hours spent in the crèche, stimulation through academic behaviour, stimulation through toys, games and books and democratic disciplining were significant contributors to the varied aspects of social and cognitive development.

Autonomy given to the child and parental pride warmth and affection were the two factors in the day care group determining both social and cognitive development. In the non-day care group in addition to these two, democratic disciplining, stimulation through toys games and books were also the factors influencing development. For the non-day care group, stimulation through toys, games and books as a significant independent variable is explanatory, as these children have to get it from the home itself; pre-school attendance did not contribute significantly to development.

The dependent measure in the study, social maturity, was not a very comprehensive indicator of social development. Results for the subscales of social maturity may not be of great significance. Bradley and Caldwell's (1979) Home Observation for the Measurement of the Environment Scale has subscales comprising of about eight items each. They too may not be adequate indices of the subscales that they represent. In the light of this, further research in this regard is essential.

The findings of this study have been summarised and some leads for further research have been suggested. The ambiguity of the direction of influence of maternal employment and day care as revealed in this and other studies points to some other factor as a determinant of development. Stimulation provided at home has been explored here as a factor and the results support it. Further, stimulation given at home by an employed mother was the same as that provided by a non-employed mother, home environment scores did not differ significantly for the day care and non-day care groups. If an employed mother/employed mother's family is providing similar stimulation as a non-employed mother's family, it means that the parents may either be paying a higher cost for child development/ rearing or that they may be handling the demands of child care very efficiently. The cost of parenting could be in terms of more financial investment, high quality day care costing more, more payments towards domestic help, more mental stress and fatigue. What the cost is needs to be explored. There may not be any cost. It could be one of efficient time management and handling of daily living hassles and stress by the working couples' family.

8

CONTEXT OF CARE AND CHILD DEVELOPMENT OUTCOMES

— Vrinda Datta

Introduction

The early life experiences of a child have immediate and long lasting impact on the child's development. Most often family is the basic unit where the child is nurtured, protected and encouraged to develop to his fullest. However in today's world, most children are exposed to other environment early in life which exert an equally important influence on their growth and development. Over the past decades there have been many changes in family structure and functioning which has impacted the way children are cared for. In the urban context, both educated and uneducated women were in wage-labour. The education of middle class girls and the widening of the service sector, and the existence of public sector has led to women being employed in manufacturing units, in service oriented occupations such as nursing and teaching. The 2001 census shows that the percentage increase in female workers between 1991 and 2001 was as high as 40.65 per cent. Further, the addition of 36 million to total female workers, 28 million (77%) was marginal workers. The shift is also seen in the number of agricultural workers—there were 67 per cent of agricultural workers in 1991, in 2001 it came down to 59 per cent.

The changes in the economic policies in the nineties and acceptance of globalisation and liberalisation has led to expansion of some sectors like the service sector. The privatisation and unprecedented entry of multi-nationals, led to expansion in such areas as trading, banking and communication. Thus of the total female workforce, around 20 per cent of women are professionals or executives (Human Development Report, 1997). Further Bhandari (2004) points out that some trends can be seen in case of married women and families of middle class in Indian society. She states that there is continuing increase of dual earning couples and that women with young children continue to be in workforce and the families, particularly nuclear families are looking for institutional support for child care.

Datta and Maheshwari (1997) found that in Mumbai, working couples across all socio-economic groups first looked for family support for child care. Out of their total sample of working couples as many as 44 per cent depended on some family member for child care, particularly the grandparents. For this, many couples were 'weekend parents' or the couple had to drop and pick up the child from grandparent's place everyday. Children benefit from the family ties which moulds them in family culture. One of the other forms of child care common among urban upper class is care by a domestic help. Working mothers find this convenient as it is in their own homes, and a lot of other domestic work also gets done. In terms of out of home care which is paid care, two forms of care are very common; the day care centre and family day care. Datta (1995) suggests that family day care is care by a woman in her own home to a group of children and that this form is more common in Mumbai as working women can depend on the neighbourhood for such service. While day care centres require infrastructure and good management to run quality services and therefore, there are few private day care centres. What exist are part of voluntary organizations like Mahila Mandals and NGOs.

Thus children of working couples are exposed to different child care environments which impact their development in many different ways. Schwartz (1983) in his study on effects of day care on children in four settings, namely home care, at-home baby sitting, sitting outside home and group care he found that the group care infants were seen as more apathetic, less attentive, more deviant and less verbally expressive. Similarly, Golden *et al.*, (1978) also concluded from his study of psychological adjustment of children in family day care, group care and home care that family day care children were more competent in communicating linguistically, emotionally and socially with adults. In contrast, Clarke-Stewart and Gruber's (1984) study showed that centre care children are higher in all measures of competence expressed in interaction with parents, strangers and ever unfamiliar peers. The study also showed that the centre care children scored higher on cognitive competence. Golden *et al.*, (1978) too reported that children in centres scored higher on Stanford-Binet and Peabody-Picture Vocabulary Test. Therefore, many such researchers showed that forms of care will influence the developmental outcome for children. However there is no empirical work in India which reflects the possible ways in which the different child care arrangements will influence children's development. This chapter reports on the study done by the author to understand the developmental differences among children under different forms of child care.

The study was done in Mumbai covering a sample across east, west, north and south wards of Mumbai.

The study was taken up with the objectives:

- To examine the differences in social development and intellectual development among pre-school children of working and non-working mothers.
- To study the effects of type of care (mother care, grandmother care, house-maid care and family day care) on the child's social development and intellectual development.
- To find out factors in type of care which effect the child's social and intellectual development.

The study was restricted only to five areas in Bombay with three schools in each area. No particular criteria was sought to select the areas from which schools should be selected. It was felt that if the sample was taken largely from suburban areas, a good representation of pre-school children with working mothers can be expected. Thus two areas in western suburbs and two from central suburb areas and one from city area were chosen for the study.

The selection of a school in a particular area was arbitrary and the only consideration was that it should be an English medium school, as the English medium schools would cover all community groups. Of the three schools to be picked in an area, one was to be a boy's school, one a girl's school and one a co-educational school, which would help in getting equal representation of females and males in the sample.

Another point kept in mind when defining the universe was to take only senior kindergarten children from the selected schools. This was felt essential because entrance to school itself is a new and at times a traumatic experience for the children. But by the time a child enters his second year of schooling, i.e. senior kindergarten, we assume that they will be adjusted to school environment and that if differences are found in their development it may be possible to associate with type of care.

Selection of Sample

The following steps were taken to arrive at a very purposively selected sample:

Step I: Any aspect of the child's development cannot be studied in isolation. The child's past experiences and his present one/s are affecting him someway or other. This study mainly worked at finding out the differences in intellectual and social development among children under different types of care, and therefore, the children had to be matched on many variables. For this, a preliminary questionnaire was formulated so as to elicit information based on which the children were to be matched. This questionnaire sought information about the pre-school child (age, sex, order of birth etc.) his family (type of family, number of members, religion etc.) and whose care he is subjected to (who looks after the child, how many hours etc.). The questionnaire was to be answered by parents. Thus all the children in the senior kindergarten class received this questionnaire to be answered by their parents. In all about 3000 children of the fifteen schools were given this questionnaire. About 2000 (60%) questionnaires were returned by parents, out of which a few were incomplete and had to be discarded. The completed questionnaires numbered 1495.

Step II: From this group of 1495, it was decided to include children who were in the age group 4-6 years. Secondly, to restrict other influences on children's development, only the first born children were taken and thirdly, to have the representation of working parents of middle and upper class it was decided to include children whose parents were educated up to SSC and above. Thus, all children who fulfilled the above three criteria were included in the sample.

Step III: To study the mentioned objective of finding differences between children of working and non-working mothers, the group formed in Step II was to be separated into two groups —(i) children of working mothers, (ii) children of non-working mothers. In the situation of having working mothers, many mothers may not be away from child as they work at home or that they work short time and are away only when the child is in school.

To avoid such a situation, the following criteria was used to consider a mother as working. (i) The mother should be a full time worker outside the home. (ii) the mother must be working for more than three years. (iii) the mother must be away from her child for at least five hours a day. For the non-working mother, care was taken to see that the mother has not worked for the past three years.

Thus with this criteria two groups of children were formed —(a) children of working mothers, (b) children of non-working mothers.

Step IV: One of the objectives of this study was to see developmental differences among children under different types of care. Thus the children of working mothers were now to be divided according to the type of care they were subjected to. Thus the groups to be formed according to type of care were:

(i) Children under grandmother care (Individual care provided by a grandmother includes own home or grandmother home).

(ii) Children under maid care in child's own home (Care provided by a domestic helper/*ayah*/maid in the child's home.

(iii) Children in group care (family day care). (Care provided by adult in a group).

To see the effects of the type of care on children, the child had/has to be subjected to that type of care for a period of time. Thus children who were in the particular care for two years and attending that care for at least five hours a day were included in the sample.

One additional point kept in mind for children attending family day care is that the family day care which the child is attending should have at least five children.

Step V: The details of 1495 pre-school children were scrutinised and all the children satisfying the conditions mentioned at every step were included in the final sample. Separate lists of children under mother, grandmother, maid and family day care crèche were made. By simple random sampling fifty children were picked up in each group.

The children in family day care numbered only 40 and hence it was decided to include all the forty. Thus, a very purposive sample was obtained from this selection procedure.

Measures

The main aim of the study was to see the developmental differences among children under different types of care. As these children were pre-schoolers, all information about them cannot be got from children itself. Thus data had to be collected from various sources. The following tools were used for data collection.

Test for Intellectual Development

The Kamat-Binet Test of Intelligence was used in this study. This test is an Indian adaptation of the Standard-Binet Scale of Intelligence. It is an individually administered test, with tests grouped into age levels extending from 3 years to 22 years. The test measures such constructs as general comprehension, visual-motor ability, arithmetic reasoning, memory and concentration, vocabulary and verbal fluency, and judgment and reasoning. Scoring is usually done based on accuracy and speed of response. The scoring and the calculations of intelligence quotient was done according to manual.

The Vineland Social Maturity Scale

The second area of development which was to be studied was social development. For this, the Vineland Social Maturity Scale (Doll, 1962) was found to be most suitable as there was the Nagpur adaptation available and also that it could be used with pre-schoolers. The scale provides an outline of detailed performances in respect to which children show a progressive capacity for looking after themselves and for participating in these activities which lead towards ultimate independence as adults. The items in the scale are arranged in order of increasing average difficulty and represent progressive maturation in self-help, self-direction, locomotion, occupation, communication and social relations. The scale helps in giving a standard schedule of normal development, it helps in measuring individual differences. The manual clearly states that for the group who cannot answer for themselves, a person who knows the child intimately should give the information. For the group of pre-schoolers, it was felt that mothers would be the best persons to give information and hence for the items on Vineland Social Maturity Scale, the mothers were respondents.

Interview Guide for Working and Non-working Mothers

The interview schedule was designed to get information on various aspects about the child and his family. There were some questions which would elicit information about the child's family that is details about his parent's age, education, occupation, income, type of family, religion, number of members in family etc. The mother was also asked to give details about her activities with children, i.e. how much time she spends with her child in various activities, which other family members spends time with child, in what areas does the child have problems etc. In addition to all this, the working mothers are asked details about the work life like hours of work is the job tiring, satisfaction with job, gains from the job etc. Besides questions on what types of child care they are using, satisfaction with it, good and bad aspects of that particular care were also included.

Data Collection

The children were already identified and selected in the various schools and were grouped according to type of care they were subjected to. However, to facilitate data collection lists of children were prepared according to the schools they were attending. Thus separate lists of children for the five areas were made. The first step taken therefore was to administer test of intelligence to children. Requests were also made that a separate room be given so that there will be no disturbances during testing. In all schools this request was granted. In all schools the kindergarten classes were functioning for about three hours. The testing had to be done in these three hours, as a result in a school a maximum of 4-5 children could be covered per day.

The second step in data collection was to administer the Vineland Social Maturity Scale. But this was to be answered by the mothers. Many of the non-working mothers come to pick up their children. It was felt that this would be a good time to call them for the interview. Letters were sent to non-working mothers through their children, requesting them to come to school on a particular day and time and in case the day and time was not suitable, they could indicate their convenient day and time. Thus most of the non-working mothers would come on weekdays to the school. All the data, intelligence testing, interview of mothers, and Vineland scale — were being collected at the same time at the school.

The difficulty was in getting the working mothers group. These mothers could come to schools only on Saturdays or Sundays. Special permission was sought from Principals to use the school premises on Sundays also. The mothers were given day and time to come to the school or indicate a suitable day and time. Many mothers could come at the requested day and time and participate very enthusiastically in the study. However, some mothers (working and non-working) did not turn up even after 2-3 reminders. Such cases were then dropped.

The sample attrition created a grave problem. With mothers having dropped out, data on intelligence test was available for all children (because it was conducted on children) while scores on Vineland Social Maturity scale were missing. Thus in all four groups of children there were many cases which had to be dropped because of incomplete data. The investigators also made attempts to visit mothers who did not come to school. However, the mothers they met were not ready to participate in the study. It was then decided that children whose parent did not participate will be dropped from the study. Thus the expected fifty in each group was drastically reduced. The final sample with all data was as follows:

Type of Care	No. of Children
Mother Care	23
Grandmother Care	23
Maid Care	21
Family Day Care	13
Total	80

Results

Education and Work Status

Of the 57 women who were working about 53 per cent were graduates, 26 per cent were educated up to SSC while some (17%) women were post-graduates. Thus about 70 per cent of the sample of the working women were well educated and were graduates and post-graduates. Among the non-working mothers group, it was noticed that about 30 per cent of them were either SSC or diploma holders; some 60 per cent were graduates and some 8 per cent were post-graduates. As we had selected working mothers who had at least completed three years of work life, the sample mothers had put in at least 4.5 years of work. About 17.5 per cent of the mothers had worked for about 4.5 years, 39 per cent of them up to 8.5 years, yet others (24%) 12.5 years and the rest (15%) 16.5 years. The average age of the women in the sample was 31 years. Thus, if on average, they start work around age of 23, they have by now completed eight years of work life. However, there was a group of women who had even completed 12.5 years of work.

About 58 per cent of these working mothers were holding clerical post, i.e. jobs like typist/clerk, steno, telephone operators, receptionist etc., while some 30 per cent of them were doing professional jobs like teaching, technical assistance, medicine and law. Just 7 of the 57 mothers reported that they were doing some business. The non-working mothers were asked whether they had worked any time in the past. Of the 23 non-working mothers in the sample, nine mothers had worked while some 14 of them had never worked. Of the nine, about four had worked for 2-3 years while the others had worked for more than three years. Two main reasons were stated by the mothers for quitting their job: one was that they got married and were not able to continue in job, while the other reason was that when the first child was born, child care problems forced them to leave the job.

Work Timings of Mothers

It is interesting to note that the working mothers started work at various timing ranging from 7 a.m. in morning to 11 a.m. Three women started at 7 a.m., some 12 started work at 8 a.m., while some of them (29) started at 9 a.m. There were 9 of them who started at 10 a.m. and a few (4) at 11 a.m. In the evening most mothers (50% of the 57) stopped work between 4 p.m. and 6 p.m. These mothers who leave early for work, if they wanted to have child care outside the home would have found it difficult because no day care opened as early as 6 a.m. or 7 a.m.

The working mothers were asked about their exact work hours. Thirty-seven per cent women worked for six hours, 35 per cent for 7 hours, 17 per cent for as long as eight hours while others (10%) worked for five hours. Thus on an average the women were working for 6.5 hours, apart from time spent on commuting to and fro. The travel time varied from less than half an hour to 2 hours or so. Some 21 per cent women spent less than ½ hour on travel, while 30 per cent spent about 45 minutes and some of them (21%) spent 1½ hours in commuting up and down. Still others (12%) spend about 2-2½ hours on travel. On an average, the women spent at least one hour in travel.

The working mothers in the sample spend about eight hours out of the home. That is if a woman's work timings are 8 a.m. to 5 p.m., she will be back home only by 6 p.m. It necessarily means that this mother will have also have very few hours with her child say 3-4 hours. But this 3-4 hours are her time at home and not necessarily with the child. She has household duties also to perform during this time. Thus, how much time the mother actually spends with the child is questionable.

Perceived Benefits of Working Mothers

In general, all the working mothers were satisfied with their work life. Secondly, when asked whether they found the job tiring or not, most women said that they do not find the job tiring. About 40 per cent mothers said that they can manage well. The working mothers said that the first and foremost benefit that the family was getting because of their working was financial help. They felt that because they were working, the financial status was better and the family can live much more comfortably and they could afford to buy luxury items also.

Working Mothers and Children's Reactions to their Working

The working mothers were also asked about their children's reactions when they left for work or when they came back from work. Contrary to our expectations of finding crying and clinging children, large number of working mothers (46 of the 57) said that there was no trauma experienced by the child each time they left for work. Some women said that their children expected a gift, while others said that their child would happily bid goodbye, some said that their child was still not adjusted and cried everyday, while some children said everyday, "don't go". Most children seem to have got used to the fact of mother being away for long periods of time and have adjusted very well to this fact. Considering reactions when mothers are back from work, most mothers reported that children were happy and expressed their happiness through hugs and kisses.

Thus adjustment to work life of the mother has been made by the children and family and does not seem to pose any problem in the life of the working mothers and their children. However it is possible that children may show problems in other areas like food habits, study habits, etc. But these problems will be discussed in comparison with the children of non-working mothers.

Time Spent by Mothers in Various Activities with Children

It was very interesting to note that through the day all working mothers spend one hour or less in feeding their pre-school child, whereas, there were quite many among non-working mothers who spend as much as two hours on feeding the child.

Among the working mothers, 21 per cent spent no time on feeding, 52 per cent spent about half an hour while another 26 per cent spent a maximum of one hour. In contrast, about 34.8 per cent non-working mothers spent about 1½ to 2 hours on feeding, another 21 per cent spent 45 minutes to 1 hour and some (26%) spent 15 minutes to ½ hour. Just 17 per cent (4) did not spend any time on feeding the child. Thus the working mothers spend on an average 25 minutes on feeding the child whereas for the same age child the non-working mothers spend about one hour.

The non-working mother is with the child for all his meals whereas the working mother is with the child for one or two meals only. Considering this one would expect more differences between the time spent by working and non-working mothers. But it is possible that because children of working mothers get their mothers for only one feed that time they may fuss over food so much that their mothers are compelled to indulge in them. Whereas, the children of non-working mothers may not strive to get the mother's attention because they are there for them, and therefore, these children may not take long with the meals. Thus the time given by mothers (both of working and non-working) does not show much difference. It is also seen that mothers who have house maids for care of child spend slightly less time on feeding activities than mothers who use other forms of child care.

All mothers spent time on bathing and dressing their children and there was not much difference in the amount of time spent by working and non-working mothers as well as mothers who used different forms of child care.

Children in crèche care and under maid care seem to require least care and attention from mothers during sleep time whereas children of mother care and relative care do require some attention during their sleep time.

In play activities, the differences were pronounced in the amount of time spent by the mothers. The non-working mothers had more time with child and therefore, indulged in play activities with the child for longer period of time (45 minutes to one hour), whereas the working mothers spent about 20 minutes with child on play activities. Among all children of working mothers, the crèche children seem to get least stimulation from mother in play activities. The reasons could be many; that the child may not feel the need for play so much as he has been with age mates all through the day, that the child has to be taken home from the crèche which may mean that the mother may not have time to indulge in special activities for her child. Besides, there will be no other members in the house except the father, the child's mother may have many more household duties which makes it difficult for her to give time for play activities.

It is interesting to note that there were many mothers who said that they do not spend any time at all on all these activities such as feeding, dressing, playing. But when came to the question of spending time on studies, there were just four of the eighty who said they did not spend time on studies with the child (Table 8.1).

Table 8.1 : Time given for Studies with Children by Type of Care (Percentages)

Time given	*Mother*	*Grandmother*	*Maid*	*Crèche*	*Total*
No time	1	2	1	–	4
	25.0	50.0	25.0		100
15 minutes to	–	1	–	1	2
½ hour		50.0		50.0	100
45 minutes to	8	4	11	8	31
1 hour	25.8	12.4	35.4	53.8	100
1.15 min. to	2	3	6	1	12
1½ hour	16.6	25.0	50.0	8.4	100
> 1½ hours	12	13	3	3	31
	38.7	41.9	9.7	9.7	100
Total	23	23	21	13	80
	28.8	28.8	26.2	16.2	100

The non-working mothers and the mothers who left their child with grandparents spent as much as 1½ hours with the child on his/her studies. As the non-working mother has the whole day at her disposal, it is easy for her to schedule her activities so that she can spend enough time on studies with her child. Similarly, the mother who lives with the child's grandparents can devote some time for the child's studies as there is someone in the house to take care of the other responsibilities. The mothers who have to depend on maid or a crèche care cannot avoid certain household responsibilities which are time consuming and have to be done by themselves and hence devote slightly less time than the other mothers (one hour).

Thus a non-working mother spends about 3½ hours in activities like feeding, dressing, sleeping and studies, whereas for the same activities, a working mother spends about 2½ hours. Apart from time spent with child on these various activities the mothers were also asked to state in all how many hours do they get to spend with the child. The non-working mothers said that they spend at least seven hours a day, with the child. While all the working mothers said that they get 4 to 4½ hours to spend with the child (Table 8.2).

All the working mothers felt that they would like to spend more time with their child. When questioned as to what would they like to do if they got more time to spend with the child, some 40 per cent said that they would like to help the child develop some hobbies and for this they would like to be with the child and encourage him. Twenty-one per cent said they would like to devote this time for studies. While another ten per cent said they feel the child gets neglected and they would like to give personal attention to the child. This response was mainly given by mothers who kept children under maid care. The few other mothers felt they would use that time to train the child in good behaviour. Thus mothers invariably seem to desire to spend more time with their child and have clearly identified in what areas the child is not getting attention and have therefore expressed a desire to indulge those things if they ever had time on hand.

Table 8.2 : Total Hours Mother Spend with Child by type of Care (in Percentages)

Hours with child	*Mother care*	*Grand-mother care*	*House Maid care*	*Family Day Care Creche Care*	*Total*
1 hour	2	2	3	1	8
	25.0	25.0	37.5	12.5	100
2 hours	2	1	3	2	8
	25.0	12.5	37.5	25.5	100
4 hours	1	9	6	4	20
	5.0	45.0	30.0	20.0	100
5 hours	3	4	5	5	17
	17.7	23.5	29.4	29.4	100
6 hours	4	5	3	1	13
	30.7	38.5	23.1	7.7	100
8 hours	4	2	–	–	6
	66.6	33.4			100
More than 8 hours	7	–	1	–	8
	87.5		12.5		100
Total	23	23	21	13	80
	28.8	28.8	26.2	16.2	100.0

Developmental Differences Among Children

Two areas of development were studied in this research. The intellectual development as measured on Kamat-Binet test of intelligence and social maturity as measured on the Vineland Social Maturity test. Both these tests are standardised on Indian samples.

The development of children was studied to understand of the effect of two main factors:

(1) work status of mother (working or non-working),

(2) the type of care (that is mother care, grandmother care,

maid care and crèche care), on intellectual and social development.

IQ Scores

The average IQ of the children in this study is about 109 with about 17 children having an IQ score of 95.5 or less and some 16 children had an IQ of 125.5 or more. Looking at the IQ scores of the males in the study (54) it was 110.00 while that of the females was (25 in number) 104.5. There appears to be no significant differences in IQ scores of children with siblings and children without siblings. Some other family background variables were also looked into when studying children's IQ scores. Education of mother and father were two such variables that were studied. Most of the mothers were either SSC or graduates. Since these were the two large groups, only these will be considered for analysis. The IQ score of children who had mothers studied up to SSC was 105.1 while those with graduates mothers had an IQ score of 110.3, thus there was a clear difference in IQ scores. The education of the mother does play an important role. Educated mothers offer better stimulation to children in terms of their interaction and materials offered to children to play and interact. It is also very interesting to see that the education of the father did not make any significant contribution to the child's IQ scores. The reason could be that the father's interaction with children is little and this could hardly influence the child's intellectual growth. However, these findings need to be studied further to draw any conclusion.

There was a difference in the IQ score of children of working mothers (112.4) and children of non-working mothers (108.1) with children of working mothers doing slightly better. It is possible that to avoid feelings of guilt and neglect toward the child, working mothers do try to give their time in the most meaningful way.

It is also important to consider the influence of type of care on IQ scores of children. The average IQ scores of children under mother, grandmother, maid and crèche care are 108.1, 114.7, 105.9 and 111.65 respectively (Fig. 8.1). The difference was found between mother care and crèche care with crèche children doing slightly

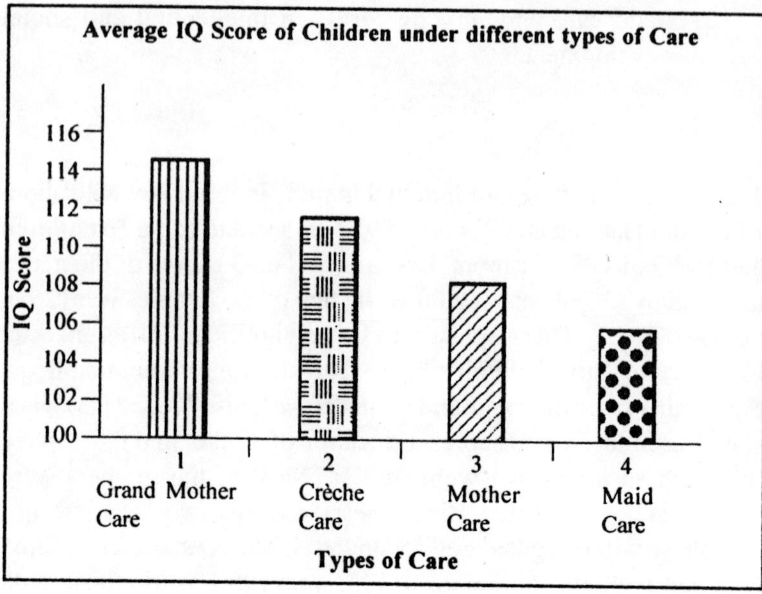

Fig. 8.1: Average IQ Score of Children under Different Types of Care

better. Here it could be said that because of the group setting and peer influence the crèche children may be doing better; but it is interesting to note that the difference between scores of grandmother care and mother care is not pronounced. The possible explanation could be that a non-working mother has many chores to perform and hence may not devote all her time with the child, whereas a grandmother will perform the major role of caregiver to the child and spend more time with the child in various activities and hence even though the peer group is absent (which is present in crèche care) the IQ scores may not show much variation. It is also seen that maid care and mother care children's scores are not varying.

Working mothers who have maids for child care will also have the same maid perform many household chores when she comes home, this releases her to be with her child and may thus contribute a little to the child's development. It must not be forgotten that the maid care group score lowest in IQ, meaning that stimulation from maid is lacking all day, because of many factors like the maid being illiterate, cultural differences and the fact that she does other household chores also and therefore whatever stimulation the child gets may be through the mother only.

The grandmother care and maid care group shows differences, with IQ scores of 114.7 and 105.9 respectively. The housemaid care group has scored low because of lack of stimulation from the caregiver, while the grandmother has the advantage of being with the grandchild most of the time and can stimulate him through activities, playing, etc. The difference between grandmother care and crèche care is not significant showing that group care is in a way beneficial to children but grandmother care is superior. The point is that apart from being in group care mothers of these children have a lot of chores to do even after picking the child and therefore are not able to give substantial time to children.

Thus in conclusion it can be said that of all, the grandmother care children do the best with an average IQ of 114.7. The advantage can be seen in a broader light that these children are coming from extended family and therefore stimulation given will be more as he/she is interacting with many more family members. Besides, the grandmother can devote much more time to be with child compared to any other caregivers in the other groups. There could be no doubt about the fact that with her intense love for grandchild, her motivation and her maturity, the grandmother will prove to be an effective caregiver. The second group which had shown a good score is that of children in family day care, their average IQ score being 111.5. The crèche care children's environment is different. The study has also shown that the caregivers do not have a programme whereby children could be learning with materials. Thus peer interaction is the only way they may learn. With a better programme in family day care the benefits for children who attend such programme will be much more. The IQ of the group cared for by the mother, shows the score of 108.1 which is low compared to grandmother care and family day care. There are two factors to be considered in this situation — one is that the mother is non-working and the fact that therefore the child is not subjected to any other child care. But the question then arises as to why do the children have such a low score if the mother herself is the caregiver. Could it be that in other groups the children are getting stimulation from mother and that their scores are high or that even though the mother is non-working, she may not be spending quality time with her child? Very often the non-working mother has a lot more household responsibilities which may make it difficult to give time when the child is at home. The maid group children suffered the most and had the lowest IQ, i.e., 105.9. The maids who take care of children can basically take care of only the child's basic needs. They are not in a position to play games and teach the child as there may be language barriers and cultural differences. Illiterate maids will not be able to play rule based games or even read to the child. Their contribution to the child's intellectual development is likely to be very limited. Thus maid care serves only as custodial care.

Thus it is important to see that proper child care is provided to children. However, the working mothers in the sample have said that after grandmother care they would prefer to have maid care. This arrangement, of course, is being viewed as per their convenience. When they have a live-in-maid apart from child care, she does a lot of chores in the house. Besides, some mothers quoted that today there is not much difference in what a family day care offers and what a maid would offer at home. They felt there is no advantage in sending their child to family day care. Therefore efforts will have to be made to convey the significance of an educated person taking care of children and to develop better family day care services so that they get accepted as a professional service which will contribute to children's development.

Social Maturity

The second aspect of development which was under study was social maturity. The Vineland Social Maturity test was used to study this aspect. The test gives a score for social maturity.

The average social maturity score of the children is 6.9. There is a difference among score of boys (6.6) and girls (7.5) indicating that socialization process has had its impact on development of social skills. That the girls score higher than boys could indicate (a) that there is more pressure for girls to develop social skills, (b) the emphasis on social skills may not be an area measured like dressing, eating, sleeping for the boy. However, it can be said socialization plays a crucial role. Comparing scores of children 5 years and 6 years does not show any significant difference making it clear that socialisation is the main factor in social maturity.

When the children of working mothers and non-working mothers are compared, it clearly shows that the non-working mothers' children (7.2) have a higher score than working mothers' children (6.8). This is contrary to the expectations. It could be expected that the working mothers' children would need to be independent and therefore score more on social maturity, and that non-working mothers since will be available to the child the need to develop self-help skills is not felt strongly. However, the results do not support this thinking. The possible reasons for non-working mothers' children doing better is that she has more time at hand and therefore can spend time with the child when he/she is learning skills (for instance, eating) and therefore these children get more opportunity to practice these skills and hence score high on their social maturity scores. In contrast, the children of working mothers have very little time to practice these. The need to save time makes mothers do things for their children and these children fall behind in their social maturity scores.

The crèche care children and the grandmother care children had an equal score of 6.9, the children under care of maid had the lowest score of 6.7. The highest score was that of children of non-working mothers (7.2). The scores of mother care children and grandmother care children were higher than that of maid care children.

The possible reason why mother care children have a higher score has been explained earlier. The grandmother may spend more time in allowing child to work on skills and therefore this group of children also have a high score.

Children under maid care may force the maids to help them in all areas of self-help and other skills. Also, the expectations of the mother that the maid should not make child do anything, for the child may make the maid do all things for the child and therefore giving the child no scope for mastering skills.

The pressure on the crèche/family day care children is different. Here the fact is there is no adult available to them all the time who will help them in all their tasks and therefore, they are forced to master some skills like dressing, eating and sleeping.

In the coming years, working mothers are going to be common feature of most families in India. At the same time family networks are becoming weaker, making it imperative that society provide the required support to allow the family to carry out its roles and responsibilities. One such important support is child care services. This study has brought to light the many issues we need to consider to give families the choices for child care and encourage appropriate services so that children get their opportunity to develop to the fullest.

The study has shown that grandmothers' care is the most beneficial to children. Young parents must realise that extended families provide a secure and stimulating environment for children and therefore should encourage child care by immediate family.

Though not an appropriate care from child development perspective, maid care is a very common form of care until parents start getting choices in quality child care, the parents will continue to use child care that is, convenient. Many parents have said that they knew that their child was not getting appropriate care, but that there was not much difference in quality of service. It is, therefore, very essential that appropriate child care alternatives be evolved. The government and private sector should create these alternative child care programmes. Employers, housing societies and neighbourhood can contribute in this endeavour. More literature will have to be generated on how good centres/programme should be run, how parents should get educated on how to choose child care.

Family day care stood next to grandmother care children in IQ scores. Very often mothers leave their jobs to be with their child because child care may not provide for all of the child's needs. The study shows that if efforts are made to create quality child care programmes, they can have a positive impact on children.

The results also show that the working mother continues to feel guilty for not doing enough for the child and therefore when the child is five years old, the mother spends a lot of time in feeding, dressing and teaching. Mothers working outside the home have to be looked at more positively by the family particularly by the husband and immediate family. This creates a supportive environment for the mother and there is better acceptance of the working mothers by the child also. If working couples get inputs on parenting they can do effective parenting, in spite of less hours of contact with the child.

In conclusion, there is no denying that the family is the most important environment for children but when children are in good quality appropriate programmes, they will benefit. Thus it is important to develop supportive child care programmes that offer quality care to children.

9

MATERNAL PERCEPTIONS ABOUT SATISFACTION IN CHILD CARE AND DEVELOPMENT OF CHILDREN*

— *Monica Gupta* and *Rajani M. Konantambigi*

Industrialisation and urbanisation in the West about a decade ago had a significant impact on the labour market. For the last three decades in India the percentage of women being employed outside the home has shown an upward trend (if one ignores the shifting criterion of employment, rural and urban definitions used in the census). The census figures show that number of employed women in urban India has increased from 7.2 per cent in 1971 to 8.3 per cent in 1981, to 9.7 per cent in 1991. This phenomenon has given rise to concerns about the possible impact of maternal employment on children.

The early studies between 1940s and the 1960s in the western context (see reviews, Hoffman, 1963; Spitze, 1988) and most of the Indian studies (Datta, 1993; 1994; Mathur and Mishra, 1993; Modi and Murthy, 1983; Motwani, 1987; Venkataramanna, 1987; Saxena, Mehrortra and Singh, 1986; 1987; Swaminathan and Parvathi, 1983) have investigated the influence of maternal employment *per se* as a status variable. A study of the western

* Re-printed with the permission of author and publisher; it first appeared in *Trends in Social Research*, 1998, 5(1), 115-130.

researchers showed that, among other findings, it was not maternal employment *per se* that was detrimental to children's growth and development, but the over all life situation of the child's family (e.g., broken homes). Indian studies have revealed mixed results; i.e., there are certain positive as well as negative effects on children due to maternal employment.

However, more recent researchers have tended to regard maternal employment as a multidimensional variable requiring un-packaging. Researchers have thus explored conditions related to maternal employment such as availability of support, maternal satisfaction with roles etc., as variables of crucial importance in influencing the child. One of the major consequences of maternal employment is the increase in the Non Parental Care (NPC) arrangements for children. These include day care centres, crèches, care by maids, etc. (Datta, 1993).

The researchers have, however, not tended to deal with the consequences of maternal employment and NPC in the same inquiry. The two different lines of researches can be related by categorizing NPC as a consequence of maternal employment. Thus, NPC related factors like quality of care, age of entry of the child may be mediating the influence of maternal employment on the child.

The theoretical basis for studying factors related to maternal employment rather than maternal employment per se for its effect on the child, can be obtained from Urie Bronfenbrenner's Ecological theory. According to Bronfenbrenner (1979; 1986), development takes place in a multi-layered context. In a complex ecology, children are seen as influenced by the nature and quality of their contact and interaction with significant others. For young children, these significant others may be their adult caretakers. The adults are in turn influenced by the context of their own lives both inside and outside the family. The contextual differences in the lives of the caretakers can influence the child's adjustment. The factors discussed in the following sections are related to maternal employment and may directly or indirectly influence the child's adjustment.

Non-Parental Care

Extensive research has been conducted in the western context to assess the influence on NPC on specifically the children's socio-emotional development. These researchers, however, differ in focus and in the research paradigms used. They can be categorized in terms of waves (Belsky, 1990; McGurk, Caplan, Henessey and Moss, 1993). Five such waves of researches are discussed below:

Wave 1: The early studies in 1970s on NPC were conducted on children in high quality, university based day care centres. These studies revealed that there was no need to be concerned about any overwhelmingly adverse consequences for children's development (Belsky, 1990).

Wave 2: In the 1980s, the research shifted to the socio-structural features of different kinds of NPC arrangements. These researches revealed that children fared well in settings that have well trained and experienced staff who work with small groups of children in safe, well-equipped premises (McGurk *et al.*, 1993).

Wave 3: The researchers done on different types of NPC arrangements also revealed that mother child attachment was at risk for children between 12 to 18 months of age (Gamble and Zigler, 1986; Belsky and Rovine, 1988; Belsky and Eggebeen, 1991). Thus, early entry into NPC arrangements became a controversial issue. McGurk, *et al.* (1993) reviewed the researches related to this controversy and concluded that the quality and consistency of care in NPC arrangements in addition to other variables like characteristics of the child and family play an important role in deciding whether early entry into NPC has an adverse impact.

Wave 4: Some researchers realized that to adequately understand the influence of NPC on children, the complex ecology of human development must be studied (Belsky, 1990).

This meant that they studied not only variation in the quality of care (Wave 2) and the age of entry on NPC (Wave 3), but also the family attitude/processes and parents' occupational experiences which could influence the child indirectly (Phillips, McCartney and Scarr, 1987; Konantambigi, 1990).

Wave 5: The studies using this paradigm were the most recent and assured that developmental processes of influence may be different in cases of children living in different settings (Howes, 1990). This also indicates that the children of employed and unemployed mothers may not be comparable as the processes in the two settings could differ.

The Indian research in the area of NPC is meagre. Besides a few studies, (Konantambigi, 1990) which take into account the family process, the list of researches focus on parental satisfaction with different kinds of NPC arrangements (Sharma, 1986; Kaur, 1988; Consul, 1990) and its relationship with children's development (Datta, 1993; 1994).

Role Satisfaction of the Mother

The adoption of multiple role by the employed women as a mother, a wife, a daughter-in-law and an employee has been the concern of sociologists and social psychologists for the past half a decade and has attracted a lot of media concern (Adhikari, 1994; Hazarika, 1994). The question here is whether the adoption of multiple roles leads to a role overload or role conflict and whether it influences the mother and the child adversely.

While the western literature is divided over whether adoption of multiple roles leads to role conflict for the mother (Gutek and Valdez, 1987); the Indian researches point towards the presence of role conflict in Indian employed mothers (Kapur, 1970; Mane, 1983; Rani, 1976). The reason given is that in India, both modernity and tradition often coexist.

The employed women are torn between traditional and modern roles and their behaviour becomes complex in terms of expected and actual conduct (Ramu, 1989). Some studies have found work role and marital satisfaction to be of consequence on child behaviour (Vanaja and Venkataramaiah, 1990; Crockenberg and Litman, 1991), others have not found work role satisfaction as a major factor influencing the child's adjustment (Greenberger and O'Neil, 1991). The issue thus remains open and undecided. The role theory (may be termed as classical role theory) posits role conflict in the presence of multiple and conflicting role demands, but empirical evidence is not unanimous in this regard, therefore, calling forth an additional dimension to the theory (Konantambigi, 1990). When role conflict is absent, factors of coping strategies and support available should be in operation.

Child Care Support

The presence of child care, emotional and financial support has been seen to be of crucial importance to an employed woman (Jaykody, Chalter and Taylor, 1993). Several recent studies have investigated the kinds of support networks available to mothers and its impact on the social and cognitive development of the child. The studies indicate that the quality and the size of the support networks may be of crucial importance in influencing the child (Jennings, Stagg and Connors, 1991; Nelson, Ladd and Hsu, 1993).

Most Indian studies in this area have tended to look at the kind of support available to the mothers and their satisfaction with support. They have not looked at how the presence or absence of support influences the child (Sharma, 1987; Kaur, 1988; Consul, 1990; Deshpande, 1992).

Career Orientation and Well-being of the Mothers

A review of literature yields that feelings of guilt and depression may influence the children's adjustment as they are at an increased risk for development of psychopathology (Cummings and Davies,

1994). The feeling of depression and guilt can have root in the career orientation of employed mothers. Researches have found that depression and feeling of guilt were high in women who preferred to be homemakers but had to work or those women who preferred employment but had to stay at home (Demeis, McBride and Hock, 1986; Hock and Demeis, 1990). Roopnarine, Talukdar, Jain, Joshi and Srivastava (1992) have gone a step further and found that maternal well-being influences the mother-child interactions.

Other Factors

Some other factors mediating the influence of maternal employment on the child include the education of the mother, her hours of employment and the gender of the child. The first factor i.e., the education of the mother has been found to be positively related to the adjustment of the child in a number of studies (Vanaja and Venkataramaiah, 1991; Bala and Upadhyaya, 1992). With reference to the second factor, i.e. the work hours of the mother, contrary to the popular beliefs, a study by Crockenberg and Litman (1991) revealed that mothers who worked longer hours were more responsive to their children. The gender of the child, a third factor, has been found to determine the consequences of maternal employment for the child. Research reveals that maternal employment is more favourable for daughters as they have higher educational aspirations and are likely to choose nontraditional career (Hoffman, 1963). Sons of unemployed mothers fared well in comparison to boys of employed mothers.

The review of research thus reveals that maternal employment is not a monolithic variable. The consequences of maternal employment on the child are multiply determined. A child could be influenced by the kind and quality of NPC arrangements; role satisfaction, career orientation and education level of the mother; the amount and quality of support available to the mother; her working hours as well as the gender of the child. However, there is a lack of Indian studies dealing with the above mentioned issues. The present study attempts to address some of these gaps.

A review of research pertaining to child outcomes as a result of maternal employment and substitute child care has shown that cognitive and social development, and issues related to mother-infant attachment have been extensively looked into (Konantambigi, 1990). Socio-emotional development of children has been relatively less researched upon, especially on Indian children. Therefore, the focus of research in this study is on socio-emotional development.

The objectives and their rationale are discussed in the following paragraphs:

1. The first objective of the study was to explore whether Global Maternal Satisfaction (GMS) was related to the Socio-Emotional Behavioural Adjustment (SEBA) of children. The GMS is a composite score of perceived maternal satisfaction in managing their emotions, support, time and finance. This gives rise to the question —'How do the employed mothers manage child care given the extra pressure of work?' Maternal satisfaction with management of emotions was seen as crucial to Indian context where a close relationship is expected between the mother and child in initial years (Kakkar, 1978). This could potentially be a source of guilt for employed mothers. Maternal satisfaction with time and financial management were explored as potentially important areas where the satisfaction level of the mother may influence the child's adjustment.
2. The second objective was to investigate the extent of contribution of different aspects of maternal satisfaction with management (i.e. emotions, support, time and finance) to SEBA of pre-schoolers.
3. The third objective was to obtain a preliminary documentation of the management strategies used by the mothers when dealing with emotion, support and time.

The study also had three secondary objectives. They were:

(1) To investigate if the employment status of the mother influenced the SEBA of children attending day school. This

objective was used to ascertain the fact that the employment status of the mother did not influence the children adversely rather than assuming this as based on the previous research. In addition, the previous research had failed to control for varying pre-school experience of children of employed and unemployed mothers. This was accomplished in the present study as children of employed and non-employed mothers attended the same day school.

(2) To investigate if the career orientation of the mother influenced the SEBA of the children. Career orientation was investigated as it has implications for the mother's well-being which can influence the adjustment of the child.

(3) The study also aimed to investigate sex differences, if any, in SEBA of children of employed and unemployed mothers. The aim here was to ascertain whether the results favouring girls in the western context were applicable to the Indian population.

Method

Sample: The sample consisted of 60, 2.5 to 5 year old children (40 children of employed mothers and 20 children of unemployed mothers) drawn from a school in Baroda, Gujarat State, which also had day care facilities for children. The children of employed mothers consisted of 20 boys and 20 girls whereas the unemployed mothers' children consisted 13 girls and 7 boys. The discrepancy was due to the fact that the children had to meet certain criteria (elaborated further in this section). These children were drawn from nursery and junior kindergarten sections, with English as a medium of instruction. The children were drawn from a day school for two major reasons. Firstly, the chosen day school combined NPC with pre-school experience. Secondly, the school could yield a sample of adequate strength. Children of both employed and unemployed mothers had to spend the entire day in the pre-school. Pre-school activities and child care were combined.

Purposive sampling technique was used to identify the sample. The two samples, i.e. families with employed and unemployed mothers were selected as matched on the following criteria:

(a) Absence of exceptional stress in the family (e.g., recent death or major illness, divorce/separation, and financial problems which could induce stress),

(b) Nuclear family type,

(c) Working hours between 6 to 8 hours, 5 to 6 days a week for employed women, and

(d) A minimum of four months spent in the school/day care by the children.

Measures

Three major measures were used for obtaining the relevant information.

Personal data sheet: The purpose of this measure was to (a) obtain relevant personal information about the mother, the child and the family (e.g., age, income, occupational details, etc.) and (b) screening/ for exceptional stress in the family — here stress induced by divorce / separation, death or fatal illness in the family and extreme financial difficulties perceived as a source of stress.

The semi-structured interview schedule: An interview schedule was constructed in order (a) to assess perceived maternal satisfaction of employed mothers when managing their emotions, support, time and finance, (b) document management strategies, used by the mother for the aforementioned aspects and (c) determine the career orientation of the mother with reference to reasons for working, commitment and continuation.

The tool was constructed as based on the review of literature and guided by the research questions. It was then given to 5 experts for feedback on content and format. Some suggestions of the experts were incorporated in the tool. The tool was then pilot tested on a sample 5 mothers and 10 children. The score categories were drawn on the basis of the semi-structured interview schedule. The score categories for maternal satisfaction with management of emotions were, "feels positively", "feels negative but copes" and "feels negative", with the scores ranging from 3 to 1. Maternal satisfaction with management of support was scored on the presence or absence of support in five areas, i.e., help from husband, outside help (relative, friends and neighbours), school/day care, job and domestic help. (a) stable routine, (b) prioritizing time satisfactorily, (c) pursuit of hobbies and activities, and (d) feels rested. The scores ranged from 0 to 4. Maternal satisfaction with financial management was scored according to whether the mother was (a) managing within the budget, (b) being able to make required investment, and (c) fulfilling all other financial responsibilities. The scores ranged from 0 to 3. As the number of items making up maternal satisfaction varied for different aspects, the scores were given equal weightage by dividing them by score of 10. The weighted scores obtained in each area, i.e. maternal satisfaction with management of emotions, support, time and finance were then added up to obtain the GMS score for each mother.

The socio-emotional behavioural adjustment scale: This scale was constructed essentially by following the same steps as in the construction of semi-structured interview schedule. It is based on the scale by Vanaja and Venkataramaiah (1990) and one by Baker and Mott (1990), described in Belsky and Eggebeen (1991). It yielded (a) parent ratings for peer interaction, adult interaction and other behavioural indicators and (b) teacher ratings for peer interaction. On the basis of pilot testing it was decided to limit teacher ratings of SEBA of children to peer rating only as the school setting did not allow for adequate adult interaction and many other behavioural indicators.

The parent rating form of the scale consisted of a total of 35 items covering aspects of social and emotional behaviours like sociability, aggression, compliance, attachment, anxiety, distractibility and activity level. Of the 35 items 16 were related to peer interaction, 8 with adult interaction and 11 with other behavioural indicators. The teacher rating form consisted of 16 items related to peer interaction only. Both the forms were four point rating scales with the categories “always”, “mostly”, “sometimes” and “never”. The items were scored 4, 3, 2 and 1 respectively for positively frame items and 1, 2, 3 and 4 respectively for negatively framed items. The scores were then added up to obtain the total score.

Procedure

The personal data sheets were sent to parents through the school. On the basis of the information obtained the families with employed and unemployed mothers were chosen as matched on the sample criteria.

For the chosen families, teacher-ratings were obtained for the SEBA of children. The respective class teachers of the children were contacted for this purpose.

The mothers were interviewed at their respective homes. Both the employed and unemployed mothers were asked to rate their children for SEBA. However, only the employed mothers were interviewed regarding career orientation and perceived maternal satisfaction in managing emotions, support, time and finance. The Hindi translation of both the interview schedule and SEBA scale were used in case the interviewees were not comfortable with English. The interviews were conducted in privacy and an effort was made to establish a rapport with the interviewee before asking questions. The responses were recorded as the mother gave them. If the mother was uncomfortable the responses were recorded immediately after the interview.

The mothers and teachers were given the SEBA scale for rating. All children utilized the day care facility as all children had to stay in school till evening.

Results

The sample of employed women comprised business women (32.5%), professional (22.5%), semi-skilled workers (20%), clerks (17.5%) or skilled workers (7.5%). A total of 55 per cent of these women were graduates and another 17.5 per cent had professional degrees. The total income of families with employed and unemployed women ranged from Rs.3,000 to above Rs.11,000. Most families with employed mother were within the income range of Rs.5,001 to Rs.11,000 and families with unemployed mothers were in the income range of Rs.3,001 to Rs.7,000.

The following were the objectives-wise results.

Objective 1

Simple correlation were computed to determine the relationship between GMS of employed mothers and SEBA of children. The low correlation coefficients of 0.1868 ($p<.05$) for the parent rating form and 0.0175 ($p<.05$) for the teacher rating form indicated that there was no significant relationship between GMS of mothers and SEBA of children on both parent and teacher rating forms. The distribution of the GMS of mothers and SEBA, however, suggests that the scores in both cases clustered around the higher ends of the continuum of GMS and SEBA for children.

Objective 2

Step-wise multiple regression was used to explore whether maternal satisfaction with management of emotions, support, time and finance predicted the SEBA of children. This analysis was done separately for the parent and the teacher rating forms. The results revealed only support to be a significant predictor of SEBA of children on the parent rating form ($R^2 = 0.166$, $p<.01$). The rest of the variables, management of emotions, time and finance were deleted during analysis as non-significant. This indicated 16 per cent of the variance in SEBA of children was contributed by maternal satisfaction with support.

Percentages were calculated to assess how mothers responded to various score categories used for assessing satisfaction with the management of emotions, support, time and finance. With regard to emotions, 45 per cent of the women felt positively about the jobs, 40 per cent felt negatively but thought they could cope and 15 per cent felt negatively. In the aspects of 87.5 per cent were satisfied with the outside help and the day school, 85 per cent felt they had support from their job, 72.5 per cent from their husbands and 60 per cent felt that they had support from their domestic help. The incidence of satisfaction was thus high for most aspects. With reference to satisfaction with time management, 85 per cent said they had stable routines, 52.5 per cent said they felt rested, 45 per cent said they prioritized their time satisfactorily and 30 per cent said they could pursue their hobbies. Maternal satisfaction with financial management was high as 87.5 per cent mothers said they could manage within self-allotted budget, 80 per cent were able to make the required investments and 77.5 per cent could fulfil other financial responsibilities.

Objective 3

Frequencies and percentages were calculated in order to document the management strategies used by mothers when dealing with emotions, support and time. Finance as an aspect was deleted, as the interviewees were not open in responding to financial matters. (For the management strategies refer to Table 9.1)

Table 9.1 : Management Strategies used by the Employed Mother

Strategy	*Frequency (of positive responses) (N=40)*	*Percentage*
1	2	3
Emotions	11	27.5
Taking a break when the child was born	13	32.5
Working for children's future	31	77.5
Long term self-need		
Giving quality time to the child		
(a) Everyday	24	60.0
(b) On weekend/holidays	33	82.5
(c) Vacations	3	7.5
Child gets adequate attention at school	13	32.5
Employment status a tradition, not anomaly	8	20.0

Contd...

Table 9.1 Contd . . .

Strategy	*Frequency (of positive responses) (N=40)*	*Percentage*
1	2	3
Support		
Taking Leave:		
Mother	26	65.0
Father	2	5.0
Both	12	30.0
Able to get help from friends and neighbours		
Yes	24	60.0
Sometimes	7	17.5
No	9	22.5
Able to get help from parents, in-laws		
Yes	25	62.5
Sometimes	11	27.5
No	4	10.0
Satisfactory role division with husband	25	62.5
Dealing satisfactorily with dissatisfaction		
with school	7	17.5
Yes	2	5.0
No	31	77.5
Not applicable		
Time		
Simultaneous handling of more than one activity	37	92.5
Dividing work between	35	87.5
Employing extra help to spend time with the child	3	7.5
Completing work and sleeping	28	70.0
Delegating Responsibilities	21	52.5

The result of the secondary objectives are reported in the following paragraphs.

Secondary Objective 1

The t-tests were computed to find out if the employment status of the mother influenced the SEBA of children. The values of 0.88 ($p<.05$) on the parent rating form and 0.48($p<.05$) on the teacher rating form revealed that the children of employed and unemployed mothers did not differ significantly on SEBA (for details see Table 9.2).

Table 9.2 : Difference between children of employed and unemployed mothers on SEBA

Group	*Mean*	*S.D.*	*t-value*
Parent Rating form Employed	110.25	8.796	0.88*
Unemployed	112.30	7.834	
Teacher rating form	51.65	6.792	0.48*
Unemployment	52.60	8.191	

*$p<0.05$. Max. possible score=140. Min. possible score =35

Secondary Objective 2

Point bi-serial correlations and t-tests were used to find out if the career orientation and t-test were used to find out if the career orientation of the employed mothers was related to the SEBA of children. Point biserial correlations are used when one of the two variables in a correlation, shows a genuine dichotomy. This was observed in career orientation as a variable which can be divided into two groups, i.e. career oriented and non-career oriented. The correlation coefficients reveal that there was no significant relationship between career orientation and SEBA of children on the parent rating form ($r = 0.02$, $p<0.05$).There was, however, a moderate negative correlation present between the two variables on the teacher rating form ($r=-0.36$, $p<.05$).The t-test results showed a significant difference between the SEBA of career of oriented and non-career oriented mothers had higher mean (54.6) than children of career oriented mothers (50.22).

Secondary Objective 3

The t-test were computed to assess the gender differences in children of employed and unemployed mothers. The t-values revealed that there were no significant difference between children of employed ($t = 0.79$, $p<.05$) or unemployed mothers ($t=0.098$, $p<.05$) on the parent rating scale or children of employed mother rating scale or children of employed mothers ($t=1.03$, $p<.05$) and unemployed mothers ($t=1.53$, $p<.05$) on the teacher rating scale.

Discussion

As there was no significant relationship between GMS of mothers and SEBA of children, it can be concluded that maternal satisfaction, a monolithic variable, was not to the SEBA of children. However, when we look at the amount of variances contributed by each of the four aspects of GMA to SEBA of children separately, maternal satisfaction with support with 16 per cent variances emerges as an important predictor variable on the parent rating form. This confirms the ecological view that family related factors could mediate the impact of maternal employment on child's adjustment. Some studies conducted in the western context have tended to support this finding (Crockenberg and Litman, 1991; Jennings, Stagg and Connors, 1991; Levitt, Weber and Clarke; 1986; Nelson, Ladd and Hsu, 1993). A research of slightly different nature, studying relations between interface of home and workplace and child care has found that different aspects of workplace characteristics were differentially related to parental disciplining behaviour (Greenberger O'Neil, and Nagel, 1995). Work challenge and complexity of works was related to positive parental behaviour, time and urgency of work to less time spent with the child, and while mood spillover did not explain parenting behaviour adequately, transfer of socializing effects from job to parenting behaviours adequately, transfer of socializing effects from job to parenting behaviour existed. Greenberger *et al.* (1995) also comment that evidence that parenting behaviour is influenced by work satisfaction and work is accumulating. In our study too we found that 87.2 per cent are perceiving positive support from there work place which helps in child care.

Another fact that came to light was that there was a high incidence of perceived maternal satisfaction reported for support from outside help, school, day care, job and husband. This partly concurs with the findings of other studies that explored maternal satisfaction with family and day care support in Baroda. These studies found the level of maternal satisfaction to be generally high (Sharma, 1987; Kaur, 1988; Consul, 1990). These findings could also be due to limitations in methodology and the phenomenon of maternal employment and support seeking for child care. Maternal employment with its attendant guilt will its attendant guilt will also not permit acceptance of that the child care support sought is inadequate or of inferior quality. There is an internal need to rationalize. There is therefore a need to explore maternal feelings at length.

Maternal satisfaction with support did not emerge as a significant predictor variable for SEBA of children on the teacher rating form. This could be attributed to the fact that the two forms did not tap exactly the same aspect of the SEBA of children. While the parent rating form assessed the peer-interaction, adult interaction and other behavioural indicators, the teacher rating form assessed peer-interaction only. In addition, it is the investigators' view that the ratings by teachers were less reliable than those done by parents. The children were rated by their respective class teachers (N=9) who showed different response sets and styles in rating the children. They also did not seem to know the children well enough. This could be attributed to a large class strength (30 to 40 children in each class) which could have limited the potential interaction of the teachers with the children. The discrepancy between the responses of teachers and parents is reflected in the low correlation coefficient ($r = 0.38$, $p<.05$) between the first 16 identical items of the two forms. Parents were found to be quite objective of their children's behaviour pointing out both positive and negative aspects.

The other three independent variables, i.e. maternal satisfaction with management of emotions, time and finance did emerge as predictor variables. This could be indicative of two possibilities. Either these variables are not important predictors of SEBA of children or further methodological refinements are needed to yield the results. For example, instead of the four categories used for scoring maternal satisfaction with time management, one could use a method that combines a wider repertoire of actual strategies used by the mother and their satisfaction with these strategies. The actual time management strategies reported by the mothers (refer Table 9.1) could form a basis for this.

With reference to management of emotions, there may be a need to further unpack the score category "feel negatively but copes" as the coping strategies reported by mothers were diverse in nature, e.g. giving quality time to the child, long term self-need etc. (refer Table 9.1). A further categorization of these strategies may yield different results *vis-à-vis* the SEBA of pre-schoolers.

The t-testing results revealed that the employment status of the employment status of the mother, and gender of the child did not influence the SEBA of children. This supports the previous findings that the employment status of the mother does not influence the child adversely as reported by Spitze (1988), and as found in a number of other studies. It should be noted that in the present study children of employed and unemployed mothers had similar pre-school experience — a factor not controlled for by many previous studies.

A moderate negative correlation between career orientation of the mother and the SEBA of children on the teacher rating scale indicates that as the career orientation of the mother increases, the SEBA of the children decreases. These results however need to be interpreted with caution as the teacher rating form may not be a reliable indicator of the SEBA of children. An explanation however may be given in terms of presence of role conflict in Indian employed women (Kapur, 1970; Mane, 1983) which may have implications for the adjustment of the child.

There were no significant gender differences in children's SEBA on either parent or teacher rating forms. Although this contradicts the research in western context which indicates negative gains for of employed mothers and girls of unemployed mothers, it is possible that for the Indian middle and upper middle class, this phenomenon does not hold true. The reasons for this need to be explored. One possible reason could be that the above findings are of earlier years. Social changes taking place could be making a change in the perceptions of maternal career pursuits by both mothers and children and of even society at large.

In sum, it could be said that family-related factor like perceived maternal satisfaction with support could mediate the impact of maternal employment on the child. This supports the ecological theoretical perspective of Bronfenbrenner (1979). The results also reveal that there was a high incidence of maternal satisfaction with support and that the employment status and the gender of the child did not influence the SEBA of the child significantly. From this study and with certain contemporary evidence, it may be concluded that in the absence of family stress, and presence of maternal satisfaction with support for child care, the developmental outcomes for children are not adverse. However, more substantiation of these findings is necessary with more refined means of getting at the reality.

10

CHILD CARE QUALITY AND PLAY AND INTERACTION PATTERNS OF CHILDREN

— *Vrinda Datta*

Introduction

Child care services can be looked at as support services for women so that she can carry on her tasks of homemaker, mother and earner. It could also be seen as supplementary care provided through health, nutrition and pre-school programme. In India, the need for child care services is emphasized in several documents. Efforts have been made to provide child care through Factories Act (1948), Plantations Act (1951) and the Government of India scheme for crèches of children of working and ailing mothers (1975). However, the services provided are inadequate and of poor quality (Rane, Naidu and Kapadia, 1986; Paranjpe and Ambosta, 1981; D'Souza, 1979). The two government documents (1988, 1989) National Perspective Plan for Women and Shram Shakti have emphasized the need for developing more child care services.

The choices in child care services for urban middle class working women are very few. Even for those mothers who are willing to pay, services are not easily available and if available are not always satisfactory in terms of quality. Children of these working women spend most of their waking hours in child care setting and therefore what happens in day care becomes crucial in determining the course of development of children. Some forms of child care are in existence today. The most common forms of out-of-home child care are day care centre and family day care. In a day care centre, a group of children are taken care of in a separate premise with specially appointed staff. In the family day care, usually a woman takes care of a few children in her own home.

There have been innumerable research studies on the particular issue about day care and children. Belsky (1984) identifies waves of research. In the first wave, the principal issue was whether day care had detrimental effects on children's development. Studies during this period were in areas of impact of child care on intellectual, emotional and social development of children. In reviewing researches in this wave, and responding to the question 'Is day care bad for children?' Belsky suggests that it may seem appropriate to conclude that it "usually is not bad and certainly does not have to be, but it can be so". In view of this conclusion, the attention of scientists and policy makers has shifted from day care impact, to the conditions of care that produce different consequences.

And so started the process of defining the quality of child care programmes. In defining quality, not only subjective values come into play but the definition often varies depending on who is defining it and what aspect of the service is being considered. Cryer (1998) identifies structural and process quality features as important aspects of defining quality in a child care programme and that they are closely linked to each other. The process variables can have a direct impact on the well-being and developmental outcomes. Thus adult-child interaction, child-child interaction, the availability of space, materials and routines all make up the process variables and are important aspects of measurement of quality. The structural variables are equally important because they provide the framework for the process variables (children's experiences). Thus staff-child ratios, group size, staff training are the important variables to be looked at in defining structural factors or quality.

The eighties has seen researches of the second wave which worked towards establishing what the best conditions for such care are or what are the conditions to be avoided. Investigations (Kontos and Fiene, 1987; Howes, 1983; Gunnarson, 1978; Goelman and Pence,

1987), have focused on the effects of day care quality on children's social and cognitive development. The study by Phillips, Scarr, and McCartney (1987) contrasted pre-schoolers who attended eight Bermudian day care centre which varied widely in quality, (with day care quality being defined in terms of physical facilities, types of activities and teachers' language to the children) found that children who were in poorer quality day care had significantly poorer language development than those in higher quality programmes. They also found social competence to be similarly affected by day care quality.

When process quality is higher, children appear happier, have closer relationship with caregivers and perform well on thinking and language tests (Peisner-Fienberg and Burchinal, 1997). Further, the staff education and training in child development are linked with high quality care (Whitebook, Phillips and Howes, 1989).

Howes and Olenich (1986) also reported more problematic development in toddlers who attended poorer quality day care. When quality was defined in terms of adult-child ratios, level of teacher training and staff turnover, children in poor quality programmes were found to be less compliant and less likely to use self-regulatory behaviour. In one of the largest National Day Care Study of the US (Ruopp, Travers, Glantz and Goelman, 1979), it was found that group size exerted significant effects on day care children —Pre-schoolers who were in smaller groups had more active adult involvement and spent less time wandering aimlessly around the room than did children who were in large groups.

The Cost Quality and Child Outcomes Study (1999) done in four states in USA found that many centres were providing poor to mediocre care and that there was a positive relationship between quality of care and child development. Further higher quality care was found in states which had stricter child care licensing norms.

Researchers are now working towards establishing whether quality of care (defined through global summary measures, or through examination of specific structural features) is related to the interactive behaviour that can be observed in the care setting. Some researchers are already saying that overall quality and specific structure quality dimensions are predictive of the emotional tone of the centres and the context of interaction observed in child care settings. The US National Child Care Staffing Study (Whitebook *et al.*, 1989) found that structural features of care were linked with the emotional tone of interactions. There was a more positive emotional climate in family day care settings in which group size was smaller, caregivers were better trained and physical space was better organized for the care of children (Howes, 1983).

Similarly using either summary measures of quality or structural dimensions as indices of quality, studies have reported that higher quality of care is associated with the enriched content of caregiver – child interaction. For example, Goleman and Pence (1987) found a global rating of care quality to predict more time spent in informational activities in both centre and family day care. Berk (1985) reported a significant association between caregivers education and time spent in enhancing children's verbal development. It has also been seen that higher quality child care appears to involve a relatively higher proportion of one-to-one caregiver–child interaction and a relatively higher proportion of time spent by children in interactions with caregiver rather than in solitary play with peers (Vandell and Powers, 1983).

Thus research studies have time and again shown that group settings for young children have the capacity to enhance the development during the early years and also after the child has entered school. Early childhood environment has both kinds of impact – immediate and long-range. Bronfenbrenner (1979) identifies adult behaviour as questioning, instructing, respecting, raising, reinforcing that will create interaction that will make children task oriented. The extent to which caregivers and personnel, in their interactions with children, engage in behaviour that stimulate, sustain and encourage task oriented activities on the part of the child will influence the development of children (Bronfenbrenner, 1979).

Bronfenbrenner (1979), however, points out that most of these researchers lack an ecological orientation. The studies all show the differences in outcomes, but give very little information about the settings themselves or the events that take place within them. He indicates that the features of a setting that have been identified as most consequential for behaviour and development; molar activities, interpersonal structures and roles — are rarely ever mentioned. He further adds that the studies on day care omit information about the child's behaviour in the situation of everyday life — at home, in the day care centre and on the playground; thus we do not know the activities that the child does or does not engage in, the role and relationships in which he becomes involved with other children, and other adults. From an ecological perspective, these are the domains in which experience in day care and pre-school is most likely to have a developmental impact. Thus the concern now is, if different settings have different developmental effects, then these effects should reflect the major ecological differences between the settings as revealed by contrasting patterns of activities, roles and relations.

This chapter compares the two environments family day care and day care centres and the differences therein and how they contribute to children's development. It also determines the quality of day care setting and gauges/observes its impact on development. The author attempts to develop indicators of quality by ascertaining what factors of a child care environment are crucial in determining the play and interaction patterns.

Objectives

- To understand the characteristics and quality of child care services.
- To study the differences between children's interaction and play patterns in day care centres and family day care and specifically of high and low quality Family Day Care (FDC) and Day Care Centres (DCC).
- To develop indicators of quality.

Operational Definitions

1. *Group care (GC):* A setting where a group of children of working parents are taken care of for the whole day.

2. *Family Day Care (FDC):* A private home providing care for five or more children for a period of five hours or more.
3. *Day Care Centre (DCC):* An organized service for the care of children away from home in a special premise with appointed staff and at least 12 children in care.
4. *Quality (Q):* The overall quality of a child care in terms of organisation, personal, care given, routine followed, materials/ equipment and activities of children as measured on the rating scale and categorized as High Quality (HQ) and Low Quality (LQ).
5. Structural Features :
   (a) *Group size:* The total number of children cared for in the day care centre/family day care.
   (b) *Age mix*: The number of age groups (infant, toddler, pre-schooler, school-aged) present in the day care/family day care.
   (c) *Adult-child ratio:* The number of children divided by the number of caregivers was calculated as adult-child ratio.

Identification and Selection of the Sample

The Children: The children in toddlerhood depend a lot on the environment and adults in the environment for stimulation and being actively occupied which helps them enhance their capabilities and therefore progress developmentally. In the child care setting these factors play an even more crucial role as children are spending most of their day time in this setting. Thus children in the age group of 1½ to 2½ years became the subjects of this study. The other reason why this age group was chosen was because children after 2½ years of age usually attend regular nursery schools and it would be difficult to differentiate the impact of nursery school and that of child care.

The Setting: The second aspect in sample selection was what child care setting should be selected. The first step, therefore, was to identify family day care (FDC) and day care centres (DCC). Since all FDC and DCC under study would be non-aided by government, there were no possibilities of obtaining any kind of listing. Thus the snow ball sampling method was used. The investigator herself had conducted survey on Family Day Care, had conducted training programmes for caregivers, and also started a Day Care Association. Due to this a large list of family day care and day care centres was available. The second source from which more addresses were obtained was from students who had done their master's thesis on child care services. Thirdly, colleagues, relatives, neighbours, friends all were approached to give addresses of any day care used by them or known to them. This yielded a large list of family day care and day care centres. From this, separate lists were made of family day care and day care centres. These were further separated according to their geographical location.

Criteria for Selection of a DCC: For a day care centre to be included in the study,

1. The DCC must have a child in age group of 1½ to 2½ years.
2. There must be at least 12 children in the setting.
3. The study child must be in the DCC for at least five hours everyday.
4. The study child has been in this DCC for at least past 4 months.

Criteria for Selection of FDC: For a family day care to be included in the study,

1. The FDC must have a child in the age group of 1½ to 2½ years.
2. There must be at least four children in the family day care.
3. The study child must be in FDC for at least five hours.
4. The study child has been in this FDC for at least past 4 months.

Fig. 10.1 : Steps in Sample Selection

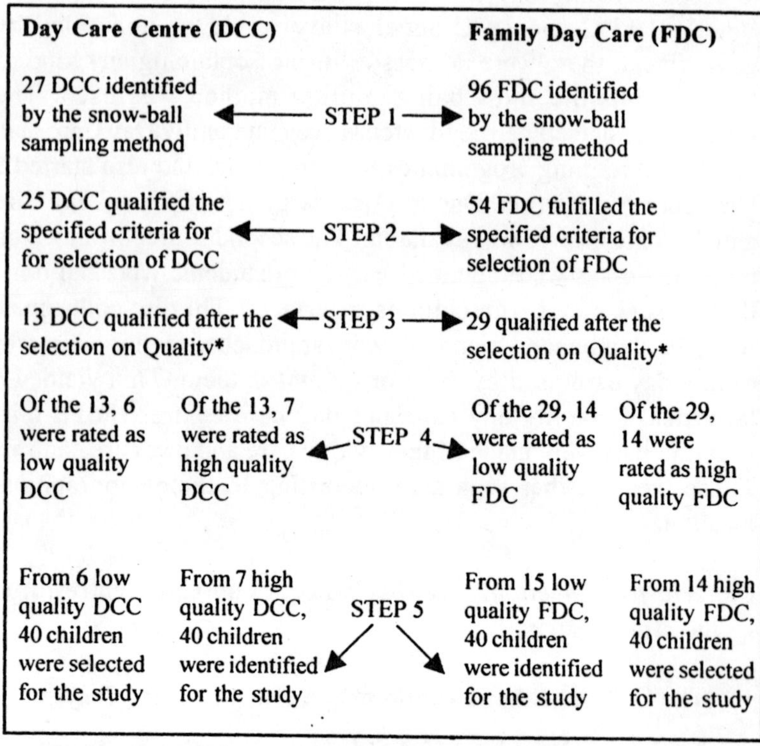

* For measuring quality the FDC and DCC were observed on rating scales developed for this study. Based on the total scores, FDC and DCC were divided as high quality, medium quality and low quality. Since two contrasting groups were needed, only low quality FDC and DCC and high quality FDC and DCC were included in the study.

During the first visit the FDC and DCC were evaluated on the set criteria. Those who fitted the required criteria were now to be evaluated for quality so that the FDC could be divided into high quality FDC and low quality FDC and similarly the DCC were to be divided into high quality and low quality.

Quality as Criteria for Selection

For getting the global rating of quality the Day Care environment rating scale and Family Day Care environment rating scale was developed on the lines of Early Childhood Environment Rating Scale developed by Harms and Clifford (1980). The Day Care Centre Environment Rating Scale developed for the study consisted of 21 items spread in 4 sectors: Organisation (5 items), personal care and routine (5 items), furnishing and equipment (4 items), and activities of children (7 items). Inter-rating reliability yielded the score of .67. Similarly the Family Day Care Environment Rating Scale was developed which consisted of 20 items spread in the same sections of day care scale. Here too inter-rating reliability was done which was 0.76. The scale requires that a day be spent in the setting and observations made on the items of the scale. Each item was marked on a seven point scale. Since description for observations were given, it facilitated in keeping uniformity in rating the child care setting. The rating scale helped in dividing the FDC and DCC as (1) low quality, (2) medium quality, (3) high quality. Since two very contrasting groups in terms of quality were required only the low quality and high quality groups were selected for the study.

Thus all FDC and DCC who fitted the first criteria were then observed for determining the quality. If any DCC and FDC obtained a score which categorised them as medium quality they had to be dropped because only low and high quality child care were to be included in the study. The children in these places were then observed for two days on the various scales that were developed for observation.

The process of identification of centre, applying the criteria and evaluating the quality was done till forty children in each group were identified. Thus the final sample had (1) 40 children High Quality Day Care Centre (HQDCC), (2) 40 children Low Quality Day Care Centre (LQDCC), (3) 40 children in High Quality Family Day Care (HQFDC), (4) 40 children in Low Quality Family Day Care (LQFDC).

Since (See Fig. 10.1) the study was looking at the effects of day care environment on children's play and interaction patterns, detailed information about the child care environment was needed. Though the rating scale gave the global quality of the environment, still factual information about child care was essential to know to know the specific factors having an impact on children's development.

The interview guide for caregivers in day care centre and for caregivers in family day care were prepared separately as some questions were very specifically meant for the day care setting or family day care setting.

Observations on Children

Tools for Observation

To bring out the social behaviour of children and to understand the emotional tone of their interactions three areas of observation were done (i) play pattern, (ii) peer interactions, (iii) adult-child interactions.

The observational method was found to be most suitable for the study. Further, it was felt that time sampling was an important method to conduct the observations. This method helps the observer to fix attention upon selected aspects of the behaviour stream as they occur within uniform intentions. The length, spacing and number of intervals are intended to secure representative 'time samples' of the target phenomena (Mussen, 1970). Usually descriptive categories are coded in advance for quick and precise judgements on the field and later efficient scoring. The observer when observing in a group setting can proceed from child to child through the scheduled intervals of times.

In a day care setting the environment will play the most crucial role in determining the child's social skills as depicted through the play patterns. The Piaget-Parten Play Scale (1932) and Carolle Howes' Scale (1980) were looked at. However since in our centres generally very little play was occurring with materials it was difficult to use Piaget-Parten's play scale. Though the Carolle Howes Scale was useful in terms of categories but the distinction between two categories like parallel play and parallel play with mutual regard were difficult to find. Thus it was felt that both these scales cannot be used directly and a new scale was developed having the following categories — (1) non-play, (2) onlooker/transition play, (3) solitary play, (4) parallel play, (5) social play, (6) group play. The non-play got the lower score of 1 and group play, a score of 6.

The second area for observation was peer interactions. All interactions could be categorized as positive and negative. Based on observation in centres and review the following categories were made. In positive interaction there were (a) giving positive attention/approval, (b) personal acceptance, (c) submission, (d) token giving, while the categories for negative interaction were non-compliance, interference, derogation and attack. The same categories were evolved for adult-child interaction. In both observation scales category of no interaction was also put.

The scoring pattern for peer interactions and adult interactions is same. For the 'no interactions' a score of zero. The negative interaction as one and positive 2.

Process

A total of three days were needed for data collection in every child care setting. However, if large number of children were present more days were spent in that particular child care, especially day care centres. Observations for every child were to be done on (1) Play patterns, (2) Peer interaction, and (3) Adult interaction.

On the first day of the visit to the child care, the quality was determined and the particular FDC or DCC was included if it was of a high or low quality. On the same day caregivers were interviewed to get further details about the day care/family day care.

Before starting observations, the caregiver was told that the observer was noting down children's activities and therefore she should follow her regular routine. Secondly, since one day had already been spent by the researcher in the setting, children were not disturbed by the presence of the observer. The observations were done when children were most active that is 9:30 a.m. to 12:30 p.m. The investigator before starting observations discussed with caregiver the routine of the study child so that the activity period of child may be fully utilized for observations. Observations were done on children on three aspects — (1) play patterns, (2) peer interaction, (3) adult-child interaction. A sequence of observations was followed, i.e. play pattern was followed by peer interactions followed by adult interaction. Between each of these observations a gap of at least 3 minutes was maintained.

Every child was observed for two days. This was felt essential as sometimes on a particular day the child's mood, or experiences of that day may interfere with his behaviour. To get a correct picture of his behaviour, two days of observations were felt necessary. Between a child's first observation and second observation of a child, a gap of at least 8 minutes was maintained. If there was more than one child to be observed, then one observation of the child was followed by one observation of the next child on all three areas (play, peer, adult). Sometimes in the day care setting more than 4 children have to observed as such times groups of children were made and observation of one group was completed before the second group was taken up. Each observation was done for two minutes and then recorded in the specified categories.

Results

Characteristics of Child Care (Family Day Care and Day Care Centres)

Family Day Care: Most of the caregivers who were running family day care were middle aged (average 42.7 years), married and educated up to SSC. Half the caregivers started family day care because of financial reasons while the other half started on the request of neighbours and friends. The family day care centres have been functioning for an average period of 7 years. There were about 9 children in family day care with a trend towards more children in older FDC. Basically no admission criteria were followed except some who felt age was an important consideration. The average charge was approximately Rs.250 p.m. Very little money was spent by caregivers on toys and materials for children. With earning of about Rs. 1800 not even 10 per cent was spent on children directly (in terms of toys, food, etc.). On an average FDCs were functioning for 9 hours.

Day Care Centres: The day care centres were either run by voluntary organizations (4), Mahila Mandal (4) or individuals (5). They were functioning for 9 years. Generally there were 5–6 staff members. Basically the staff was not much educated. The average schooling of the helpers (*Ayahs*) was 7 years of schooling. Only 6 of them were trained while they had experience of as many as 7 years. The remuneration was low (Rs. 500 p.m.). With average number of children being 26, the staff child ratio comes to 1: 6. All day care centres had children from 6 months to school age children. There were no admission criteria. About 1000 sq.ft. was available for the day care centres with only half centres having outdoor space. All centres functioned for about 10–11 hours.

Quality

Results showed that except for two items on the rating scale, family day care and day care centres had no differences in scores on the rating scale used to measure quality. It was found that the day care centres had significantly higher score than family day care on the item of staff qualification (t = 1.92, P < .10). There were many more staff trained with DCCs than the FDCs. With regard to group size, it was found that the FDCs had a higher score that DCCs. Generally the group size of the DCCs was very high (26) and therefore very often the space staff and materials were inadequate and hence DCC scores low on group size attributes. The results also showed that in terms of the child activities generally the score was very low as most FDCs and DCCs did not have many or varied activities with children.

Regression analysis indicated the effects of variables like years of functioning, staff qualification, age-mix, adult-child ratio and group size. The analysis showed that 39 per cent of variation in quality was explained by these variables. (F value 4.6, significant at 5% probability level). The results also showed that group size was very significant determinant of quality. Similarly, it was also seen that staff qualification was a correlate of quality and that for every unit increase in score on staff qualification there was 5.3 units increases in quality score. It was interesting to note that years of functioning had a negative relationship with quality score, i.e. longer years of functioning had a negative relationship with quality score, i.e. longer years of functioning did not reflect a positive impact in terms of quality of services. The variable age mix and adult-child ratio did not significantly explain the variation in quality score.

Table 10.1 : Regression Coefficients Explaining Impact of Structural Features on Quality

Independent	*Regression Variable**	*T - Value Coefficients*	*Significance of T*
Years of Functioning (YF)	-.55316	-1.862	.0707
Staff Qualification (SQ)	5.30301	3.005	.0048
Age Mix (AM)	.42415	.198	.8438
Adult Child Ratio (ACR)	1.17747	.464	.6456
Group Size (GS)	5.39625	2.601	.0134
Constant	34.41532	2.661	.0116
R^2		.39126	
F Value		4.627	

* Dependent variable = quality score

Type of Care and Children's Development

Play Patterns : In FDCs there were 11 per cent children who had majority of the 15 observations as non-play while among the DCCs group only 2 per cent had this. The FDC children generally had at least 2-3 observations in non-play category while the DCC group did not have any observation in the non-play category (t value 2.45 $P < 0.5$). In all other categories of play, the scores were near equal in both the groups and thus the scores on total play patterns are also not varying among FDC and DCC children.

Adult-Child Interaction: More FDC children had positive adult - child interaction scores than DCC children. There were 55 per cent children of FDC who had maximum positive interactions (majority of the 10 observations) while only 45 per cent of the DCC children had most interactions as positive interactions. The average score of FDC children on positive interaction was 9.2 while for DCC children it was 7.5. This difference was found to be statistically significant ($t = 2.08$ $P < .05$). Similarly the scores of FDC and DCC children for negative interactions with adult were significantly different (Table 10.2). These results clearly indicate that for the age group 1½ - 2½ years, the FDC helps in getting the opportunities to interact with adults, whereas in the DCC setting with large number of children and large staff the young child (1½ - 2½ years) may find it difficult to relate to adults. Also, in DCC as many adults are present over the whole day, no one adult may feel responsible to interact with children and therefore children do not experience adult - child interactions at all.

Peer Interactions: It was found that there is no differences in the peer interaction patterns among FDC and DCC children.

Quality and Development of Children

Play Patterns: It is interesting to note that there was a very significant difference between the High Quality (HQ) child care (family day care and day care centre) on the total score for play patterns ($t = 3.13$, $P < .01$). This finding clearly shows that the environment of HQ and LQ child care are very different. The differences could be in terms of space materials available or number of children using play materials etc. The differences between high quality and low quality child care were also seen in non-play score ($t = 3.65$, $P < .01$.) onlooker play ($t = 1.96$, $P < .10$). These differences in categories of play between high quality child care children and low quality child care children shows that basically, low quality child does not give opportunities to child for play. Both forms of play, non-play and onlooker/transition imply that neither children nor their playmates were doing any thing. The HQ child care children and LQ child care children did not vary much on their score on parallel play and solitary play. The HQ child care children indulged more in

Table 10.2 : Difference in Adult-Child Interaction Scores between Children in FDC and DCC

Items on Rating Scale	*Family Day Care Average Score*	*Day Care Centre Average Score*	*T-Value*	*Level of Significance*
Positive adult child interaction score	9.27	7.50	2.08	.05
Negative adult-child interaction score	.62	1.00	1.85	.10
Total adult child interaction score	9.90	8.8	1.78	.10

group and social play. This may be because adults participate in play or that there are toys and materials which encourage group activities.

Adult-Child Interaction: In the HQ child care the average score of children on positive adult-child interaction was 9.7 while LQ child care was 7.0 which was statistically significant (t - 3.2, P < .01). Also, the HQ child care children score higher on negative adult-child interaction score than LQ child care children. Thus it shows that HQ child care provide opportunities for children to interact with adult. In high quality child care availability of adult for interaction and situations for interactions (routine care and play) gives scope for more interactions. The total score of HQ child care children (10.75) is also statistically (See Table 10.3) different from LQ child care children's score (7.5).

Peer interactions: The HQ child and LQ child care had significantly different score of positive peer interactions (t = 3.32, P < .01) negative peer interaction (t - 2.49, P < .01) and also total peer interactions (t = 2.90, P < .01). The HQ child care had an average score of 14 while the LQ child care had an average score of 10 on the peer positive interaction score (Table 10.4). 82 per cent of the

Table 10.3 : Difference in Adult Child Interaction Scores between Children in High and Low Quality Child Care

Items on Rating Scale	*High Quality Child Care Average Score*	*Low Quality Child Care Average Score*	*T-Value*	*Level of Significance*
Positive adult-child interaction score	9.77	7.00	3.32	.01
Negative adult-child interaction score	1.06	0.56	2.49	.01
Total adult child interaction score	10.76	7.56	3.86	.01

LQ child care had some negative interactions. Thus HQ child care encourages peer interactions but due to availability of some materials the children do have negative interaction which is equally important.

Effects of type of Care and Quality on Development of Children

Play pattern: The results indicated that high quality family day care (HQFDC) and high quality day care centre (HQDCC) both offer opportunities for higher forms of play like group play and social play. Due to lack of adult involvement, space materials and large number of children the low quality family day and day care centres do not provide appropriate environment for children. Among the HQDCC and HQFDC, the significant differences in score ($t = 1.75$, $P < .10$) implies that HQDC offers more opportunities for group play than HQFDC. Non-play was mostly observed in LQFDC.

Adult-Child Interaction: The HQDCC and HQFDC and LQFDC children had significantly higher scores with regard to adult-child interactions than LQDCC children. The results have shown that with family day care environment, the quality does not make much difference to adult-child interaction scores but within day care environment, the quality has a greater impact.

Table 10.4 : Difference in peer interaction score between children in High Quality (HQ) and Low Quality (LQ) Child Care

Items on Rating Scale	*High Quality Child Care Average Score*	*Low Quality Child Care Average Score*	*T-Value Significance*	*Level of*
Positive Peer interaction score	13.30	10.32	2.90	.02
Negative Peer interaction score	.950	.225	4.48	.01
Total Peer interaction score	14.25	10.68	3.56	.01

Peer interaction: The most opportunities for peer interactions were given by HQDCC.

Quality Variables and Child Development

Regression analysis was done to see the impact of group size, adult-child ratio, age-mix, caregiver education experiences, training on the scores of children on play patterns, adult-child interaction and peer interaction.

The results showed that 25 per cent variation in peer interaction in explained by these variables. The findings also show that adult-child ratio, age mix and group size have a negative relationship with peer interaction scores. This implies that as adult-child ratio, age-groups in care and group size decreases, there will be increase in peer-interactions.

Similarly, about 16 per cent variations in adult-child interaction were explained by the above variables. The negative relationship with respect to adult-child ratio and age-mix indicates that with decrease in these two there will be an increase in adult-child interaction.

Conclusion

The study has demonstrated that high quality child care is better than low quality child care on all aspects namely organization, personal care and routine, furniture and equipment and activities with children. The quality of all child care services was quite low in terms of activities with children, schedule of activities/routine and hygienic practices. These aspects have to definitely be improved upon by both FDC and DCC, both of high and low quality.

The study has brought to light that group size has greater impact on quality than adult child ratio. This was in agreement with studies like Ruopp. *et al.*, (1979) which showed that caretaker child ratio cannot by itself be the principal mechanism for guaranteeing benefits to children, although it may be an important indicator of staff burden. It also showed that effects of staff-child ratio were small compared to group size.

Thus if children are to have an environment responding to their needs, then group size should be maintained at the appropriate level. With appropriate group size, the caregiver will be spending more time interacting with children. It would also help children to take more interest and participate in activity and also indulge in behaviour that involves language such as considering, contemplating, contributing ideas, giving opinions and cooperating. It is possible for a caregiver in small groups to be more stimulating and encouraging and appreciative of initiatives. It was also found that group size had a negative impact on the adult-child interaction, that is with increased group size there was decrease in positive adult interactions and increase in negative interaction or 'no interactions'. Thus as group size becomes smaller adults will engage in more task-oriented activities and spend less time in management and control activities.

Similarly, for peer interactions the results showed that group size would affect the peer interaction and that if there are more children per adult, the greater the peer interaction. Even though at toddler age, children are dependent on a one-to-one relationship with an adult, the group care environment with a large number of children and high adult-child ratio forces children to be more with peers.

Another important factor which determined the quality of child care was staff qualification. Serious efforts must be made to enhance the capabilities of caregivers through training and other forms of interaction. It is not enough to rely on the experience of the caregiver. This research has demonstrated that education and training play a more important role than past experience. Training must be made easily accessible and methods like in-service and on site training etc. should be availed. It is important to keep in mind that training must not only help caregivers develop a professional identity and appropriate skills but it should also provide appropriate recognition for training received.

Unless appropriate incentives are offered to child care workers such as higher wages, service benefits, and better work environment, child care workers will not be motivated to take an interest in their work. As Whitebook *et al.* (1989) have pointed out that these factors contribute in improving quality of child care.

The results have shown a reciprocal relationship between years of experience and quality. This finding has tremendous implications and breaks the myth that experience is a good teacher. In spite of many years of functioning, crucial factors that are important to improve quality have not been identified. The main reasons are that there is a general lack of knowledge on the part of authorities and no development of literature by academicians and professionals based on which caregivers can understand their problems and attempt to solve them.

The second important reason for this finding could be the 'burnout syndrome' which the caregivers may experience after years of functioning in the same setting and same job routine. Thus efforts by professionals and academicians in disseminating information about child care issues seems to be imperative.

The findings reveal that children who had higher adult interaction had less peer interaction. But then the alarming finding was that many children who had no adult interaction had no peer interaction at all. Besides, half the children with no adult interaction indulged most in non-play or onlooker play. It is important that all child care maintain a balance in the kinds of experiences that children have. Children of 1½ - 2½ years definitely need more adult attention and encouragement to do varied and stimulating activities. Efforts must be made to develop appropriate programmes for all ages so that children do not spend the six to eight hours in the day care in boredom and lethargy which is bound to influence their later life.

Children in FDCs had more interactions with adults than children in DCCs did, irrespective of the quality of FDC/DCC. This finding is similar to Golden *et al.* (1978) who reported that FDC programmes were superior on amount of social interaction and individual attention children receive from caregiver and in the degree of positive social-emotional stimulation provided by caregiver to children during noon-meal. For the young ones (1½ - 2½) FDCs proved to be a better environment as it encourages adult-child interaction which is so essential for these children who depend on adults to stimulate and guide them in their development. Efforts should be made to encourage the development of more family day care services.

With regard to play activities, it was found that children in DCC and particularly HQDCC had higher forms of play like social and group play while the LQFDC children indulged in non-play and onlooker play. In general because of more space, more materials and a large age mix, children in DCC had more varied and higher forms of play while the FDC children had lower forms of play. Efforts have to be made to make the caregiver realise the importance of providing toys and materials for young children. The caregivers must spend a part of their earnings in buying new materials regularly for the children. All caregivers should also encourage children to use these materials rather than try to preserve them.

This study has taken the first step in studying child care from an ecological perspective. This study has helped in understanding every aspect of the two day care environments, namely family day care and day care centres. The study has helped in knowing the similarities and differences of these settings and also the quality variations within these settings.

For the toddlers, it appears that family day care helps them to get individual attention and a positive social emotional climate compared to day care centre. It is unquestionable that quality is the most important factor whether we have family day care or day care centres. Efforts to develop quality programmes have to be made by all stakeholders. The researcher should help identify the features of quality programmes; the government should work out policies and strategies to develop quality control measures; and the practitioners must look at the quality indicators in their programme, so that child care services work towards and reach the ultimate goal of supporting holistic development of child.

SECTION-IV

Towards Quality in Child Care

11

TRAINING PERSONNEL FOR CHILD CARE

— *Mridula Bajaj*

> *She has 4 children aged 10, 8, 4 and 2. The two older ones go to a municipal school nearby. The younger two stayed with their grandmother, who passed away recently after a brief illness. Kasturi is determined to ensure that her older children continue with their schooling. But what does she do with her younger two? She cannot afford to leave her job —the earnings are too precious and needed to sustain the family of six.*

Thousands of women across the country are in a similar plight, facing the same dilemma:

To stay at home and look after their young children.

Or

To work and feed and sustain the family's needs.

Many women find solutions out of the limited options they have. They get their older children to look after the younger ones either by not enrolling them in school or withdrawing them from school – an all too familiar scenario! Others just lock out their young children or lock them in their homes and carry on with their "jobs". A fortunate few are able to work from their homes on piece meal contracts and try to do justice towards their multifarious home and child rearing responsibilities.

Deprived of the love and essential care that is its due, the young child is left in the hands of children who themselves need support or have to fend for themselves. In a study conducted by Samuel and Arulraj (1995), it was found that the average age of child minders was as low as four years and that 58 per cent of the children under sibling care were 2 years and less. It was also found that 56 per cent of sibling care givers did not attend school and 81 per cent of the above were girls. One wonders if this is what is promised to the child within the constitutional framework of India.

Under the Convention on the Rights of the Child, ratified by India in 1992, every attempt will be made to ensure the Survival, Protection, Development and Participation of the Child. And yet about 60 million children in the 0-6 years age group living below the poverty line continue to be deprived of their rightful share of care during their childhood.

What is Child Care all About?

It is all about providing an environment that will ensure the protection and development of all children, providing every child an opportunity to develop to his/her full potential. It is about giving attention given to all aspects of development so that the child grows up to be a confident, competent individual, with self-respect and high self-esteem.

Early child care thus involves the provision of a safe, protective, nurturing and stimulating environment where children can grow. It thus aims to provide a substitute for the family and the nurturant, enabling environment similar to that available within the institutional framework of a family. Early Childhood Development theories testify to the crucial importance of the child's earliest years. There is ample evidence to show that healthy children who have experienced good early development and learning programmes are more likely to remain in primary school and achieve their life goals. Early learning therefore forms the essential base on which any later learning is built. The Warangal experiment, whilst reinforcing the above provides a clear direction by indicating that a multi-pronged integrated approach is necessary and has been found to be more efficient in promoting the development of women and children (Kielman *et al.*, 1983).

Need for Training

Quality childcare thus assumes significance as it addresses a host of problems associated with poverty. It can be attained only through a conscious investment of human and material resources. Commenting on the Mobile Crèches programme in "In Sight, on Site", Swaminathan points out that "low cost" in material terms can achieve little without "high cost" in human terms, though the latter may often be undervalued. Current policies and budgets have not prioritised ECCE, nor looked at the grave implications of this low priority. Khullar (1991), identifies "gaps in training" as one of the most important factors responsible for the shortcomings in existing day care services.

Early childhood care is visualised as a specialised activity which requires specific skills and competencies to carry out a range of multiple tasks for children in the age group 0-6 years living in difficult and deprived conditions. This can be attained through a planned and systematic programme with theoretical and practical inputs.

Since early childhood is a critical period, it is not advisable for state policy to leave childcare to the happy coincidence of finding a wise and caring caregiver. Instead it is vital that the issue of training receive high priority as it is training which will enable a child care worker to provide development care as opposed to just custodial care. A conscious orientation and training for skills in early child care is essential to sustain quality of services at the field level.

Box 11.1 : The Mobile Crèches Programme

The Mobile Crèches Programme

Set up in 1969 at Gandhi Darshan, in response to neglected, migrant children at construction sites, Mobile Crèches has grown into a leading resource in Early Childhood Care and Development.

Apart from providing day care services to children of working mothers at slums and construction sites in the three cities of Delhi, Mumbai and Pune, the programme has expanded its activities to include training, research, documentation, community communication and advocacy.

Its Core Day-care Programme Comprises

- Physical care: cleaning, bathing, feeding, putting to sleep
- Supplementary nutritional interventions: breakfast, lunch and snacks (approx. 500 kcal/day)
- Preventive and curative medical care: doctors' visits, growth monitoring, vitamin supplements, first-aid, hospital referrals, special health camps and check-ups
- Educational and recreational facilities: stimulating activities, organised games, well designed pre-school programme, school enrollment and tutorial support.

* To run an integrated programme comprising of such diversified activities catering to children from birth to 12 years, requires an intensive preparation which is acquired through a comprehensive in house training programme.

The Child Care Worker

The provision of developmental care can be made possible by a person

- who is aware of *what* the needs of children are
- who knows *how* to address those needs
- who understands *why* it is important and critical to address those needs.

Box 11.2 : Key Components Underlying a Successful Training Programme

The Child Care Worker should be equipped with	The Child Care Worker is expected to carry out activities related to
1. Basic **knowledge** and understanding of – – principles of child development – health and hygiene requirements – teaching methodology. 2. **Skills** to – interact and play with children of different age groups – organise activities and materials for the children – look after their children's physical, nutritional needs – maintain excellent interpersonal relations with the children and community. 3. A positive **attitude,** which is reflected in all aspects of work – – respect for the children – dignity of labour – ability to find creative solutions to problems – value and self-respect for one's own work.	(a) Look after children, feeding, cleaning. (b) Ensure basic standards of hygiene and sanitation for the children. (c) Ensure basic preventive and curative health care for children including immunization. (d) Play and interact with the children, and provide them with age appropriate equipment and opportunities to learn and develop. (e) Provide readiness skills for children through the play-way approach – for entry into formal school. (f) Identify children with special needs. (g) Communicate with and create awareness on critical issues in the community to sustain the impact of interventions with children. (h) Adopt simple systems and procedures to manage the day-to-day functions of the child care centre/facility

A training programme is successful when certain *basic principles of adult learning are adopted consciously as part of the training strategy.*

The trainers should ensure that the training is *learner centred* –

— it takes off from what the trainee already knows.

— it actively involves the trainee in the learning process (on-the-job).

— the theoretical framework and knowledge is periodically reiterated (through repeated workshops).

— the training process is participatory with space for learning through sharing of experiences and discussions.

— the techniques adopted engage the maximum number of senses to ensure lasting retention (through use of different media).

— the curriculum has scope for flexibility within the larger parameters, that is, training syllabus and curriculum is responsive to trainee needs and specific field situations.

— there is space for undertaking mid-training evaluation, based on assessment and feedback from the trainees; specific components may be introduced or repeated within the larger training objectives.

The specifics for *ECCD Training* include a high component of skill development, information and building up of empathy and respect for the child living in deprived conditions (Box 11.2). Keeping the above principles as a guideline an outline of a specimen training programme has been presented below. (Table 11.1).

The programme is designed to enhance competencies in the areas of Knowledge, Skills and Attitudes of the trainee.

This is only an illustration and may be modified to respond to the objectives of training, trainee profile and needs of the target group.

Extracurricular Inputs

It has been observed that even the most comprehensively designed programme fails to deliver because certain key inputs are not taken into account whilst conducting the training. These are *invisible, non-articulated, intangibles* which are the backbone of any successful training programme. It forms part of a *sensitised communication skills package* which a trainer incorporates into his/her training, but which is not documented or manifested in any official reporting. These are:

Table 11.1 : Curriculum for the ECCD Training Programme

Topic/Head	*Topic*	*Assignment*	*Media/Method*
Knowledge	1. Understanding the need for a crèche/child care • Communicating need to community • Awareness of Child Rights	• Visit to a crèche/child care centre • Community visit • Conducting a survey/ assessing child care needs	• Focused group discussions • Visits • Role play • Any other medium that the trainer finds useful in the context
	2. Characteristics of children 0-3 years • Developmental Milestones • Indications of normal growth 0-3 yrs.	• Controlled observation of children of different age groups at play • Solitary • Group • With toy (specified), • Outdoor • Learn to weigh/measure growth	• Observations • Focused group discussion • Case studies • Slide/tape show • Flash cards • Charts
	3. Understanding children's needs. • Physical care at different stages • Ante natal care (pregnancy) • Delivery • Post natal care	• Interacting with women with prepared questions on pregnancy • Visit to a nearby dispensary • Collection of materials/ drawing of materials necessary for delivery Mother's feeding	• Film • Slide show • Group discussion • Songs/*Katha* • Local medium

Contd . . .

Table 11.1 Contd . . .

Topic/Head	*Topic*	*Assignment*	*Media/Method*
	4. Nutritional Needs • Imp of lactation • Imp of weaning • Supplementary nutrition and feeding • Feeding schedules, preparation and delivery of food	• Recognising malnutrition • Preparation of weaning foods • Identifying pictures of food items in all groups	• Flash Cards • Special medium • Songs • Group discussion • Role Play
	5. Health related needs/ requirements • Need for hygiene and cleanliness • Systems required to maintain cleanliness • Common childhood illnesses and household remedies • Malnutrition. Growth charts recognising malnutrition and ways of overcoming it • Immunisation — schedule • Motivating community	• Collection of photographs to identify common illnesses – polio, malnutrition, deficiency diseases etc. • Observing the behaviour pattern of a malnourished child in the community • Making an immunization schedule	• Local medium • Songs • Mother/community meetings

Contd . . .

Table 11.1 Contd...

Topic/Head	*Topic*	*Assignment*	*Media/Method*
	6. Stimulating activities for fostering all round developmental activities for sensorial development • Physical development • Cognitive development • Language development • Social and emotional development • Preparation and development of low cost indigenous materials	• Making of toys • Organizing activities • Puppets • Use of local material • Creating and using new teaching materials	• Group discussion • Practical demonstration • Audio visuals
	7. Understanding Children with special needs • Children at risk • Their special needs • How are they identified • Need for referral	• Collection of children's pictures at risk • Identification and recognition	• Group discussions • Role plays • Case Studies • Audio visuals

Contd...

Table 11.1 Contd...

Topic/Head	*Topic*	*Assignment*	*Media/Method*
Skills	Organisation of day care centres • Materials required • Setting up/storage of materials • Time management — why it is important • Planning a day schedule • Keeping of records/ inventories of stores.	• Setting up of work areas • Working out ways of maintaining records • Attendance • Immunization • Ways of keeping track of time • Making of a clock	• Group discussions • Exposure visits — different models
Attitudes	• Role and responsibilities of a child worker • Rights of Children • Gender awareness Modernity/Traditionalism • Awareness regarding superstition and social differences • Eliciting community support and working towards sustainability • Importance of body language gestures, etc.	• Planning and acting out a play on specific issues	• Group discussions • Role play • Puppetry • Case studies • Flash cards

- *Providing Support and Building-up of Relationship with the Trainees:* Very often the trainee, who comes from an underprivileged, deprived background is faced with conflicting situations which need to be resolved before the positive impact of attitude building can start. A nurturant supportive environment enables to build on the confidence and self-esteem of the trainees, for example, (if we are expecting the trainee to incorporate the basics of gender equality in his/her work, it is important to facilitate sensitivity orientation to gender discrimination or exploitation that he/she may be facing in his/her life at a personal level).

- *Enhancing the Confidence of Trainees:* Providing opportunities in the field through specific assignment increases confidence and competencies. This is consciously included as part of the training process wherein trainees are observed and provided feedback, for example, conducting a household survey, planning and organising celebration of festivals etc.

- *Exposure to Wider Issues:* Awareness of national programmes and priorities on related topics contributes to understanding the rationale and importance of ones contribution. It provides value to ones role as an ECCD worker. The linkages to other issues provides the context — "Why" is it important to do what one is doing? "What" is the impact of one's contribution? "This should be part of an on-going training effort and should not be seen as contributing to knowledge alone. In fact it takes on the role of a motivational tool and thus merits serious and focused consideration in the design of a training programme.

- *Exposure to Different Models:* An *exposure to alternative* models of community development programmes is enlightening. The enriching experiences bring creativity and innovation to one's work and should be consciously incorporated.

A successful ECCD training programme thus takes into account the following techniques of imbibing knowledge, skills and attitudes.

Box 11.3 : Successful Techniques in ECCD Training

1. **Exposure** - an initial orientation to the field programme with limited participation.
2. **Experiential learning** - field training under the guidance of experienced staff and consists of acquiring basic skills, procedures and routines through a process of drilling, repetition and role modelling.
3. **Rationalisation** - through workshop sessions and discussions to arrive at an understanding of the different components of the programme.
4. **Problem solving** - an on going process to bring in creativity and innovation.

Organising a Successful Training Programme

The following key elements need to be kept as basic guidelines whilst planning for training in ECCD to ensure its success.

- *The objectives of training* need to be identified and stated in terms of specific measurable goals, for example, the trainee will gain knowledge in (specify), the trainee will be able to run a *balwadi.*
- *Time and resource allocation including budgets* should be spelt out clearly.
- *Coordination with the administrative department,* at the initial stages of planning should be ensured to eliminate any dysfunctional elements. An understanding of the training process only helps to sustain and complement the training activity.
- Adequate attention needs to be given to *communication techniques and strategies* as these help to translate plans

into action. They help to establish the link between the trainer and the trainee. Techniques and methodology will vary according to clientele and topic, but should be within the participatory and experiential framework.

- Training should be designed so that there are spaces for physical activity, involvement, sharing and discussion. It is important to have stimulation of more than one sense concurrently as research has established that better learning and retention takes place through adoption of such an approach.
- Thus care should be taken to ensure that the *resource persons*/trainers believe in the above guidelines and *have adequate knowledge and field experience.*
- There should be space for flexibility in the design. There should be feedback to make the training more effective and responsive.
- *Evaluation strategies* should be built into the design to consolidate feedback from trainees, which can strengthen future training.

Model of a Successful Training Strategy

The following example, illustrates how all the factors discussed in the preceding section have been adopted and put into practice. The fact that the Mobile Crèches training expertise is highly appreciated and in demand proves that the strategies can be adopted and replicated in different situations as varied as urban slums, remote villages or challenging circumstances.

Training Child Care Workers at Mobile Crèches

Building on its rich, grassroots experience of providing day care services to the underprivileged children, Mobile Crèches has developed a comprehensive programme to train workers to work in harsh conditions and care skilfully for neglected sections of children. The training programme is the product of a dialogue between the sound principles enunciated by academicians and practical experience demonstrated by fieldworkers. A cadre of trainers has been developed over a period of time, where field experience and first hand knowledge are extensively used for training.

Mobile Crèches at present provides training in ECCD at three levels.

1. A regular Bal Palika Training Programme for girls who have passed Standard X to prepare a cadre of professionally competent and skilled child care workers.
2. Training and organisational support to other organisations engaged in providing ECCD, through customised, need packages.
3. Building local capacities in ECCD through training of non/semi-literate women as a means of empowering women and extending outreach of ECCD.

Mobile Crèches firmly believes that the specific skills required for quality child care can be built up provided the trainee has a positive attitude and willingness to work hard. The internalisation of values and principles leading to a high degree of discipline is developed through a regular process of discussion and reflection.

1. **The Bal Palika Training Programme** has a clearly outlined syllabus on integrated child care, which focuses on all aspects of ECCD, that is, the crèche, the balwadi, NFE and community awareness and communication. About 70 per cent of the learning takes place through placements in the field and the remaining takes place through workshops to build a sound theoretical base.

   Training is invariably participatory in nature. Field experience through regular sharing assumes prime importance. Thus group discussions and innovative strategies form the core elements of training.

2. Through its **Extension Training,** Mobile Crèches extends and shares its expertise with other organisations. These programmes are not pre-packaged, but are need-based depending on the specific requirement of the client organisation. Therefore, they vary in frequency and duration, but here too the core belief of participatory non-didactic approach is adhered to. Challenges arising out of the extension training experiences include

    - providing training to trainees with different literacy competencies,
    - developing material for training on new topics that arise from the needs expressed by the trainees,
    - designing appropriate training for workers playing multiple roles of balwadi workers, NFE teacher and remedial education teacher,
    - developing appropriate child care programme for organisations with special needs and constraints such as within a prison.

3. Mobile Crèches firmly believes that **training for the non/semi-literate community women** is essential for a country where 90 per cent of its 12 crore working women work in the unorganised sector. The need for crèches is great and therefore, the employment possibilities for child care workers are immense. The challenge lay in modifying the Mobile Crèches training process creatively, to ensure that learning takes place for trainees who do not have formal education and therefore are not literate.

This training has evolved to a stage where the trainers through constant innovations are in a position to undertake training for different groups of women in varied situations and locations. The training is largely activity based. Principles of child development are imparted through innovative techniques like games, drawings, discussions and activity based assignments (Box 11.4).

Khalakdina (1995) in her case study "In Sight On Site" attributes the development of "the work ethos, the team spirit, the willingness to take on multi-purpose tasks, the positive attitude towards doing things — in a nurturing environment" to the intangibles, of the unique hands — on training of Mobile Crèches.

Box 11.4 : Key Elements of Mobile Crèches Training

- Well designed and comprehensive syllabus.
- Training duration —one year Integrated child care training.
- Field placements — 20 days/month.
- Workshops — 4 days/month.
- Tutorials — 1 day/month.
- Exposure visits to other organisations — 15 days.
- Trainers have rich and long field experience and therefore understand problems and offer practical and pragmatic solutions.
- Covers the entire range from antenatal — 12 years.
- About 70 per cent of the training takes place through field placement where learning takes place through exposure, role modelling supportive practice and close supervision.
- Fieldwork is reinforced through training workshops wherein practical learning is reinforced and supported by sound child development principles and theoretical inputs.
- All field assignments are closely related to and complemented by the theoretical inputs given during the training workshops.
- Has a high component of community communication techniques built into each topic.

ICDS Training for ECCD

Today ICDS is one of the world's largest outreach programme for ECCD. It constitutes the major convergent interface between disadvantaged communities and different sectoral programmes of the government.

A very significant resource component of ICDS is the training of its workers and partners at various levels. It is through these human resources that the programme vision is realized and strategies implemented. The training aims at strengthening the capability of its functionaries to understand the community situation, need, resources, perceptions for improved programme, quality and sustenance.

Looking at the ICDS training model, what strikes one immediately is the total absence of role modelling and field placements during the training tenure.

The training comprising largely of workshops is conducted by specialists or resource persons who have had no exposure in the field. The result is a highly academic and theoretical input, imparted in isolated packages, with little or no relevance to the field realities. The training is conducted in centralised regional institutions, which do not take into account the local variations. The result is a patchy field programme of poor quality which reflects the confusion and lack of clarity of the anganwadi/child care worker.

Recently the government has felt the need to reorient the curriculum to the changing needs of the community and strengthen the methodology and pedagogy of training and to develop appropriate training strategies to implement social development programmes effectively.

UDISHA (1997), the national initiative for quality improvement in training of child care functionaries of ICDS has been launched recently with the assistance of the World Bank. UDISHA (1997) aims at making training more participatory, field based and locally relevant. It envisages a key transformation training child care functionaries through a holistic approach to the young child. The new child-centred curriculum is being structured along the lifecycle and development continuum of the child by pulling together different sectoral interventions in a rights perspective.

The ICDS Programme can pick up some of the key elements responsible for the success of the Mobile Crèches Training Programme — mainly field based trainers, a high component of supervised field placement and employment of more participatory techniques. This may involve a major shift from current practices and may have implication for changes in policies. With the vast geographical areas and regional variation that ICDS training has to respond to, it may well have to adopt a more flexible and decentralised approach —with the core syllabus being built upon by local trainers.

Thus the course content, assignments, practical sessions may vary from region to region, responding to local needs and in this lies the key to preparing well trained ECCD personnel.

A comparison of the two different strategies employed in the training of child care professionals illustrates all too clearly, the key ingredients contributing to the success of the training. How these can be adopted and implemented at a national level, is a challenge that can best be resolved by decentralising the training process, and making allowances for diversity and flexibility. Feedback from the field needs to be given its rightful share in the planning and designing of training. These and other issues of concern are taken up at length in the following section.

Training for ECCD – Issues of Concern

Child care is considered to be a job requiring minimal skill which can be picked up in the course of growing up. If no special skills are required for child care, then no training is required either. This attitude is responsible for the low priority given to training of ECCD workers.

The lack of appreciation of the need for training has affected the development of child care services in the country profoundly.

The factor of training is crucial to the improvement of quality of Early Child Care Programme, because it is in the hands of the field worker that objectives get translated into outcome. However, there are a few issues that need to be addressed, before one can hope for a quantum leap in ECCD programmes, both qualitatively and quantitatively.

Advocacy for ECCD

Recognising the importance of ECCD is a critical factor which may indirectly impact the quality of training. The creation of a need for adequate and appropriate Early Child Care has to be enunciated by all the stakeholders –primarily the parents, women's groups, peoples' movements and employers. However, it has been observed that the need for ECCD is not felt or expressed by the people who would benefit by the provision of such services, only because these have not been in their repertoire of experiences. People at the bottom most rung of the ladder, do not feel in control and are in no position to make demands or expect access to their entitlements or justified demands. Most of them work in the unorganised sector and are therefore not members of any organised group or movement.

What therefore emerges is an urgent need to create awareness of the beneficial impact of ECCD, on the young child? It is important for parents to realise that the very survival and development of the young child cannot be left to chance and that *they have a right to demand appropriate child care either from the employers or from the government.*

At the other end of the continuum, it is also important to actively lobby with the principal employers, and the Government for the provision of adequate and appropriate child care services. This will have a positive impact on the development of good training strategies and techniques.

Increase in demand for ECCD therefore has a direct relationship to the professionlisation of child care. The casual approach to accepting low quality child care will be superseded or replaced by a demand for trained and skilled child care workers.

Understanding ECCD

It is important to come to a broad understanding of what constitutes 'good' ECCD. The various constituents comprising child care need to be spelt out clearly and a common understanding of the different component of quality child care will bring clarity and focus in designing the training programme for ECCD.

Instituting Parameters for Quality Training

Once the parameters for quality early Child Care are recognised and accepted, an understanding of *quality training* will emerge. It is important to identify the critical components of a good training programme with room for local variation and innovation.

Certain key components have been listed, but these are neither exhaustive nor mutually exclusive.

(a) **The Trainer** — It is imperative to recognise the role of the trainer. The value of any training programme is enhanced manifold by the presence of a skilled and competent trainer – *a person who has had vast and varied field experiences, who has been exposed to wider issues and who has a good conceptual understanding of ECCD.*

The trainer should be sensitive to and understand the socio-cultural background of the trainees. He/she should be receptive and be willing to listen and interact rather than instruct and react. This would help the trainer to accommodate to the changes and demands made during the training sessions. The trainer should be conscious of the importance of body language or the non-verbal aspects of communication and ensure that both the verbal and non-verbal cues are consistent. It is important that the trainer possess the ability to establish a bond with the trainees, communicate effectively in the local dialects and be adept at using a variety of techniques to get the message across. Very often, the trainer has to take on the role of a model, possess and display high standards of work and behaviour thus initiating the process of absorption of attitudes and values. A trainer who is mobile, offering advice guidance and skill up-gradation on the spot and on the job is highly desirable. The ability to assess and evaluate critically at all times with a positive attitude is an important skill which helps the trainer to turn every situation into a learning experience.

The need to update one's knowledge and keep abreast of the latest technology and skills is essential for a good trainer. Thus a conscious orientation to and planning for a training of trainers has to be kept in mind: exposure to specialised courses of repute and opportunities for interaction with professionals and specialists should constitute a part of the trainers' career schedule.

(b) **Opportunity for Field Based, Practical Training** — Training which is on the job and rooted in experiential reality is more likely to be meaningful and enduring. It is important to provide opportunities to the trainees for on-the-job training, to put into practice what has been learnt and to be given a feedback and guidance whilst at work. Field placements offer an opportunity for role modelling and skill development through repetitive carrying out of tasks and assignments. The development of appropriate values and a positive attitude so essential when working in isolation and in difficult situations takes place when one is provided with hands-on training.

It also offers the trainee an opportunity to clarify doubts and find solutions to practical field based problems. On the job training saves effort and the need for repetition, and is thus more cost effective in the long run.

(c) **Training apparatus/strategies** should include adequate provision for monitoring, supervision and professional guidance, but care should be taken to ensure that these are diversified, flexible and multilayered to respond to diverse needs.

Diversity in Training

In the designing of any training programme it is important to keep in mind the need for responding to local needs, to having a component of flexibility built in which can incorporate the basics and yet be able to customize to specific requirements.

Status of Child Care Workers

Khullar (1991) in her review of child care services in seven states, comes to the conclusion that child care "unfortunately is a low status occupation and its members are still invisible to society". All the seven case studies reported that the remuneration and working conditions of the child care workers were found to be shockingly poor. ICDS workers are still referred to as volunteers, who therefore are only eligible for an honorarium as opposed to a salary for a well-defined job and its corresponding duties. The inadequate remuneration is largely responsible for the poor quality of child care services in the field.

Secondly, the child care worker feels isolated in the field. The cursory visits by the senior staff take on the role of supervision and checking rather than offering support and guidance. No attempt at problem solving is made nor is any importance given to institutionalising systems of formal feedback of the experiences of child care workers.

All this leaves the child care worker in a situation where working conditions are dismal and tough, and there is total absence of adequate support in the form of material goods, equipment or even guidance. Compounding and adding to the dismal scenario is the lack of opportunities for growth and advancement. All this reflects the poor status accorded to the child care worker and unless their contribution is recognised as meaningful, there is every danger of the situation remaining *status quo* and child care workers being deprived of their justified role as a dignified worker.

In short, as Swaminathan states: "Low Cost cannot be achieved through low salaries." Child care is a skilled job and must therefore be given its due.

Recognition

Accordingly recognition to training programmes for child care or institutions which provide quality training is important as this will provide the much needed support for quality child care. It will add value to the training and enable trainees to take pride in their training and get good jobs with adequate remuneration. At present there are very few ECCD training programmes which are recognised or affiliated to institutions. Some post-graduate, highly specialised courses are available in some universities, but none offer ECCD as part of the vocational stream.

High quality, widely recognised and acclaimed training programmes offered by NGOs and field based organisations find it difficult to sustain their efforts due to lack of financial support and problems in getting affiliation.

Training for ECCD for Semi-non-literate Community Women

The delivery of ECCD services by the government has been planned through the ICDS system, which has been observed to be unimodular and incapable of responding to specific, regional variations.

The answer to universalising access to ECCD lies in developing community capacities for ECCD. The challenge lies in harnessing the untapped potential of millions of women across the country and imparting appropriate training to them. Literacy or competency in the three Rs is not an essential requirement for ECCD and therefore is not a limiting feature for developing community based child care workers.

What is required urgently is a skill based field oriented training programme which relies heavily on the oral tradition and other innovative techniques of communication. The challenge lies in developing trail blazing efforts which will guide others to replicate such experiments to make ECCD accessible to every child in India.

12

THE CHILD CARE WORKFORCE

— *Vrinda Datta*

Introduction

Early childhood programmes are considered essential input for child's development. Trends show that investment in early childhood programmes enhances the efficacy of investment in education, human capital formation, fosters social development and therefore reduces later costs on welfare. However, there are different viewpoints/opinions on what constitutes early childhood programmes. In India there is a clear divide between early child education and early childhood care programmes. The main goal of early childhood education programme is education and very often have the downwards extension of primary curriculum. For the disadvantaged children, these programme are generally integrated to provide for health, nutrition and education. The child care programmes emerged from the needs of a large number of women in the workforce. However, there has been very little attention for its expansion and quality. One of the most important dimensions of quality early childhood programmes is the workforce. Studies point out that the staff is the most significant factor in determining the quality of early childhood programmes (Whitebook, Howes and Phillips, 1989; Datta, 1994; Moss, 2000).

Child care workers with appropriate skills and knowledge are of the most essential ingredients of quality child care programme.

Yet there appears to be a complete disregard for this section of workers. It still prevails that any woman can do this job, since a woman is a mother and that since she has cared for a child, she has sufficient knowledge and skill to take care of a group of children. However, being a child care worker is much more. This chapter looks at some research studies which have tried to understand the child care worker. It identifies key factors that impact the job performance of child care workers and analyses how to address the issues through policy formulation. The chapter covers issues related to workers in child day care programme.

Who Constitute the Child Care Workforce?

In India, child care workers are associated with the government or state sector, private sector and voluntary sector. The services within these sectors are many and vary in the way they are organised catering to the needs of both education and child care. The private sector provides early childhood programmes under the nomenclature of play groups, nursery schools, pre primary centres and kindergarten. Children as young as one-and-half years are introduced to such programmes. While there may be no separate training for teachers in various programmes, all are called 'teachers'. The child care services under the private sector are run as day care centres and family day care. Here again there are few, who may be trained as 'crèche workers' as there are few opportunities for training. The voluntary sector has a pre-school programme for 3 -5 years old and is run by voluntary organisations mainly for the disadvantaged. Similarly for child care services, the voluntary sector has group care services with crèche workers in the workforce. The state run early childhood programmes are generally integrated with emphasis on health, nutrition and education. The state programme has its own training inputs for both its pre-school and child care programmes. Thus such diversities in programmes call for a closer look at the workforce in these programmes.

(i) *The Person:* The child care workers are generally women. The tasks related to care and education of young children is considered an extension of the mother's role. Secondly, many families still believe in allowing women to work in 'safe' occupations and therefore, doing a job in an early childhood programme clearly pointed out that they are in this job because it is convenient, it is in the same neighbourhood, and it has short hours of work (Datta, 2001). Many of the workers of the government programme who interacted with the community felt that they enjoyed the respect and recognition that this job had given them. Thus there is an intrinsic reward which seems to be important in determining the child care workers continuing to be in these jobs. The voluntary organisations run early childhood programmes in the community and very often view it as a women's empowerment programme as girls and women from the community run these centres and find a new avenue for income generation.

(ii) *Family Background:* Across many states, the child development workers were generally 35-40 years of age (Datta, 2002; Shanmugavelayuthan and Nirmala, 2004). Most of them come from nuclear families with generally four to five family members. Only 11 per cent of the families were single earner families, most others (58%) were two-earner families and 25 per cent were three-earner families (Datta, 2002). It was seen that the per capita income of the families of child development workers was Rs.1561 per month. The child development worker seemed to contribute 43 per cent to the family income. However, the Tamil Nadu study on anganwadi workers showed that 80 per cent of the families had indebtedness. The husbands of child development workers were generally in low paying jobs and many were casual labourers. Thus the child development worker comes from low socio-economic status, but they are not women in distress or complete poverty who depend only on this income for their livelihood.

(iii) *Education and Training:* Generally child care workers are educated till Standard X or higher secondary. However,

> today in cities like Mumbai (Datta, 2002), Chennai, Shanmuganvelayuthan (2004) one does find some graduates in the government programmes like ICDS. It was also seen that women who take up family day care for 6-10 children in their own homes, were educated up to high school or junior college. It is interesting to note that workers with high school degrees run the programmes much better than the higher qualified workers and the explanation offered was that probably when a person is highly qualified, she may feel that her skills are underutilised or not appreciated (Gupta, 2001). Along with education, competence development of the early childhood workers has to be addressed through training.

Training for early childhood workers is mainly pre-service and in-service programme. Muralidharan and Kaul (1993) suggest that there is a need for a multi-model programme to fit the needs of the variety of early childhood programmes. Besides training has to be made context relevant and with a lot of continuous inputs through refresher courses. Some of the significant training programmes of child care workers have been the five weeks crèche training programme for crèche workers working for the crèche scheme of the Central Social Welfare Board, and the training programme run by NGOs like Mobile crèches.

The five weeks crèche workers training programme blends theory and practice and yet the competencies of staff related to child development were found to be inadequate (Pandit, 1993). Pandit also pointed out that the duration of training was related to competencies and those undergoing a longer duration of training were at a higher level of competency than the group which attended short duration programme. Thus she suggests that the competencies to be developed through training programmes should be associated with the specific tasks to be performed. Since the present training is not adequate, there needs to be effective supervision and monitoring systems to help enhance the performance of the worker. Pandit also suggests that it is important to determine the minimum level of education necessary for different levels of child development workers as this will determine the working capability in curriculum building and methodology adopted in the programme.

Mobile crèches provides training to equip the child care workers, for instance, *Balwadis* and crèche workers with formal learning in child development but also emphasise on developing sensitivity to needs of young children. Mobile crèches believes that quality training can happen when factors such as experienced and well qualified trainers, diversity of training are all taken into consideration. The training programme evolved through evaluation and monitoring and with lot a field inputs, stands today as one of the most effective training programmes in child care. The organisation has contributed towards developing many individualised training programmes for voluntary organisations and the government.

Though the ICDS is not a day care programme, it has the component of health, nutrition and stimulation for children less than three years. As it is an integrated programme, the child development worker needs knowledge and skills to reach the mothers and those children in the age group 0 - 6 years. Though training has been an integral part of the ICDS programme, it has been seen that the job performance of *anganwadi* workers is far from satisfactory (Datta, 2001). Issues regarding ineffectiveness of training are related to the content, training and its quality. Many changes have emerged in the training modules. Holistic approach to the child is reflected in the new child-centred curriculum that is structured along the lifecycle and development continuum.

Overall, the training of early childhood workers is far from adequate. Firstly, even though government efforts are seen for an in service training for early childhood workers, the private sector makes no demands to have trained teachers. Besides, some of the private programme which claim to have trained staff, have teachers who are trained by unprofessional training centres where one sees short duration training, lack of appropriately qualified and experienced staff and poor support through continued training inputs. Besides, due to poor funding most training centres, whether government or private, have little curriculum material.

Work Environment

Features

The adult worker in the child development programme will work efficiently when certain aspects of structural and process variables are taken care of. Three factors which directly impinge on effective functioning are group size, staff child ratio and age-mix. A large group size along with a mix of all age groups creates situations where the adult worker is forced to select tasks which are serving the immediate and urgent needs of children. Observations in such centres showed that older children faced a lot of restriction in their movements and activities when infants were also present in the centre. Constant instruction to these children was, "Be quiet, don't run around"! It was also noticed that the toddler group was the most neglected, while the pre-schoolers with their language skills and mobility were able to attend to their needs themselves or ask for help. The toddlers were not able to get attention because of their limited abilities of language and movement (Datta, 1994).

In terms of staff-child ratio, it was seen that the average staff child ratio across all types of programmes was 1 : 9 (Datta, 2002). This means that irrespective of the age group combination in the centre, the caregiver has to give attention to nine children! Such a ratio prohibits adults from giving quality care to the children. In such situations, if one infant is being fed, there are eight other children who are on their own waiting in a non-stimulating environment.

Visits to various child development programme reinforces the point that structural features play a very important role in increasing the efficiency of workers and reducing staff burden. Many centres are located in unsafe areas due to which workers have to restrict children's movements and at times children (large number) are forced to stay indoor all day. In Mumbai, the centres in the slums have no water facilities and at times due to lack of storage facility, workers bring water from their homes or neighbourhood.

Similarly, we find that lack of space gives little scope for workers to conduct all the activities. Moving from one activity to another means cleaning and clearing up after every activity. Therefore, very often workers do not have a variety of activities. Even toys/materials are not given as taking them out and putting them away requires a lot of effort. Non-availability of materials and equipment add further barriers in functioning. Many child care workers use this as an excuse for not doing any activities with children, while there are a few who think hard and try to be creative to find ways and means to occupy children. Similarly, as cleaning up after food or serving it requires time, many workers asked children to bring *dabbas* so that they do not have to clean up. Such an approach will not create child appropriate programmes. To work with these difficulties and yet create a quality programme calls for a lot of effort and creativity on the part of worker. But with limited exposure, poor training and lack of guidance many workers find easy methods of coping with the situation.

Skills

Child care workers have generally completed high school and more often than not, they are untrained and are workers in programmes which require multiple skills. Some of these skills they acquire on the job and some of the skills they never acquire instead, they learn how to avoid doing those tasks which they find so difficult. In both NGO and government programmes, the worker has a lot of administrative responsibilities, such as filling up records and registers, asking for supplies, special reports related to children regarding growth, health, nutrition and progress reports (monthly, quarterly, yearly). Some of these require only time but not much skill, for instance, maintaining an attendance or stock register. But when it comes to child related records, they require skills of observation, knowledge regarding child development and also skills to measure child's weight and so on. Much of these records are used for evaluating the impact of the programme and also in planning further interventions for children. The records become a measure of the worker's performance. So very often, workers put in incorrect data to cover the flaws in their centre. Such acts impact the measures taken to enhance the programme and often fail to address the real issues that need to be tackled.

The second area in which skills are needed is health and nutrition. Child care practices, particularly in infancy, impact on the child's well-being and therefore due attention needs to be paid to the skills. It has been observed that child care workers find ways to do these tasks which consume less time. It has been seen in some centres that many toddlers are fed by one adult from one plate at the same time, or that adult holds infants in postures where the child is forced to gulp the food or he/she will choke. One question whether the workers evolve easy methods to function after a few years of experience. However, inculcating the right skills of feeding a child are important and constant observation and guidance is required. The same goes for hygienic practices which are related to health and nutrition skills. Pandit (1993) and Datta (1993) both point out that inadequate knowledge of workers related to immunisation and health reduces the efficacy of the programme.

The effectiveness of a programme is determined by the actual practices. It is important that a teacher evolves a programme, and develops skills to conduct the programme, but the skills have to go beyond this. He/she has to be observant to see which children do not participate and how do draw them into the group, how to create a good combination of activities with children's ideas, individual choices and structured activities. The child care worker needs skills to recognise changes in children over time, and identify areas that need further stimulation. Pandit (1993) found that in spite of the training, crèche workers were poor on aspects related to child development and infant stimulation. Further Datta (2001) pointed out that even though the child care workers knew of certain activities, they could not associate them with particular aspects of development. Therefore, the programme paid little attention to the development of children.

The third major area regarding skills is working with groups such as colleagues, parents and management. This aspects gets least inputs in training but is a very important dimension for the success of the programme. The efficiency of programme implementation depends on interpersonal skills which one has to evolve. In every centre there are generally three levels of workers supervisors, teachers, crèche workers/helper. It has been observed that very often in government programmes, hierarchy comes in the way of sharing tasks, and also in creating a positive environment in the centre. How the staff approach parents when the child begins life in the centre, the types of interaction they have everyday, the planned interaction and intervention are serious aspects of the programme that determine the child's adjustment, participation and progress in the programme. Interaction with parents has shown that they always feel threatened by the centre staff because they always have complaints about the child and if there are no complaints there is little or no communication. But again talks with caregivers reveals that parents feel that once the parents leave the child at the centre, they do not want to know anything, they are casual in their attitude and at times believe that it is their right to get the services. Communication between parents and staff is necessary to maintain continuity in the routine.

Work Status

The low status of child care workers is reflected in the low earnings, poor benefits and very few opportunities for a career growth. The study on Maharashtra child care workers (Datta, 2001) showed that the workers in government and NGO sector are paid as low as Rs. 500 p.m. while the private centres earn about Rs. 2400 p.m. the NGO salaries are slightly better than that of government workers but on the whole, most workers get less than minimum wages in spite of being better educated than average labourers. Very few organisations had a system of yearly increments. Some workers have been on the same salary for five to eight years. The jobs of child care workers are not of a permanent nature. There are no benefits such as provident funds or pension. So in spite of working for many years they do not have any savings to fall on back at the end of their career. There are also no health insurance which adds to their problems. Thus with low salaries and no benefits the child care worker is in indeed in a very sorry state. Added to this are the other aspects of work conditions. Most caregivers work 8 -10 hours a day. Observations have shown that when the group size is large and the adult-child ratio is high, the workers do not get time to eat their meals at a fixed time nor do they get any respite from the continuous chores that they have to do. Most centres do not allow for an yearly vacation. Workers get a few days causal leave. In some places they are allowed to take compensatory off.

Considering these work conditions, to expect motivation, commitment and efficiency is asking for the impossible. Studies have shown that the quality of work is dependent on appropriate work conditions and salaries and therefore this dimension of work conditions will also have to be addressed if one wants to enhance workforce effectiveness.

Steps to Move Ahead

In the context of Structural Adjustment Programme and New Economic Policy, the state's investment and also concern for the social sector has been reduced. However, without political will and commitment there can be no change expected in this field. It is high time that government recognises that child workers form a large part of the workforce and due recognition to them as workers should be established. Secondly, the workers need to be recognised as professionals. First of all it is expected even in the ICDS programme, that the workers are high school graduates and that they undergo specialised training. These two factors should make it possible to call it a 'profession'. If these factors are recognised and attended to, then three major issues need to be addressed. Each of these factors have to be worked on simultaneously.

- It is imperative that child care funding needs to be increased.
- The government cannot talk of empowering women without looking into the issues of child care.
- Funding is needed not only for expanding the outreach of programmes but also giving enough funding to improve quality of programme by giving appropriate wages and adequate per child costs to run quality programmes.

The second major area where reforms are needed is regarding the work conditions of child care. In the era where low wage labour market is readily available, the number of women available to do child care jobs for a very low remuneration is high. Because of this, there never seems to be pressure from any front for increase in wages. Honorary workers do not get a decent salary or benefits such as increments, provident fund. It has to be understood that appropriate salaries and work conditions make significant differences to the workers' performance and therefore, the quality of a programme. It is not only the government but many NGOs who seem to make innocent women feel that the organisation has no money so how can they afford better salaries?

Training of child care workers is an important factor. Datta (1994) has shown that teacher's training is a more important factor impacting quality than just years of experience. Training is not declared as 'essential' for child workers and therefore be it government, NGO or private organisation, not much importance is given to having trained staff. We need accredited training institutes who will impart quality training which will ensure better work performance. The whole idea of need-based, community-based training sounds good but this so called flexibility has resulted in training which brings no betterment of knowledge and skills of child care workers. Another major hurdle in training is the lack of uniformity in training inputs received. The training programme needs to be accredited so that only training programme which give the right input sustain in the field.

Along with all this, it is very important to improve the overall quality of a child care environment in terms of the space, materials, staff-child ratio and group size. All these factors determine the workload of the worker which has to be above fatigue level. We need to ask ourselves whether we need regulation to evolve some standards for programmes.

One of the significant findings of Datta (1992) has been that long years of functioning of a centre do not ensure high quality because most centres work in isolation and therefore continue to function at a level of quality for a long time, the reason being lack of opportunities to interact and learn from group interactions. As an answer to this, networks started emerging. Networks help to enhance knowledge and skills of the members through interactions and information sharing. Secondly, since all who network have a common agenda it becomes easier to identify the common issues and find solutions by way of advocacy, policy recommendations and training inputs. Many examples of local, regional and national networks can be seen, for example, Shishu Palak Vrind of Baroda, FORCES – Tamil Nadu and National FORCES. However, it has been very difficult to influence the policy and programme. But with global pressure on government to address Child's Rights, one can be optimistic and hope to find early childhood programme get their due recognition.

In conclusion, the issue of child care workforce cannot be looked at in isolation. The whole field of early childhood programme needs serious changes – in programme practices, funding, workers' status and strong network so that the early childhood programme are recognised as important for the future of the nation.

13

ENSURING QUALITY IN CHILD CARE

— *Vrinda Datta*

The Indian Context of Child Care Provision

Services to provide care for children with working/employed parents have not been much on the political agenda in India. From the beginning early childhood programmes in India have been a part of the welfare programme. Many government documents have emphasised on the need for creation of crèches to guarantee child's education and protection. The industrial legislation like the Factories Act (1948), the Plantations Act (1951), State Migrant Workers Act (1980) lay down that crèches are a statutory obligation. The setting up of Central Social Welfare Board (1956) gave a new impetus to the balwadi and crèche programmes through their grant in aid programme. Recommendations were made by many committees like the working group on employment of women which recommended setting up child care centres as part of minimum needs programme and the committee for the status of women in India which felt there was complete neglect of women in the unorganised sector. The National Perspective Plan for Women (NPP 1988) recommends the provision of crèche services to all women in organised and informal sectors and so also the Shramshakti Report (1989) of the National Commission on Self-employed Women and Women in the Informal sector which emphasised that child care was major cause of concern of women in the unorganized sector and child care services must be created in the interest of the mother and child.

In spite of such strong recommendations by various bodies from time to time the status of child care programmes has remained dismal. The problems of children are inextricably linked with the entire gamut of social political ailment of the country (Prasad 1997; see this volume also). Over the past decade there has been hardly any visible change in the outreach of child care programmes. In the context of the New Economic Policy (NEP) and Structural Adjustment Programme (SAP), the social, political and economic environments are found to affect the child's survival, growth and development. Unemployment, income loss and rising prices of essential goods could impair the family's capabilities for providing for children's development. Also, reduced budget allocation for child development programmes, could have serious consequences for children's development. Saleth (1992) has identified three mechanisms by which NEP and SAP would impact investment in child development programmes. Reduction of investments through the elimination of certain components of programme or the scaling down of the size/coverage of the child development programmes. It has been seen that two major programmes that is grant-in-aid programme of Central Social Welfare Advisory Board for nutrition programme and even Balwadis programme have been completely stopped. Also, there is no expansion for a long time in grant-in-aid crèche scheme. This was rationalised by saying that there is duplications of programmes and the national ICDS programme will give the required inputs as it is being universalised. However not many changes are seen either in the budget allocation to each ICDS project or in the expansion of ICDS. One can also observe the changing pattern of financial sources for child development investment. One trend emerging is that the government is encouraging NGO and international organisations to participate to a large extent, in the name of partnership and secondly, there are changes in the State-Central allocations for Child Development Programmes. Due to lack of effort by government, efforts were made by private industry/organisation to develop child care service. In urban areas where need is more, child minding centres have mushroomed everywhere, with no regulation in place they follow few practices that would help children in their development. Thus today we have the public and the private enterprise providing for child care services in the country. Though the services may be highly inadequate, what exists is of great concern to people who are concerned for young children. What happens in these centres? Are we giving enough attention health and safety? Is the staff trained to understand the needs of young children? How are the children occupied/stimulated. If one visits any centre with these questions, one can see the great divide between what should be provided and what is provided. The concern for quality of programmes is absent. There is no awareness among all stakeholders about implications of poor quality care for children and therefore, there is no effort on any front to ensure quality. This chapter explores the issues related to quality and discusses the possible ways to bring quality in our child care programme.

Dimensions of Quality

Quality programmes is the new buzz word for people working in the field of early childhood. However, the problem begins when we start defining quality for the definition would be influenced by subjective values or perhaps it would depend on what aspects the programme are being addressed. One of the earliest attempts to understand how to look at quality was given by National Day Care Study of U.S. (Ruopp *et al.*, 1979) where they said that quality programmes by definition must promote healthy normal, social, emotional and cognitive development and that quality judgements should be based on direct assessment of child's daily experience and its impact on developments. From the regulatory framework quality was looked at as a continuum of care with minimum safeguards at lower level and provision of services to meet all needs of children at the highest level. According to Moss (1994) early childhood programme quality is a relative concept, not an objective reality, and that definitions change over time, according to values, belief, needs and involvement of other stakeholders. Definition of quality will also be influenced by the developmental goals that are laid down in the cultural context and therefore Smith (1996) points out that richer, more meaningful and active is children's participation in culturally diverse activities the greater then its contribution to child's cognitive and social goals of development.

Through review of research Love, Schobert and Meckstroth (2002) tried to understand the ingredients of quality care and education, the supports needed to attain quality, the linkage between quality and child development. The authors came to the conclusion that investments in the following five areas are likely to have great benefit, (a) Well trained staff who are motivated and want to work with young children, (b) Physical environments which are safe, sanitary and accessible to parents, (c) Ratios and group sizes that make it possible to interact appropriately with children, (d) Consistency in the supervision and staff development that encourages continuing and improving quality. This analysis clearly shows that both the structural and process variables impact the quality of a programme. However, its important to recognize that the structural variables impact the process variables. Further Tietze, Burchinal, Leal and Palacios (1999) categorize the structural variables as proximal that is having a more direct impact on process and distal as variables that impact the process indirectly.

Various researches have been done to identify specific impact of both structural and process variables. Among the structural variables staff ratio and group size are considered very crucial, however group size seems to have a greater impact on quality of programme (Ruopp, 1979; Datta, 1993). Datta's study further showed that with increased group size there was decrease in positive adult interactions and increase in negative interaction or no interaction.

Cryer (1998) has shown that one of the important predictors of process quality was wages. The US National child care staffing study (Whitebook, *et al.*, 1989) indicates a relation between aspects of quality and child development outcomes. For example children were found to spend more time in purposeful play rather than aimless wandering when teachers were more responsive and had more intense interactions with children. Similarly, the cost, quality and child outcomes study (Persner-Feinberg, *et al.*, 1999) found that the quality of centre-based care was related to pre-school children's concurrent development across all domains studied some of them being academic skills, classroom behaviour. This study has highlighted that the children who may be at risk for school failure particularly children from disadvantaged background were more susceptible to the effects of child care quality. Further the study also identified in the sample many centres as 'poor to mediocre' raising a lot of concern for Quality in Early Childhood Programmes.

The efforts to evolve methodologies to bring quality in practice was seen in many fronts. Organisations like National Association for Education of the Young Child (NAEYC) focused on developing systematic methods to identify quality in early childhood programmes while academician contributed in developing indicators of quality. The NAEYC efforts to extensively disseminate the Development Appropriate Practices brought to awareness the many process within early childhood programmes that need to be understood.

The pioneering efforts of Harms and Cliffords (1980) to measure quality in programmes, initiated a numerous studies to systematically understand quality across USA and other countries and also creation of more tools to measure quality. The most widely used scales to measure quality in child care is Harms and Cliffords Early Childhood Environment Rating Scale (1980) and later they did specific tools for Infant/Toddler environment rating scale and also the family environment rating scale. In 1998 the Early Childhood Environment Scale was revised to incorporate new findings from research and also cater to issues related to special needs children but the basic principles remain the same. Based on these scales the Indian adaptations to measure quality in day care centres and family day care was done by Datta (1993). These scales had a five point rating scale with description for ratings of 1, 3, 5. The scale established a high inter-rater reliability (.67 and .76 respectively), An adaptation of Bradley and Caldwell's (1979) HOME inventory was done by Konantambigi which was a scale to measure quality of home and child care setting. In India the Indian Association for Pre-school Education (IAPE) which is the largest association in field of early childhood, has nearly two decades ago showed its great concern for issues related to quality in early childhood programmes. The National Council of Educational Research and Training (NCERT) has been able to put together a very significant document on minimum standards for early childhood programmes in India. There were many criticisms to this concept of minimum standards as it would mean we are asking for 'acceptable' programmes but are not moving towards quality programmes.

How to Ensure Quality?

Williams (1995) identified three approaches for regulating quality in early childhood programmes. The first approach is the total quality approach which expects that all those involved in the programme have to take responsibility for running quality programme. Thus all stakeholders have to work for quality programme. The management creates the environment for conducting quality programmes, the teacher has to give major inputs to implement the programme, the children's responses to the programme guides the functionaries for further programming, while the parents create a demand for quality programmes by making informed choices. In quality assurance certain procedures like supervision and monitoring, staff training and child outcomes and evaluations help in looking at individual programme in their abilities to deliver the programme. The criteria and procedures could be evolved that are specific to programmes depending on their objectives and outreach. Such processes help to identify specific issues and develop procedures to increase efficiency.

Quality control basically addresses regulation for ensuring that not only minimum standards are met but also the existing standards of quality are raised. Therefore, regulation could be said to be the rules, strategies and standards that govern early childhood programmes. Morgan (1985) in describing methods for regulating quality talks of licensing as the lowest form and accreditation as one of the highest forms of quality control; in between are other forms like registration, staff credentials and monitoring.

Regulatory Child Care

Gwen Morgan (1985) has described licensing as the lowest form of regulation while the accreditation as the highest form of regulation. In between in these two are various methods of regulating and bringing in quality in ECE programmes.

Licensing

Generally licensing applies to early childhood to programmes operated in the private sector. It appears that licensing is a powerful legal protection for children. Licensing basically describes the minimum that early childhood programmes have to adhere to for obtaining licence for running early childhood programmes. For example, staff child ratio, space, safety, staff training etc., are some of the items on the basis of which licences are issued. For licensing to be successful there has to be the will of the public. The government is dependent on the consent of the people. Also, licensing requirement cannot be made unless the programmes are able and willing to meet them; parents should be willing to pay for them and overall public should be willing to support their enforcement. In this aspect it appears that in India we are not yet ready for licensing. It is only now that pressure is being built by the professionals for developing quality programmes. But parents still are not sure what to expect from the programmes and we need to go a long way in bringing about a change in parents thinking. The concern of the government for quality in private ECE programmes is completely absent. Thus in such a situation, to initiate licensing may ensure failure of this regulatory system. The setting up of standards itself is, therefore, an important requirement to make everybody aware about where to set the base line of requirements. The efforts of NCERT in developing minimum standard for pre-school programmes marked a beginning in developing standards for ECE programmes in India. Another major issue in licensing is the massive machinery that will be required to achieve routine inspections before and after the issue of licence. The Indian experience in other sectors have shown high level of malpractices in inspections and in the issue of licence. If this happen in Early Childhood Programmes, it will create even greater dangers as promoting or legalising wrong practices in dealing with children could create lasting impact on children's development.

As mentioned earlier the licensing standards are applicable to programmes operated in private sector whereas state itself operates a programme. But it is important to see that these programmes do not operate at standards lower than those of licensing standards for private centres. And, therefore, such public programmes are "Approved" programmes (Morgan, 1985). The approving agency can be the licensing agency itself. How far a government would allow its programmes to be scrutinised and approved is questionable but one must agree that this procedure will help to bring all programmes at common standards for quality. Very often because it is a government programme ICDS is excused for the sub-standard quality of its delivery of service but if it has to be a 'approved' programme then even ICDS would have good quality.

In India there are many legislations which have relevance for the field of Early Childhood Programmes. For example, the Factories Act, the Plantations Act are some which provide for child care facilities for children of working parents. These Acts do lay down minimum requirements from these crèches. However, the emphasis is on staffing and space only with no specifications on kind of care. Therefore, such legal provisions cannot help in bringing quality programmes. The Maharashtra Pre-school Admission Act (1996) (which was later withdrawn) was an attempt to bring in some control on the malpractice existing in the field of ECCE. For the first time the issues which were affecting children's development were being considered and this indeed was a very encouraging step. For example, issues like admission tests, use of work books, school bag burden etc. were some issues highlighted in the Act. These issues are very important as they all are influencing the quality of ECCE programmes. In any law the implementation is important and will of the public should be present. Unfortunately the many issues in implementing this Act were not envisaged creating protests on all fronts — from practitioners, parents, researchers and academicians. Legislations can bring in some minimum standard. But only the combination of regulatory and non-regulatory methods will help us enhance quality of programmes.

Registration

One of the alternatives to licensing is registration which primarily rests on self-regulation. The state could describe standards and persons running programmes should submit documents that they meet the standards and then the programme is registered. This midway path may seem a better option for India as it requires not much manpower. However the success of registration system could be ensured by entrusting the role of registration to academic institution or ECCE training colleges who would perhaps not only do the required paper work but would also take responsibility to enhance the quality of centres, registered with them by starting resource and referral cell. Involvement of people from the field will ensure that expectations are realistic and professional inputs are ever present. A beginning has been made by Ram Joshi Committee Report of Pre-school Education in Maharashtra by talking of registration as an important step in quality of ECE Programmes. The commitment of registering body, the honesty and integrity of registering agency are big question marks in the registration system. But rather than having 'care a dam' attitude, a regulatory method like registration may help bring about some change in quality of programmes.

Staff Credentials

Very often in emphasising programme standards and requirements, the qualification of staff is often neglected. The US Day Care Staffing Study (Whitebook, *et al.*, 1989) has shown that the staff is the single most important factor in determining the quality of a child care programme. There are two factors in considering issues related to staffing. The first is the significance of the training for personnel in early childhood programmes and the second is the work conditions which will determine the motivation and commitment of the staff to the job and the programme.

The notion that any person who likes children or is herself a mother will be a good staff in early childhood programme, still prevails in the Indian context. The discrepancies in the duration of training, methodology, exposure to theory and practice are so many that the levels in functioning of the personnel is also varying tremendously. On one extreme we have university and government recognised courses with fixed curricula duration and some standards set for trainers and the organisation and on the other extreme we have the private institutions who run their own courses with no standards for teaching curriculum or duration resulting in bringing out 'professionals' who are unable to develop healthy programmes for young children. In the hope of developing need based training programmes and in the hope of indigenizing training, NGOs were encouraged to develop their own training programmes. This step has lead to even more chaos in the training of early childhood educators. What emerged from this strategy is that any kind of training is good enough training. This is where the role of the government comes in terms of regulating staff credentials. One of the recent steps of government of setting up the National Centre for Teacher Education (NCTE) has recognised early childhood educators training under its auspices. This has given hope that the NCTE will scrutinise and grant recognition to only those organisations which are competent to impact ECE training. It is also the government's responsibility to see that the training imparted to personnel in programmes like ICDS also have appropriate training of similar standards. The experience has been that government talks only in terms of targets to be met and therefore, entrust things like training responsibility to anyone and everyone who is willing to take up. This has resulted in resources being wasted and also bringing about a low quality programmes run by government.

The second important aspect regarding personnel is their work conditions. Large number of staff in ECE programmes, especially government programmes are 'honorary' workers which denotes that they have no salary but an honorarium, they don't have the benefits of permanent workers nor the hope of having a career ladder. The status of workers in NGOs and private enterprise is no better. When staff has to deal with young child's overall development, the motivation and commitment will make a lot of difference to their approach to the task. This calls for recognition of these people as a workforce.

Monitoring and Evaluation

When government buys or creates a service through grant or contract, it can establish specifications for the quality it wishes to support. For example, the ICDS has a built in monitoring system. The Management Information System ensures a regular flow of information upward from each Anganwadi to the project — to the state — to the Government of India. Information on funds, supports, staff, coverage, health and nutrition indicators are some information put on monthly monitoring report (Sharma, 1987). Basically such monitoring helps in understanding the mechanisms and problems therein in the implementation of the programme and therefore such monitoring system does not cover quality aspects. However, within the same framework inputs for quality could also be included giving more meaning and effectiveness to monitoring system. For example, the indicators of nutritional status are used in monitoring system to identify special intervention strategies for nutrition. However, along with this if one could also have inputs on issues like kind and quality of food, distribution of food etc. such information would help to identify the exact cause of problem and show the quality of services delivered.

Similarly, the experiences of monitoring and evaluation of crèches under the scheme of crèches for children of working and ailing women shows that the government's concern is not so much for quality but to get information on targets reached and achieved. Such kind of monitoring offers no inputs to staff and programmes to resolve their problems on even in terms of suggestions for better functioning. Thus monitoring is basically done by funders to see the appropriate utilization of funds. Evaluation too is a strategy for quality programmes. The funds or sponsor generally use evaluation to understand efficiency and accountability of the programme based on which decision are made regarding further funding. The decision-makers of a programme are also interested in evaluation to understand what changes should be made in the programme. Lastly, evaluation is also done to measure the effectiveness of the programme in terms of outcomes. However, most often evaluations are done for funding. Very often the qualitative information required regarding practices, children's interactions and activities is lacking due to which many factors that need to be addressed to bring in quality in programme remain untouched in the process of evaluation. Thus evaluation needs to be used with caution.

Accreditation

Accreditation perhaps is a method to bring in highest standards of quality in early childhood programmes. Very broadly accreditation means a stamp for quality. Three characteristics of accreditation are (1) that it is usually done by professional bodies from the same field, (2) organisation voluntarily choose to participate in the accreditation process, and (3) the organisations have to do a self-study as a requirement of accreditation.

First of all for an accreditation system to be initiated, a professional body has to develop the standards for good quality programmes. This would call for an understanding of the programme variety and diversity and also scientific understanding of all the issues that make up quality of early childhood programmes. Once these items for evaluation are identified and levels of standards agreed upon, the accreditation process could begin. The process itself requires that self-study be done by the organisation so that they become involved in a process that will facilitate real and lasting improvements in the quality of the programme. The organisation is also visited, observed and studied so as to validate the information received from the organisation. If the organisation receives accreditation it is for a period of three years only so as to ensure that there is no lapse in quality after some time.

Applying accreditation system in the Indian context seems to be a very difficult proposition. For example, accreditation requires a recognized professional body to implement the process. In India, though IAPE has been a professional body, it has not been given a national recognition. Considering the diversities in programmes and practices it would require large amount of research and scientific input to understand how to set the standards for accreditation, calling for investment in time and money. One very crucial factor is that the people in the field of ECCE are yet not convinced of the need for quality programme and do not feel the need of quality control systems like accreditation. However accreditation gains a very important place in the methods for bringing quality in ECCE.

Non-regulatory Methods

Besides these very specific methods to ensure quality there is a need to look at other practices which would help in the process of changing the quality of programmes and these could be termed as non-regulatory methods. Professionals in the field of ECCE programmes can and must play a very important role in ensuring quality ECCE programme. The concept Developmental Appropriate Practices (DAP) as developed by National Association for Education of Young Child (USA, NAEYC, 1990) and the concept of practices appropriate to context of early development (PACED) as given by Woodhead (1996) are important to be understood and brought into practice.

The efforts have to be made to make programmes age appropriate and individual appropriate with definite attention to the context in which the programme is functioning. The efforts will have to be at two levels. One is in the training programmes which need to emphasize on these aspects and give practice inputs during the training. Secondly the practitioners need to evolve methods to see that within the given resources how the programme can be adapted to bring in DAP practices. There has to be rigorous efforts by academicians and researchers to provide scientific inputs towards standards for quality, more involvement with government and NGOs to bridge the gap between research and practice. They also need to take leadership in advocacy for quality programmes. The networking of organisations and developing a common agenda for advocacy by practitioner, researcher, NGOs might built enough pressure for getting quality programmes by changes in policy and programme practices.

Tshe parents who are the consumers of ECE programmes are never considered to be as important change-agents. It would go a long way to get parental support by educating them and involving in understanding need for quality programmes and to help them be part of the advocacy groups. Parents can be very crucial in forcing change in practices and even developing of policies and legislation. The reason for the many problems in implementing the Maharashtra Pre-school Admission Act was that there was no importance given to parental needs and opinion in spite of them being the programme-users.

To bring in standards in Early Childhood Programmes (through regulatory or non-regulatory methods) is indeed a tremendous challenge. The effort by FORCES (Forum for Crèche and Child Care Services) in advocacy for funding more programmes and quality has indeed been remarkable. The efforts of M.S. Swaminathan Research Foundation in disseminating information on the various efforts by NGOs, individuals and government to bring in more effective programmes has created much more understanding and awareness about the richness and variety in ECCE programmes, identify issues of concern and has helped to bring on Agenda the issue of quality in ECCE programmes. The contribution of NCERT and home science colleges in evolving research and literature are worth appreciating. The role of NGOs in ECCE just cannot be ignored as they have taken a large responsibility in reaching out to children. Co-ordination, networking and developing a national agenda for strategies for quality in ECCE programmes should now be worked out so that appropriate policies and programme practices are encouraged.

14

STRENGTHENING THE ARMS OF DAY CARE : NETWORKING AND ADVOCACY

— Rajalakshmi Sriram

Introduction: Quality and the Private Child Care Scenario

The need for support services for child care outside the home is an accepted fact in the present Indian scenario. There has been a growing realisation among child development professionals, practitioners and policy-makers about the importance of a supportive environment. It includes provision of good quality services for promoting the interlinked goals of healthy and optimal development of children (with special focus on the girl child) and also facilitates women's development within and outside the context of the family.

An analysis of the practical realities of the child care (especially day care) situation, however, reflects the wide gaps that exist between intention and action. Child care services have developed in a piecemeal fashion in response to diverse needs and conceptual viewpoints that have emerged at different times. This is truer of the urban and unorganised sector, which is a private domain with no regulatory mechanisms of any nature. The resulting situation is described vividly by Swaminathan with reference to the general Early Childhood Care and Education services:

> "Casual observation can vouch for the spread of innumerable such institutions, going by varying names, which are generally characterised by untrained teachers, in ill-equipped classrooms,

cramming the three R's forcibly down the throats of unwilling children, while ignorant managements enforce inappropriate curriculum and methods of teaching; at the cost of parents, who ironically often pay fees they can ill afford" (1998:22).

Though this seems to be a sweeping generalization, it is quite applicable to "day care" services in the "for profit" sector which encompasses both the very best and the very worst, in terms of quality.

Research studies, though limited, give us some clues to the existing features related to quality parameters. This detail of quality and its impact on children are available in other chapters of the book, and hence only a brief illustration based on a framework (model) of Dorothy (1991) adapted by Sriram is provided here to highlight key features of privatised urban day care (see Figure 14.1).

Why is Quality Important and How can it be Regulated ?

Good quality child care support and ECE has been recognised as an important intervention, not only for optimal child development but as a strategy for community development by effectively meeting the intersecting needs of women, families and the broader society. This is summarised in Box 14.1.

Recognising the importance of quality, a variety of regulatory and voluntary mechanisms have been in operation across the globe. What is used generally in the social sectors especially in other developed countries (Canada, USA, Australia or parts of Europe) fall into three categories, the details of which are described in Figure 14.2 (Morgan cited in Doherty)

- Regulatory methods, such as licensing/sanction approval.
- Voluntary standards of professional practice such as accreditation.
- Other non-regulatory methods including public education, training, advisory committees, improving motivation through continuous support and so on.

Caregiver Chacteristics

- *Education :* Mostly high school or graduate for teachers and illiterate to primary for helpers.
- *Training :* No training or qualification in child development.
- *Age & Experience :* 26 years onwards to middle age, with experience of 5-15 years.

Contextual Factors

- ***funded*** mostly by user fees/or care providers
- absence of ***licensing***/monitoring
- absence of ***minimal standards***
- little or no active ***parental involvement***
- ***treated as a private*** enterprise and not a social service

Child's Environment

- ***Inadequate*** health and safety provisions.
- ***Wide variation*** in physical environment. Many centres found lacking in terms of ***adequate space***, lack of attention to ***hygiene*** and sanitation.
- ***High density*** and over-crowding in some centres.
- High ***caregiver turnover***.
- Staffing pattern, where **bai's** are responsible for ***care*** and ***teachers*** for ***programme***.
- Lack of attention to a ***developmentally appropriate programme*** curriculum/focus on select regimented activities.

Child's well being: Some positive benefits reported but usage of bad words, aggression, also becoming illness prone are reported.

Day care centres rate fair to poor in quality leaving much scope for improvement across dimensions.

Caregiver Child Interaction

- Generally ***affectionate and loving relationship,*** offering security to children.
- Both ***negative and positive*** strategies of interaction equally prevalent.
- Wide range in ***staff child ratio*** ranging from 1:5 to 1:20.
- Lack of ***individual attention*** to children (especially cleanliness and hygiene).

Adult Work Environment

- ***Insufficient wages*** ranging from Rs. 500-1500/month.
- Little or no opportunity for ***training or advancement***.
- Job taken up due to ***personal interest*** in children or as ***"time pass"***.
- ***Feeling of isolation*** due to absence of a system where one can belong.

Fig. 14.1 : An Overview of Quality of Childcare Programme in Private Urban (On key indicators). *Source:* Datta, V. (1995); Sriram, R. (1993); Sriram and Rashmi, (1996); Sriram and Shukla, (1999); Christina (1999); Shanta (1997); Narayanan (1994).

Box 14.1 : Benefits of Good Quality Child Care

For Children

- Promotes positive developmental opportunities, for example, greater social competence, higher levels of language development, better ability to regulate their own behaviour, greater compliance with adults and fewer behavioural problems (Western Research quoted in Doherty, 1991).

For Women/Girls

- Permits pursuit of economic and social equality by providing.
- – opportunities to participate in employment, school or training.
- – helps to balance work and family responsibilities.

For Families and Broader Society

- Allows parents to make better contributions to economic productivity as workers.
- Improves efficiency in work by reducing work family tension.
- Provides
- – support and resources for parenting.
- – a solid foundation for future education.

Source : Adapted from Friendly, 1994

It is important to note that two aspects of quality that is the programme and caregiver child interaction which are most related to the outcomes, are most difficult to regulate. Regulatory methods focus mostly on structural features and requirements.

A study/survey of research on successful innovative experiments in child care programmes in India reinforce and highlight the need for sustained inputs into the following features as a means towards attaining quality (Datta, V.,1995; Sriram, 1995; Pandit, 1995; Shanta, 1996).

Programme Design

- Building programmes based on multiple needs of children, women, girls and the community.
- Working towards setting up information and referral services.
- Choice of place, worker and timings in consultation with the users.
- Developing norms collectively and following the same.

Regulatory Methods
- Fiscal regulation
- Licensing or registration
- By laws/code of conduct and standards

Voluntary Standards
- Accreditation : Where a recognised body sets standards.
- Credentialising or certification for staff and programme.
- Self or peer review for continuous reflection and upgradation.

Non-regulatory Methods
- Staff training
- Public education
- User education/parent awareness
- Parent advisory committee
- Consultation from other professionals
- Resource support
- Referrals
- Membership in professional organisations.

Fig. 14.2 : Multiple Ways of Promoting Quality (Adapted from Morgan, 1979)

Monitoring and Control

- Control of service by parents and community or Sangha *(women and community groups).*
- Clear understanding and sharing of responsibility between parents and providers.
- On field support by resource persons for supervision.

Training and Liaison with Child Care Workers

- Promoting interaction between care providers through a variety of means and improving their status.

- Providing professional support by forming groups or associations.
- Addressing emerging needs through regular in-service training programmes.

Systematic progress towards the attainment of quality requires that we form structures and initiate processes that take into account the strengths of the current situation. The principles and concepts of Total Quality Management (TQM) towards which the corporate sectors are moving to ensure excellence, is worth considering for application in suitable ways to the private sector of child care.

TQM focuses on reducing defects, improving productivity, improving customer service and innovation and these are achieved by involving the entire workforce in the process (Shanta, 1997). The concept is about the quality in each one of the processes involved, emphasising on teamwork motivation of management and staff. In such a case, quality assumes a subjective and dynamic judgment influenced by all stakeholders including users and providers, staff and the community involved. It becomes a negotiable component changing over time to reflect the improved understanding of stakeholders and to address dynamic needs instead of a prescribed uniform standard. Therefore, reinforcing quality parameters through voluntary and non-regulatory mechanisms, seems to be a possible approach not only to improve quality and accessibility but also to empower women through awareness, training and supportive resources.

In countries like Canada and Australia, there are associations formed by family day care providers, which serve the dual purpose of offering visibility to their issues and concerns and also support providers to work towards up gradation of their services by procuring funds for training, education and creating resource support (Dunster, Personal communication with author, and visits to associations, 1991, 1994).

Networking offers much scope in empowering home or centre based providers operating in an isolated environment, to focus on the development of services of a reasonable quality that benefit children and families. Figure 14.3 helps to summarise the key benefits of a system of networking of child care services based on the experiences of other countries and forums within the country. The dimensions of benefits include strong support and motivation to providers, assistance for up gradation of day care environment, mobilisation of resources and a platform for collective action.

This chapter describes a small experiment of forming a day care providers association in the city of Baroda and some of its activities and approaches. An effort has been made to use some of the aforesaid ideas for enabling the effective functioning of services.

Formation of Child Care Providers' Association: Experiences of Shishu Palak Vrund

Critical reflections on the existing situation, inspiration from observation and interactions, with professionals in the field of child care from across the country and other countries culminated in the formation of a network by initiating an association of child care providers at the local level. The Child Care Providers Association, named Shishu Palak Vrund was formed under the auspices of the Child Development Trust which is an alumni association of the Department of Human Development and Family Studies at M.S. University, Baroda. Since its formation in 1995-96, an intervention process, that is slow but steady has been initiated and sustained through a variety of activities.

Listening to Voices Within and Without

The existing day care centre of the department was used as a pad to launch activities such as meetings to initiate a dialogue about the need for networking and training workshops for child care workers. Sporadic attendance, lack of clarity of mutual interests and goals, busy schedules of care providers were serious impediments to the process. However during one of the meetings, around 15-17 group members, coined the name SHISHU PALAK VRUND which means a circle of people who rear children. Subsequently, the group

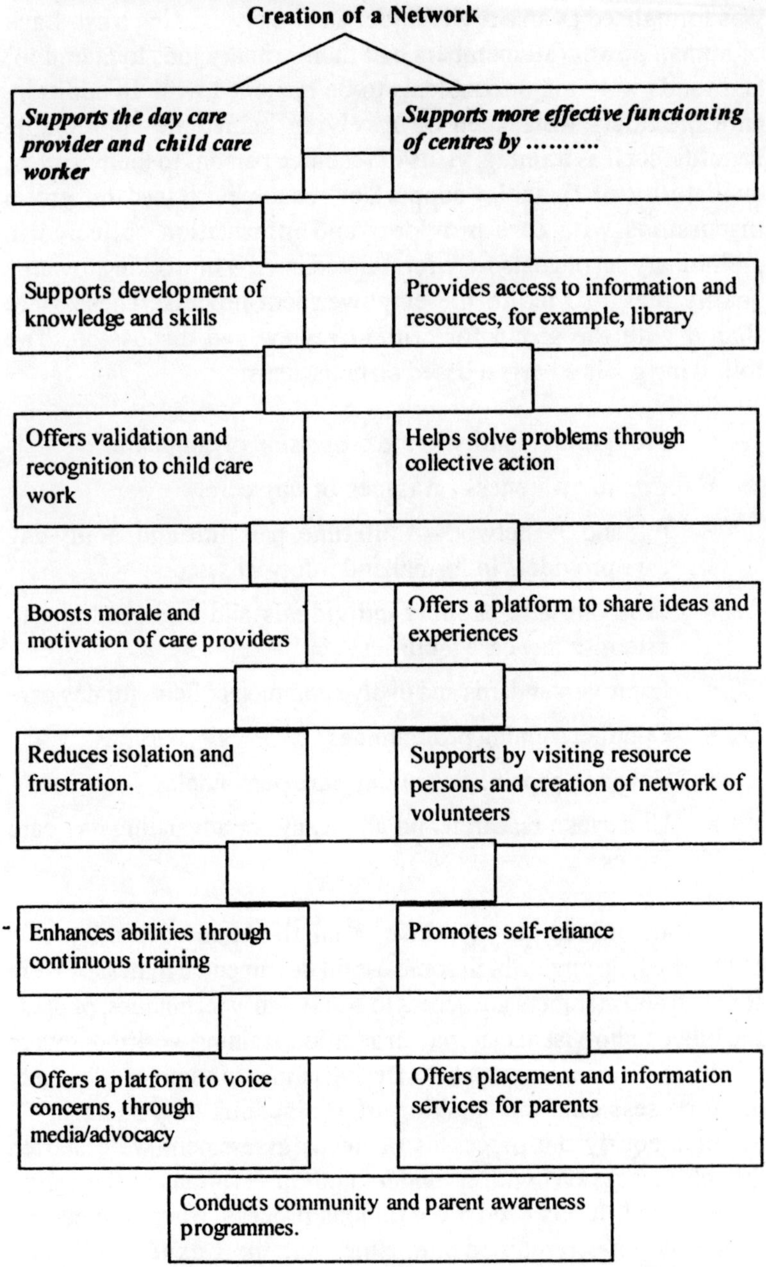

Fig. 14.3 : Muliple benefits of forming a Network of Child care Providers

was formalised as an activity under an already existing trust. Lack of human power (all members had their primary jobs to attend to) and funds were major problems to be reckoned with. In addition, care providers were keen on receiving immediate appreciable benefits, such as training, visits of resource persons to their centres, availability of financial support or resources. Based on group discussions with care providers and information collected, a preliminary set of goals were formulated in view of working towards quality that also led to the empowerment process. These were shared with the group for critical review and discussion. The following goals emerged based on consensus:

- Provide an identity to the profession of childcare.
- Create awareness on issues of day care.
- Expand the network of full time, part time and family day care providers in formal and informal sectors.
- Motivate and support individuals and organisations to establish day care facilities.
- Improve standards and evolve common policies for day care
- Conduct training programmes.
- Enhance capabilities of day care personnel.
- Undertake research and advocacy for advancing day care issues.

As an immediate response, a small resource library was established, through which some useful documented materials were supplied and members got access to books, story techniques, puppets and other audio-visual material. In addition, training workshops were conducted on themes such as "offering games in summer," "variety in story sessions" or "making of indigenous play materials". Simultaneously the processes of needs assessment were started though discussions with providers and observations at the centre were started. It has been a continuous process, where the central concerns have remained the same, but their expressions and frequency have varied. Box 14.2 provides an overview of these concerns.

Box 14.2 : Problems and Concerns : An Overview

With parents	*With staff*
• Delay or non-payment of fees as expected • Overexpectation about children's learning. • Non-compliance to rules by some parents.	• Quick turnover especially helpers due to poor salary • Unprofessional attitude • Lack of skills and knowledge of child development.
In administration	*With children*
• Problems with neighbours due to vehicular and noise disturbance. • Electricity charged on commercial basis. • Space and finance in some cases.	• Inability to handle special needs or behavioural problems. • Caregiver child interactions

Providers and child care workers were eager to receive help from Shishu Palak Vrund in solving some of their problems. The Figure 14.3 describes the nature of support expected which formed the basis for designing interventions. Most of them desired support in training care providers, in improving the quality of the programme, and in improving management and communication with parents. Others desired additional assistance in enhancing commercial, social and legal security, planning of meals and counselling to parents where they felt that they had very limited competencies.

Some insecurity came to light during informal discussions on a one-to-one basis:

- Will I have to declare my income?
- I do not know much about child development? What will the others say?
- Will my workers go away to other centres, for a higher salary or better working conditions, if I send them for training?

- Will the benefits derived from attending meetings and training session be worth the time and expenditure?
- Will others come to know of my centre's weaknesses?
- What if there are questions that I do not want to answer?

These dimensions had to be taken into account while planning activities so as to be able to build on existing strengths, being fully aware of constraints and limitations related to time, finance and attitudes. A successful intervention to improve the functioning of childcare centres needs inputs in many areas addressing both parents' and care providers' needs.

Interventions with Childcare Providers

Training Sessions with Caregivers

Needs assessment in centres indicated that the major input required was to promote positive strategies of interaction and support children's adjustment in the centres, so that both care providers and children felt secure. Care givers requested that they be oriented to provide variety of stimulation especially for toddlers. (For additional details refer Chapter V on Childcare in the Service Sector).

The underlying philosophy of training was based on experiential learning that recognised the innate strength of caregivers many of whom had 5-7 years of experience and promoted reflection on their own practices. This process became more meaningful and beneficial to the group with inputs from a master's research student, who was developing a methodology and a resource manual for such a training. It contributed to some extent in building group solidarity. The focus was on making the group more sensitive to the needs of children, based on developmental principles and on orienting the group to appropriate practices, so that they could evolve and adapt their practices accordingly. These sessions were spread over a period of one year, as the group could participate only in afternoon sessions of 2-3 hours each, once a month. A brief overview of the themes of sessions is presented in Box 14.3.

Box 14.3 : Training Session — Themes

Knowing the caregivers and their perceptions of day care: • Introducing oneself • Knowing each other • Sharing feelings • What is day care • Caregivers' perceptions	In support of children's adjustment to the centre: • Feelings in an unknown place • Understanding children's fears, feelings and thoughts • Special needs during adjustment • Helping your children adjust to the centre.
Sharing for better caring: Positive Interaction and overcoming difficulties: • Draw and dialogue : Children's problems • In search of solutions to problems • Why, when and how instructions to children • Routine instruction not again • As children view it: Maximizing do's and minimising don'ts • Logical reasoning: Does it help • Interaction: Does it promote self-expression in children • Helping children co-operate • Revisiting children's errors.	In support of children's stimulation in day care: (A) Understanding children's developmental needs and characteristics • What children can and cannot do • Identifying children's needs • Meeting developmental needs of children : Caregivers' role (B) Promoting children's body co-ordination • Body co-ordination : A look at activities in the centre • Activities: What skills do they promote • Discovering together : The effects of activities • Exercising the unexercised body parts • Learning from each other • One object : Multiple uses (C) There is more to music than nursery rhymes • What do caregivers and children think of music • Implementing music session : Overcoming barriers • Music can be introduced in many ways (D) Stories and conversation : A means of enhancing children's language skills • Knowing what you give and what you want· Why stories • Story session —facing hurdles • Is it the right story - How can it be narrated • There is more to a story session than stories. • Stories can be fun.

The training sessions used a variety of participatory exercises which not only promoted critical reflection but also brought out practices, needs of care givers and multiple viewpoints for solutions and follow up.

Such an approach helped in enhancing care providers' sensitivity to their own roles, needs of children and some ways of meeting these efficiently within the existing situation. Training was a recursive cycle as reflected in Fig. 14.4.

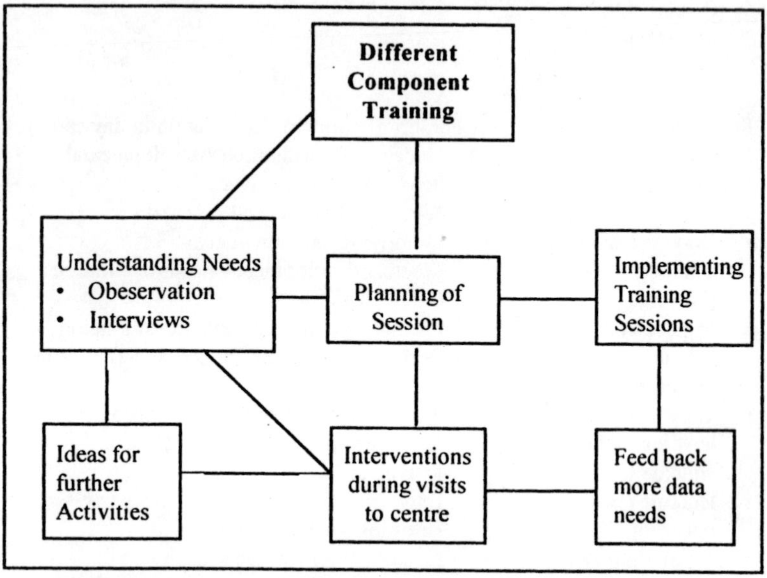

Fig. 14.4 : The Recursive Cycle of Training

In addition to these sessions for training, meetings were organised for care providers to solve their problems related to the running of the centre and to address other emerging issues. Some discussion sessions were arranged on selected themes and care providers were given an opportunity to participate in activities organised by others some of which are enumerated in Box 14.4. Approximately 50 programme in-charge persons and caregivers participated in these meetings. The meetings helped to facilitate discussions on common problems and come up with solutions by a consultation process.

Box 14.4 : Activities carried out with urban care providers

- Workshop on safety in and around the centre with the doctor.
- Film show on a quality childcare centre.
- Film show on the development milestones and age appropriate activities.
- Communicating with parents issues and solutions.
- Common policies: A discussion.
- The open house organised by the faculty of home science helped them know many different creative activities such as dance, music, story telling and so on.

New opportunities for training and awareness were created at this stage of networking in liaison with other organisations that offered ongoing training by sending information to providers. Members could use their discretion to participate in these workshops.

Perceptions of Programme

A strong common voice that was heard directly and indirectly from caregivers was that they would benefit much from the regular visits of resource persons, since it would be difficult for some of them to leave their homes and care giving duties and attend training programme. The field investigator of the project visited each centre at least 5-7 times during the period of one-and-a-half years and visited some centres more than ten times. She observed the ongoing sessions of the centres and offered constructive suggestions to care providers on field, to enhance teachers skills and support them in running a centre successfully. In addition the visiting resource person had discussions with the parents regarding their concerns and issues, not only related to children's development but also about the organisation of the centres About 20 centres and 35-40 caregivers benefited from these activities.

Since the resource person was young and unassuming (a masters degree holder in human development), the field visit provided an opportunity to care providers for free discussion without anxiety or inhibitions (which they had during the training sessions). On the

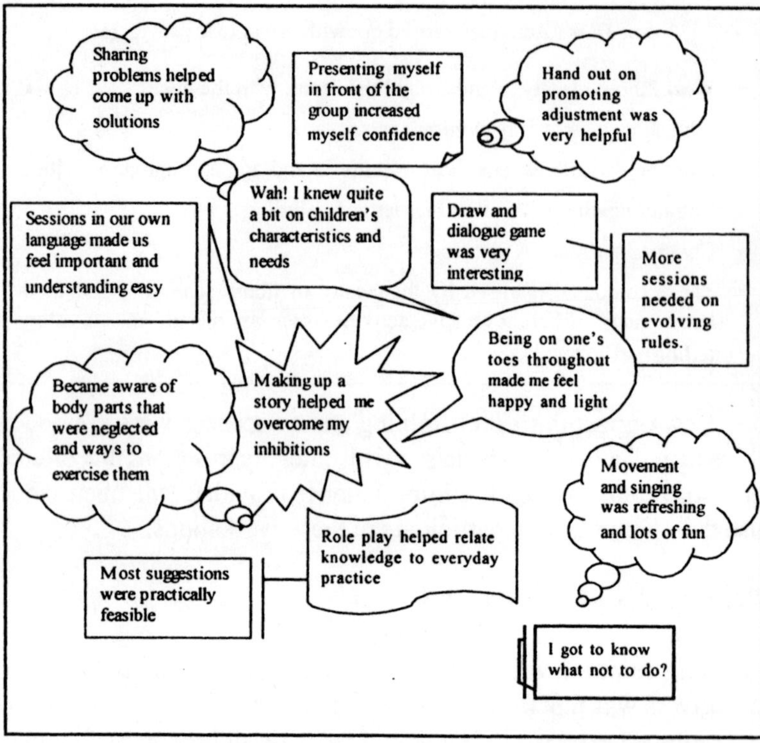

Figure 14.5 : Benefits of training : Care provider's voice

spot suggestions were taken positively. Also some queries that were difficult for care providers were answered on the spot. This process helped communicate the maintainance of quality parameters to them indirectly. Care providers responses in Box 14.6 give a glimpse into the benefits of the initiative/programme.

There were a number of interventions to involve all the players, the caregivers, the parents and the children.

Interventions with Parents

A variety of activities were conducted on a continuous basis for parents, care providers of different centres participated in the planning and execution of each activity which enhanced the partnership process. Each strategy of intervention complemented the other, thus converging towards a holistic approach.

Box 14.5 : Activities carried out during visits

- ***Demonstrate*** creative activities (10) Story telling (20) dramatisation (5) discussion, theme talk with children (7) plan a project for the week.
- ***Demonstrate*** strategies for communication with children - talking, listening, playing, explaining, soothing and solving disputes among children.
- ***Support care providers to plan*** the programme activities and environment which is child friendly.
- **Understand** parents' needs and expectations and approach them.
- **Respond** parents' queries related to the child's development care and education.
- **Feedback** on the activities and approaches of caregivers, thus helping them make appropriate changes through demonstration.

(Figures in parenthesis indicate number of centres where this support was offered).

Box 14.6 : Responses of Care Providers to Field Visits by Resource Person

Thanks for visiting my centre!	*Your visit helped my staff to behave properly with the children.*
We learned how to arrange the board according to the child's need and theme	*Can you please visit again and demonstrate the story dramatisation*
Is the environment as per the child's need ?	*Please give us a feedback on our centre's environmental setting to make it more child friendly.*
You convinced that difficult parent, which was a relief for me.	*I feel so much more confident when you appreciate the little changes you have made.*
Now that you have shown me how to make play materials for the centre, I can do much more! Thus I can avoid buying them.	*Now the neighbours bother me less about vehicles coming in after you supported my explanation. They know we have an association.*

Parents' Meetings

The study revealed that care providers face considerable pressure to introduce reading, writing, numbers and verbal skills to children in a formal way. They were also very anxious about admission, health, development issues and behaviour problems. As a response to this, geographical area-wise parents meetings and "Vali Mela" were arranged by Shishu Palak Vrund.

The parents' meetings had the following goals:

- To provide a platform for parents and providers to come together to reflect the concerns of their children.
- To be an eye-opener to the care providers limitations and restrictions in running a centre.
- A forum for parents to express their anxieties and tensions in relation to their children.

Providers from centres in each area were to reach out to the parents in and around Vadodara city. Parents were contacted through letters and display of posters in child care centres. Decisions about time and place were made in consultation with the providers of that area. The panel of resource persons included were:

- Paediatrician
- Principal/Supervisor of the school.
- Child development professionals.
- A member of Shishu Palak Vrund.
- In-charge, teacher of centres in that particular area.
- Parents

Around 250-300 parents participated across the centres. The meetings helped parents and providers ponder over

(a) Issues related to school readiness/admission.
(b) Child's health (physical and mental).
(c) Behaviour problems, faced by child care centres.
(d) Child's overall development.

A child's admission to a good school is a major issue. Children and parents undergo the traumas of interviews for admission. The principals/supervisors discussed the procedure followed in their schools for admission, the criteria followed, and reasons for refusal. Many issues related to admissions and teaching such as donations, more emphasis on reading and writing and the medium of instruction were discussed.

Parents emphasised on reading and writing in the child care centre to facilitate school readiness. Resource persons discussed the importance of play in the development of children. In this context, there was a discussion on the need for children to explore the world around them through experience. Parents also discussed on the medium of instruction quite intensively.

Child's Health (Physical/Mental) Development and Behaviour

Paediatricians and child development personnel were invited to answer issues and queries of parents regarding the child's health. Parents were primarily concerned with the appropriate growth of the child and doctors informed them about the developmental milestones of children. Parents were also concerned about inappropriate personal and social behaviour such as bed-wetting, thumb sucking, temper tantrums, holding the breath and so on.

These questions were discussed in detail both from the medical and child developmental perspectives. It has been summarised as general tips for parents in Box 14.7.

Box 14.7 : General Tips for Parents

- Parents should understand the reason for inappropriate or unexpected behaviour of children.
- With appropriate reinforcement the action/behaviour (expected) can be elicited from children.
- Parents should not be harsh and show children that they are panicky.
- Children should be kept away from various tensions experienced by parents/family members.
- Parents should not induce unnecessary fears in children (fear of teachers, wicked women).
- Children's needs should be understood and changes can be made accordingly in the family.

The cluster-wise meetings facilitated the initiation of an open dialogue on certain issues that otherwise antagonised parents. It helped providers communicate to them about their concern for their children's welfare. Parents expressed the need for such meetings more frequently to solve problems and be a help to providers. Some parents enrolled themselves as members of Shishu Palak Vrund.

Parents Fair (Vali Mela)

This activity aimed at social mobilisation. It was organised as part of celebration of International Women's Day in collaboration with Lions Club of Vadodara (South zone). The major aims of the *mela* were to

- Create a common platform to facilitate interaction between parents and care providers.
- Provide an opportunity for caregivers to share the activities of their centre with the parents.
- Sensitise parents towards the experiences that children gain in child care centres.
- Provide a common platform for care providers to offer an exposure to childcare issues.

Thirteen centres of the city took part in the fair and had their stalls. Each stall had different activities such as printing, painting, college, origami, *rangoli*, music, story telling, science and maths experiments, language concepts, different indoor and outdoor games, sand and water play. In addition, puppet shows and mimicry were arranged. This *mela* helped to reach out to about four hundred parents in Vadodara.

A significant feature of this event was that parents participated in activities that children do, so that they experienced the pleasure of childhood, relaxed and enjoyed themselves. This process made parents aware of the amount of learning that is fostered through play and hence there was no need to force the centres for an early introduction to the three.

Support through Literature (Posters, Brochures, Policies)

Literature helped reach out to a number of parents and also bring to surface certain dormant issues for discussion. It catered to both parents and care providers. The data of the study was fed into literature. A set of posters were evolved about caregivers concerns with reference to organisational and programmatic issues. In addition brochures on the following themes were evolved, offering practical tips to providers and parents to grow towards a common view point.

Child's Adjustment to the Centre

Our data indicated that parents expect children to adjust to the centre immediately and some times use unhealthy practices due to worry and anxiety. As a means to support parents and caregivers to respond to the individual behaviours and needs of children, a pamphlet on child adjustment was prepared. Some tips of do's and don'ts are also provided, enabling both care provider and parents for positive action.

A Glimpse into Day Care/Play Care Centre

The major purpose is to orient parents to the goals and programme of a child care centre so as to enable them to develop realistic expectations.

Safety Measures in the Centre

This leaflet offers tips to create a safe and secure environment for the child both at the centre and at home. It describes precautions to be taken to prevent accidents

Childcare Worker : A Glimpse into her Life

In general this evolved out of a concern to make people aware of the work and feelings of a care provider and the multiple demands of her job.

How to Choose a Child Care Centre?

This was an indirect means to convey to providers, the need to maintain particular standards and educate parents about important features of good centres. This promoted voluntary setting of standards.

Rules and Policies

A study of rules and policies of each of the centres indicated considerable variations in approach. Some centres were extremely clear in the communications about rules to parents whereas others were not. They often faced the problem of delay in fee payment, late pick ups, inappropriate dressing and high expectations. As a response, the group decided to evolve common rules that were prepared by the investigator on which consensus was obtained. There are now four aspects of policy and rules that have been evolved.

(1) General rules to be followed in centres.

(2) Child care agreement form.

(3) Health policy information to be sought during admission.

(4) Parental versus caregiver responsibilities.

The initial response indicates that these have been helpful for seeking parental cooperation. However, it needs wide dissemination across the centres uniformly. Leaflets were a means of awareness generation for parents and providers. Common rules and policies helped in enhancing the image of the centre and also contributed to smooth administration and better communication with parents.

Unfolded Key Concerns

This project has been a slow process. Though one cannot claim that major changes to have occurred, it has begun a dialogue within

SPV between providers and parents. It has unfolded certain key concerns and has reinforced the need for continuous input for maintenance of quality in day care. They are as follows:

(a) Need for methods to overcome parental pressures on providers for early initiation into the three R's at day care and play care centres.

(b) Dilemmas related to rules and policies for admission, maintenance and need for formalising the same.

- Contractual agreements for care.
- Health policy.
- Supportive information for parents.
- Seeking cooperation from neighbourhood.

(c) Need for continuous communication with parents, to reinforce the beliefs, values of SPV and promote desirable, caregiver friendly and child friendly behaviour.

(d) Need for communication with parents about organisational and quality issues in day care such as:

- Where does your money go in a day care?
- A day in the life of a providers.
- How to choose a day care/play care centre?
- Collective action for advocacy related childcare issues.

(e) Need for active involvement of parents, and continuous communication as data indicates that they are not only competent (possess skills for a variety of activities) but are also willing to participate in the running of the centre (for details refer to appendix). Hence it is worth while to generate a pool of resource persons for each centre.

This experience has brought forth many difficulties that are closely associated with sustaining group processes over extended periods of time. Following are some of the sessions for the future:

Enabling the Leadership

Nature of Leadership: Leadership and initiative from an academic institution has had the advantage of a strong research/academic and philosophical base for action. At the same time limited resources hinder the process, inputs get limited in terms of resources of time and finances, as teaching and training are basic priorities.

Philosophical Orientation: One is quite frequently faced with the dilemma of giving priority to addressing practical needs that are the concern of care providers, which might run contrary to the philosophy of the intervention. For example, care providers wish to know how to teach the three R's or conversational English to young children in three months and would be happy if such an activity were supported. But the association attempts to discourage such a practice thus creating mixed or even hostile feelings among care providers about the benefits of membership or involvement.

Methods of Intervention: The visit of resource persons to centres is appreciated and also found beneficial as there is a high turnover of staff who need continuous orientation; but it is very resource intensive and hence cannot be undertaken for continuous periods of time. Similarly, participatory learning approaches adapted by SPV brings about gradual changes in attitudes and level of commitment of care providers; people are used to receiving a package of information during training sessions and hence often find it difficult to undertake a true reflection on their own practices/or may not turn up for training sessions on a continuous basis .

Hidden Fears: Initially SPV planned to offer trainings to functionaries at all levels, such as *bai's* (helper, care providers and teachers). But it has not been possible to organise for group sessions as the directors, people in-charge of centres do not wish that their staff interact with staff of other centres. They fear that these people may disclose certain secrets or start working for an other centre for better rewards or for more pay.

Cost vs. Benefits: Most child care centres in the private sector stagger the timings of their staff in view of the financial situation. Hence they sometimes find it difficult to participate in meetings or attend training due to their inability to leave the centre unattended. They weigh the benefits of participation against the cost of travel.

Day-to-day practical problems in centres are many and these deter them from participating in an activity which has few immediate tangible benefits.

Difficulty in Addressing Delicate but Crucial Practical Issues: Since these child care centres are run in providers homes in residential areas, many face practical problems, such as complaints from neighbours about noise, traffic, parking of vehicles etc, or commercial enterprise rates for electricity rates or house tax. It has been extremely difficult to tackle this issue as getting true data on income and expenditure which is a requirement for convincing the municipality of a city has been very difficult. Further, all communities have their own politics and their own governing boards and hence interfering in their affairs is a difficult task.

15

STRATEGIES FOR NETWORKING AND ADVOCACY FOR CHILD CARE

— K. Shanmugavelayutham

Introduction

FORCES, an acronym for Forum for Crèche and Child Care Services, is a network of organisations working for the care and education of children in the 0-6 years age group. There is a National FORCES, and there are State Chapters. State Chapters exist in Tamil Nadu, Gujarat, Orissa, Karnataka, Maharashtra and Rajasthan. The rationale for a networking body is that, while there are organisations working for the care and welfare of children, the efforts are not in unison, and there is a need to lobby vociferously for and advocate for this vulnerable group of children's needs. Though the Constitution sanctions for the care of the most vulnerable groups, the resources are not allocated or do not reach the children.

This chapter covers the strategies that TN Forces used to achieve its objectives, and the impact created by the strategies. These experiences over 8 to 9 years have made one realise that any advocacy work requires a lot of efforts to bring the people together, to appreciate and to work towards common goals. Sustaining such an advocacy network requires financial and institutional support which are difficult to get, as child care is not a prime issue for many funders. Networking for child care is up against many odds.

The Tamil Nadu Chapter of FORCES, (TN-FORCES) since its initiation in 1992, has been advocating the cause of effective early childhood care and development (ECCD) services for children below six years, especially the children of those mothers who are employed in the unorganised labour sectors. With its varied memberships like Trade Unions, NGOs, Research and Professional Institutions, Women's Organisations, TN-FORCES has become a strong mechanism in lobbying and advocacy with the Government. There are at present 95 organisations who are members of the network.

Objective

The objective of TN-FORCES is to lobby for better care of the young child in Tamil Nadu. As the Government is a major provider of child care services, the network, works closely with the Government. With this mandate, TN-FORCES has been working in the areas of maternity and child welfare, empowering working women to breastfeed, empowerment of the family, gender concerns and other policy related issues, apart from having training programmes for various functionaries involved in the delivery of child care services both from the Government and NGOs. TN-FORCES is a pressure group committed to the survival and development of the children of Tamil Nadu , the majority of whom live in circumstances of poverty. Since 1997, the Department of Social Work of Loyola College, Chennai, is the Secretariat for TN-FORCES.

Basic Premises

These are:

(1) Childcare is a basic support to working women and the right of children.

(2) Day Care is an important strategy for poverty prevention and 'development'.

(3) Adequate resources are vital to child care services.

(4) People's planning and participation are vital to the success of the programmes.

(5) Child care workers need recognition, adequate remuneration and capacity building.

In order to reach and influence a wide range of people involved namely, policy makers, legislators, employers, programme planners, implementers, and the general public, TN-FORCES used a variety of strategies, namely advocacy, lobbying, information sharing, capacity building, strategizing and carrying out joint activities.

Advocacy

Advocacy is a type of intervention where TN-FORCES acts on behalf of young children to redress the injustice by seeking through legitimate authority, to bring about changes in the laws and programmes that are causing the injustice.

Advocacy is the process of working with/or and on behalf of young children

- To obtain services or resources for young children that would otherwise not be provided.
- To modify existing policies, procedures or practices that have an adverse impact on young children.
- To promote new legislation or policies that will result in the provision of needed resources or services.

Advocacy Strategies

Memorandum

The first major advocacy activity was the presentation of a Memorandum to the State Minister for Social Welfare in 1992; on the need to improve child care services in the State. Nothing much came out of this, as the Government did not respond to any suggestion on the follow-up.

In May 1994, following a meeting with legislators and based on the network theme for the year, a Memorandum on 'supporting working mothers to breastfeed their children' was submitted to the government. Four important demands were made in the memorandum:

- Extension of maternity leave from three months to four months from the date of delivery.
- Two nursing breaks with a minimum of 45 minutes a day.
- Sufficient increase in the cash benefit under the Muthulakshmi Reddy Scheme from Rs. 300 to Rs. 1600.
- Removing the income ceiling and restrictions on number of children for obtaining benefits.

The memorandum apart from being widely circulated among legislators, women's organisations, trade unions and in conferences, was also reproduced in newsletters and the magazines of network members. Another Memorandum submitted to the State Finance Commission called for decentralisation of child care services at the Panchayat level and recommended allocation of adequate resources to the Panchayats for managing the services. Advocacy on this issue started in 1992 when a Methodology Note on 'parent mobilisation and decentralisation' for strengthening child care services in Tamil Nadu, was widely circulated. This was revised in 1997 in view of the election to the local bodies in the State. The Chairperson of the Commission assured that the Memorandum would be included in his report to the Government.

The other Memoranda were

- ✓ A Memorandum on the inclusion of childcare services in National Women's policy, submitted to the Department of Women and Child Development, Government of India.
- ✓ A Memorandum calling for a separate Directorate for pre-schools submitted to the Education Minister, Government of Tamil Nadu.

✓ A Memorandum on the rights of women workers including maternity benefits, child care services and equal pay submitted to the Labour Ministry, Government of India.

✓ A Memorandum on the burden on pre-school children submitted to the Government constituted High Level Committee on reducing the burden on school curriculum.

A Memorandum to revise the Scheme of Assistance for crèches for children of Working and Ailing mothers Scheme was given to the Minister, Secretary and Director of the Department of Social Welfare and to the Chairperson of State Social Welfare Board. The following demands were presented to the Government.

- Honorarium of the care taker and the helper to be increased to Rs. 1100 and Rs.600 respectively.
- The grant for supplementary feed to be increased to Rs. 9 per child per day from the existing Rs. 1.05
- To relax the terms and condition that resources should not be raised from other sources for this purpose.

This form of advocacy mainly targets bureaucrats and politicians in their capacity as policy makers. Memoranda have been fairly successful in gaining their attention as well as orienting them on the issue. Memoranda have also been used for multiple forms of advocacy. They are part of training kits, conference materials, meeting handouts or more plainly as an information note on the issue.

Care was taken in the process of preparation of these memoranda. The first step is the preparation of a brief outline of what could be included in the memorandum. This is circulated following which extensive discussions are held with member organisations before the memorandum is finalised. In some cases, the thinking of the Government on the issue is also sought before the memorandum is finalised, as was the case with the one submitted to the State Finance Commission.

Pre-election Appeal

Pre-election appeal was given to the political parties that were contesting in the Parliamentary and Assembly elections. An opportunity to influence politicians came up on the eve of the elections to the State Assembly in early 1996, and Parliamentary elections in 1998 and 1999. A memorandum on inclusion of issues related to women and children in the election manifestos of political parties was submitted to all major political parties. It was a good occasion for advocacy, as the manifesto draft committees who were looking for ideas to be packaged into promises, picked up points from the memorandum for inclusion in their manifestos. Three major parties included some of the issues in their manifestos, while all the parties agreed that these are important issues. Two parties published the contents in the manifesto which were used up by party speakers and raised in pre-election campaign meetings. The memorandum was also sent through partners to several districts for distribution to party cadres at the local level. Simultaneously, the memorandum was released to the press and due coverage was given both by the English and the vernacular press. This also ensured that the issues were in the agenda at the political level as well as the public level paving the way for a continuous debate on the issues. Seeing the same issue appearing in the press reinforced the importance of considering them seriously. The memorandum was later distributed along with other materials to elected members of the Assembly. Though, pre-election campaigns are possible once in five years, they have enormous potential to generate awareness. A press meet was held and the appeal was given to the parties which also appeared in the dailies.

The following were the issues for inclusion in their party manifesto:

- Inclusion of child care services under the Minimum Needs Programme.
- Setting up of a Special Fund for crèches and childcare services.

- Allocation of a minimum annual amount calculated as a fixed share of the GNP for child care services, keeping in mind that children below six years constitute 18 per cent of the population.
- Child care workers must be paid at least minimum wages.
- Review and amendment of existing labour laws to make childcare services effective in both the unorganised and organised sectors.
- Provision of adequate facilities in the existing childcare centres and allocation of Rs. 9 per child per day for nutrition.

Public Hearing Strategy

A Public Hearing programme on child care services was organised by TN-FORCES on the June 2, 1998 at Chennai. The purpose of this programme was to highlight the need for childcare services and the problems faced by the women in the unorganised sector due to the lack of these services and the problems faced by child care workers.

In the Public Hearing programme 600 women from throughout the State of Tamil Nadu representing the sectors of agriculture, *beedi* workers, construction labourers, pavement dwellers and domestic workers participated.

The women labourers (30 of them) deposed their cases in front of the panel which consisted of eminent people from the field of child welfare and Government officials from the Departments of Social Welfare and Labour. The case presentations were classified based on the following issues:

- Lack of child care services.
- Deficiencies in the existing services.
- Problems in the support services.
- Problems faced by child care workers.

Lack of Child Care Services

There are several areas where child care services are not available and this is due to the problem of distance and accessibility. Women working in the remote areas found it difficult to take care of their children and go to work. The children are thus exposed to hazards at work, get affected by accidents and contract diseases. In some areas, the women have to travel long distances to gain access to the nearest child care service centre.

Deficiencies in the Existing Services

The women pointed out the lacunae in the existing child care services. The issues that were raised included:

- *Food:* The quality of food was poor and low in nutritional content. The quantity was also not sufficient.
- *Unhygienic Conditions:* The centres are not maintained properly and the *ayahs* do not keep the place clean. Clean drinking water is often not made available and the children often grow up in unhygienic surroundings.
- *Availability of Materials:* The women expressed their view that the materials they require are not available on time and therefore, they are unable to perform their duties properly.
- *Improper Implementation:* Antenatal and prenatal care services are not implemented properly. There is no proper monitoring of all the existing services.

Problems in the Support Services

The support schemes that were available for the girl child were inadequate. The amount that was given to pregnant women under the Muthulakshmi Reddy Scheme was very minimal and the actual benefits were limited due to bureaucratic delays, corruption and diversion of money for other purposes.

Problems Faced by Child Care Workers

The timings of the child care centres are not suitable for the child care workers. They are not consulted while major decisions are taken for running the centres. Their problems are not heard to and they face difficulty in running the centres.

Follow-up of Public Hearing

The proceeding of the Public Hearing was printed in book form, both in Tamil and English. A meeting was held on July 16, 1998 at the Secretariat with the Minister of Social Welfare, Government of Tamil Nadu. The recommendations that were brought out from the seminar on Child Care Workers in the Twenty-first Century, held on May 7, 1998 and the public hearing programme on child care services held on June 2, 1998 were presented to the Minister.

The Minister agreed to consider the following demands put forward by TN-FORCES:

- An advisory committee would be set up to oversee the functioning of the child care services throughout Tamil Nadu (ICDS, TNIP and other support schemes). The members of this committee, its functioning and other details would be decided at a later meeting.
- The norm that the female only would have to undergo family planning will now be relaxed. Both, the male or the female, will be responsible and it will not be thrust on the females alone.
- Under the Muthulakshmi Reddy Scheme, from now on either the ration card or the Village Administrative Officer (VAO) certificate will suffice to get to know the income of the family. This will help to lessen the burden faced by women in availing the facilities of this scheme.
- The State Government will consider giving additional funds to the crèches run by NGOs aided by the Central Social

Welfare Board (CSWB) under the Scheme of Crèches for Working and Ailing Mothers.

Public Hearings at District Levels

Public Hearing was held in the Districts of Nagapattinam, Dindigul, Tirunelveli, Kanchipuram, Villupuram, Pudukottai, Thiruvellore and Perambalur respectively. The problems faced by the women working in unorganised sectors due to lack of child care services, inadequacies in existing services, difficulties faced in availing themselves of the Government Schemes and the status of child care workers were the issues that were focused during the programme.

The district representatives from the Departments of Labour, Health, Social Welfare, ICDS and District Collector participated in the programme. The women came forward to express their problems in caring for their young child. In each of these programmes, around 700 women participated and the NGOs at the local level came forward to organise the programme.

Follow-up Activities

The sub-group formed at Thiruvallur District was doing an intensive survey of the child care centres in their district and was planning to submit it to the District Collector. The sub-group at Nagapattinam District planned to meet the Government Officials at District levels to follow up the petitions that were received during the Public Hearings and were submitted to the Collector.

Lobbying

Manual to the Members of the Legislative Assembly

With the resource support of Project ACCESS, MSSRF, a manual descriptive of the rights of the children below six years, the Government programmes available, the lacunae in the same and the reasons for demanding a revision of the existing same were given to the members of the Legislative Assembly. It suggests what the MLAs can do in their capacity for better delivery of child care services.

Advisory Committee on Childcare Services

TN-FORCES submitted a proposal for an Advisory Committee for child care services to the Department of Social Welfare in September 1998. Since there was no response from the Government regarding this, a reminder letter was sent to the Department. A petition regarding this was also sent to the Governor, the Chief Secretary and the Chief Minister of Tamil Nadu. Advocacy through the media was also made to expedite the process.

Lobbying with Legislators during the Budget Sessions

On the eve of the Budget Session of the Tamil Nadu Legislative Assembly, TN-FORCES lobbied with leaders of the opposition parties and presented a Charter of Demand justifying the rationale for increase in budget allocation for crèches and child care support services by the State Social Welfare Board. The demands also focused on upgrading the quality of nutritional mix, repair and maintenance of the buildings of crèches, provision of toilets and drinking water facilities.

Capacity Building

TN-FORCES organised Advocacy workshop on Early Childhood Care and Development for its member organisations.

Seminars and Workshops

A series of seminars on Child Rights were organised at Thanjavur, Madurai and Kanyakumari Districts on "Child Rights also Human Rights", "Child Rights Violation in Educational Institutions and Residential Homes for Children", "Child rights violation in family settings". "Child Rights Violation in Government Programmes and Services". NGOs and activists from the respective districts participated in the programme. The seminar highlighted the rights of children below six years, which are mostly overlooked. A workshop for pre-school teachers were organised at Coimbatore and Thiruvannamali. These seminar-cum-workshops focused on strategies for healthy childcare services in the future. A similar seminar was held at Chennai in 1999. The Minister for Fisheries participated in the seminar. A workshop on the status of childcare workers in the voluntary sectors was jointly organised by MSSRF and TN-FORCES on 1999 itself.

Strategizing and Carrying Out Joint Activities

The pre-school sub-group of TN-FORCES has been working towards issues concerning pre-school education. TN-FORCES developed an alternate early childhood education curriculum, described as "activity-based", "developmentally appropriate" and "child centred". An effective tool for advocacy has thus been provided which the TN-FORCES network planned to disseminate in the voluntary sectors, as part of its campaign for regulation of ECE in all sectors to strengthen the rights of the young child. The pre-school sub-group of TN-FORCES with the expertise of India Association of Pre-school Education (IAPE) has formulated an activity-based, developmentally appropriate curriculum for young children.

Other Strategies

Rally

A rally of around 500 anganwadi workers was organised in 1999 projecting various demands. The rally started at Valluvar Kottam and culminated at Panagal Park with a public meeting.

Taskforce

As a follow-up of the Seminar on the Status of child care Workers in the Voluntary Sector jointly organised by MSSRF and TN-FORCES, a Task Force was formed. As suggested in the Task Force meeting held in the middle of 1999, efforts were taken to have a dialogue with the Department of Labour. This was organised in January 2000 with a purpose to create awareness in the Labour Department about women labourers need for child care services.

Token Fast

As there was no response from the Government regarding the revision of the Assistance for Crèches for the Children of Working and Ailing Mothers, the NGOs receiving grants from the Central/ State Social Welfare Board observed a token fast was held in front of the State Guest House at Chennai in December, 1999. About 200 Crèche Teachers and ayahs and NGO representatives participated in the fast. A memorandum was presented to the Secretary, Department of Social Welfare to revise the scheme. The Government agreed to revise the scheme and elicit the opinion of voluntary organisations. This itself is a major achievement for the TN-FORCES.

TN-FORCES organised a meeting to finalise the suggestion regarding the scheme to the Government. The suggestions were sent to the all the organisations and they were asked to send the same to the Government and Tamil Nadu State Social Welfare Board.

Cradle Demonstration

Sixty women belonging to the unorganised labour sector converged at the Labour Welfare Commission building along with their children for a 'cradle demonstration' demanding that Labour Welfare Board, other welfare boards and schemes for the workers in the unorganised sector recognise the need for crèches.

Street Play

During the Breastfeeding Week, programmes encouraging women to breastfeed, necessity of the family's support and creating awareness for the young on the importance of breast feeding, were organised through street plays. This programme was organised in the Madurai district by the Madurai sub-group of TN-FORCES.

Building Alliances

The issue of TN-FORCES was pushed through various other bodies that campaign for the child rights, in their own capacities. CACL included the issue of the need for quality of ECCD programmes and crèches for children of women in the unorganised labour sectors in their pre-election appeal given to the various political parties that contested in the Parliamentary elections.

The National Alliance for the Fundamental Right to Education has accepted to address the issue of education of children six years in the 83rd Amendment through a legislative process. It was put forth by TN-FORCES.

The TN-FORCES also made efforts to interact with National Commission for Women, to put forth the need for child care services for women. A meeting was held with the former Chairperson of the National Commission for Women. In this meeting, the demands of TN-FORCES were presented to her, which were forwarded to the Chief Minister of Tamil Nadu.

The PHA Campaign seeks to strengthen Primary Health Centre which is the basic strategy to achieve goal of "Health for All". The campaign demands policy change at the international, national, and regional levels that will stave off the danger posed to the poor and make health accessible and affordable to all. TN--FORCES with the help of the Tamil Nadu Science Forum organised Districts Convention at Villupuram and Pudukottai in the form of an open interactive face to face programme between the peoples' representatives of self-help groups and the head of the District Health Department, ICDS, TINP and Social Welfare Department. During the above interface the existing lacuna and the lack of adequate of services in child care and the Primary Health Centres were debated.

The people from the respective blocks submitted their demands and grievances pertaining to the above said problems in their areas to the District Collector who was present at the interface. The focus of their demands centred around the necessity of the Government ensuring provision of quality and adequate PHCs and Child Care Services accessible to people, especially to the weaker sections.

Strengths of TN-FORCES

- Flexibility of strategies and implementation is imperative if strategies are to do justice to the variety and peculiarity of childcare needs across various communities.
- *Network — Means and Ends:* TN-FORCES was formed as a vehicle to address issues and to help the network grow and flourish. TN-FORCES' campaigns function as both, ends and means. TN-FORCES' campaigns had the twin goals of obtaining a major achievement and in the process got organisational mileage. Therefore, when choosing an issue, the TN-FORCES has been concerned with not only whether it can be achieved but also how the campaign can be used to develop the network.
- The strategy is as important as the goal itself. No social strategy can be static. The advocacy strategy is the refinement of the earlier strategies.
- Use of local media including folk-theatre as a means of communication was encouraged.
- TN-FORCES also brings in other member organisations like trade unions to involve them in organised efforts.

The process of advocacy in TN-FORCES is summarised in the chart 15.1.

Impact of Advocacy

Sustained campaigning on this issue by TN-FORCES and the network members resulted in number of concrete benefits:

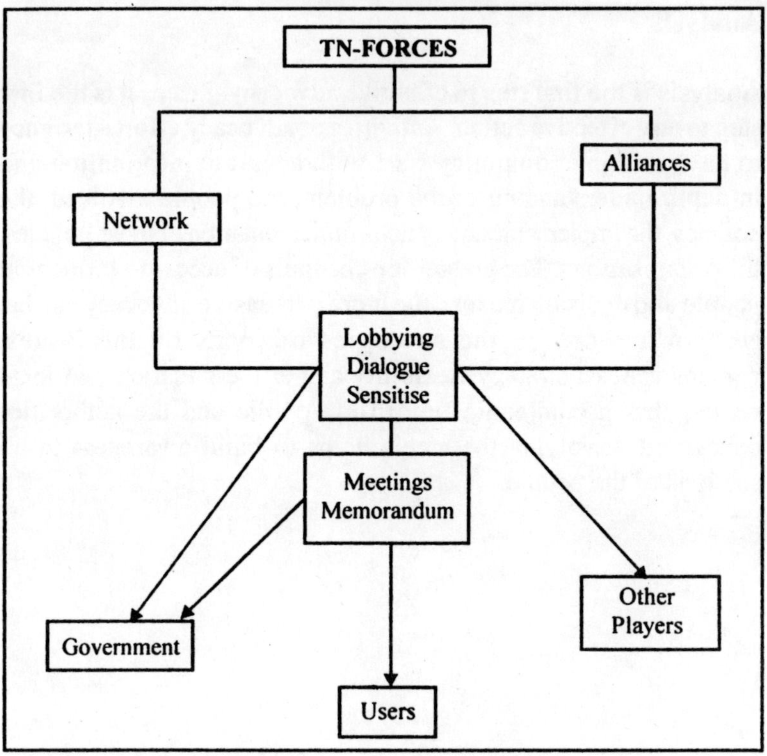

Fig. 15.1 : TN Advocacy Process

- Six months maternity leave to women workers in the unorganised sector.
- Extension on noon meals to pregnant women and lactating mothers for six months.
- The campaign has created a favourable opinion about the ECCD through media.

Research Studies

TN-FORCES conducted two Research studies, namely child care needs of the Urban Poor in Chennai and Infrastructure facilities of the ICDS. The findings of these studies are used in advocacy activities.

Analysis

Analysis is the first step to effective advocacy, just as it is the first step to any effective action. Activities or advocacy efforts designed to have a impact on policy start with accurate information and in-depth understanding of the problem, the people involved, the policies, the implementation or non-implementation of those policies, the organisations. The greater the channels of access to influential people and decision makers, the more persuasive advocacy can be. Networks work on the strategies of focus on the issues, persuasiveness, strategy flexibility as per the situation and local needs, strong communication to the public and the authorities concerned. Involving the media helps to build awareness in all sections of the people.

SECTION-V

Future Perspectives

16

FUTURE PERSPECTIVES

— *Vrinda Datta* and *Rajani M. Konantambigi*

Indian society largely believes that child-rearing and socialisation of the child are the prime responsibilities of the family. Parents and extended family provide the care and attention needed by children to give them opportunities for growth and development. With rapid socio-economic changes there has been a change in this notion and the way children are being reared. The emergence of a new social structure (women-headed households, nuclear families), technological changes, changes in labour markets and also migration to urban areas have created situations where parents are not solely responsible for child rearing, but external support systems have started playing an important role.

Child day care services can be seen as an important intervention to provide women the right and the opportunity to participate in employment and to carry out the task of being a home-maker and a mother. The last decade has seen that more women are in the labour market, work longer hours and very often are prime breadwinners in the family. Thus creation of child care services has become essential for supporting these women. In the context of women's rights and gender equity, child care is also viewed as very important to release young girls from the task of child care of their siblings and seek education so as to enhance her opportunities in life and also to create a future generation of educated mothers who would then be empowered to change the life of their children (Combes, 2001). Thus child care programmes must be viewed as programmes that strengthen the mothers as the primary caregivers and as important systems to support young girls' development.

The Convention on the Rights of Children recognises the importance of care and development of young children, and family as the fundamental group of society which is the natural environment for the growth and well being of all its members, particularly children. Combes (2001) clarifies that this does not mean that the Convention puts children against adults, but its basic aim is to call attention to the importance of childhood and to the responsibility of all adults to care for them. But one can see a general lack of commitment to this important function of society. The so-called more urgent social and economic issues gain importance at the cost of expansion of services and programmes for young children. As Swaminathan (2000) points out that even after twenty years of existence of the government scheme for crèches for children for working women, only 13,700 crèches exists all over India which cater to about 3,50,000 children. Further the government in its process of economic reforms also rationalises budget cuts in these schemes as they are duplicating services provided by the national scheme, Integrated Child Development Services Scheme (ICDS). However ICDS does not provide child care *per se* but the government proposed that by 2000, 25 per cent *anganwadis* would be *anganwadi*-cum-crèche programmes. However, this did not happen. Thus the policies and programmes of the government inadequately fulfil the obligation of providing the support to families in the care and development of children.

The statutory sector too has seen no new provisions. The existing laws make provision for crèches for women in some sectors such as mines and plantations but in spite of clear lacunae identified by researchers and practitioners, the services rendered even today are inadequate and of poor quality. The dearth of services is a cause of concern in today's context where more and more women are in the unorganised labour which makes tremendous demands on their time and energy. Besides, when child care is not available, a woman worker is forced to depend on her girl child or leave the child unattended. Thus even though there is a demand for child care, child care facilities are not being created and the alternatives that families think of may not always be appropriate.

The age at which mothers will send their children to a child care setting will depend on the support she gets from her employer as maternal entitlement. In piece rate work or daily wages, there is loss of earnings for a family when the women is in the post-parturition stage. Therefore, many women get back to work at the earliest and at the cost of the health of self and child. In her analysis of maternity entitlements, Swaminathan (2000) says that some legislations do exist but among them there are such, which are restrictive rather than enabling in nature. At times it is difficult to establish the eligibility of the women under some schemes or it even restricts certain women from getting benefits and further there are many women who are unaware of their entitlements. In such a situation maternity entitlements will not be utilised and women and young children will continue to suffer.

Stronger efforts will have to be made to give working women their maternity entitlements. It must be understood that for mother and child, it is essential that mother stays off work/labour for sometime. Wage protection is needed for the time period that women are away for which, both, the employer and the government need to take responsibility. Unless this happens, she will return to work quite immediately after delivery and the infant will be under care of young siblings or in a child care setting.

Women in the organised sector are much privileged in this respect as there are legislation (Maternity Benefit Act and Employees State Insurance Act) which offer some health care and leave to these women. However, not much has been changed in these Acts and may not meet needs of today's families. Efforts to create policy for paternity leave is needed so that there is greater involvement of both parents in care of the young infant. Some states have considered increasing the maternity leave so that mothers can continue breast feeding for a longer time.

The dilemma of who will care for the child ultimately is faced by all women. It has been noted by researchers (Clarke-Stewart, 1989) that early and extensive hours of non-maternal care were related to insecure attachments of infants with their mothers.

However, this must be viewed in the context of quality of care and stability. Most mothers would want care by some family member. Datta (Chapter 8, in this volume) has pointed out that among the middle class the grandmother care is the most preferred form of child care and children under such care do well on social and IQ measures. When grandmothers are not available, these women prefer individual care in their own houses. However, such care does not help in the child's development outcome and therefore should be viewed with caution as alternate child care arrangements. It has been seen through various studies that very young children benefit from family day care settings which offer warmth and security of a home. The most important factor one should look for stability and quality in the child care that is chosen. The women in the unorganised sector do not get much choice in how they will arrange for child care. Wherever possible, women carry their infants to work or delegate the care to siblings of the child as most other adults in family are also at work.

Mothers who are away from children for long hours experience profound guilt which has many implications for parenting and the subsequent effects on children. As Datta (1993) pointed out, mothers because of their guilt often feel they must do everything for children. When parents leave their children behind in a child care setting for the entire day, they are seeking a high stimulating home-like environment for their children (Konantambigi and Sriram, this volume, Chapter 5). Further, Arulraj and Samuel (this volume, Chapter 4) also point out that even the rural women have expressed that when their children are with them, it creates dependency and therefore their children are poor even in self-help skills. Maternal/parental guilt can have many more implications apart from the above. The situation is not any different when we look at paid child care. Women have very few choices. Family day care is a very urban phenomenon and one of the preferred forms of out of home care. Day care centres exist but are difficult to sustain as they entail a lot of expense.

Konantambigi (Chapter 2) elucidates that children, at every stage in life, have specific developmental needs for which child care settings play a vital role. There are no specifications given as to what should comprise a child care programme under the statutory crèches or even by the government and private centres. So there is no understanding of the concept of needs of children and to provide for them through a planned programme. Caregivers seem to lack comprehension of developmental needs ranging from physical care to individual differences in child sensitivities and temperament. But the fact is that child care impacts child's development and there is need to evolve an appropriate stimulating programme. Vandell, Dadisman and Gallagher (2000) identified over-time effects that need to be considered; effects may not be initially apparent but emerge later in children's development effects may be transitory but dissipate over time and effects may reflect the cumulative impact of care over time.

The efforts to understand development outcomes for children in child care is seen through the many researches presented in this book. Much more systematic and serious cross-sectional and longitudinal studies will have to be undertaken to analyse the issues of child outcome. The earlier model by Gamble and Zigler (1986) gave us hope that if one developmental context is of poor quality it is compensated for in another set up. And therefore one gave parents inputs to spend quality time so that somewhere there will be compensation for the poor child care environment he/she is likely to face. However, today's literature takes the view that poor quality environment can have a detrimental effect on children's development and therefore the inevitable need that child care programmes have to be of good quality.

Over the last two decades, child care research has tried very hard to create a scientific understanding of the concept of quality and also find methods by which quality can be measured and subsequently, guide programme regulation and monitoring (Datta, Chapter 13). The review of literature in the Indian context shows that there are wide variations in the quality of child care programmes across the country. The study in Mumbai showed that good quality family day care had the potential to create an environment which encouraged adult and peer interactions (both positive and negative). This is one of the most important components of a child care programme. Further, the Bangalore study (Konantambigi, this volume

Chapter 7) reiterated that day care centres are of varied quality and both day care and home environment contribute to strengthen the quality of care. Thus quality is a factor that needs to be understood and implemented in our child care programmes.

Quality issues can be addressed in two ways. Quality in terms of a minimum standard because it is essential to recognize that programmes below the minimum standards are unacceptable as an environment for children. It is also a method to make all programmes accept the concept of quality programme even though this is one of the lowest forms of quality. Context studies/researches exploring into indicators of quality (Cryer, 1998) have found time and again certain key variables as the most important in impacting quality in child care and perhaps these should be accepted as some indicators to develop minimum standards. Issues related to child protection and safety (safety and hygiene) cognitive stimulation, emotional needs and caregiver characteristics are some factors that can be considered for minimum standards. In most countries, minimum standards are related to licensing and very often focus only on structural features (as staff-child ratio, group size, age group). However, some aspects of process variables are important to monitor even though they are difficult.

The second outlook to quality is to identify the indicators of quality which relate to structural and process variables and place them on a continuum so that its possible for practitioners to understand the level at which they are functioning on every indicator and how far they are from optimum quality. The efforts of Maharashtra FORCES and that of National Task Force to develop such tools could soon lead to an Indian tool to measure quality in early childhood programmes. However, the whole issue of quality is complex. It indeed requires much discussion and reflection to develop an understanding of the concept of quality in the Indian context.

Viruru (2002) raises important points for discussion of our acceptance of concepts in early childhood from the developed world without questioning them and without recognising our needs, strengths and weaknesses in early childhood programmes. This applies also to the whole issue of quality and its indicators. Certain issues need to be debated, discussed and reviewed. Do the quality indicators developed fit our programmes? Do we need to look at new indicators that benefit our programmes? Do we need to create new ways to measure quality? The diversity in the programmes, the various stakeholders involved, the varying child care needs of working mothers across sectors – all this makes it inevitable that a new thinking needs to emerge from Asian countries like India in understanding the issues concerning our early childhood programmes.

The understanding and enhancement of the field of child care can occur only when we have all stakeholders interested in the task. The recognition of the importance of child care services has to come from the government, employers and society at large. It must be emphasised that child care is not a substitute to family care but a support service to families who need it and such families are growing in numbers. So then who should take responsibility for provision of child care? In India the public and private partnership in such fields have to be encouraged, while the government's role would be to reach to all the marginalised families. The private sector initiates programmes for populations who can pay for them. The Government should encourage employer involvement in child care by way of tax benefits and/or other exemptions and this should apply to employees in both the organised and unorganised sectors. Perhaps the government may evolve a child care cess so as to avoid the excuse of always not having funding for such important programmes. The grant-in-aid schemes and programmes were/are an excellent example of government and NGO partnership. However, today in the name of partnership, the government is clearly handing over its own responsibility to the other stakeholders. It would be essential not to fall into such traps and be alert and push the government to take on its prime responsibility of protecting children's rights. Funding is one of the issues that needs to be addressed amongst other policies along with recognising child care quality, regulation through legislation and other methods.

Serious efforts are needed to develop systematic and scientific understanding of how these programmes need to operate. Contribution of the academicians and practitioners in creating a national understanding on child care programmes which will guide all stakeholders in operating such programmes is essential. Further such a document should be endorsed by the government so that there is national acceptance on how early childhood programmes should operate.

So far the government has never looked into issues of quality of programme, be it their own programme or those of the private sector. That poor quality programmes can be detrimental to children's development is a fact which has to be understood and taken seriously by all of us. Therefore, there have to be methods of monitoring programmes that deal with young children. Datta's (Chapter 13) analysis of various regulatory methods and its application to Indian context shows that a combination of methods may have to be used to regulate the many diverse programmes that are in existence.

The workforce in child care programmes is also a prime issue in evolving quality programme. It has been seen (Datta, Chapter 8; Konantambigi and Sriram, Chapter 5; Gupta and Konantambigi, Chapter 9) that the caregiver strongly influences the quality of child care programme and that training and education contribute positively rather than just experience. People's thinking needs to change to accept that caregivers are to be considered as professionals who require training and perform a different role than that of a mother. In this context appropriate training models need to emerge. Bajaj (this volume, Chapter 11) clearly brings out this issue that how training needs to be imparted to fulfil the many responsibilities in child care. Further Datta discusses how the lack of uniformity in training inputs has led to acceptance of any training as adequate with implications for caregiver performance and therefore, quality of a programme. Appropriate training institutions should be given recognition in order to avoid incompetent staff from entering child care programmes.

To sum up, stakeholders need to focus on:

- Creating resources to train and pay the child care giver/ child care workers adequately.
- Providing an efficient and effective governing system that will supply, regulate and guide child care programmes.
- Changing existing legislation, policies, programmes in view of the changes in the society related to labour market, family and needs of children. *Contd....*

- Advocating changes in knowledge base and conceptual shifts.
- Creating new directions through legislations, policies and programmes to evolve strategies to develop appropriate programmes and quality practice.
- Working towards inter-sectoral collaboration and coordination.
- Scaling-up of innovative programme.

These may ensure that the children get developmentally appropriate care that is undoubtedly their due.

LIST OF ABBREVIATIONS

A.P.L.	:	Above Poverty Line.
A.W.Cs	:	Anganwadi Centres.
A.G.	:	Autonomy Given to the Child.
B.P.L.	:	Below Poverty Line.
C.E.	:	Stimulation through Toys, Games and Books.
C.E.D.A.W.	:	Convention for Elimination of All Forms of Discrimination Against Women.
C.M.	:	Child Mortality.
C.R.C.	:	Convention on the Rights of the Child.
D.P.	:	Disciplining Methods.
D.P.T.	:	Diphetheria Pertussis Typhoid.
E.C.E.	:	Early Childhood Education.
E.C.C.D.	:	Early Childhood Care and Development.
FORCES	:	Forum for Crèche and Child Care Services.
F.W.P.R.	:	Female Work Participation Rate.
G.M.S.	:	Global Maternal Satisfaction.
I.A.P.E.	:	Indian Association for Pre-school Education.
I.M.R.	:	Infant Mortality Rate.
I.C.D.S.	:	Integrated Child Development Services.
I.D.A.	:	International Development Association.
I.Q.	:	Intelligence Quotient.
L.S.	:	Language Stimulation.

M.S.S.R.F.	:	M.S. Swaminathan Research Foundation.
N.A.E.Y.C.	:	National Association for Education of the Young Child.
N.C.A.E.R.	:	National Council of Applied Economic Research.
N.C.E.R.T.	:	National Council for Educational Research and Training.
N.C.F.	:	National Crèche Fund.
N.E.P.	:	National Economic Policy.
N.F.H.S.	:	National Family Health Survey.
N.G.O.	:	Non-Governmental Organisation.
N.M.	:	Neonatal Mortality.
N.P.C.	:	Non Parental Care.
N.P.P.	:	National Perspective Plan for Women.
O.A.	:	Stimulation through Outdoor Activities.
P.A.C.E.D.	:	Practices Appropriate to the Context of Early Development.
P.D.S.	:	Public Distribution System
P.E.	:	Physical Environment.
P.H.C.	:	Primary Health Centre.
P.N.N.	:	Post-Neonatal Mortality.
P.W.A.	:	Parental Pride, Warmth and Affection.
R.C.H.	:	Reproductive and Child Health.
S.A.B.	:	Stimulation through Academic Behaviour.
S.A.P.	:	Structural Adjustment Programme.
S.E.B.A.	:	Socio-Emotional Behavioural Adjustment.
S.S.C.	:	Secondary School Leaving Certificate.
S.E.S.	:	Socio-Economic Status.
S.T.	:	Scheduled Tribe
T.B.	:	Tuberculosis.

TN-FORCES : Tamil Nadu Forum for Crèche and Child Care Services.

T.N.I.P. : Tamil Nadu Integrated Programme.

U.F.M.R. : Under Five Mortality Rate.

U.N.I.C.E.F.: United Nation's International Children's Emergency Fund.

W.P.I. : Wholesale Price Index.

W.P.R. : Work Participation Rate.

GLOSSARY

Anganwadi: "Anganwadi" literally means courtyard. Anganwdi is a courtyard pre-school, grassroot level unit of the Integrated Child Development Services (ICDS) Scheme of the Government of India.

Anganwadi Worker: Field level worker of the ICDS scheme of the Government.

Ashram School: In the ancient Indian education system, a pupil boarded with a teacher of repute, received education and in return rendered domestic or other services. The term is also used for residential schools run by the Government of India for children hailing from under privileged sections of society.

Ayah: A hired female caretaker generally for children, in the children's own home.

Balwadi: literally the term means "children's garden". The term is used to refer to the pre-school education programme for three to six year old children.

Coolie: A person making a living by carrying or transporting goods on his/her person.

Crèche: A term to indicate group care for children generally in the age group of 3 months to school age.

Day Care Centre: An organised setting for the substitute care for a group of young children away from home in a special premise with appointed staff, for some part of the day.

Dyads: An interpersonal interaction setting between two individuals; for example, child-mother dyad.

Ethology: A study of the role of critical period in development.

Exosystem: The social setting that the individual never experiences directly but that can still influence his or her development. For example, a child generally does not experience the work site of his parents. But what transpires there could be satisfying or dissatisfying to the parents and could in turn impact the child. Similarly what transpires in school could be brought to the family interactions by the child.

Family Day Care: A form of substitute child care for young children at the caregiver's residence for some part of the day.

Group Care: A setting where a group of young children are taken care of during some part of the day.

Headstart: An early childhood programme of the Federal Government of the United States of America which has the overall development of the child as its goal. Involvement of the parents and the community is also sought in its implementation.

Jowar: A cereal grown and consumed in parts of Karnataka, Maharashtra and Andhra Pradesh.

Junior Kindergarten: A pre-school programme for children of 3½ to 4½ years.

Macrosystem: The larger subcultural and cultural contexts in which the microsystem, mesosystem and exosystem are embedded. Indirect impact of the cultural, societal context on the individual is explained by the macro context.

Mahila Mandal: A congregation group of women formed within a community for achieving their social and/or family/community related needs.

Mahila Samakhya: Is a government initiative to mobilise and empower rural women within a clearly worked out ideological framework. The programme is need-based and the components of the project are designed to facilitate collective reflection/

action and expand opportunities for basic education in rural areas.

Malayalees: A person originating from the state of Kerala, in South India.

Matrilineal Family System: A familial system where a woman in the head of the household and the female children/female members inherit the property rights.

Matrilocal Pattern: A society system in which descent is reckoned in the female line.

Mobile Crèches: A voluntary organisation running child care centres, and schools for children (aged 3 months to 14 years) of migrant labourers. Mobile crèches is operational in various cities of India.

Mesosystem: The inter-relationships or linkages between microsystems. For example, unpleasant experiences at the pre-school could upset a child, and in turn disturb the relationships with parents.

Microsystem: The immediate environment in which the individual functions. For example, for an infant it is generally the family, day care centre. Within any microsystem individuals contribute to their own development by affecting their companions, who in turn influence them in new ways.

Nuclear Families: The smallest family unit comprising a married couple and their unmarried children.

Nursery School: An early stimulation and early learning programme for children aged 2½ to 3½.

Role Theory: The premise that when an individual has two or more roles to play, each making incompatible demands, not only is there role-strain, but role-effectiveness is reduced as well.

Sanskritization: A social process wherein persons belonging to lower social strata look up to and imitate the mores and values of the upper caste persons in a society. The term was coined by M.N. Srinivas.

Senior Kindergarten: A pre-school programme for children of 4½ to 5½ years.

Statutory Crèches: Child care setting/s under the law for children aged 3 months to school age.
(Legal provision for child care. Specific categories are covered under the provision like Factories, Mines, other organised sectors).

Tamilians: A person originated from the South Indian state of Tamil Nadu.

Triads: An interaction setting, face-to-face among three individuals; e.g. child-mother-father.

Tuwar: A pulse commonly grown in Southern and Western India, and consumed in various parts of the country.

UDISHA: literally means, 'a new dawn', and is the name of current training programme for functionaries under the Integrated Child Development Services Scheme, India.

Unorganised Sector: Work settings which are informal in nature and where labour practices are not entirely governed by legal provisions.

Zamindars: landlords of India, in the pre-independence days.

REFERENCES

Adhikari, S. (1994) The leisure gap. *The Sunday Times of India*, March 6, p.11.

Ainsworth. M.D., Blehar, M.C., Waters, E., and Wall, S. (1978) *Patterns of Attachment* Hillsdale, NJ: Erlbaum.

Ainsworth, M.D.S. (1979) Mother infant attachment. *American Psychologist, 24*, 932 - 937.

Anandlakshmy, S. (1994) The Girl Child and the Family, An Action Research Study, sponsored by the Department of Women and Child Development, HRD Ministry, Govt. of India, New Delhi, p. 127.

Arulraj, M.R. and R.S. Samuel. (1995) *Balancing Multiple Roles. Child Care Strategies of Women Working in the Unroganised Sector in Tamil Nadu* (Research Report No. 1), Chennai: M.S. Swaminathan Research Foundation.

Atkinson, A.M. (1987) A comparison of mothers' and providers' preferences and evaluations of day care centre services. *Child and Youth Care Quarterly, 16D, Spring 1987*, 35-47.

Atkinson, A.M. (1992) Stress levels of family day care providers, mothers employed outside the home, and mothers at home. *Journal of Marriage and the Family*, 54, 379-386.

Bala, P. and Upadhyaya, K. (1992) Behaviour problems in pre-school children and the education and employment of their mothers. *Indian Psychological Review, 39*, 25-29.

Balasubramanium D. (3.6.1999). 'The hope and the hype', in *The Hindu*, New Delhi: Science and Technology Supplement.

Belsky, J. and Eggebeen, D. (1991). Early and extensive maternal employment and young children's socio-emotional development: Children of National Longitudinal Survey of Youth. *Journal of Marriage and Family, 3*, 1083-1110.

Belsky, J. (1990). Parental and non-parental child care and children's socio-emotional development: A decade of review. *Journal of Marriage and Family, 52*, 885-903.

Belsky, J. and Rovine, M.J. (1988). Non-maternal care in the first year of life and the security of infant-parent attachment. *Child Development, 59*, 157-167.

Belsky, J. (1984) Two waves of day care research: Developmental effects and conditions of quality in R. Ainsle (ed.) *The Child in the Day Care Setting,* N.Y.: Praeger.

Belsky, J. and Steinberg, L. (1978). The effects of day care: A critical review. *Child Development, 49,* 929-949.

Berk, L. (1985). Relationships of educational attainment, child oriented attitude, job satisfaction and career commitment to caregiver behaviour towards children. *Child Care Quarterly, 14,* 103-129.

Bhandari, M. (2004). The relationship between economic and social dimensions of work — A case study of women executives. Paper presented at National Seminar on Globalization and Women's Work, March 25-26, India.

Bjorkman, S. Poteat, G.M. and Snow, C.W. (1986). Environment ratings and children's social behaviour: Implications for the assessment of day care quality. *American Journal of Orthopsychiatry, 56* (2).

Blalock, H.M. (1979). *Statistics for Social Scientists.* New York: McGraw Hill Book Company.

Bogota, A.G., and Gensheimer, C.K. (1986). *Child Care Quarterly,* 15(3), Fall, 159-169.

Bradley, R.H. Caldwell, B.M., Rock, S.L. Ramey, C.T., Barnard, K.E., Gray, C., Hammond, M.A., Mitchell, S., Gottfried, A.W., Siegel, L., and Johnson, D.L. (1989). Home environment and cognitive development in the first three years of life: A collaborative study involving six sites and three ethnic groups in North America. *Development Psychology, 25,* 217-235.

Bradley, R.C. and Caldwell, B.M. (1979). Home observation for the measurement of environment: Revision of the pre-school scale. *American Journal of Mental Deficiency, 84,* 235-244.

Bradley, R.H., Caldwell, B.M. and Rock, S.K. (1988). Home environment and school performance: A ten year follow-up and examination of three models of environment action. *Child Development, 59,* 852-867.

Bredecamp, S. and Coppre, C. (eds.) (1997). Developmentally appropriate practice in early childhood programmes (Rev. ed.) Washington D.C.: National Association for Education of Young Children.

Bronfenbrenner, U. (1986). Ecology of the family as a context for human development. Research perspective. *Developmental Psychology, 22,* 723-242.

Bronfenbrenner, U. and Crouter, A. (1982). Work and family through time and space in S. Kamerman and C. Hayes, (eds.) *Families that work: children in a changing world.* Washington: National Academy Press.

Bronfenbrenner, U. (1979). *The ecology of human development: Experiments by nature and design,* Cambridge: Harvard University Press.

Burchinal, M., Lee, M., and Ramey, C. (1989). Type of day care and pre-school intellectual development in disadvantaged children. *Child Development, 60,* 128-137.

Caldwell, Wright, Honig and Tannenbaum. (1970). Substitute child care satisfaction and the parent child relationship: Only one study. *American Journal of Ortho Psychiatry. 40,* 397 - 412.

Census of India. (1991). *Provisional population totals: Workers and their distribution, Series-I,* New Delhi, Government of India.

Chaudhary, D.P. (1996). *A dynamic profile of child labour in India* - (1951) - (1991), New Delhi CLASP - ILO.

Chaudhari, S.N. (1990). *Study on work pattern of women and its impact on health and nutrition.* Calcutta: Child in Need Institute.

Cherry, F.F. and Eaton, E.L. (1977). Physical and cognitive development in children in low-income mother working in the child's early years. *Child Development, 48,* 158-166.

Cheung, F.M. and Chau, B.T.W. (1984). Caretaking forms and styles in urban Hong Kong: A pilot study on three-year old children. Mimeograph. Hong Kong: The Chinese University of Hong Kong.

Christina, J. (1999). The first teacher: Childcare workers in the voluntary sector of Tamilnadu. Chennai: M. S. Swaminathan Research Foundation.

Clarke-Stewart, K.A. (1989). Infant day care: Maligned or Malignant? *American Psychology, 44,* 266-273.

Clarke-Stewart, A. and Gruber, C. (1984). Day care forms and features in R.C. Ainslie (Ed.). Quality Variations in Day Care. New York: Praeger.

Cochran, M.M. (1977). A comparison of group day-care and family child rearing patterns in Sweden. *Child Development, 48,* 702-707.

Combes, B.P.Y. (2001). Linking children's and women's rights: An early childhood perspective. *Development, 44(2),* 35-40.

Consul, M. (1990). Child care support of employed mothers' satisfaction and desire for alternatives. Unpublished Masters Thesis, M.S. University of Baroda.

Cost, Quality and Outcomes Study Team. (1999). The Children of cost quality outcomes study go to school. Executive Summary. www.fpg.unc.edu / WCEDL/PAGES/ equas.htm

Crockenberg, S. and Litman, C. (1991). Effect of maternal employment on maternal and two-year old child behaviour. *Child Development, 62,* 930-953.

Cryer, D. (1998). Defining and Assessing Early Childhood Programme Quality. *The Annals of American Quarterly of Political and Social Science, 563,* May 1999, 39-44.

Cummings, E.M. (1980). Caregivers stability and day care. *Development Psychology, 16*, 31-37.

Cummings, E.M. and Davies, P.T. (1994). Maternal depression and child development. *Journal of Child Psychology and Psychiatry and Allied Disciplines, 35*, 73-112.

Datta, V.R., (2002). Child Development Workers in Maharashtra. Mimeograph. Mumbai: TISS.

Datta, V.R., (2002). Factors Affecting Job Performance of Anganwadi Workers — A Study of Three Districts in Maharashtra. A Study sponsored by UNICEF. Mumbai, TISS.

Datta, V.R., (2001). A Study of Urban Early Childhood Programmes. Study sponsored by UNICEF. Mumbai, TISS.

Datta, V.R. (1995). *Home away from home: Family day care in India.* Suraksha Series No.1, Chennai, M.S. Swaminathan Research Foundation.

Datta, V. R. (1995). Developmental differences among pre-school children in group and at-home care. Bombay: Tata Institute of Social Sciences.

Datta, V.R. (1994). Group care as a context for child development. Unpublished Ph.D. Thesis, SNDT Women's University, Mumbai.

Datta, V.R. (1994). Development differences among pre-school children in group and at-home care. Mimeography. Bombay: Tata Institute of Social Sciences.

Datta, V.R. (1993). Developmental differences among pre-school children in group care and in home care. Mimeograph, Mumbai: Tata Institute of Social Sciences.

Datta, V.R. (1991). A perspective on child day care services in India. Unpublished manuscript. Bombay: Tata Institute of Social Sciences.

Datta, V.R. (1989). Services in crèches (under the Government Scheme of crèches for working and Ailing Women). Supervision and Monitoring of Creches Projects, Ministry of H.R.D., Government of India, New Delhi.

Datta, V.R. and Maheshwari, P. (1997). Working parents and family life in Mumbai. Project of Ministry of Welfare, Government of India, Tata Institute of Social Sciences, Mumbai.

Demeis, D.K., McBride, S.L. and Hock, E. (1986). The balance of employment and motherhood: A longitudinal study of mothers' feelings about separation from their first born infants. *Development Psychology, 22*, 627-632.

Department of Women and Child Development, *Annual Report 1997-98*, New Delhi: Ministry of HRD.

Deshpande, L.P. (1992). Problems of working wives: A study of family adjustment pattern of married women workers of GIDC. Makarpura, Baroda. Unpublished Masters Thesis, M.S. University, Baroda.

Dixon-Mueller, R. and R. Anker. (1988). *Assessing women's economic contributions to development* (Paper No. 6). In Background papers for training in population, human resources and development planning, New York: II.O.

Doan, R.M. and B.M. Popkin. (1989). *'Women's work and child care arrangements in the Philippines'*, Maryland: Population Association of America, Baltimore.

Doll, E. (1963). *Vineland's social maturity scale.* New Jersey: Vineland Training Centre.

Dorothy, G. (1991). Quality matters in child care. Oakville: Jesmond Publishing.

Douvan, E. (1963). Employment and the adolescent. In Hoffman, L.W. and Nye, F.I. (Eds.) *The Employed Mother in America.* Chicago: Rand McNally and Co.

D'Souza, A. (1979). Day care for underprivileged children: A study of crèches in Delhi, in D'Souza (ed.), *Children in India: Critical issues in human development,* New Delhi: Manohar Publications.

Dunster, L. (1993). *Caregiver to caregiver: A handbook on developing family day care provider groups.* Ottawa: Childcare Providers Association.

Easterbrooks, M.A., and Goldberg, W.A. (1985). Effects of early maternal employment on toddlers, mothers and fathers. *Developmental Psychology, 21,* 744-783.

Engle, P.L. (1981). *Maternal care, maternal substitutes and children's welfare in the developed and developing countries.*

Etaugh, C. (1980). Effects of non-maternal care on children: Research evidence and popular views. *American Psychologist, 51*, 179-186.

Etaugh, G.G, and Clarke-Stewart, A. (1973). *Day care in context.* New York: John Wiley and Sons.

Fanai, E. (1993). Child care needs in rural south district of Mizoram. Unpublished master's thesis, Department of HDFS, M.S. University, Baroda.

Farel, A.M. (1980). Effects of preferred maternal roles, maternal employment and socio-demographic status on school adjustment and competence. *Child Development, 51*, 1179-1186.

Fein, G.G. and Clarke-Stewart, A. (1973). *Day care in context,* New York : John Wiley and Sons.

FORCES (1999a). Reports of the Three FORCES National Consultations 1990-97 and Seminar on Maternity Child Care and Development, 1999, IMA, Delhi.

FORCES (1999b). FORCES Gazette, No.12, Jan-April 1999, New Delhi.

FORCES, (1997). Report of Third National Consultation 8-10 September 1997, FORCES, (Forum for Crèche and Child Care Services) New Delhi.

FORCES (1997). 'Population stabilisation; Issue or non issue?', Report of A Workshop on Proposed National Population Policy, 24 November 1997, FORCES, New Delhi

Friendly, M. (1994). *Childcare policy in Canada: Putting the pieces together.* Ontario: Addison -Wesley Publishers.

Galambos, N.L. and Maggs, J.L. (1991). Out of school care of young adolescents and self-reported behaviour. *Development Psychology, 27*, 64 - 4 - 655.

Gamble, T.J., Zigler, E. (1986). Effects of infant day care: Another look at the evidence. *American Journal of Orthopsychiatry, 56(1)*, 26-42.

Ganapathy, H. (1992). Some child care management strategies used to cope with motherhood and income generation — The tea plucker's story. Unpublished master's thesis, Department of HDFS, M.S. University, Baroda.

Garrey, W.M.(1993). Child care needs in rural West Garo Hills district of Meghalaya. Unpublished master's thesis, Department of HDFS, M.S. University, Baroda.

Gold, D. and Anders, D. (1978). Developmental comparisons between ten-year-old children with employed and non - employed mothers. *Child Development, 49*, 75 - 85.

Golden M., Rosenbluth, L. and Grossi, M. (1978). *The New York City infant day care study.* Medical and Health Association of New York City.

Goleman, H. and Pence, A.R. (1987). Effects of child care, family and individual characteristics on children's language development: The Victoria Day Care Research In D.A. Philips (ed.). *Quality in child care: What does research tell us?* Washington NAEYC 89-103.

Gopal, A.K. (1992). *Crèches in plantations.* New Delhi: National Institute of Public Cooperation and Child Development.

Gopal, A.K. and Khan, N. (1998). *Crèche services in India.* New Delhi: National Institute of Public Cooperation and Child Development.

Government of India. (2000). Draft country report on birth registration in India *Plan International - India Chapter*, New Delhi: Author.

Government of India. (1989). *Shramshakti, Report of the National Commission on Self-employed Women and Women in the informal sector*, New Delhi: Author.

Government of India. (1998). *Handbook of Civil Registration*, Office of the Registrar General, India, Ministry of Home Affairs, New Delhi: GOI.

Government of India. (1988). *National Perspective Plan for Women 1988-2000 AD*, Department of Women and Child Development, New Delhi: Author.

Government of India: *Census of India. (1981 and 1991), Registrar General of India.* New Delhi: Author.

Government of India. (1989). *Shramshakti. Report of the National Commission on Self-Employed Women and Women in Informal Sector*, New Delhi: GOI.

Government of India: *National Policy of Education. (1986) - Programme of Action,* Ministry of Human Resource Development, 1992.

Greenberger, E., O'Neil, R. and Nagel, S.K. (1995). Linking workplace and home-place: Relations between the adults' work and parenting behaviours. *Development Psychology, 30*, 990-1002.

Greenberger, E., and O'Neil, R. (1990). Parents' concerns about their child's development: Implications for fathers' and mothers' well being and attitudes towards work. *Journal of Marriage and Family, 52,* 431-448.

Gunnarson, (1978). Children in day care and family day care in Sweden: A Follow-up. Cited in Brofenbenner, U. (1979). *Ecology of Human Development,* Harvard Press, MA.

Gupta, A. (2001). Governing population: The integrated child development service programme in India. In Thomas Blom Hansen and Finn Stepputateds. States of Imagination : Ethnographic Explorations of the Post-colonial State. Durham : Duke University Press, 2001, pp. 65-96.

Gupta, M. and Konantambigi, R.M. (1998). Perceived maternal satisfaction and socio-emotional behavioural adjustment of children. *Trends in Social Research, 5*(1), 115-130.

Gupta, M. (1994). Maternal Satisfaction: Consequences for the child. Unpublished master's thesis, M. S. University of Baroda.

Gutek, B.A. and Valdez, R.L. (1987). Family roles: A help or a hindrance for working women. In, A.B. Gutek and Larwood, C. (Eds.), *Women's Career Development,* (pp. 157-169). London: Sage Publication.

Harms, T. and Clifford, D. (1980). *Early Childhood Environment Rating Scale.* New York, Teachers College Press.

Hazarika, Y. (1994). Mothers of all minions. *The Sunday Times of India*, March 6, p.11.

Himes, J.R., C. Landers and J. Leslie (1991). Women, Work and Child Care (Summary), *Proceedings of the Innocent Global Seminar,* Florence: UNICEF.

Hindustan Times, (24.5.1999), 'Town and country planning organisation', *Hindustran Times*, (24-5-1999), New Delhi: Author

Hock, E. and Demeis, D.K. (1990). Depression in mothers of infants: The role of maternal employment. *Development Psychology, 26*, 285-291.

Hofferth, S. L., and Wissoker, D.A. (1992). Price, quality and income in child care choice. *Journal of Human Resources, XXVII,* 70-111.

Hoffman, L.W. (1963). Effects on children: Summary and discussion. In L.W. Hoffman and F.I. Nye (Eds.). *The employed mother in America.* Chicago Rand McNally and Co.

Hoffman, L.W. (1979). Maternal employment: 1979. *American Psychologist, 34,* 859-865.

Howes, C. (1990). Can the age of entry into child care and the quality of child care predict adjustment in Kindergarten? *Development Psychology, 26*, 292 - 303.

Howes, C. (1988). Relations between early child care and schooling. *Development Psychology, 24*, 53 - 57.

Howes, C. and Stewart, P. (1987). Child's play with adults, toys, and peers: An examination of family and child care influences. *Development Psychology, 23*, 423-430.

Howes, C. and Olenick, M. (1986). Family and child influence on toddler compliance, *Child Development, 57*, 202-216.

Howes, C. (1983). Caregiver behaviour in centre and family day care. *Journal of Applied Developmental Psychology, 4*, 99-107.

Howes, C. (1980). Peer play scale as an index of complexity of peer interactions. *Developmental Psychology*, 371-372.

Huffman, S.L. (1985). Women's activities and impact on childhood nutrition. Department of International Health, John Hopkins University School of Hygiene and Public Health, Baltimore.

Jain D. and M. Chand. (1981). Patterns of female work — Implications for statistical design, economic classification and social priorities. Paper presented at the National Conference on Women's Studies, April, Bombay.

Jaykody, R., Chalter. L.M. and Taylor, R. (1993). Family support to single and married African American mothers: The provision for financial, emotional and child care assistance. *Child Development, 55*, 260-267.

Jennings, K.D., Stagg, V. and Connors, R.E. (1991). Social networks and mothers' interactions with their pre-school children. *Child Development, 62*, 966-978.

Jensen, A., (1983). Again, how much can we boost IQ? *Contemporary Psychology, 28*, 756 - 758.

Jhabvala, R., (1998). *'Making women count', women at work*, New Delhi: Commission for Women.

Kabra, Kamal Nayan. (1999). *Macro scenario, Alternative Economic Survey 1991-98; Seven Years of Structural Adjustment*, New Delhi.

Kagan. J. (1984). *The nature of the child*. New York: Basic Books Inc. Publishers.

Kagan, J., Kearsley, R.B. and Zelazo, P.R. (1979). The effects of infant day care and psychological development. In J. Kagan (Ed.) *The growth of the child*. London: Methuen and Co. Ltd.

Kagan, J. and Klein, R. (1973). Cross-cultural perspectives on early development. *American Psychologist, 28* : 947.

Kakkar, S. (1978). *The inner world: a psycho-analysis study of childhood and society in India*. Delhi: Oxford University Press.

Kaneda, T., Suwa, K, and Hijikata, H. (1994). A study of the quality of day care for children under the age of three in terms of teacher's awareness (Series 3): Day nursery teachers' image of "good care". Paper presented at the XIII Biennial Meetings of the ISSBD, 28th June-2nd July 94, Amsterdam.

Kapur, P. (1970). *Marriage and the working women in India.* Delhi: Vikas Publishing House.

Karat, Brinda. (1999). Summary of outcomes from the one day convention of women on food rights, Research Foundation for Science, Technology and Ecology, New Delhi.

Karat, Brinda. (1999). *Women in the new economic order.* AIDWA Publication Series, New Delhi: AIDWA.

Kaur, H. (1988). Support availed for child care and household tasks by nurses and its relationship to their perception of role performance. Unpublished Masters Thesis, M.S. University, Baroda.

Khosla, Renu. (1999). Report on the National Seminar on Campaign for Maternity, Child Care and Development, 21-22nd Jan 1999, National Institute of Urban Affairs, New Delhi.

Khosla, Renu. (1998). Personal Communication. New Delhi: NIUA.

Khullar, M. (ed). (1991). *Whither child care service?* New Delhi: Centre for Women's Development Studies.

Kielman, *et al.* (1983). *Child and maternal health services in rural India: The Warangal experiment,* New York: World Bank Research Publications, USA.

Konantambigi, R.M. (1990). Cognitive and social development of pre-school children in home and day care environments. Unpublished Doctoral Dissertation, Bombay: Tata Institute of Social Sciences.

Konantambigi, R.M. (2000). Home school transition and performance and adjustment of children. Unpublished research report, Mumbai : TISS.

Kontos, S. and Fiene, R. (1987). Child care quality, compliance with regulations and children's development: The Pennsylvania Study in D.A. Phillips (ed.), *Quality in Child Care What does research tell us?* Washington, D.C.: NAEYC.

Kumar, S.K. (1978). *Role of the household economy in child nutrition at low incomes: a case study in Kerala,* Occasional Paper No. 95, Cornell University, New York.

Lamb, M.E., Hwang. A.G., Sternberg and K.J. Broberg, and G.Hwang (eds) (1992). *Child Care in Context,* Lawrence Erilbaum Associates, New Jersey.

Lamb, M.E. and Sternberg, K.J. (1990). Do we really know how day care affects children? *Journal of Applied Development Psychology, 11,* 351-379.

Lamb, M.E. Hwang, C.P., Bookstein, F.L. Broberg, A., Hult, G., and Fordi, M. (1988). Determinants of social competent in Swedishi pre-schoolers. *Developmental Psychology, 24,* 58-70.

Leonard, A. and C. Landers (1995). 'Child care: meeting the needs of working mothers and their children, in A. Leonard' (ed), *Seeds 2: Supporting Women's Work around the World* (pp 169-205), New York: Feminist Press.

Leslie, J. (1989). "Women's work and child nutrition in the third world' in J. Leslie and M. Paolisso (eds.) *Women, Work and Child Welfare in the Third World American Association for the Advancement of Science.*

Lerner, J.V. and Galambos, N.L. (1985). Maternal role satisfaction, mother child interaction and child temperament. *Development Psychology, 6,* 1157 - 1164.

Levita, M.J. Weber, R.A. and Clarke, M.C. (1986) Social support relationships as sources of maternal support and well-being. *Developmental Psychology, 22,* 310-316.

Love, J. Schochet, and P. Meckstorm, A. (2002). Investing in effective child care and education: lessons from research. In M. Young (Ed.) *From Early Child Development to Human Development: Investing in our Children's Future.* Washington D.C.: World Bank, pp. 145-193.

M. S. Swaminathan Research Foundation. (2000). '*Quality matters' understanding the relationship between quality of early childhood education and learning competencies in children.* Chennai: Author.

Madras School of Social Work. (1970). *Working mothers in white collar occupations.* Madras: Author.

Main, M. and Cassidy, J. (1988). Categories of response to reunion with the parent at age 6: Predictable from infant attachment classifications and stable over a 1-month period, *Developmental Psychology, 24,* 415-426.

Mane, P.N. (1983). Women at work: a study of women employees at the Mantralaya. Unpublished Doctoral Dissertation. Bombay: Tata Institute of Social Sciences.

Marantz, S.A. and Mansfield, A.F. (1977). Maternal employment and the development of sex-role stereotyping in five to eleven year old girls. *Child Development, 48.* 668 - 673.

Mathur, K. and Misra, G. (1993). Maternal Employment and Personality Functioning in Children. Unpublished manuscript. Barkatullah University, Bhopal.

McBride, S. and Belsky, J., (1988). Characteristics, determinants, and consequences of maternal separation anxiety. *Developmental Psychology, 24,* 407 - 414.

McCartney, K., and Galanopoulos, A. (1988). Child care and attachment: A new frontier the second time around. *American Journal of Ortho - Psychiatry,* 58 (1) January 1988, 16 - 24.

McGurk, H., Caplan, M. Hennessy, E., and Moss, P. (1993). Controversy, theory and social context in contemporary day care research. *Journal of Child Psychology 34(1),* 3-23.

Ministry of Human Resource - Government of India. October, (1997). UDISHA - the new Dawn in ICDS Training, Department of Women and Child Development, New Delhi: Author.

Ministry of Human Resource Development (Government of India). May, 1986. *National Policy of Education, 1986.* New Delhi: Author.

Mobile Crèches. (1989). *Mobile Crèches annual report, 1987-88.* Bombay: Mobile Crèches.

Mody, S.N. and Murthy, V.N. (1988). The study of mental health of children of working mothers. *Journal of Personality and Clinical Studies, 4*, 161-164.

Moore, B.F., Snow, C., and Poteat, G.M. (1988). Effects of variant types of child care experience on the adaptive behaviour of kindergarten children. *American Journal of Orthopsychiatry, 58*(2), 279-203.

Moore, T.W. (1963). Effects on the children (b) A report from the Child Study Centre in, Yudkin, S. and Holme, A. (Ed.s) *Working mothers and their children.* London : Michael Joseph.

Moorehouse, M.J. (1991). Linking maternal employment patterns to mother child activities and children's school competence. *Developmental Psychology, 27,* 295-303.

Morgan, G. (1985). The Government perspective on quality in early childhood programmes. High Scope Early Childhood Policy Paper No.3. Ypsilanti: Michigan

Morgan, G. (1979). Regulation: One approach to quality childcare . *Young children, 34*(6) 22-27.

Moss, P. (2003). Beyond caring. The Case for reforming the Child care and Early Years Workforce Facing the future policy papers.

Moss, P. (2000). Workforce issues in early childhood education and care. Paper presented at consultative meeting on International Development in Early Childhood Education and Care, Columbia University, New York (May 11-12).

Motwani, M. (1987). A study of the effect of child-rearing practices of working and non-working women on extrovert and neurotic behaviour of their children. Unpublished Masters Thesis, Punjab University, Chandigarh.

Mukhopadhyay, S. (1981). *Work and women: Some pertinent issues,* Delhi: Institute of Economic Growth.

Muralidharan, V. and Kaul, B. (1993). Early childhood care and education: current status and problem. In T.S. Saraswathi and Baljit Kaur. (Eds.), *Human Development and Family Studies in India.* Ist Edition, New Delhi: Sage Publications.

Muralidharan, R., and Kaur, B. (1983). The impact of an intervention programme on the language and cognitive development on tribal pre-school children. Mimeograph. New Delhi: N.C.E.R.T.

Mussen, P.H. (1970). Carmichael's manual of child psychology. New York: John Wiley and Sons.

Mussen, P.N. (1970). Handbook of research methods in child development, New Delhi: Wiley Eastern.

Myers, R. and Indriso, C. (1987). *Women's work and child care: Supporting and integration of women's productive roles in resource poor households in development countries.* Paper prepared for the Rockefeller Foundations IDRC Workshop on Gender, Technology and Development, February, 1987.

Naidu, U.S. and Nakhate, V.S. (1985). *Child development studies in India.* Bombay: Tata Institute of Social Sciences.

Narayanan, R. (1994). *Issues in implementation of child care services in policy for the young child* (proceedings no.10) Chennai: M.S. Swaminathan Research Foundation.

National Council of Applied Economic Research (NCAER). (1998). 'Findings of the pilot survey on ICDS Scheme' Annexure X, Annual report 1997-98, Department of Women and Child Development Ministry of Human Resource Development.

National Council of Applied Economic Research (NCAER), (1994). *Study of 33,000 Households,* New Delhi: Author.

National Family and Health Survey (1992-93). India Report, New Delhi, pp. 273-77, New Delhi.

National Institute of Nutrition. (1995). Report of the National Nutrition Monitoring Bureau, Hyderabad: Author.

National Institute of Public Cooperation and Child Development. (1978). *Working mothers and early childhood education.* New Delhi : Author.

Nelson, G.F., Ladd, G.W. and Hsu, H. (1993). Maternal support networks, maternal cognitions, and young children's social and cognitive development. *Child Development, 64*, 1401-1417.

O'Donnell, H. (1994). *Women and the family,* World Development Series, Zen Books, New Jersey.

Oppenhiem, D., Sagi, A. and Lamb, M.E. (1988). Infant adult attachments on the kibbutz and their relation to socio-emotional development 4 years later. *Developmental Psychology, 24,* 427-433.

Pandit, B. (1993). Competences for crèche workers and an appraisal of training programmes. Unpublished M.Phil dissertation. Mumbai, SNDT University.

Paranjpe, R. and Ambosta, D. (1981). Evaluation study of the crèches for children of working and ailing mothers in Maharashtra, Mumbai: Bombay College of Social Work, Nirmala Niketan (Mimeo).

Parten, M.B. (1932). Social participation among pre-school children. *Journal of Abnormal and Social Psychology, 27,* 243-269.

Pasquali, L., and Callegri, A.I. (1978). Working mothers and daughters sex-role identification in Brazil. *Child Development, 49,* 902-905.

Peisner-Feinberg, E.S. and Burchinae, M., (1997). Relations between pre-school children. Child care experiences and concurrent development: The cost, quality and outcomes study, *Merill Palmer Quality, 43,* 451-77.

Philips, D., McCartney, K. and Scarr, S. (1987). Child care quality and children's social development. *Development Psychology, 23,* 537-543.

Phillips, D.A.; Scars, S. and McCartney, K. (1987). Dimensions and effects of child care quality: The Bermuda Study in D.A. Phillips (ed.), *Quality in Child Care. What Does Research Tell Us*? Washington D.C.: National Association for Education of Young Children.(43-55).

Piotrkowski, C.S. and Katz, M.H. (1982). Indirect socialization of children: The effects of mothers' job on academic behaviours. *Child Development, 53,* 1520-1529.

Poresky, L.H. and Whitsitt, T.M. (1985). Young girls intelligence and motivation : Links with maternal employment and education but not systems theory. *The Journal of Psychology: Interdisciplinary and Applied, 119,* 475 - 480.

Prasad, Vandana. (1998). 'Health and nutrition of the girl child; A broad look at status, linkages and consequences', *Women's Link, (Indian Social Institute), 4*(3).

Prasad, Vandana. (1998). 'Children and the State: The politics of child care': in *Childhood, a symposium on early childhood care and education:* Issue No.: 462, New Delhi.

Prasad, Vandana. (1997). "A study of an urban slum", Unpublished Study, NOIDA (U.P).

Ramalingaswami, V., Jonson, U., and Rohde, J. (1996). 'The Asian Enigma' in *Progress of Nations*, pp 11-17, UNICEF, UK.

Ramesh, B.M. (1987). Behavioural correlates of contraceptive use. Unpublished Ph.D. Thesis, International Institute of Population Sciences, Mumbai.

Ramu, G.N. (1985). *Working wives, working husbands.* New Delhi: Sage Publications.

Ranade, S.N. and Ramchandran, P. (1970). *Women and Employment.* Bombay: Tata Institute of Social Sciences.

Rane, A. (1979). A new look at factory crèches. *Eklavya: Mobile crèches annual. 1979.*

Rane, A.J.; Naidu, U.S. and Kapadia, K. (1986). Children in difficult situation: A review. Bombay: Tata Institute of Social Sciences, (Mimeo).

Rani, K. (1976). *Role conflict in working women.* New Delhi: Chetna Publications.

Robinson, R. and Robinson, N. (1971). Longitudinal development of very young children in a comprehensive day care programme. *Child Development, 42,* 1673-1683.

Rodman, H., Pratto, D.J., and Nelson, R.S. (1985). Child care arrangement and children's functioning: A comparison of self-care and adult-care children. *Development Psychology, 21,* 413-418.

Roopnarine, J.L., Talukdar, E., Jain, D., Joshi, P. and Srivastava, P. (1992). Personal well-being, kinship tie and mother-infant and father-infant interactions in single-wage and dual-wage families in New Delhi, India. *Journal of Marriage and Family, 54,* 293-301.

Roopnarine, J.L., and Lamb, M.E., (1977). The effects of day care on attachment and exploratory behaviour in a strange situation. *Merrill-Palmer Quarterly, 24,* 85-89.

Rubenstein, J.L. and Howes, C. (1979). Caregiving and infant behaviour in day care and in homes, *Development Psychology. 15,* 1-24.

Ruopp, R. (1979). Children at the centre: The final report of National Day Care Study. Boston: Abt Association.

Saleth, M. (1992). Coping with the impact of structural adjustment on child welfare in India. In proceedings of the seminar 'Structural Adjustment Policies and Child in India'. Chennai: M.S. Swaminathan Research Foundation.

Saraswathi, T.S., Radhika, S. and Biswas, U. (1995). Woman, Work and Child Care — The Need for Options, Working paper No. 13, Women Household Studies Information Centre, Baroda.

Saxena, A.K., Mehrotra, S.N. and Singh, S.B. (1987). Maternal employment and personality of Child. *Indian Pediatrics, 24,* 127-132.

Saxena, A.K., Mehrotra, S.N. and Singh, S.B. (1986). A psychological study of children of working mothers and the effect of providing an alternative care. *Child Psychiatry Quarterly, 19,* 128-137.

Schachter, F.F. (1981). Toddlers with employed mothers. *Child Development, 52,* 958 - 964.

Schwartz, J. (1983). Length of day care attendance and attachment behaviour in eighteen month old infants. *Child Development, 54,* 1073-1078.

Sen Amartya and James D. Wolfensohn. (1999). 'Development; a coin with two sides', *The Hindu* 6.5.99, New Delhi: Author.

Shanmugavelayutham, K. and Nirmala, (2004). Status of anganwadi worker in Tamil Nadu. Executive Summary. Chennai: Loyola College.

Shanmugavelayutham, K., (1998). Social legislation and social change. Chennai: Vazhga Valamudan Publishers.

Shanta, E.V. (1997). *Services that matter: An overview of childcare services in Tamilnadu.* (Monograph no 7). Chennai: M. S. Swaminathan Research Foundation.

Sharma, N. (1987). Child care support of primary school teachers with pre-school children. Unpublished Masters Thesis, M.S. University of Baroda.

Shiva, M. (1977). Personal communication. Head of Public Policy Division, VHAI, New Delhi.

Shiva, V. (1999). Summary of outcomes from the one day convention of women on food rights, 23.2.99, Research Foundation for Science, Technology and Ecology, New Delhi.

Shramshakti. (1988). 'Report of the National Commission on Self-Employed Women and Women in the Informal Sector', Government of India.

Smith, A. (1996). Is quality a subjective or objective matter? Paper presented at the National Seminar on 'Assessing and Improving Quality of Early Childhood Centres'. School of Medicine. Wellington, New Zealand.

Spitz, G. (1988). Women's employment and family relations: A review. *Journal of Marriage and Family, 50,* 505-618.

Sriram, R. (in press). 'Child care and women's empowerment: The interface' in M. Swaminathan (ed), *Innovations in ECCE,* Sage, New Delhi.

Sriram, R. (1998). Women's empowerment and childcare: The interface in M. Swaminathan (Ed.). *The first five years: Critical perspectives in ECCE in India* (240-271) New Delhi, Sage.

Sriram, R. (1997). Report of a preliminary survey on sources of income and expenditure of day care, play care centre in Baroda, unpublished paper, Shishu Palak Vrund: Department of Human Development. M. S. University, Baroda.

Sriram, R. (1995). Another kind of child care: Alternatives for rural women, Chennai: M.S. Swaminathan Research Foundation.

Sriram, R. (1993). Situation of urban day care and play care in Baroda. Unpublished research report, Development of HDFS, M.S. University, Baroda.

Sriram, R. (1992). Women's development and child care: Experience at evolving flexible models, Department of Human Development and Family Studies, M.S.University, Baroda.

Sriram, R. (1991). Child care support patterns of middle class employed women. Paper presented at the 3rd International Family Day Care Organisation Conference Sydney, Australia.

Sriram, R. and Shukla, A. (1999). *What do parents expect from day care: Supporting providers to respond.* A research report. (Mimeo) Shishu Palak Vrund, Department of Human Development and Family Studies, Baroda: M.S. University.

Sriram, R., and Ganapathy, H. (1998). 'Child care options in agricultural contexts", *Economic and Political Weekly, XXXII*(43), WS-64-72.

Sriram, R., Ganapathy, H. (1998). *The dismal status of childcare in Gujarat: Time for action.* (Unpublished paper) Ahmedabad: Gujarat Shishu Sangh (Forum for Crèche and Childcare Services, Gujarat Chapter).

Sriram, R. and Rashmi, K. (1996). Needs assessment for starting a resource centre, unpublished report, Shishu Palak Vrund, Baroda.

Stith, S.M. and Davis, A.J. (1984). Employed mothers and family day-care substitute caregivers: A comparative analysis of infant care. *Child Development, 55*, 1340-1348.

Super, C.M. and Harkness, S. (1986). The development niche: A conceptualization at the interface of child and culture. *International Journal of Behavioural Development, 9*, 545-569.

Suraksha Series, (1995). Early childhood care and education in India, Chennai: M.S Swaminathan Research Foundation, Chennai.

Swaminathan, M.S. (2000). Quality matters: An exploratory study in Tamil Nadu, Chennai: M.S. Swaminathan Research Foundation.

Swaminathan, M. (1997). *The first five years: A critical perspective on early childcare and education in India.* New Delhi: Sage.

Swaminathan, M. (1996). Innovative child care programmes in India. *International Journal of Early Years Education, 49(2)*, 41-55.

Swaminathan, M. (1993). 'Current issues in early childhood care and education' in T.S. Saraswathi and B. Kaur. (eds.), *Human Development and Family Studies in India: An Agenda for Research and Policy,* Sage, New Delhi.

Swaminathan, M. (1985). *Who Cares? A study of Child care facilities for low income women in India,* Centre for Women's Development Studies, New Delhi.

Swaminathan, V.D. and Parvathi, S. (1983). Occupational aspirations of adolescent boys and girls of working and non-working mothers. *Indian Journal of Applied Psychology, 20*, 23-28.

Thakkar, A. (1991). Evolving needs of daycare provision and training, Bombay, India. Paper presented at the 3rd International Family Daycare Organisation Conference. Sydney, Australia.

The Hindu. (1999). 'Tirade against GM crops', *The Hindu* 15.2.99. New Delhi: Author.

The Hindu. (1999). 'Beyond Malthus: Nineteen dimensions of the population challenge', Worldwatch Institute, Washington, *The Hindu,* 23.4.99. New Delhi: Author.

The Hindustan Times (1999). 'Indians' Food Security under Threat'. *The Hindustan Times,* 4.3.1999. New Delhi: Author.

The Independent Commission on Health in India, Voluntary Health Association of India, 1997.

Prasad, A. (1999). The sections on breast feeding, malnutrition and mortality indicators have been taken from. "Economic Reforms and the Child". FORCES (unpublished), New Delhi.

The Sunday Times. (1999). 'Europe experts fear gene tinkered food', *The Sunday Times* 14.2.99. New Delhi: Author.

Thomas Blom Hansen and Funn Stepputat (eds.). (2001). *States of imagination: Ethnographic exploration of the post-colonial states*, 65-76, Durhan: Duke University Press.

Thomas, T. N. (1999). 'The urban sector', In, *Alternative Economic Survey 1991-98; Seven Years of Structural Adjustment*, New Delhi.

Tietze, W.; Burchinal, M.; Leal, T. and Palacios, J. (1999). Predicting process quality from structural quality in preschool programmes: Across country comparison. *Early Childhood Quarterly*, 339-361.

Times of India, (1997). 'NGOs demand provision for child care in 9th plan', 16.9.97. New Delhi: Author.

TN-FORCES. (1998). Proceedings of the Workshop Advocacy Strategies in Early Childhood Care and Development, TN-FORCES, Department of Social Work, Chennai: Loyola College.

TN-FORCES. (1998). Public Hearing on Child Care Services, Chennai: Department of Social Work, Loyola College.

UNICEF. (2005). www.unicef.orgi/info by country India.html

UNICEF. (2000). *State of the world's children - 2000*, New York: Author.

United Nations Development Programme (UNDP). (1997). Human Development Report 1997. New York: Oxford University Press.

Upadhyaya, V. (1999). 'Prices', in *Alternative Economic Survey* 1991-98, New Delhi.

Vanaja, M. and Venkataramaiah, S.R. (1990). Effect of marital satisfaction and employment status of mothers on behavioural problems of their children, *Indian Journal of Clinical Psychology, 17*, 8-11.

Vandell, D.L., Dadisman, K. and Ballagherk. (2000). Another look at the elephant child care in the ninetees. In R. Taylor (Ed.) *Resilience across contexts: Family, work, culture and community. 91*-120, New Jersey: Erblaun.

Vandell, D.L., Henderson, V.K. and Wilson, K.S. (1988). A longitudinal study of children with day care experiences of varying quality. *Child Development, 59*, 1286-1292.

Vaughan, B., Gove, F. and Egeland, B. (1980). The relationship between out of home care and the quality of mother infant attachment in an economically deprived population. *Child Development, 51*, 1203-1214.

Venkataramana, H.L. (1987). Professional employment of mothers: Impact on personality and parent-child interaction. *Indian Journal of Psychology, (1 and 2),* 13-23.

VHAI. (1997). *Report of the Independent Commission on Health in India,* Voluntary Health Association of India, New Delhi, pp.200-202.

Viruru, R. (2001). Early childhood education: Post-colonial perspectives from India. New Delhi: Sage Publications.

Whitebook, M.; Howes, C. and Phillips, D. (1989). Who cares? Child care teachers and the quality of care in America. Executive summary: National Child Care, Staffing Study, Oakland, CA.

Woodhead, M. (1996). In search of the Rambow: Pathways to quality in large scale programmes for disadvantaged children. *Early Childhood Practices and reflection, 10.* The Hague: Bernard Van Leer Foundation.

World Bank. (2000). Growth alone not enough to check poverty says World Bank Report', 14.2.99, *The Times of India:* New Delhi.

World Bank. (1997). *Reproductive and child health project. Project Appraisal, India Document,* South Asia Region, p.iii.

Yarrow, M.R. Scott, P., Leeuw, L., and Heing, C. (1962). Child rearing in families of working and non - working mothers. *Sociometry, 25,* 1962, 122 - 140.

ABOUT THE CONTRIBUTORS

Mridula Bajaj, a child development professional has been working with and on children's issues for the last 25 years. Her experience covers a vast repertoire of activities ranging from field research to teaching and pedagogy issues for the young child. A genuine concern for children living in poverty has drawn her into the Civil Society movement since the last 10 years. As Executive Director of Mobile Crèches, a leading NGO working with the young child with a special focus on the migrant child, Mridula Bajaj has been instrumental in strengthening the advocacy agenda for the organization. Her rich field experience feeds into her recommendations as a member of several working groups and committees constituted by the Planning Commission and Government to plan, frame guidelines and lay down policies for the young child. She has to her credit important papers and presentations made at several national and international conferences and seminars.

CLAP (Committee for Legal Aid to the Poor) is a non-profit NGO, specialised in giving professional legal support. It is operating in Orissa, India and is registered under the Societies Act. It exists for promotion and protection of human rights and rule of law. Right from the beginning CLAP has placed highest priority on the Rights of the Children through strategic intervention through programmes like in Defence of the Child. CLAP promotes advocacy in favour of young children so as to bring about change in the policies and legislation in order to protect the children form all forms of discrimination, exploitation and injustice and promote the best interest of the children, particularly in the nutrition, health, housing, clothing and education entitlements.

Dr. Hemalatha Ganapathy is currently Assistant Professor in the Department of Educational and School of Psychology, Indiana State University, USA. She has worked in the Centre for Health Education, Training, and Nutrition Awareness (CHETNA), Ahmedabad, India, before teaching at the Department of Human Development and Family Studies, Maharaja Sayajirao University of Baroda. Her research interests are parenting and childcare in culturally diverse contexts, rearticulated discourses of ethnic identity as a result of migration, and research philosophies and paradigms in culturally sensitive research. Dr. Ganapathy received her Master's degree in Human Development and Family Studies from Maharaja Sayajirao University, Baroda, India.

Ms. Monica Gupta has a background in Child Development and Educational Psychology. She is a lecturer in the Department of Elementary Education, Gargi College, University of Delhi. She has also taught at the Department of Psychology, University of Delhi. Her current work is on Integral Psychology based on the works of Sri Aurobindo and its applications to the areas of human development, educational psychology and self development.

OMVS (Orissa Mahila Vikash Samiti) is a local NGO in Orissa, India. It has a stake in the mining area of Sukinda, Jajpur. Sukinda is considered as one of the largest mining area of Orissa. OMVS has coordinated with FORCES and CLAP in conducting the research on child care in Orissa Mines.

Orissa FORCES is a state chapter of National FORCES (Forum for Crèche and Childcare Services). FORCES was formed in 1989 following the efforts of a group of concerned individuals/organisations to lobby for more, accessible and good quality child care as well as to assist in policy formation and implementation. It is committed to the care of children below the age of 6, of poor and underprivileged sections of society.

Dr. Vanadana Prasad is a community paediatrician working with women and children in an urban slum. She has been an active member of National FORCES. She is a working mother and practising doctor for 17 years, of which nearly 6 years were spent working in Britain. She is actively involved with the organisations working for the advocacy of young children.

Mr. M.R. Arulraj is a senior faculty in the Department of Social Work, Loyola College, Chennai with an M.Phil. in Population Sciences from the International Institute for Population Sciences, Mumbai. Mr. Arulraj is actively involved in research and training in various areas like Planning, Decision-making, Communication, Interpersonal Relationships and Leader Effectiveness. Community Based Emergency Preparedness has been one of the important evaluation studies that he has undertaken. Currently he is also the Co-oirdinator of the Pondicherry University and Loyola College Twinning Programme for MBA and other post-graduate degrees.

Mr. S. Raja Samuel, MSW, currently teaches at the Madras School of Social Work, Chennai. He is Involved in research and training in social development for the past 14 years. The topics of research have been on varied issues like, female infanticide, charities administration and psychosocial interventions in disaster situations. He is also conducts training on leadership and communication, networking for development and social research. His currently research is on NGO networks.

Dr. K. Shanmugavelayutham, is currently Reader in the Department of Social Work, Loyola College, Chennai and the convenor of Tamil Nadu-FORCES. Dr. Velayutham is also the coordinator for the Chennai Slum Dwellers Rights' Movement. His other area of interest is special education, and he is Honorary Director of BVSN Murthy Centre for Special Children.

Dr. Rajalakshmi Sriram is Reader at the Department of Human Development and Family Studies, Maharaja Sayaji Rao University of Baroda. Her current research focus is on innovative interventions and advocacy related to childcare issues, fatherhood, motherhood, domestic violence, reproductive and child health issues. She is part of a national task force that is attempting to put together a tool to measure quality in early childhood environments in India. She has been nominated in advisory capacities to state level bodies such as Mahila Samakhya and has been invited by NGOs like Plan International to evaluate their early childhood programmes and training using participatory empowerment strategies. She was awarded the International Fellowship for Research from the Shastri Indo Canadian Institute to carry out research at Canadian Universities.

INDEX